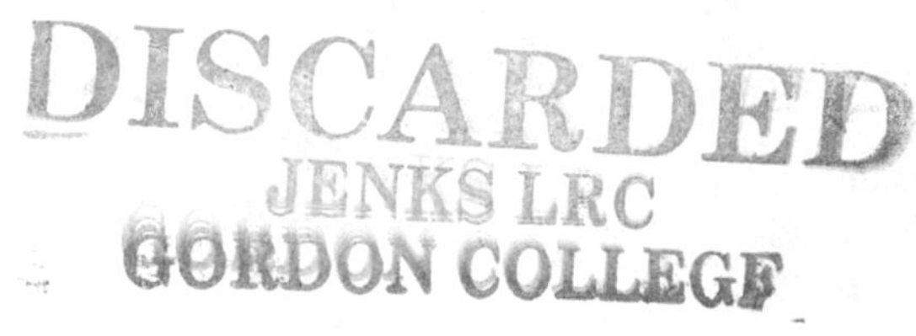

thomson.com

EARTH ONLINE

An Internet Guide for Earth Science

MICHAEL E. RITTER
University of Wisconsin, Stevens Point

WADSWORTH PUBLISHING COMPANY
I(T)P® An International Thomson Publishing Company

Belmont, CA • Albany, NY • Bonn • Boston • Cincinnati • Detroit • Johannesburg • London
Madrid • Melbourne • Mexico City • New York • Paris • Singapore • Tokyo • Toronto • Washington

Earth Sciences Editor: Kim Leistner
Editorial Assistant: Elizabeth Norbringa
Marketing Manager: Halee Dinsey
Project Editor: Karen Garrison
Print Buyer: Stacey Weinberger
Permissions Editor: Peggy Meehan
Advertising Project Manager: Joseph Jodar
Cover Design: Craig Hansen
Cover Photographs: Images ©1996 PhotoDisc, Inc.
Printer: Malloy Lithographing

Printed in the United States of America
3 4 5 6 7 8 9 10

For more information, contact Wadsworth Publishing Company, 10 Davis Drive, Belmont, CA 94002, or electronically at http://www.thomson.com/wadsworth.html

International Thomson Publishing Europe
Berkshire House 168-173
High Holborn
London, WC1V 7AA, England

Thomas Nelson Australia
102 Dodds Street
South Melbourne 3205
Victoria, Australia

Nelson Canada
1120 Birchmount Road
Scarborough, Ontario
Canada M1K 5G4

International Thomson Publishing GmbH
Königswinterer Strasse 418
53227 Bonn, Germany

International Thomson Editores
Campos Eliseos 385, Piso 7
Col. Polanco
11560 México D.F. México

International Thomson Publishing Asia
221 Henderson Road
#05-10 Henderson Building
Singapore 0315

International Thomson Publishing Japan
Hirakawacho Kyowa Building, 3F
2-2-1 Hirakawacho
Chiyoda-ku, Tokyo 102, Japan

International Thomson Publishing Southern Africa
Building 18, Constantia Park
240 Old Pretoria Road
Halfway House, 1685 South Africa

Library of Congress Cataloging-in-Publication Data

Ritter, Michael E.
Earth online : an Internet guide for earth science / Michael E. Ritter
p. cm.
Includes bibliographical references (p. 257) and index.
ISBN 0-534-51707-2 (alk. paper)
1. Earth sciences—Computer network resources. 2. Internet (Computer network) I. Title.
QE48.87.R57 1997
025.06'55—dc20 96-34516

CONTENTS

Chapter 8 Putting the Internet to Work 201

Chapter 9 Where to Go from Here 227

Chapter 10 Internet Resources for Earth Science 236

PREFACE

The information age is evolving before our eyes aided by the ever expanding connectivity and resources of the Internet. Success in our information-based age requires effective reading, writing and computing skills. Computing is no longer a tool that we apply to our work. Computing is more than a knowledge of computer languages and software. Today, computing is an environment within which we conduct our daily work, study and leisure time activities. Computing is a way to facilitate the conceptualization and framing of problems. Computing is a way of locating and accessing information. Computing involves the management and communication of information. The vast amount of information we are exposed to each day requires computer tools to archive, retrieve and display information in ways that are suitable for a variety of users with different needs and computer skills. The complexity of earth systems science requires earth scientists in particular to have well-developed computer skills to be a productive element in today's research and education communities. The development of the global communication network called the Internet has placed a new set of tools at the hands of earth scientists to study the earth. As your companion and guide, *Earth Online* helps you gain access to earth science resources on the Internet.

The investigation of earth systems demands a framework whereby students and professionals can successfully integrate information from a variety of disciplines and perspectives into a unified whole. The earth scientist rarely investigates a problem within the confines of that particular discipline. Information from allied disciplines are required to grasp the complexity of earth systems. The vast resources and connectivity of the Internet give earth scientists an "information framework" to conduct their work. Like the earth system, the Internet is a system of interconnected resources (documents, data, images) that are transported between the system components (servers and clients) along information pathways. The Internet is more than that. The Internet is

> . . . a sort of power loom, providing the framework and resources from which is being woven an enormously complex tapestry of new information, relationships, services, and—potentially—ways of working and interacting within a global society. (Watson, 1995)

Earth Online is for students, educators and professional earth scientists wishing to become active participants in the Internet earth science community. This book is intended for the novice, or casual Internet user. ***Earth Online*** cuts through the technical details of networking common to many Internet user guides. ***Earth Online's*** goal is to make you familiar with earth science resources on the Internet and how to effectively use them. To this end, I have minimized the amount of information dealing with the creation and growth of the Internet, the technical details of networking, and the various systems and services offered over the

Internet. Instead, you find valuable information about how to use the Internet for earth science education and research. Numerous real-world examples demonstrate the effectiveness of the Internet in getting our jobs done.

Audience

I wrote this book specifically for students of earth science, whether in the classroom or in the professional world. For the professional earth scientist, ***Earth Online*** serves as an introduction to, and a resource for, earth science information on the Internet. In ***Earth Online*** you'll find a variety of examples of how professional earth scientists are using the Internet to conduct their work. For students enrolled in earth science classes and programs, you'll find ways to use the Internet to locate information for class projects and research papers. ***Earth Online*** might even help you find a job! Educators will find ***Earth Online*** to be an effective tool to enrich earth science classes, and even if you are not a student or professional earth scientist, you'll probably find something of use because ***Earth Online*** is a "tool-oriented" book. As a tool, ***Earth Online*** helps you get your job done, whether this is studying the eruptive history of North American volcanoes, writing a research paper about the environmental effects of ozone depletion, publishing your work in electronic form or simply keeping in touch with your instructor or colleagues.

I assume that you have an elementary knowledge of computers. That is, you know what a mouse is, what a prompt on a computer screen means, and what a file directory looks like. If not, don't worry because the illustrations and examples provided in the book will probably give you enough information to figure this out on your own. ***Earth Online*** assumes that you've had a limited exposure to the Internet or possibly none at all. Your familiarity with the Internet is not really important. Actually ***Earth Online*** has value to all levels of Internet users, or "Internauts" as we are sometimes called. Even the most experienced Internet user will find something of value. What is important is a willingness to learn new things and "boldly go where you have not gone before." The problem for most Internet neophytes is navigating the vast and largely uncharted "space" that is the Internet.

Approaching the Internet for the first time can be an exasperating experience. Ed Krol described the Internet very well:

> . . . the Internet is a lot like grabbing a handful of Jell-O-the more firm you think your grasp is, the more oozes down your arm. You don't need to deal with the Internet in this manner to eat it, you just need the right tool: a spoon. And you need to dig in and start eating. The same is true of the Internet. You don't need to be an expert . . . for it to be useful. You just need to know how to use some tools, and to start working with them. (Krol, E., 1994)

Earth Online will get you into earth science Internet resources from the very first chapter.

Earth Online will be your tool, and several places have been provided in the book for you to start digging into the Internet. Each chapter is profusely illustrated with examples of exemplary resources available on the Internet. I give you a chance to work hands-on with the Internet in the "Try It Out!" sections that accompany each chapter. But you need to start working with it!

What's Required to Use *Earth Online*

You will glean many new ideas and techniques by reading through the text of ***Earth Online***. However, to get the most out of ***Earth Online*** you will want to equip yourself with a few tools. First would be to establish an Internet connection. Several choices are available these days, and Chapter 1, "Getting to Know the Internet," explains some of those choices.

To try out the services discussed in ***Earth Online*** you'll also need access to a variety of different Internet client software, the software used to connect to the various services over the Internet like electronic mail, file transfer and the World Wide Web. Internet software is usually provided by the organization providing your Internet connection. You computer operating system may have come bundled with Internet software, such as WARP OS/2 or Microsoft Windows 95. The ***Earth Online*** Web site is **http://ritter.wadsworth.com**.

It is impossible to provide examples of how different computer operating systems and their client software interact with the Internet. The PC-Windows client software and UNIX examples are used throughout ***Earth Online***. Though other operating system software may look and feel somewhat different, they perform the same basic functions as those used in ***Earth Online***. The Netscape Navigator is used throughout ***Earth Online*** for exploring the Internet. Practically all services offered over the Internet can be accessed with this one piece of software, or "helper" applications connected to it. ***Earth Online*** uses Netscape Navigator to demonstrate how to use a particular Internet service or activity in each chapter.

How to Use *Earth Online*

The way you use this book depends on your level of Internet expertise and what you're looking for. Here are a few suggestions for making the best use of this book.

If you are new to the Internet . . .

Start at the beginning with the first chapter and follow through until the end to get the most benefit out of the book. Work through the various "Try It Out!" sections. Take a look at how earth scientists are using the Internet in the "Focus on the Internet" feature in each chapter. Stop in at the ***Earth Online*** World Wide Web site (URL - http://ritter.wadsworth.com) to get easy access to Internet earth science resources.

If you have done some "surfing" and want to know more . . .

Check out the chapters about tools that you haven't used before. If you've been Internet surfing and can't seem to find what you want, turn to Chapter 8, "Putting the Internet to Work." This chapter can cut down on your frustration level.

If you want to keep in contact with people . . .

Electronic mail is one of the best ways to keep in contact with people without playing "phone tag." Check out Chapter 3, "Communicating over the Internet." Here you'll find out how to send an electronic message and participate in online group "discussions."

If you are working on a research project/paper . . .

The Internet is a vast, up-to-date resource for finding information for a research project or paper. Before jumping into your next project, take a look at Chapter 8, "Putting the Internet to Work." This chapter will focus your efforts to make the most of Internet resources and tools. Then move to Chapter 6, "Searching the Internet."

If you want to get started publishing on the Internet ...

Chapter 8, "Putting the Internet to Work," introduces you to HyperText Markup Language, the language of the World Wide Web. In this chapter you'll examine what goes into publishing a "home page" and how to design one. Step-by-step instructions show you how to create a personal Web resource page with links to earth science resources.

If you just want to browse . . .

Browsing the Internet can be one of the most exciting activities on the Net. There's nothing like coming upon a gold mine of information by chance. Several tools aid your browsing or "surfing" adventures. Chapter 2, "Browsing the Internet," is your initial link to browsing on the Internet.

If you are an experienced "Internaut" . . .

Experienced users will certainly benefit from checking out the extensive list of resources in Chapter 10, "Internet Resources for Earth Science." You might want to get right to the ***Earth Online*** World Wide Web site by connecting to **http://ritter.wadsworth.com**. The ***Earth Online*** site will keep you current with what's new in earth science Internet resources. At the Web site, experienced users are invited to share their experiences using the Internet.

Special Features

Earth Online helps you get online and using Internet earth science resources from the very first chapter. Chapters 1 through 8 have Apply It! sections. Here is where you take what you have learned in a particular chapter and apply it toward finding resources concerning the issue of climate change. You'll apply what you've learned using the Netscape Navigator World Wide Web browser in a step-by-step fashion. For instance, in Chapter 1 you'll learn how to navigate the Internet with Netscape and visit the Virtual Earth Web site. Chapter 3, "Communicating over the Internet," shows you how to send electronic mail with the Navigator Web browser. In Chapter 8, "Putting the Internet to Work," you'll learn how to publish the climate change resources you've found in each chapter on the World Wide Web. Additionally, each chapter has a "Try It Out!" section suggesting other activities utilizing the various Internet tools and services available.

Earth Online and Wadsworth Publishing will help you navigate the Internet with the ***Earth Online*** World Wide Web site (**http://ritter.wadsworth.com**). The ***Earth Online*** page is located on the Wadsworth World Wide Web server and is your link to the ever expanding universe of earth science information on the Internet. The ***Earth Online*** page contains all the examples used in the book. Educators can access the book examples as they instruct their students about the use of the Internet. All the "Try It Out!" exercises are also here. Links to the extensive catalog of earth science resources described in Chapter 10 are accessible from the ***Earth Online*** World Wide Web site. The ***Earth Online*** site is updated on a monthly basis, but we'll do it sooner if we find resources that you'll need right away. I would also like to hear from you, the ***Earth Online*** user. Let me know when you find online resources to add to the resource catalog. We would also like to hear about how you are using ***Earth Online*** or the Internet in your classes or work. We will post your ideas or links on the ***Earth Online*** site. One of the disadvantages of publishing a book about a fluid medium like the Internet is that the technology and online resources change rapidly. The ***Earth Online*** page will serve as a way of keeping the ***Earth Online*** book up-to-date so that you can keep abreast of the latest developments and any changes in the book's example sites.

Conventions

I have adopted a set of text formatting conventions that represent different operations that you would perform on your computer to interact with the Internet. Commands issued to start an application or perform some operation via your keyboard are in *boldface* type. (e.g., **gopher, get, exit**). Generic placeholders or "variables"—text that the user would replace with a specific value or word—are printed in *italic* between the greater-than and less-than characters. For example, in the command

get *<filename>*

the reader replaces *<filename>* with the actual name of the file he or she wants to get.

Internet addresses are in bold and use the Uniform Resource Locator (URL) format. For example:

A World Wide Web address: **URL - http://address here**
A Telnet address: **URL - telnet://address here**
A Gopher address: **URL - gopher://address here**

To use these addresses with a World Wide Web browser you use everything after the "URL - . " When using other Internet applications (e.g., Telnet , Gopher, FTP client programs) use everything after the double slashes "//." Electronic mail addresses are printed in bold. For example,

mritter@uwsp.edu

Acknowledgments

I would like to acknowledge several people who helped bring this book into print. First, thanks to Kim Leistner and Karen Garrison, whose patience is limitless, and to the following reviewers who helped to craft this book:

Herbert Adams, California State University, Northridge (Geological Sciences)
John Arnfield, Ohio State University (Geography)
Lawrence Boenigk, Indiana State University (Geography/Geology)
Arthur B. Busbey III, Texas Christian University (Geology)
John C. Butler, University of Houston (Geology)
Joe Engeln, University of Missouri (Geological Sciences)
Leonard Gaydos, San Jose State University (Geography)
Michael A. Gibson, The University of Tennessee at Martin (Geology/Geography)
David Greenland, University of Oregon (Geography)
Greg Guyer, Iowa State University (Geology)
Kevin Kloesel, Florida State University (Meteorology)
Michelle Lamberson, The University of British Columbia (Geological Sciences)
Marc Plowman, University of Missouri at Kansas City (Computational Services)
Lisa Sloan, University of California, Santa Cruz (Earth and Marine Science)
Ken Windom, Iowa State University (Geological Sciences).

I owe a debt of gratitude to the University College of London Remote Sensing Lab for providing me with an Internet connection while in London writing the first draft, and the International Students House-London for a comfortable place to write. A special thanks to Mr. Tom Neuhauser, University of Wisconsin-Stevens Point, without whose help getting me online and keeping me online I couldn't have finished this book. I would especially like to thank my wife, Sarah, who missed out on several art museums in London while I worked on the book. A special thanks goes to my son Nathan, who came up with the title for ***Earth Online,*** and missed a Dad on many evenings and weekends.

Michael Ritter

EARTH ONLINE

CHAPTER 1

Getting to Know the Internet

Computing, the Information Age and Earth Science

Over the last few decades the world has experienced a revolution in computing technology. First has been the advances made in personal computing technology through the shrinking of powerful computers down to the desktop. Computer users have more powerful computers in their homes than what many research institutions had five years ago. Desktop computers equipped with powerful microprocessors, huge storage devices and peripheral equipment like CD-ROM drives, sound cards, and video overlay cards are making their way into households, home offices and dorm rooms. Second has been the creation of globally networked computing environments. Network computing permits the exchange of information and ideas across transmission lines between computers located in the same building or in different parts of the world. Connecting various regional networks together, or Internetworking, has created the global computer network that we call the Internet today. The explosive development of global computer communications networks has tied information on far-flung computers together for anybody to access, whether they are a professional researcher, educator, student or any other individual just wanting to keep abreast of the latest developments in our information age. By connecting computers in a networked environment, our computing activities can reach out beyond the desktop to much larger audiences than what we might have expected, or possibly even intended.

Our ability to reach out to so many people is a result of the development of powerful, yet easy-to-use, Internet software tools. Graphical user interfaces (GUIs), employed in operating systems like the Macintosh and Windows computing environments, have been created for many of the services offered over the Internet. The most notable examples are GUI interfaces like Netscape Navigator, Microsoft Explorer and NCSA Mosaic. The "point and click" operation of these interfaces makes it easy for users to become proficient at interacting with the Internet.

Internetworked computer resources bring powerful tools to our desktop. But ignoring the data, documents and other files located on computer servers around the world, the huge community of Internet users itself is a global resource for information. The key to using the Internet is to open yourself up to the entire electronic earth science community that the Internet has helped create. The earth science Internet community is one of many virtual communities that are bonded together by networks, whether electronic or human. Calling on the human resources behind the Internet is just as important, and in some cases more so, than the digital resources the Internet provides. We often neglect people as a type of Internet tool or resource. No one knows for sure how many people are connected to the Internet, but estimates range to 8 million or more. Communications between people with electronic mail maintains a personal touch when using online information resources, as opposed to interacting with an inanimate computer service. Calling on the human resources in the earth science Internet community makes navigating through the gigabytes and terabytes of information much easier. Never in our history has the average person had a tool to reach out to such a large number of people and resources with such relative ease. The global computer network that is the Internet allows people to seek out information in new ways and to access information that has never been available to them in the past.

In many ways the Internet is structurally similar to the earth system. The earth, like any system, is often conceptualized as a number of components, all interacting together between pathways of energy. The Internet is a system of interconnected computers sharing information along nonlinear electronic pathways. Earth scientists have long recognized the power of computers in studying earth systems, and have been at the forefront in using them in research and education. Computers are an invaluable tool for manipulating data, creating and running simulations and forecasting changes in earth systems. Earth science educators have used computer-mediated learning to facilitate a deeper understanding of earth systems at all levels of education. Technologies like video disks, CD-ROM and digital video are visually stimulating ways to learn about the earth and its dynamic processes. Today, the vast resources residing on computers connected to the Internet enable earth scientists to investigate earth systems with powerful new research and communication tools. In a networked environment, earth scientists can pull materials together from many different sources to form an integrative picture of our earth system.

Earth scientists recognize that the earth environment is comprised of a complex web of interconnected systems. To study earth systems one must integrate information from a variety of different sources and disciplines. For instance, to study hydrological systems one must draw on knowledge encapsulated in disciplines like engineering, hydrology, geomorphology, geology, and climatology. The difficulty in approaching such integrative problems is gaining access to the appropriate sources of information and tools. The study of earth systems greatly benefits from having the ability to link earth science information and data together. This means that the large amounts of data that are required to study earth systems can be distributed among several computers and drawn upon when needed. Mass storage problems on single computers diminish as data and programs can be distributed across several computers to share. For instance, hydrologic information located on computers at the United States Geological Society can be matched to data residing on computers at the National Oceanic and Atmospheric Administration and input into models running on a desktop computer located in your office (Figure 1.1). Accessing data in this way reduces the burden and costs on any one particular computer user. Interconnectivity of computer resources encourages information sharing and integration within and between disciplines that fall under the broad rubric of what we call earth science.

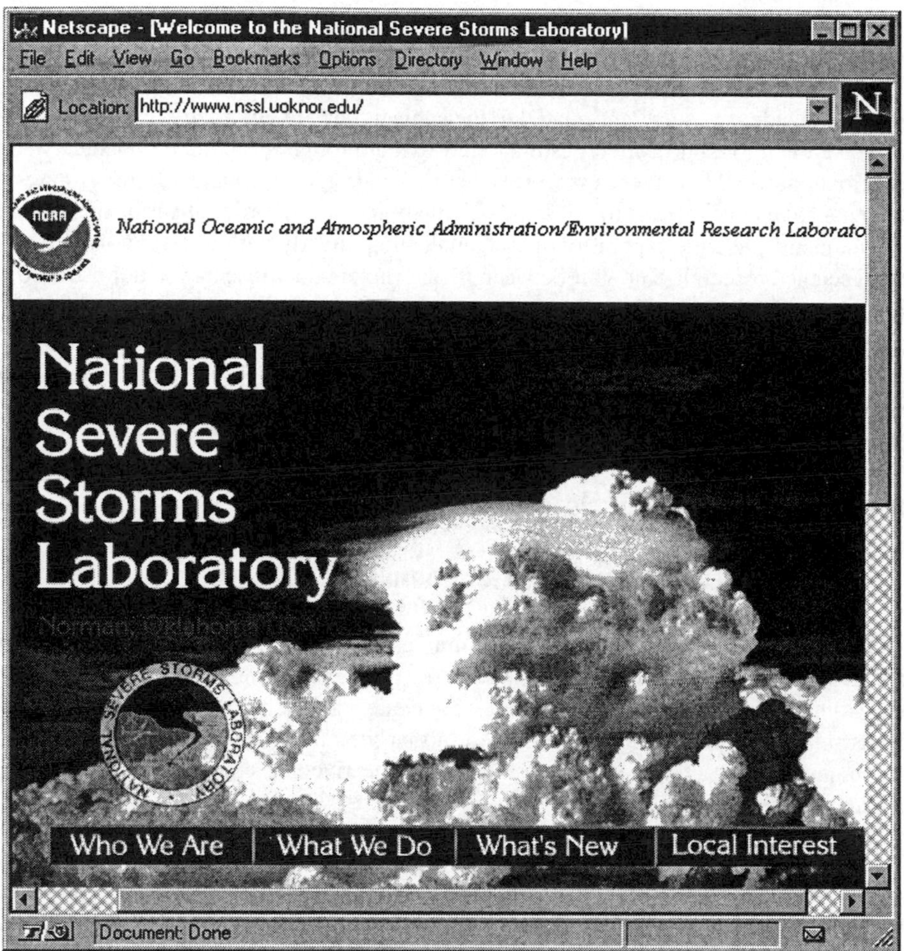

***Figure 1.1 National Severe Storms Laboratory World Wide Web site* (URL - http://www.nssl.uoknor.edu/)**

From an educational standpoint, the Internet provides many new opportunities for teachers and students to become active learners and participants in the information age. Having personal access to networked resources lets users explore information at any time and from any place, so long as they have a connection to the Internet (see "Connecting to and Navigating the Internet" later in this chapter). Having networked computers means that the information stored on them can be tied together in a endless web of electronic connections. Students have the opportunity to seek out information on their own terms. They become active learners rather than passive ones waiting for an instructor or video program to dispense the information to them. Giving control of learning to the student forces changes in the role of the educator. Educators are no longer dispensers of information but facilitators of it. Educators help point students in the direction of information and toward the goals they are trying to achieve. Students choose a path best suited to them. Students may take a direct path to the desired goal or may be detoured along the way by interesting side roads that are related to the subject they are studying but that nevertheless will take them to their desired destination. Moving through these interconnected webs of information, users discover new worlds that they didn't know existed. In many cases, students have equal access to the same information that professional earth scientists have. In fact, students have the capability of communicating directly with those involved with basic earth science research. The gulf between those who conduct research and those who study and teach it is closing with the help of communication tools like the Internet. The Internet is tying such information located on different computers together for earth scientists to use to bring about an understanding of our earth system. For whatever our intended goal is, the Internet can get us to our destination quicker. We might be detoured now and then, but you never know what gems you might run across on your way there.

The Internet and the Earth Scientist

The Internet Earth Science Community

Much has been written about the virtual communities that have arisen with the evolution of the Internet (Rheingold, 1995). The Internet earth science community is comprised of individuals, professional organizations and societies, academic institutions, businesses, and government agencies using the Internet to further their respective goals. Each member of the community brings a different dimension and perspective to the earth science Internet community.

- *Individuals* within the Internet earth science community are involved in electronic discussion groups—scientists bound together by a common interest and willing to share their views and opinions with each other via electronic mail. Individuals have entered the World Wide Web by creating personal Web pages with information pertinent to the earth science community. Many of these pages contain extensive lists of online resources of interests to earth scientists.
- *Professional organizations and societies* utilize the Internet to keep in contact with, and offer services to, their members while promoting their respective discipline and the objectives of their organization. To this end, professional societies and organizations have created Gopher and World Wide Web sites to access this information. Organization home pages link to online membership information, conference announcements and proceedings. Electronic mail discussion lists are maintained to provide a forum for the discussion of subjects relevant to their particular discipline or organization.
- *Academic institutions* participate in the Internet earth science community by creating Gopher or World Wide Web sites that contain information about academic programs, career opportunities, ongoing research programs, and links to other

online resources. They are actively involved in using the Internet for distance education as well.

- *Businesses* in the Internet earth science community use the Internet to distribute information about products of value to earth scientists. Businesses also distribute online help information and software upgrades through the Internet. Many are using the Internet to distribute online electronic publications.
- *Government agencies* play a very active role in the Internet earth science community. Governments use the Internet to archive and distribute data to their employees, as well as the general public. They create clearinghouses for online earth science information. Many government agencies pursue educational activities through the Internet as well.

During your pursuits of information take advantage of the networked human resources. The Internet is more than just a network of computers. Behind those computers lies a human being, someone who has programmed, mounted and maintained information on an Internetworked computer. It takes time to convert analog data into digital form. The human resources Internet community can point in the direction of offline information as well as online. Much government data is archived on CD-ROM or at least on computer tape. Web data sites at NASA, for instance, point to these offline sources of information as well as online NASA data.

What Can You Do with the Internet?

Those unfamiliar with the Internet probably wonder what the fuss is all about. Students and professional earth scientists are finding that the Internet is radically changing the way they conduct their lives. Having access to the kinds of information outlined in the discussion above makes the Internet a rich environment in which to conduct one's work. Knowing that you have access to all this information and data is one thing, but how can you integrate the various tools and resources available to conduct your work?

Let me show you how students and professionals are using global communications networks to conduct their education and work. First, let's look at how a student might use the Internet to research a term paper about the greenhouse effect. Sitting in his dorm room, the student logs on to his campuswide area network. The local campus network gives the student access to the university's electronic library card catalog. While connected he searches the card catalog for information concerning the greenhouse effect and locates a few books. He copies and pastes the references into a word processing document for later perusal at the library and for his term paper bibliography. Not finding many up-to-date resources, he starts up a Telnet remote login program and connects to the CARL UnCover bibliographic database of journal articles. Here he discovers several entries in journals not found in the local library. The student goes to the library's online interlibrary loan form and electronically sends the reference information to the library, which will contact him by electronic mail when the material arrives. Next he enters the World Wide Web and follow a

***Figure 1.2 World Wide Web document from USGS Model of Three Faults online activity* (URL - http://www.usgs.gov/education/learnweb/EarthS.html)**

series of hyperlinks to Internet search engines. He chooses the WebCrawler to search for World Wide Web resources. The search brings him to the United Nations World Wide Web home page, where he finds nearly a hundred online documents dealing with the science, economics, and societal impacts of the greenhouse effect. Among the documents is a particularly informative one about the distinction between the greenhouse effect and climate change. With a few clicks of the mouse, the document is transferred to his computer for later reading. After browsing some of the documents, he creates a personal annotation and bookmark link so he can return directly to the documents at a later time. Proceeding back to the WebCrawler search results, a link to the National Climate Data Center is established.The

NCDC provides interactive access to global temperature anomaly data. Within seconds of filling out the electronic data request form, a map of global temperature anomalies is sent to the student's workstation. The student copies and pastes the map into his word processing document. Going back to the NCDC, he then retrieves a graph of North Hemisphere temperature anomalies. Next he accesses an Archie service, finds a computer server that has the 1990 Clean Air Amendments and transfers the text to his desktop to see what legislation has been written to safeguard against global warming. Finally a stop at the Greenpeace Web site informs him about how he can get involved in environmental activism. Having collected these materials the student completes his paper and delivers it electronically to his instructor via electronic mail. What might have taken hours, days and maybe weeks in the past is now accomplished in a fast and efficient way with globally networked information sources.

The effective use of the Internet in the scenario presented above applies equally well to the professional earth scientist or educator. Networked communications in particular is changing the way scholarly communication and publication is done. For example, in the initial or prepublication stage of research one often spends considerable time engaged in communication with like-minded peers or circulating ideas and proposals for review. Conventionally, much of this activity occurs by direct contact, telephone communications, fax and surface mail. Each one of these methods has particular disadvantages that can be overcome through using the Internet. Busy personal schedules makes it difficult to communicate with people in person and over the phone. Fax is a better way of communicating information that does not require immediate input or interaction from another individual. Fax machines however, are often located in places that are not secure, fax transmissions can involve expensive long-distance charges and the transmission can be interrupted or fail. Communication is effectively carried out over high-speed networks using electronic mail where the cost of transmission is minimal, retransmission can be easily accomplished, and addressees can access messages to suit their schedule. Digital messaging, like electronic mail, does not require the individual to be online to receive the message. Conference calling can be cumbersome and expensive to organize. Electronic mail discussion groups, people who subscribe to a subject-oriented electronic mail service, are an alternative that has become popular over the past decade as a means of exchanging ideas between groups of people.

The Internet has opened new outlets for scholars to communicate their ideas and research. Research finds its way to the scientific community more rapidly as authors can transmit copy-ready text and graphics directly to a publisher through electronic mail. Papers can be revised, and journals quickly put into print. The electronic journal and virtual conference are two notable examples. The electronic journal requires no paper or printer, does not need ink and can be accessed by a much larger audience than a conventional print journal. Immediate feedback to the author or publisher can be implemented from hypertext documents placed on the World Wide Web. Colleagues can submit questions or comments directly to the author via electronic mail by including electronic links to the author's email address. Professional organizations find the Internet a useful place to announce professional conferences and call for papers. In addition, the World Wide Web is seen as a venue for conducting virtual conferences. Virtual conferences offered over the World Wide Web offer several advantages over conventional conferences. Virtual conferences can be "attended" on any day and at any time. Lodging and transportation costs are no longer an impediment to attendance. Conducting the conference over the multimedia-enhanced World Wide Web permits demonstrations of research results that might not have been possible under conventional circumstances. Video and sound can be effectively integrated into the conference "papers" and presentations. Interactivity can be established with the audience through electronic mail. We will examine examples of these activities in the following chapters and show you how to take advantage of them.

Increasingly research reports and electronic books and journals are making their way onto the Internet. In some cases, the Internet is the only place where you'll find this electronic "print" media. For instance, the Electronic Green Journal is a professional journal devoted to disseminating information on international environmental topics. The journal can be sent to subscribers by electronic mail or read online through the Gopher service **(URL - gopher.uidaho.edu)**, menu choice: University of Idaho Electronic Publications) or the World Wide Web **(URL - http://gopher.uidaho.edu /1/UI_gopher/library/egj)**. You can download a copy via anonymous FTP, the file transfer service of the Internet **(URL - ftp. uidaho. edu/ pub/docs/publications/EGJ).**

Professional earth scientists, and earth science students for that matter, have a considerable body of professional resources located on the Internet. The tireless efforts of innumerable people have put an enormous amount of information literally at our fingertips. Over the past few years the United States has made the distribution of data via computer networks a high priority. For instance, the National Geospatial Data Clearinghouse **(URL - http://fgdc.er.usgs.gov/clearover2.html)** is a distributed, electronically connected network of geospatial data producers, managers, and users. The clearinghouse enables its users to determine what geospatial data exists, helps find the data they need, evaluates the usefulness of the data for their applications, and tells how to obtain or order the data as economically as possible. President Clinton's Executive Order 12906 instructs federal agencies to provide this metadata to other agencies and to the public through the clearinghouse. The clearinghouse uses the Internet to link computers that archive the geospatial data. For instance, Internet users can download monthly sea ice concentration data for the Arctic Ocean (1901-1990) and southern oceans (1973-1990) from the National Snow and Ice Data Center **(URL - http://nsidc.colorado.edu/NSIDC/data_announcements/ice_concentration_01 -90.html).**

The Internet contains some of the most up-to-date information available to the earth science community. The ability of the Internet to respond to world events was demonstrated during the 1995 earthquake that struck Kobi, Japan (now referred to as the Hyougo-ken Nanbu quake). Within hours of the tremor, news of its destruction rapidly spread through the Internet community. The USGS earthquake information center released data on the epicenter of the earthquake almost immediately. Soon, a World Wide Web site came online with information and links to data about the quake. Images that had appeared only hours before on Japanese TV were put online for the rest of the world to see (**URL - http://www.niksula.cs.hut.fi/~haa/kobe.html**). The Internet community has closely monitored the effects in both physical and human terms. English teachers at Kobe University made student compositions about their personal experience with the quake available on the World Wide Web. Sharing these personal reflections over the Internet added an important human dimension to the disaster that many people would not otherwise have been able to experience or know about.

The Internet is useful for finding information for conventional communication as well. Many universities are putting faculty, staff, and student information databases online. Office and home addresses, email addresses, and phone numbers can be searched for, and retrieved, from these databases, and communication can be established. For example, in preparation for this book I needed a colleague's phone number. I opened up a connection to his university's online phone book and used the search service to locate the number. Once I found the number I copied and pasted it into my phone-dialing software and let the computer dial the number. I soon had my colleague on the phone and my questions answered.

When properly designed, interactive computer-mediated learning motivates people to explore topics to which they have never been exposed before. "Computers teach by involvement of audio, visual and tactile experience. The use of computers as a teaching tool improves daily due to multimedia capabilities" (Pool et al., 1995). Educators of all ilk, and especially earth science educators, have taken to using the Internet in many interesting and unique ways. Earth science educators are using the Internet to distribute class notes, enrich their classes with up-to-date and exciting earth science-related information, for computer-mediated instruction and communication. Students can even take online virtual field trips to places like the Costa Rican rain forest, Hawaii, and even outer space in the cabin of the NASA space shuttle.

There are powerful personal reasons to use the Internet. As monetary and human resources diminish due to ever-tightening budgets, we are asked to do more with less. Economies of time and space can be redefined in a digital world. Knowing how to effectively use the Internet will make you a more productive earth scientist. Productivity increases when you can do the same things you do now only more quickly and efficiently. The connectivity of information theoretically permits you to get at what you need faster. In digital form, information of any type (text, graphic, numeric) is much easier to manipulate and work with. Clearly, if you can communicate information to more people with less effort, then you will be more productive. If information can be accessed more efficiently and incorporated into your tasks then you will be more productive. The tight coupling of computer software like Microsoft Office and Lotus Notes enables computer users to seamlessly move data from one application to another. Text and graphics copied from your computer or one connected to the Internet can be pasted into a word processing document or electronic mail message and sent off to a colleague located halfway around the world or on the floor just beneath you.

Networked information technologies like the Internet are the wave of the future. The much-talked-about "information superhighway" will explode into our lives much faster than we might think. Few could have predicted the rapid rise of personal computer ownership. Even fewer could predict the accelerated rate at which computer technology has changed, continually placing more computing power on our desktops. Those of us willing to tap these technologies will be at a major advantage over those who decide not to.

What Is the Internet?

Before launching into your Internet journeys, a brief explanation of what the Internet is might help you understand how the Net works. Physically speaking, the Internet is comprised of many regional and local area networks connected together to form an integrated, global network of computers or "a network of networks." The Internet is often regarded as a "digital library" because of the vast digital holdings it makes available to those who have access to it (Comer, 1995). In many respects it is like a conventional library because it contains many different kinds of resources and has tools that are used to search through its holdings. The Internet has the added advantage of being able to deliver its resources to your desktop in a fast and efficient manner. Though the Internet is a network through which information is exchanged, it also presents us with a new framework for working and interacting with our global society.

Creating the Internet

Over twenty years ago, the Advanced Research Projects Agency of the U.S. Defense Department created the ARPAnet as an experimental network for supporting military research. The Defense Department was interested in creating a computer network that could withstand partial power outages and still provide communications between command and research facilities. The network had to be able to reroute information between computers even when portions of the network might be down or destroyed. ARPAnet software was designed to require the least amount of information from computers to exchange data between them. These computers used specialized software to split data into small packets called Internet Protocol (IP) packets and send them across the network (Figure 1.3). Each packet had encoded information to tell network hardware the origin and destination of the data. IP packets find their way through the Internet by passing through *routers*, computers that read the packet destination information and determine a network path for it. The packets are sorted out and data reassembled into their original form upon reaching their destination. And it all happens with remarkable speed and accuracy.

Several years after ARPAnet was established, computer workstations connected to each other by local area networks (LANs) began appearing on desktops of academicians and

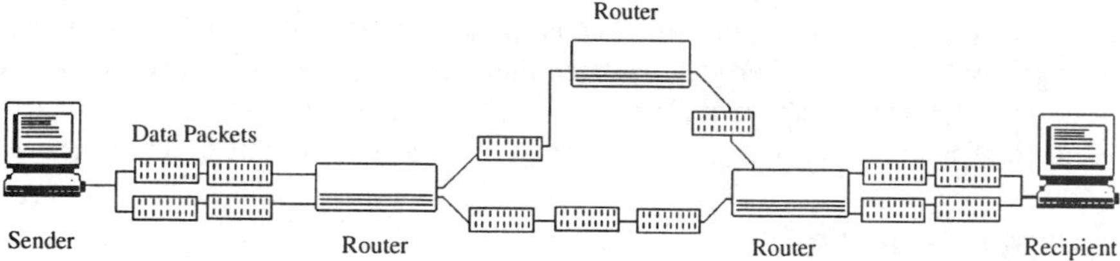

Figure 1.3 Internet packets being transferred across the Internet

researchers. These people soon recognized the potential for sharing networked computer resources and sought to be connected to the ARPAnet. Other large networks sprang up, among which was NSFnet, sponsored by the National Science Foundation (NSF), a research grant-funding agency of the United States government. NSFnet was charged with connecting the computer facilities of major universities and research institutes to one another. ARPA quickly realized the need to develop software that could handle the various networks that were emerging. The main problem was that many computer systems and their local networks were incompatible with each other. ARPA sponsored a program to develop a new set of protocols suitable for the interconnection of these different packet networks. Soon, Transmission Control Protocol (TCP) was born. The protocols that link networks together and determine how communication is accomplished across networks is collectively known as TCP/IP (Transmission Control Protocol/Internet Protocol). TCP/IP permitted the interconnectivity, or *internetworking*, of different networks through devices called *gateways*. Thus the name Internet was penned for the "network of networks" that was beginning to form.

During the mid-1980s the National Science Foundation created a program to provide access to its five supercomputer centers in support of high-powered computing capabilities for scholarly research. Due to the enormous expense of hooking every university to a supercomputer, the NSF implemented several regional networks. Nearby universities were connected to each other as a regional network. Each regional network was then connected to a supercomputer center, and the supercomputer centers connected to each other. This arrangement permitted any two computers to communicate with one another by routing information from the originating computer through the regional network to a supercomputer center and then to the destination computer.

Those working in the networking community saw NSFnet as the next step toward a U.S.-wide skeleton of high-speed networks.. The new network was originally called the National Research Network (NRN), and was later retitled the National Research and Education Network (NREN) to emphasize the educational uses of the Internet. NREN is a government-sponsored program to meet the future computer network needs of the scientific and education communities.

The United States is not the only country actively involved in the networking business. By 1991 many European countries were developing networks using TCP/IP. University and research groups throughout Europe organized themselves into a cooperative for the creation of a high-speed computer network called EBONE. The EBONE is a wide-area network that spans much of Europe and connects locations to what we can call the global Internet.

Internet Addresses

In order to communicate over the Internet, each computer is identified by its Internet Protocol (IP) address. The address tells a router where the information comes from and where it is to be delivered. Proceeding from left to right, the first set of numbers tells the router what part of the network you belong to. An Internet address consists of four groups of numbers, each separated by a period—123.345.67.8, for example. There are two parts to the address: the network portion and the local portion. Numerical IP addresses are difficult to remember, and you will rarely need to use them. The domain name system was implemented to overcome the difficulty of numerical addresses. Each computer on the Internet is assigned a domain name address as well. The domain name system uses plain English text separated by periods to address a computer. For instance, www.usgs.gov is the domain name of the United States Geological Survey World Wide Web server. The domain name is divided into separate parts and identifies the computer's unique location. The structure of a domain name is:

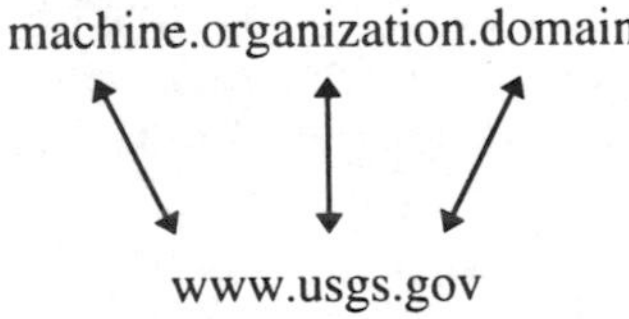

A computer can have any machine name, from very imaginative ones to those that accurately describe the type of server like the USGS Web server. In the USGS's Web server domain name, the www indicates that the machine is a World Wide Web server. The organization is the United States Geological Survey, and it is a government domain. There are a number of domains including:

com	commercial organization
edu	educational site
gov	government site
mil	military
net	network resources
org	organization

Domains also can indicate the country the computer is located in:

ca	Canada
jp	Japan
uk	United Kingdom

There is no correlation between the domain name and the numbers assigned in the numerical IP address. When you use a domain name address, a domain name server on the Internet will correlate the domain name to the numerical IP address and send you to the right destination.

Connecting to and Navigating the Internet

Internet Connections and Accounts

The burgeoning interest in the Internet and the growth of Internet service providers make getting connected easier every day. Right now your organization may have a connection to the Internet. Many universities and colleges are or are getting connected to the Internet. Some public libraries offer service to the Internet. There is an ever growing number of commercial Internet providers too. Many commercial online services like CompuServe or America Online provide Internet access. Even cable television is jumping into the act. Regardless of the provider, the type of connection you have will determine how and how fast you interact with the Internet. The type of connection you make to the Internet sometimes determines the types of services that are available to you and how you can interact with them. At schools and universities, larger business and government institutions, the local area network (LAN) is hooked into the Internet in some way. Because there are so many different LANs and operating systems, you should contact your computer system administrator to see if and how your computer connects to the Internet.

Basically, there are three kinds of connections: direct, direct through a host, and dial-up via telephone or cable lines to an Internet provider. A *direct connection* (Figure 1.4) means that your desktop computer is hooked directly into a communications network. A direct connection can be made through a host computer too (Figure 1.5). In this case your desktop computer has a network connection to a host computer, which is connected to the Internet.

A *dial-up connection* (Figure 1.6) is made over telephone lines using a modem connected to your computer. To access the Internet, your modem dials a telephone number that connects to an Internet service provider. If you are at home or in a dorm without a local area network connection, you'll probably use a dial-up method for getting online. A dial-up connection via modem is how you connect to many of the commercial online services too. Educational institutions are offering dial-up services to faculty and students wishing to connect to their campus network and the Internet from off-campus locations.

The kind of connection you have determines the speed at which information is exchanged between your computer and the remote computer you are in communication with

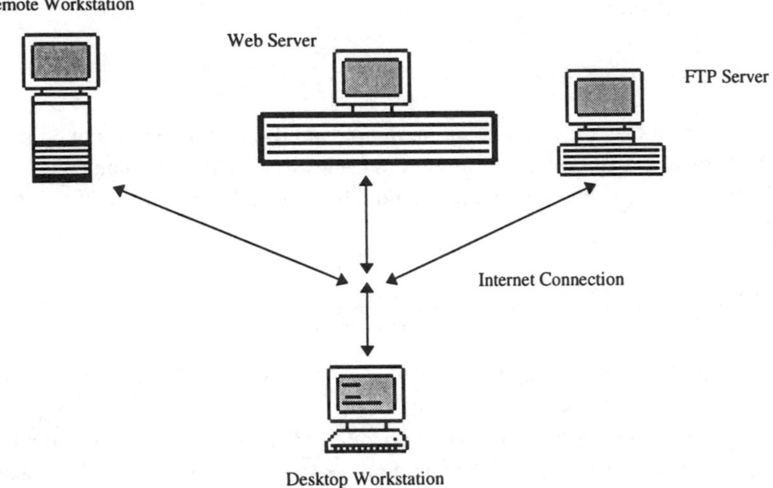

Figure 1.4 Direct connection to the Internet

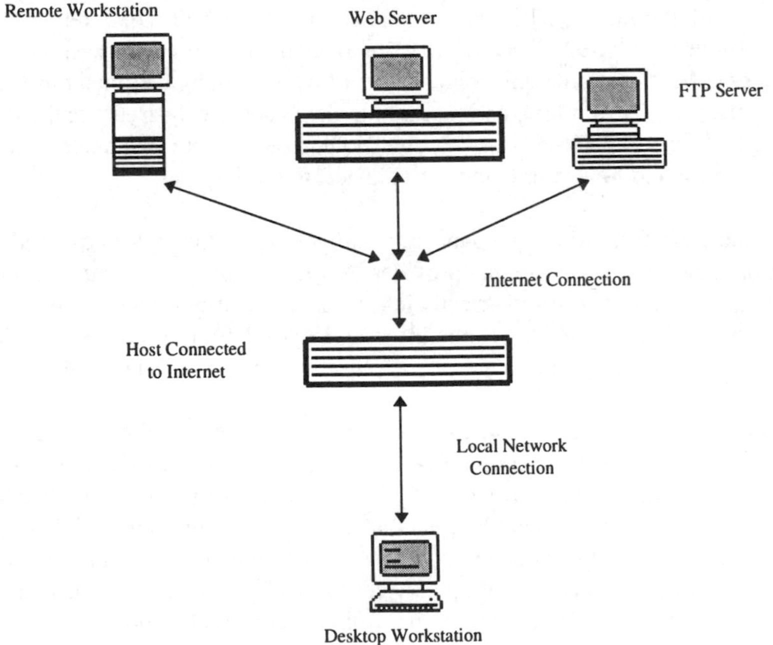

Figure 1.5 Direct connection through a host

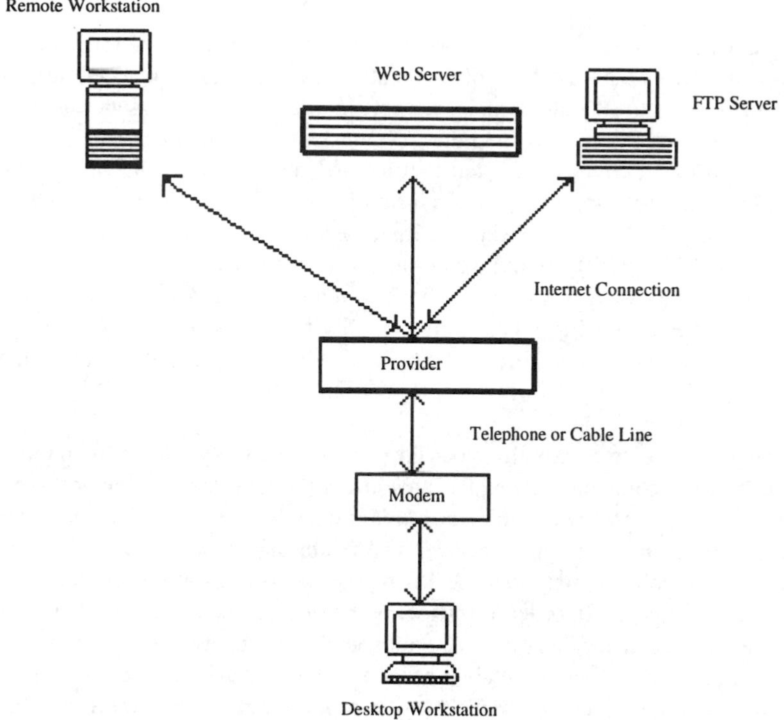

Figure 1.6 Dial-up connection to the Internet

on the Internet. Several variables affect the speed at which information is passed to your computer. Certainly the power of your computer processor will affect the speed at which information is displayed across the screen. Computer processing power, and in particular your video card, will impact the drawing of graphical information across your computer screen.

Factors beyond your desktop affect the speed with which you can interact with the Internet. Network traffic can slow your communications. Because the "road space" (the bandwidth) permitted along the communication network is limited, the information highway gets bogged down as more and more people use it. During peak day-time hours the speed of your communication slows, much the way your trip to work slows during the morning and evening rush hours. The number of people trying to access a particular computer server can affect your ability to connect to it.

Some servers have a limited number of communication lines to them, making it difficult to get a connection with them. The likelihood of getting a connection can depend on the time of day. It used to be that evening and early morning hours were times when access to remote computers was better. However, the Internet is a global network, and it's always prime time somewhere. There may be no good time for some servers. The rabid popularity of the Netscape browser made it difficult for potential customers to gain access to Netscape Communication's server to download their Internet Navigator. For some services, there may be no good time to reach them. One thing that you must have is patience when trying to connect. If you don't get connected on your first try, you may get in on the very next try or shortly thereafter. The one thing that you will have to have is PATIENCE. (When you see all the words capitalized like this in an electronic mail message, it means that you're shouting; Yes, I'm shouting PATIENCE.) I'm quite confident your patience will be tested from time to time when using the Internet. Infrastructure changes in the network have not kept up with demand, and our expectations for uninterrupted, quality service is constantly being tested. But I guarantee that with continued use you'll be increasingly amazed at what the Internet has to offer.

Access from your home or possibly your dorm room is usually gained by dialing into a computer server that is connected to and has an address on the Internet. You will log on to one of two kinds of dial-up accounts, either a *shell* or a *SLIP/PPP*. A *shell account* is an account where an area on the Internet provider's computer has been allocated for your use. When logging into a shell account, your local computer becomes somewhat like a terminal hooked to the host computer. In order to interact with the Internet you use software located on the host computer, not your computer. Any movement of data across the Internet is between the host computer where your shell account is located and other computers connected to the Internet. When you transfer a file from a remote computer, it will be sent to your allocated disk area on the service provider's computer rather than directly to your desktop computer. You must use your modem's communication software to transfer the data from your shell account to your desktop computer.

Earth Online Tip: Keep the files in your shell account to a minimum. Download files to your desktop computer's hard drive and routinely scan your computer for viruses.

A *SLIP* (Serial Line Internet Protocol) or *PPP* (Point-to-Point Protocol) account enables the allocation of an Internet address to your desktop computer. This means that any communication you have with the Internet is passing through the service provider's computer directly to you. You communicate with computers on the Internet by running software on your desktop computer rather than using software on your Internet provider's computer (although you can do that). A SLIP/PPP account is preferable because file downloads come directly to your computer hard drive, bypassing your dial-in server. There are software packages like SLIP KNOT that emulate some of the features of a SLIP/PPP account over a shell account. You should check with your Internet provider as to the feasibility of using a SLIP emulation package.

Whatever type of dial-up account you have, you will be issued a user name and password to log on to your account. These two items are initially provided by your Internet system administrator. Your user name will rarely if ever change. You should change your password from time to time in order to keep it secure. Keeping your password secure is important. Unscrupulous hackers could gain entry into your files or do damage to someone else's in your name if they obtained your user name and password. To create a secure password you should:

- use a punctuation mark or number in it
- refrain from using common words or any part of your name
- create a word not in a dictionary
- use a word 7 or 8 characters long
- never give it out

Some systems have restrictions on the length and content of passwords; some don't allow punctuation, for instance. Contact your system administrator if you're in doubt about your password.

Navigating the Internet

Once you get connected, how do you "surf the Internet" for the multitude of information available to you? There are any number of ways of navigating through the Internet depending on what you're looking for. Your information needs will determine how you use the Internet. Before logging on, take some time to consider what you're after. The vast and relatively uncharted resources of the Internet make it a daunting environment to work in if you are not prepared with a plan of action or have not identified what you are after. Actually, you can log on to the Internet without any particular goal in mind to simply see what's out there. Browsing the Internet can be quite exciting, especially when you uncover a great site of information by simply stumbling onto it. Browsing is *time consuming*. Situations arise when you need to get on the Internet with a very specific goal in mind—say, to find a data set of world temperatures. In this case, your approach and navigation will be quite different from serendipitously browsing through the Net.

Each Internet service will determine what information is available to you and how you interact with it. In the following chapters you'll experience a good deal of what the Internet has to offer the earth scientist. The most popular and fastest growing part of the Internet is the multimedia rich environment of the World Wide Web (Chapter 2). Web software is capable of displaying color images, digital movies and sound, which make the World Wide Web an exciting environment in which to conduct research and education. Context-sensitive, electronic linkages between information give users control over the ways in which they move through the World Wide Web. Web browsers have evolved into "one-stop shopping" software for accessing information from the Internet. World Wide Web browser software permits you to access different kinds of Internet services with one program. With a Web browser client you can connect to gopher servers, do file transfers, and even send electronic mail. It's no wonder the use of the World Wide Web is exploding before our eyes.

Gopher (Chapter 2) service enables users to browse the Internet in a structured, menu-system approach. Gopher enables you to seek out information, view it on screen, save it to your hard disk or print it off, or simply "tag" it for later review.

Electronic mail is the most commonly used service over the Internet. Electronic mail (Chapter 3) allows you to transmit messages to individuals or groups of people quickly and efficiently. Virtual seminars and discussions can be conducted via electronic mail over the Internet. If you're looking for some assistance in finding earth science information, an electronic mail discussion list or a Usenet group like sci.geo.geology is a good place to start.

Over 6,000 gigabytes of files are being stored on computers connected to the Internet. File Transfer Protocol (FTP) (Chapter 4) is the service by which you transfer files to your local computer or send files to FTP servers. FTP servers are an excellent source of freeware and shareware programs for earth science research and education, help or frequently-asked-question files (FAQs), and earth science data of all sorts.

Telnet (Chapter 5) is the means by which many Internet users connect to remote computer systems. Telnet software basically turns your desktop computer into a terminal that interacts with a remote computer. With Telnet, you can access and search online university card catalogs.

Search engines and Internet directories (Chapter 6) are popular starting points for navigating the Internet. A number of World Wide Web search engines, or a Veronica Gopher search engine, can conduct Boolean searches on Internet resource databases. Directory services provide linkages to resources on the Web through linked menu lists. There are general resource directories like Yahoo **(URL - http://www. yahoo.com)** discipline-specific ones like the Virtual Earth **(URL - http://atlas.es.mq.edu.au/users/pingram/v_earth.html)** and locally grown like those found on university home pages **(URL - http://www.uwsp.acaddept/geog/res.htm).**

Finally, the ***Earth Online*** World Wide Web page **(URL - http://ritter.wadsworth.com)** is an excellent starting place for navigating through earth science resources on the Internet. The easy-to-use menu structure and user-friendly interface provided by World Wide Web browsers make navigating the Internet easy and fun.

The users of this book will log onto the Internet using different computer platforms. The Internet programs available for each platform will perform basically the same task, albeit in their own special way. Macintosh users might want to pick up Bernard Robin's article "Supporting Geoscience with Graphical-User-Interface Internet Tools for The Macintosh" (Robin, 1995). This article is a good overview of the various software tools available for the Macintosh computer environment, like the Eudora email program, NewsWatcher newsreader program, Fetch for transferring files via FTP and Mosaic for the World Wide Web. IBM-compatible PC users might want to look at Alex Woronow and

Scott Dare's article "On the Internet with a PC" (Woronow and Dare, 1995). Their article discusses some of the nuances of configuring software for DOS and Windows-based systems to run a variety of Internet applications like WSGOPHER to connect to Gopher servers, Eudora email for the PC, and WS_FTP for doing file transfers.

➤➤ Focus on the Internet: *The Longterm Ecological Research Program*

Throughout ***Earth Online*** you will encounter a multitude of ways that earth scientists are using the Internet. The U.S. Longterm Ecological Research Program (LTER) is a good starting point to show how the Internet, and in particular the World Wide Web, is being used to distribute information about the earth environment. You will need to be online to fully explore the information that LTER has provided. Use a graphical user interface World Wide Web browser like Netscape Navigator, Microsoft Explorer or Mosaic to connect to **http://lternet.edu/**. See your computer systems administrator or Internet provider if you don't have these programs.

The Longterm Ecological Research Program is composed of over 775 scientists and students at 18 different sites throughout North America. LTER's mission is to conduct and nurture ecological research by:

- understanding general ecological phenomena that occur over time
- creating a legacy of well-designed and documented long-term experiments and observations for the use of future generations
- conducting major synthetic and theoretical efforts
- providing information for the identification and solution of societal problems (LTER, 1995)

Each site within the LTER network represents a particular ecosystem, and all share a common commitment to long-term ecological research with regard to:

- patterns and control of primary production
- spatial and temporal distribution of populations selected to represent trophic structure
- patterns and control of organic matter accumulation in surface layers and sediments
- patterns of inorganic inputs and movements of nutrients through soils, groundwater and surface waters
- patterns and frequency of site disturbances (LTER, 1995)

The commitment to the core areas of research means that similar measurements are being made, enabling cross-comparisons between sites. Intersite research projects include process studies of climate forcing, analyses of temporal and spatial data, and the upward

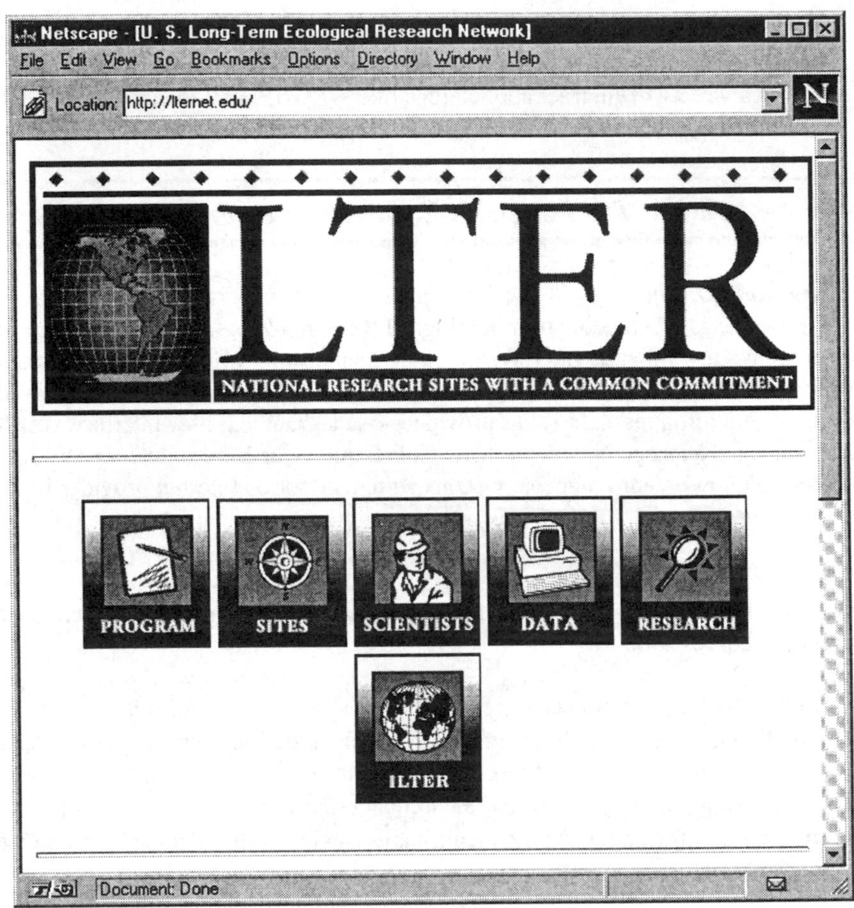

Figure 1.7 Longterm Ecological Research Program home page

scaling to continental and global scales. Ongoing climate research projects include measurements of micro- and mesoscale variables. Integrative studies involve the exchange of information, and the long-term Ecological Research Program wisely uses the Internet to accomplish this.

The LTER home page (Figure 1.7) provides access to background information, gives LTER site descriptions, and connects users to the network office **(URL - http://lternet.edu/)**. The "point and click" graphical interface to the World Wide Web shown in Figure 1.7 makes it easy for users to navigate through the information provided. Links to other resources are implemented through "hot words" or "hot areas" on an image. Hot items, or hyperlinks as they are called, are highlighted in a color different from that of standard text. Icons, or pictures that serve as hyperlinks to other resources, are similarly outlined. The "Research" link connects to descriptions of the core areas of research, current intersite

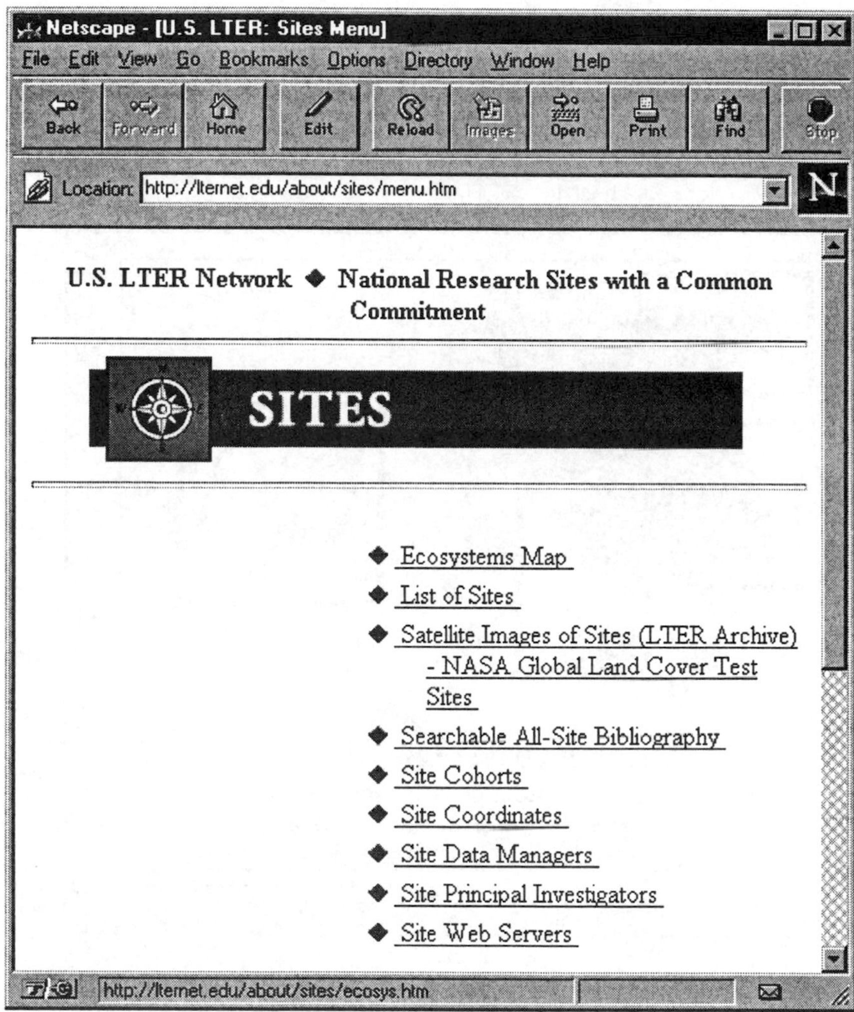

Figure 1.8 LTER Sites page

research activities and LTER Web servers. The last icon, ILTER, is the link to the International Long-Term Ecological Research Program. ILTER is an extension of the LTER in North America. The main ILTER Web site links to other ILTER sites located in Argentina, Australia, Canada, China, Costa Rica, Hungary, Taiwan, and the United Kingdom.

Leaving the Main Menu, I link to the "Sites" page (Figure 1.8) by clicking on the Sites icon. From this page LTER site information is accessible via graphical browse through LTER Site information. To obtain information about the HJ Andrews Experimental Forest

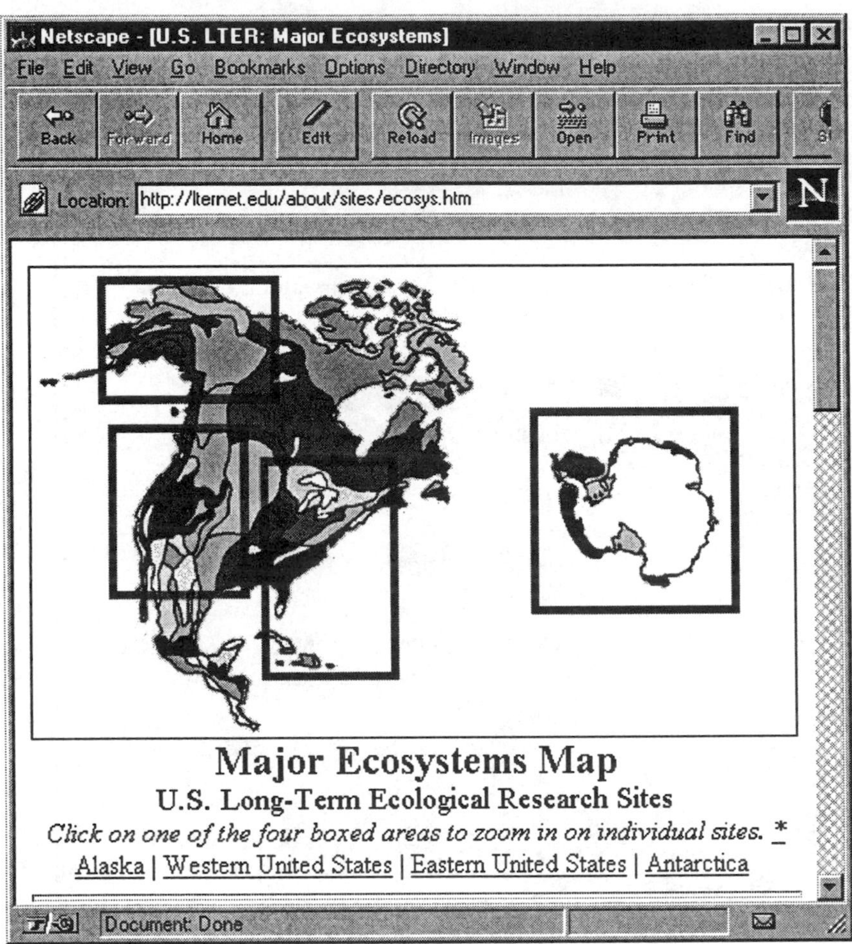

Figure 1.9 LTER Ecosystems Map

site, I'll navigate my way to specific site information by choosing the Ecosystems Map link. The boxed areas on the Ecosystems Map (Figure 1.9) are hot areas. That is, you retrieve information about a particular region by clicking your mouse inside the box. Doing so on the northwestern portion of the United States retrieves a closer view of the area. Clicking on the location of the Andrews site displays information about the principal biotic and abiotic elements of the site, ongoing research topics, and affiliations. A click at the bottom of the page sends me to the H.J. Andrews Web site (Figure 1.10). The Andrews LTER site uses its home page as a resource center for information about the site. In addition to program information, the home page has links to researcher profiles. Specialty areas, research interests, surface mail addresses, phone numbers and email addresses are all available online, making it easy for readers to contact someone about their research activity.

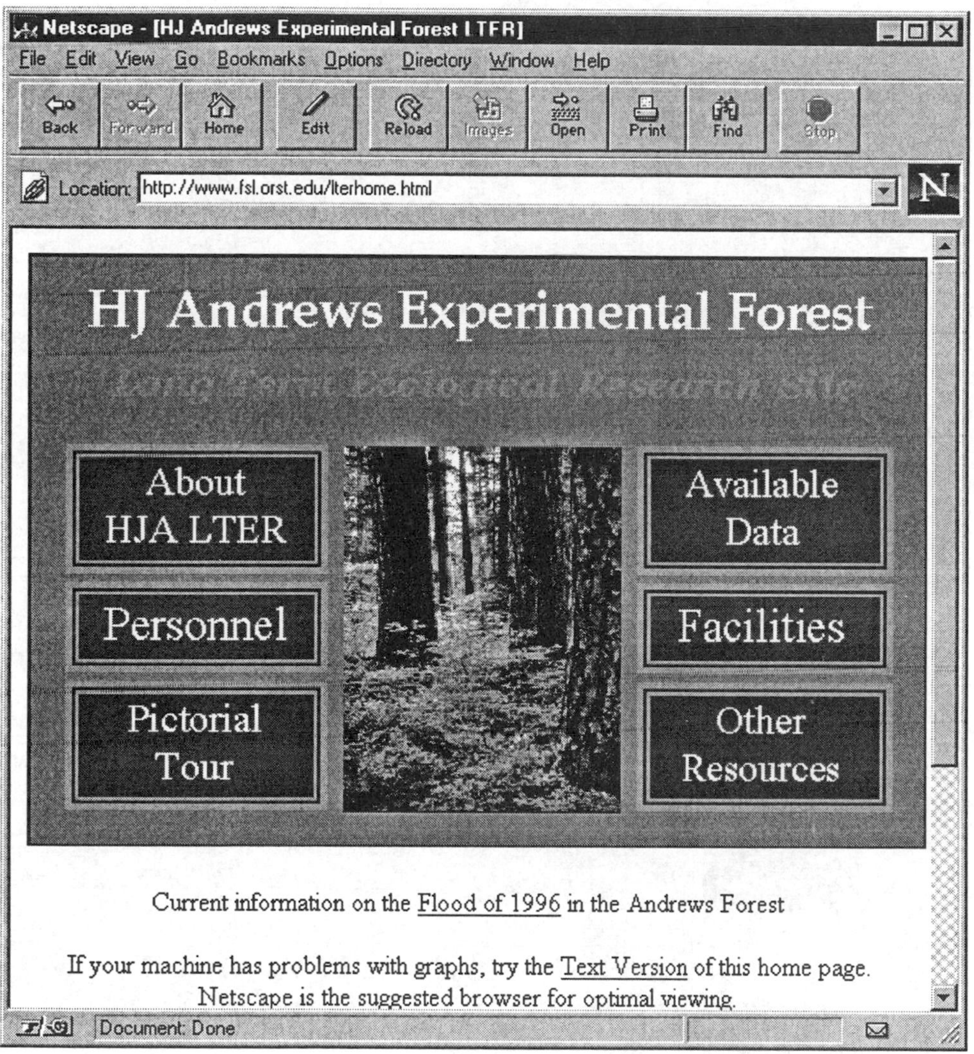

Figure 1.10 HJ Andrews LTER site

Behind the "Available Data" link is the site's archive of data sets in text and mapped format. Visitors to the Data section of the Andrews Web site can download ecological (e.g.,biodiversity, forest succession, carbon dynamics, primary productivity), hydrological (e.g., suspended sediment, daily and monthly stream flow), and climatological data (e.g., precipitation chemistry and acid rain, daily temperature and precipitation, solar radiation) sets. Going to the "Pictorial Tour" link brings up a number of potential tour choices. Visitors to the Web site can take a "virtual tour" describing the landscape, vegetation and wildlife of the Andrews site. Thumbnail images with accompanying descriptive text

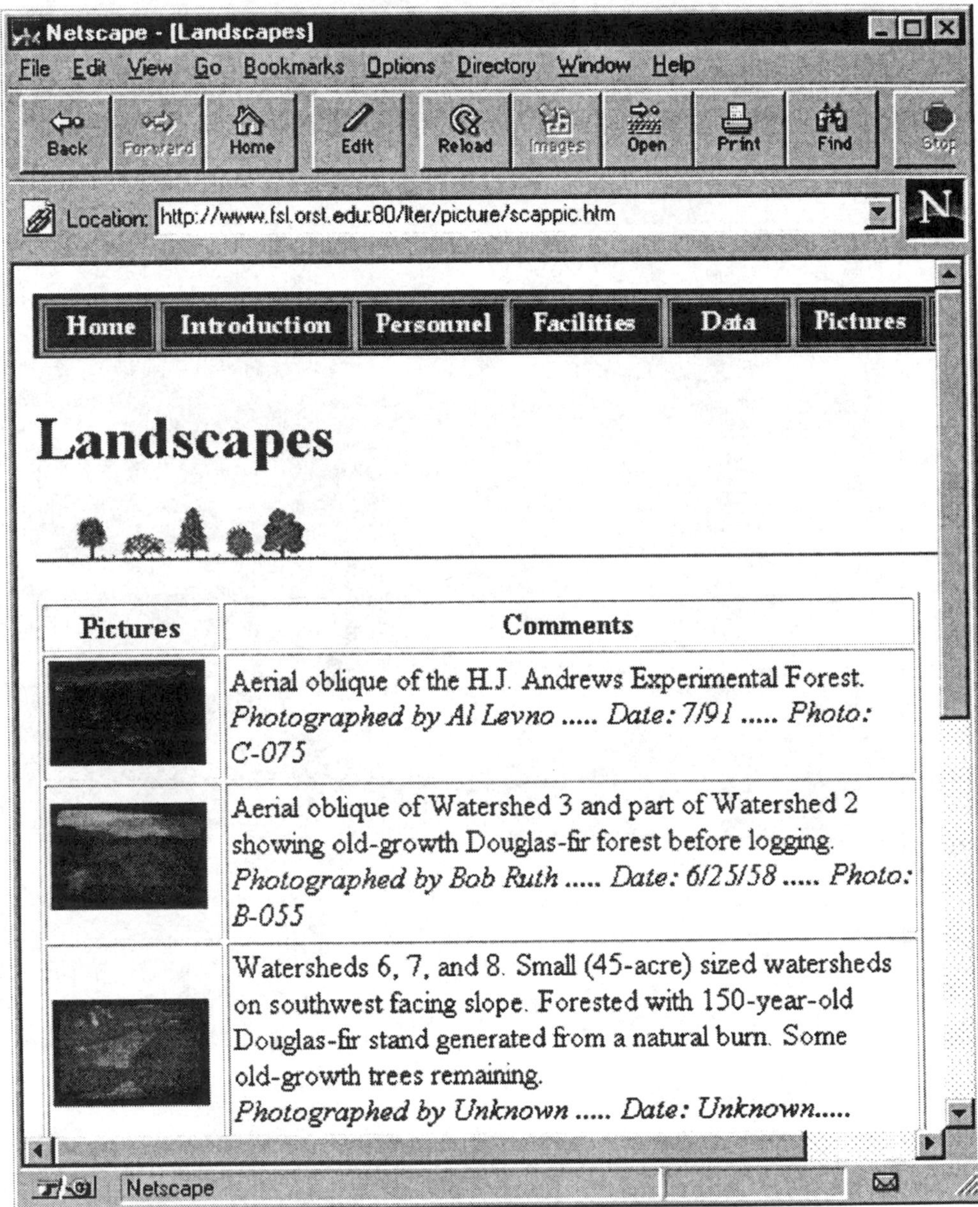

Figure 1.11 HJ Andrews "Landscapes Pictorial Tour" Page

illustrate the topography of the Andrews sites on the "Landscapes" page (Figure 1.11). Clicking on one of the small pictures brings the full-sized image to screen.

Similar home pages and information are available for the other LTER sites. Interconnectivity of online site information supports the cooperative efforts of the program participants to further LTER's mission and goals.

What You Have Learned

- The Internet is a computer "network of networks."
- The Internet encourages information sharing.
- Information discovery and retrieval over the Internet encourages self-motivated learning.
- The Internet provides time-saving and cost-effective means of communication in educational, professional and personal activities.
- Direct and dial-up connections are the primary means of connecting to the Internet.
- SLIP/PPP accounts permit the user's computer to have a physical address on the Internet, which is not possible with a shell account.
- PATIENCE is important.
- Electronic mail is an efficient means of communication.
- Telnet is a means of communicating with remote databases in a variety of forms.
- Gopher and the World Wide Web provide means of linking related data, permitting browsing for information.
- File Transfer Protocol (FTP) is used to transfer data across the Internet.

Apply It!

The goal of ***Earth Online*** is to get you "plugged into" earth science resources on the Internet, and the Apply It! sections are designed to accomplish that very purpose. In our first Apply It! we'll get you on the Internet and using it to create a resource base for studying the impact of the greenhouse effect on hydrological systems. The best way to get started exploring online resources is through the World Wide Web (Chapter 2). It is easy to explore digital information with the "point and click" graphical interface of programs like Microsoft Explorer (Figure 1.12) and Netscape Navigator (Figure. 1.13). We'll use both programs to navigate through the Internet.

The first site you'll visit is the Virtual Earth. The Virtual Earth highlights what is good and bad about online geoscience materials. The Virtual Earth is a "tour through the World Wide Web for earth scientists" intended to "illustrate the potential of the Web as an information retrieval system." Museums, libraries, company sites and Usenet newsgroups and more are accessible from the Virtual Earth.

To explore the Virtual Earth World Wide Web site you'll need access to an Internet-ready computer and a World Wide Web browser. ***Earth Online*** uses the Netscape Navigator graphical user interface (GUI) as its means of maneuvering around the Internet in the

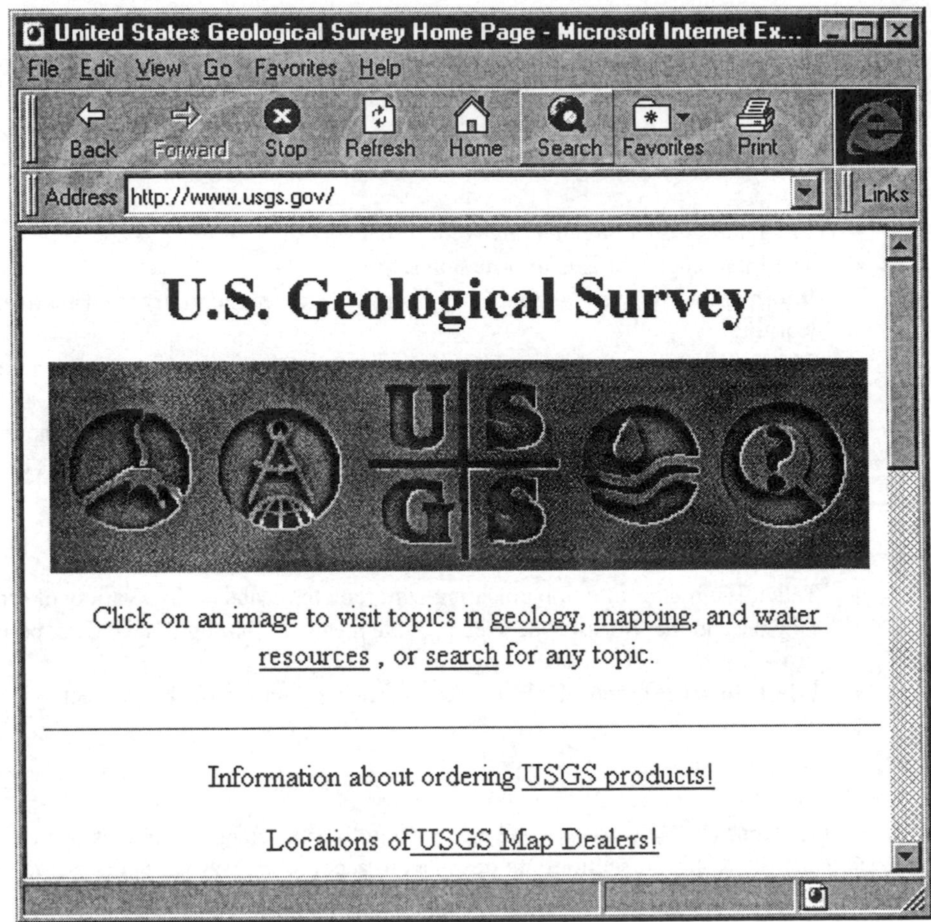

Figure 1.12 Microsoft Internet Explorer World Wide Web browser

Apply It! sections. GUI uses icons, buttons, and menus rather than keyboarded text to perform actions. Graphical user interfaces have the ability to display pictures too. Several versions of the Netscape Navigator are readily available for downloading over the Internet. See Chapter 10 for an Internet software archive to download it from. Check with your computersystem administrator or Internet provider if you don't have these programs. Netscape Navigator Gold for Windows 95 is shown in Figure 1.13.

You only need to know a few functions of a Web browser like Netscape Navigator to explore the Internet. Drop-down menus that perform various actions are located beneath the window title bar. Beneath the menu bar is the toolbar. Buttons on the toolbar perform specific tasks. For instance, the "Open" button is used to connect to sites on the Internet. When you click this button, Netscape will request an Internet address. "Forward" and

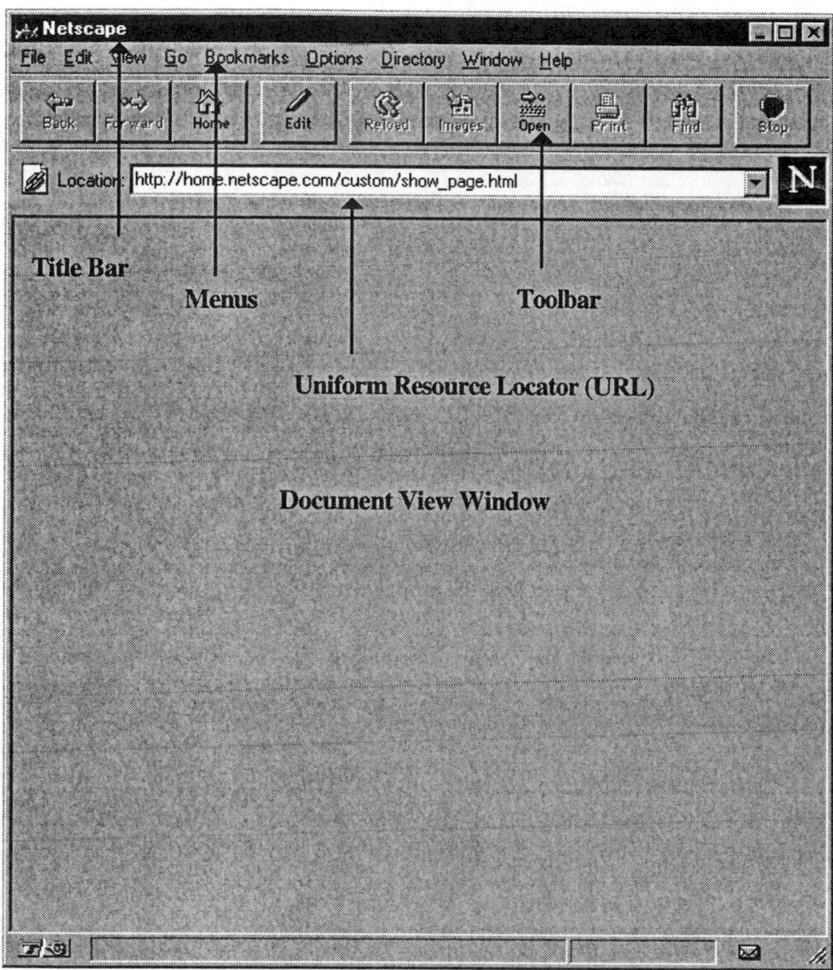

Figure 1.13 The Netscape Navigator World Wide Web browser software

"Back" buttons send you to previously visited sites ahead or behind the one visible in the document view window. The "Home" button will send you to the home page configured for the browser. A home page is the first document loaded at a Web site or the first document read into your browser upon start-up. The "Stop" button stops the transfer of information to your browser. A "Reload" button is used to refresh the document in the document display window. There are many other buttons and menus you can test as we proceed through **Earth Online**.

Next comes the Uniform Resource Locator or Location (URL) window. This is where the address of the site you are connected to is displayed. A connection can be made by

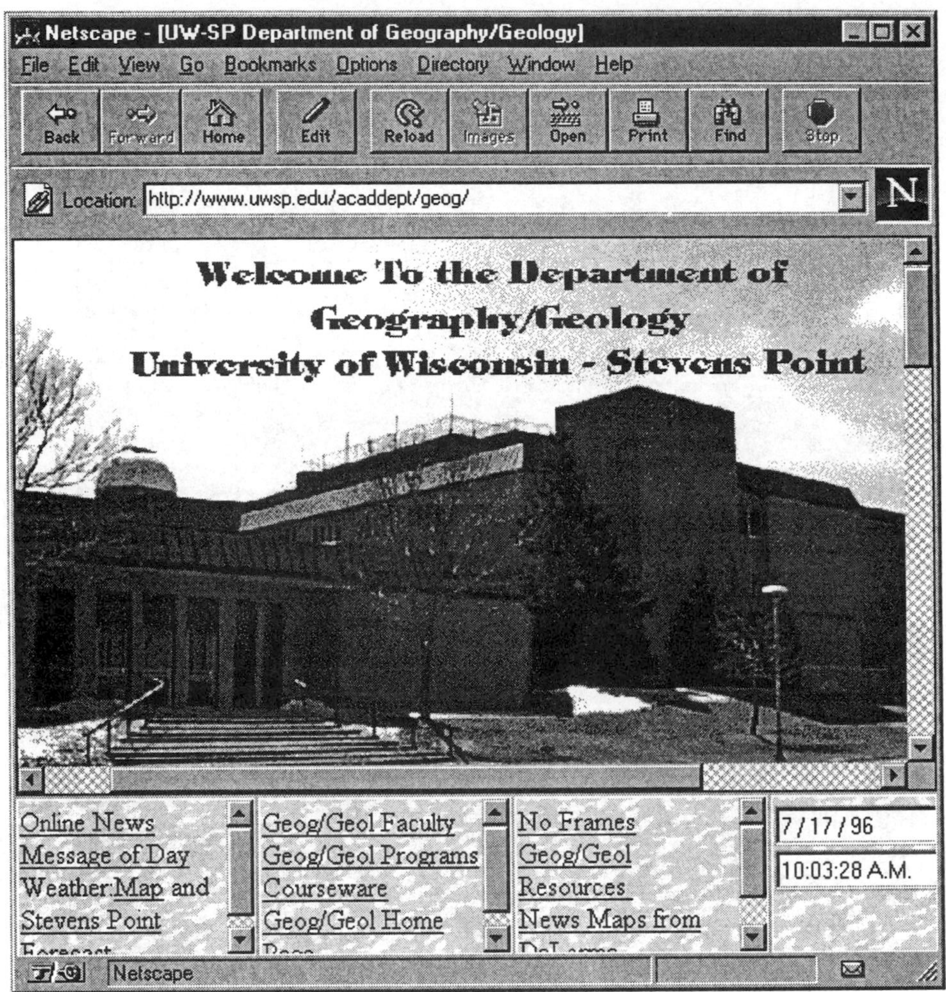

Figure 1.14 Framed document view window

typing the address into this window and pressing return. The small arrow to the left of the window drops a menu down to display previously visited sites. A new development in browser software is the use of frames. The document view window can be divided up into a number of frames.

Each frame displays an online document. Individual frames can be targeted to retrieve information. For instance, the bottom row of frames on the home page in Figure 1.14

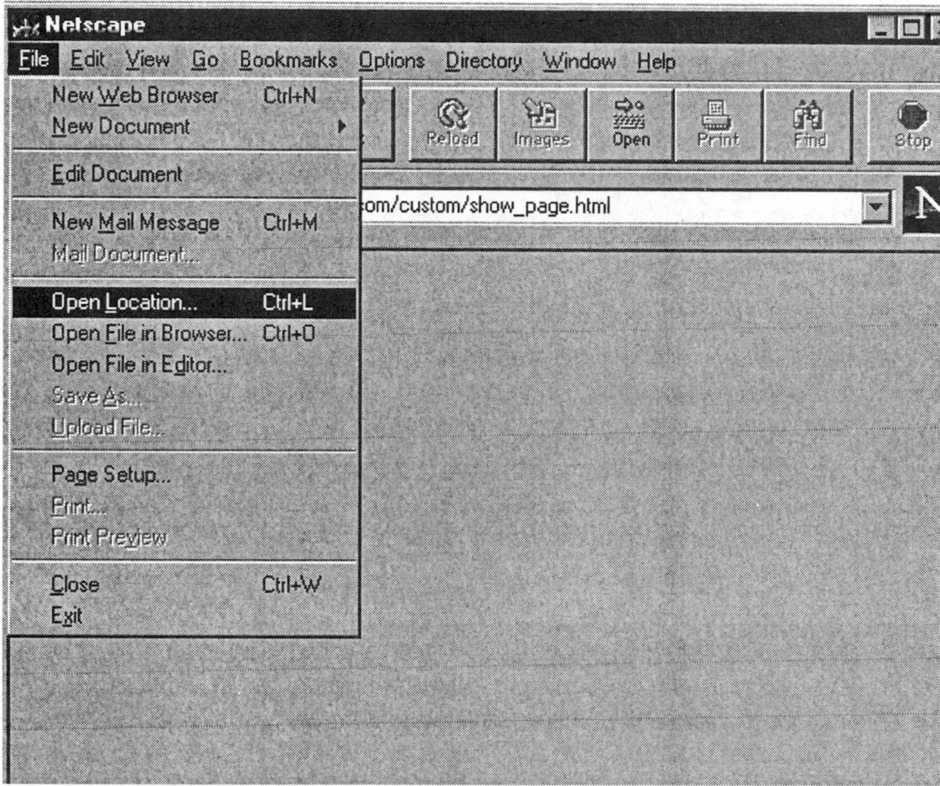

Figure 1.15 Opening a connection to a Web site

display their linked resources in the larger "display" frame above. Some World Wide Web sites use frames to keep a table of contents on screen while the user browses the site.

To connect to the Virtual Earth home page click the "Open" button or use the "File" drop-down menu to bring up the "Open Location" dialog box (Figure 1.15). Type the URL for the Virtual Earth given below into the field and click the "OK" button.

http://atlas.es.mq.edu.au/users/pingram/v_earth.htm

If all goes well you'll soon have the Virtual Earth home page displayed in your browser (Figure 1.16).

Notice that some of the text is highlighted and underlined. These are "hyperlinks," which are discussed in greater detail in Chapter 2. Suffice it to say that when clicked, a

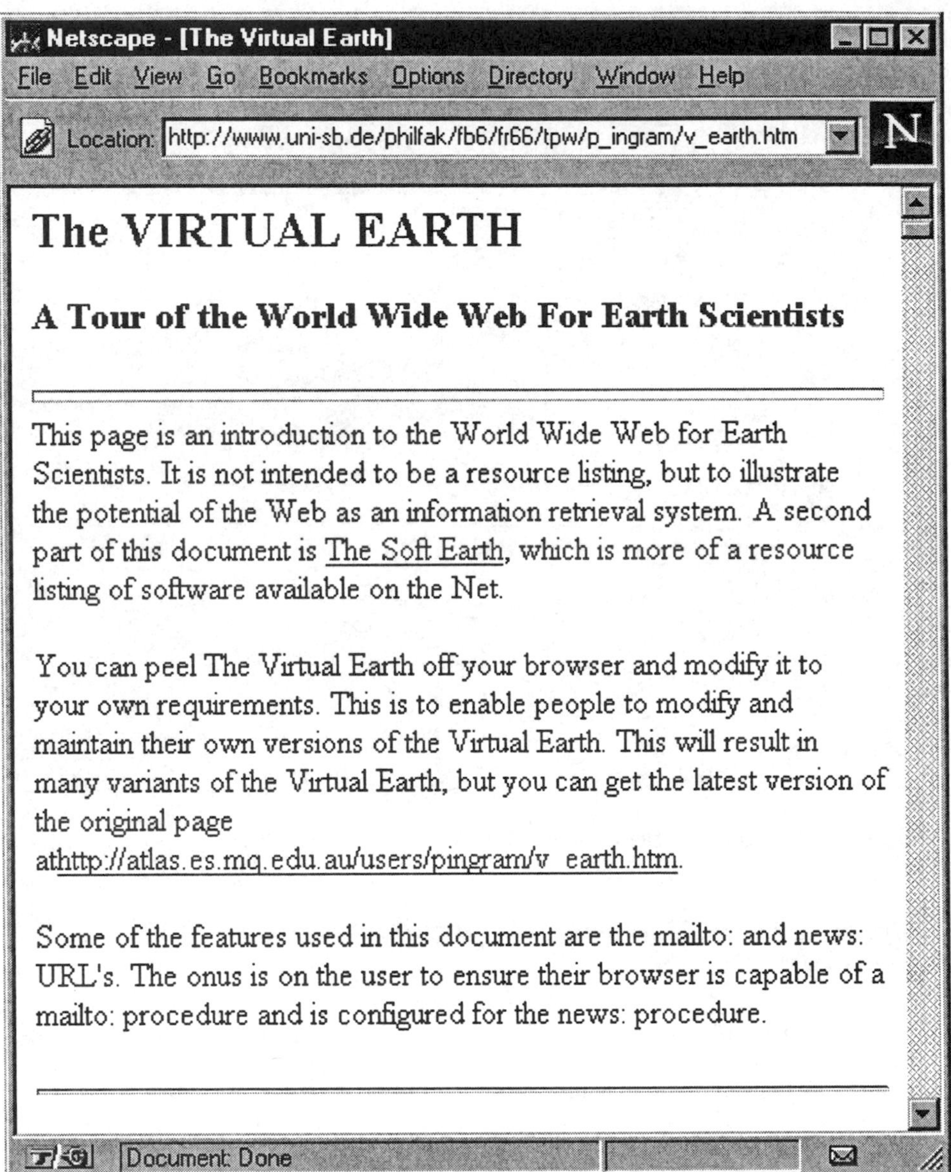

Figure 1.16 The Virtual Earth Home Page

hyperlink connects you to a related resource somewhere else on the Internet. Scrolling down the document brings you to the Table of Contents, which is a list of hyperlinks. Clicking on the "Earth Science Connections" retrieves a description of various earth science resources on the World Wide Web. After scrolling down a bit we encounter a link to the Global

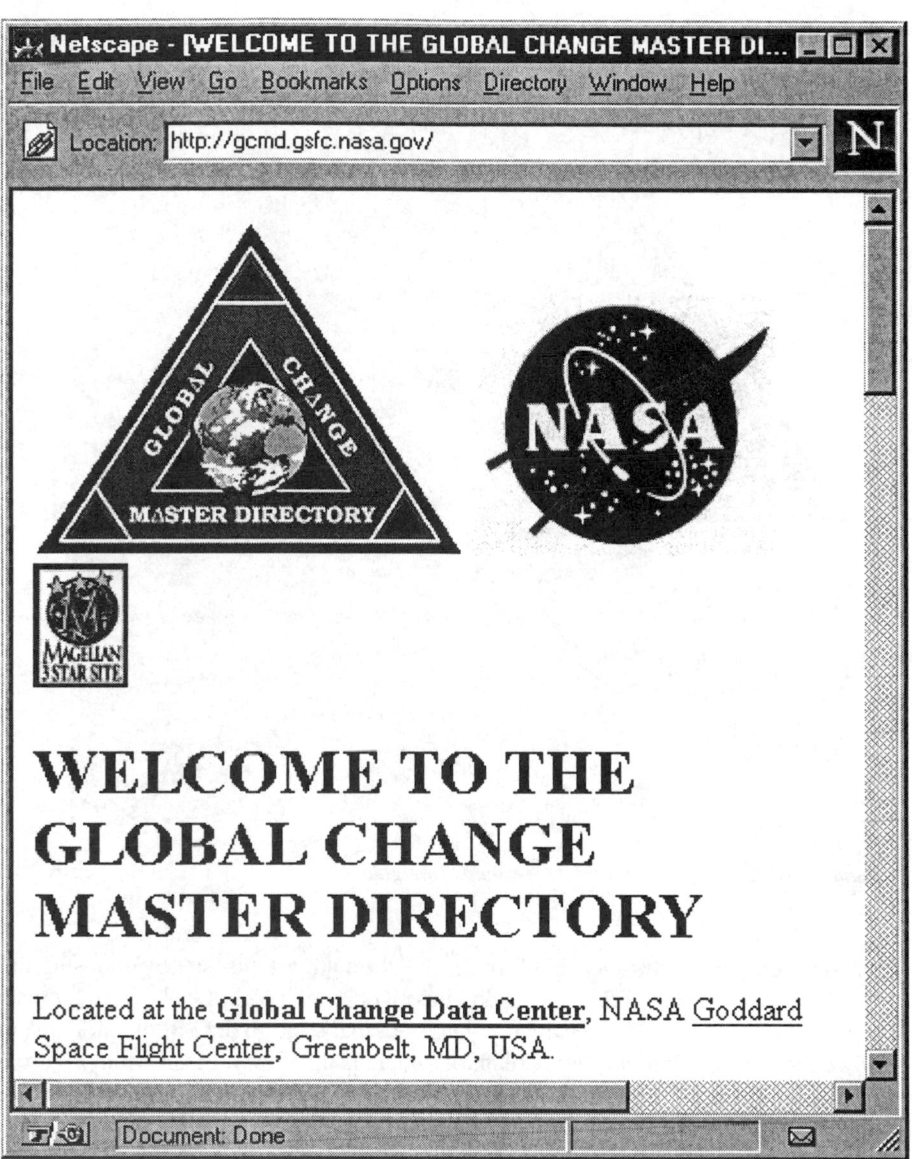

Figure 1.17 Global Change Master Directory home page

Change Master Directory (**URL - http://gcmd.gsfc.nasa.gov/**). Choosing the GCMD hyperlink connects to its home page located at NASA's Goddard Space Flight Center in Greenbelt, Maryland (Figure 1.17). The GCMD provides a comprehensive repository of information about worldwide earth science data holdings and is an excellent place to start

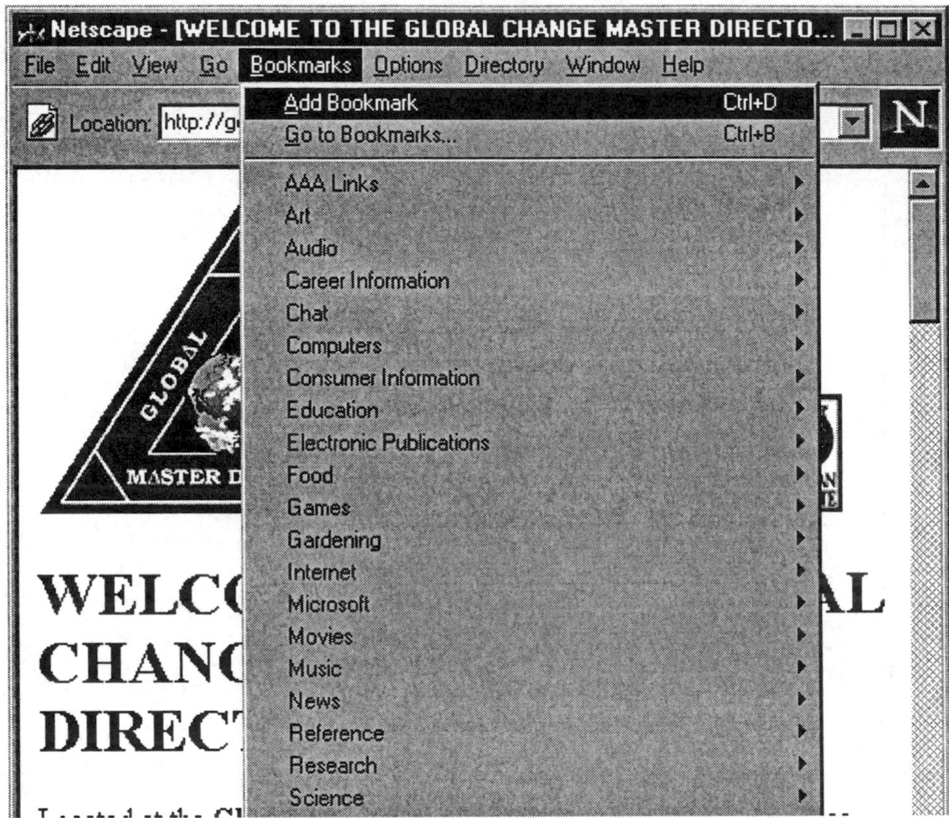

Figure 1.18 Adding a bookmark to Netscape Navigator

when looking for earth science information. I'll bookmark this site by choosing the "Bookmarks" menu and then the "Add bookmark" menu pick. Bookmarking creates a"shortcut" to a site. To view and use your bookmarks go to the "Bookmark" menu. A drop-down menu of bookmarks and bookmark folders is displayed, as shown in Figure 1.18. Edit your bookmarks by choosing the "Go to Bookmarks" menu pick to open the bookmark window. You'll read more about bookmarks in Chapter 2, "Browsing the Internet with Gopher and the World Wide Web."

Having taken this short journey into "cyberspace," you've gotten a feel for navigating the Internet. There is much more to see and do on the Internet and the World Wide Web. Apply It! sections in the chapters to come will show you how to find and gather resources from the Internet. We'll develop a way to organize these resources in Chapter 8, "Putting the Internet to Work."

Try It Out!

1. If you haven't done so yet, get connected! If you're connecting from a school or business, ask your computer system administrator how you get your office computer connected to the Internet. If you're connecting from home, you'll need to find an Internet service provider. Internet service providers are popping up all over the place. Most large communities have an Internet provider.

2. Explore the Wadsworth Publishing Earth System Science Resource site (**URL - http://zelda.thomson.com/rcenters/earthnet/earth_sci.html**). Here you'll find links to other Internet "hotlists," access to earth science data, virtual field trips and more. Check in from time to time as new resources are being added.

3. Connect to the ***Earth Online*** Web site (**URL - http://ritter.wadsworth.com**) and get updates on the ***Earth Online*** text. The ***Earth Online*** Web site has one of the most extensive lists of online geoscience references on the Internet, and we're adding more each month.

4. Offline browsing can pay big dividends in finding online resources. Peruse the professional journals in your area of interest to see what others are doing on the Internet. Some journals routinely publish articles about new online resources. For example, GIS World publishes a regular column called "Netlink." And many new and popular Internet magazines, like NetGuide, publish directories of Internet resources on a monthly basis.

5. Read ahead in ***Earth Online*** for exciting digital roads to earth science information online.

CHAPTER 2

Browsing the Internet with Gopher and the World Wide Web

Internet browsing systems differ from ones like FTP because they allow a user to interactively locate and evaluate information stored on a remote computer without having to retrieve the contents of a file or directory to know what it contains. More importantly, browsing systems connect information on one computer to related information stored on the same computer or on another computer located somewhere else. In this chapter we will look at two means of browsing the Internet, a simple browsing system like Gopher and the more advanced World Wide Web. Gopher uses a series of menus to navigate between information on the Internet while the World Wide Web uses context-sensitive links embedded in documents to branch off to related Internet resources. Earth science organizations have taken great advantage of the resources that Gopher and the World Wide Web have to offer. For instance:

- The Earthquake Information Gopher server **(URL - gopher://nisee.ce.berkeley.edu)** is provided as a public service of the University of California-Berkeley's National Information Service for Earthquake Engineering Research Institute (NISEE). The NISEE Gopher provides information about earthquake engineering, disaster response, and hazards mitigation.
- NASA's Earth Observing System Data and Information System (EOSDIS) **(URL - http://gcmd.gsfc.nasa.gov/gcmdeos.html)** maintains several World Wide Web sites to provide researchers with access to the entire NASA Earth Science Data Collection through the Distributed Active Archive Centers (DAACs).
- The University of California-Berkeley ushers you through an online tour of its Paleontology Museum **(URL - http://ucmpl.berkeley.edu)**, complete with full-color images of dinosaurs, sound files, and instructive text.
- The Texas Natural Resources Information System **(URL - http://www.twdb.state.txus/www/tnris/tnris_hp.html)** provides access to an extensive catalog of data like GIS coverage at the county level of transportation routes, water features, remotely sensed images and a variety of socioeconomic data.

Searching and Browsing for Information

Searching and browsing are two different approaches for seeking out information on the Internet. *Searching* implies that a particular piece of information, say, a groundwater geochemical data set for central Wisconsin, is being sought. When searching for the data set you look for it on a specific computer or use a searching service to help you find its location. In *browsing* for information you usually have no specific goal in mind; that is, you are merely "looking around" to see what you can find. Actually, browsing involves one of three different methods or strategies depending on the job you are trying to complete. First, *search browsing* is a directed search where the goal is known. You are in effect looking for something in particular but not necessarily employing a distinct search methodology. Second, *general purpose browsing* is the act of consulting sources that have a high probability for finding items of interest. In this case you might be using a broad keyword search to turn up possible sources of information or perusing documents that are related to the subject at hand. Finally, those who randomly move through the Internet without any particular goal in mind use *serendipitous browsing*. You might say that you're just "shopping around" for information when you employ serendipitous browsing. Serendipitous browsing requires the most time, but it can pay great dividends when you chance upon that great site of information. Some of my greatest finds have occurred this way. Accidentally running into information just might spark that idea for your next research project or term paper or force you to look at a problem in a way you hadn't considered before. Browsing for information is a natural approach to information discovery for a distributed information system like the Internet.

Browsing systems generally fall into one of two categories, *simple browsing* or *advanced browsing*. Simple browsing and advanced browsing have similar abilities to connect to remote computers and browse information without having to retrieve the file to view its contents. Simple browsing is accomplished with a well-defined menu structure that includes descriptions of the contents of menu items. The Gopher system uses a simple menu-based browsing technique to navigate through resources on the Internet. Even though Gopher is limited by this approach, it remains a powerful tool for navigating the Internet.

Advanced Browsing and Hypermedia

Advanced browsing permits uniform access to many Internet services and uses links, embedded in the text of documents, to connect information. The World Wide Web is a notable example of an advanced browsing system. Advanced graphical user interface browsers permit the display of inline graphics. Browsing is encouraged when the user is engaged in a hypertext or hypermedia environment like the World Wide Web. A hypertext document is like any other text document in that it can be read, edited and stored. Hypertext, however, contains embedded links between related information located in the same document or information residing in different documents. The information links are called *hyperlinks*. *Hypertext* refers to a text document that contains hyperlinked information. *Hypermedia* goes beyond mere text linkages to include links between images, sound files, or digital video. Pictures can serve as links to text and vice versa. Hypermedia is an exciting way to empower individuals to become active players in the information age.

Using a hypertext document or hypermedia is really not much different than the way many earth scientists interact with "conventional" media. When we use a textbook to find information we usually turn to the index to find its location. While we read the material we might come upon a reference to a picture or statement on another page or to the bibliography. We turn to the "linked" information, process it and either return to our starting point or continue investigating related information. Electronic hypermedia has programmed links between information, making navigation much faster and more efficient. At the click of a button a user moves directly to the new information, processes it, moves to another bit of information or returns to the starting point. For instance, World Wide Web browsers, the software you use to interact with the World Wide Web, highlight linkages to related information with a color different from the standard text and with underlines. For example, a document might describe sedimentary rock layers that comprise the Grand Canyon. Within the text the words "sedimentary rock" are a hyperlink. When the user clicks on "sedimentary rock" she is sent to a definition of sedimentary rocks located in another document. Arriving at the definition, she sees a hyperlink to "sandstone." This link displays an image of sandstone on her computer screen.

Hypermedia has several advantages over conventional, linear forms of communication. First and foremost, hypermedia makes the user an active participant in the information discovery/learning process. The path through many texts or computer-aided instructional materials is defined by the author or programmer. Hypermedia lets users choose their own path through the material and encourages exploration of information in ways that authors might not anticipate. Hypermedia lets users navigate the information in ways that suit their style of learning. It lets them skip past irrelevant information and get to the information they seek. By following various pathways through information, users uncover new ways of approaching a topic or uncover related information by accident.

Digging Through the Internet with Gopher

Gopher is a simple, yet powerful, browsing system for Internet information. Gopher gets its name from the school mascot of the University of Minnesota, the Golden Gophers, where the software was developed. This menu-driven system allows the user to successively access information down through a set of structured paths similar to the file/directory structure on a computer. This feature makes it very useful for Internet neophytes. If you can navigate through your computer directory structure, you can use Gopher. Once you find the information you're looking for, Gopher knows which application (Telnet, FTP, Internet white pages, etc.) to use and starts it for you.

There are hundreds of computer servers running Gopher server software for you to access on the Internet. You can connect to a Gopher:

- by running Gopher from your local Internet provider
- by remotely logging in to a Gopher site with Telnet

- by running a client program on your desktop computer
- by accessing Gopher through a World Wide Web browser

Connecting to Gopher from your local Internet provider may be as simple as typing

```
%gopher <return>
```

at the system prompt. To access most public-access Gophers, you open a remote login session using Telnet. For example:

```
%telnet uxl.cso.uiuc.edu
```

The Telnet server responds with

```
Trying 128.174.5.59 ...
Connected to uxl.cso.uiuc.edu.
Escape character is '^]'.

UofI CCSO - Sequent S81 (uxl.cso.uiuc.edu - ttytz)
4.2+ BSD/5.3 UNIX - Dynix 3.1.2
```

At the login prompt type

```
login: gopher
```

No password is required when you Telnet into a public access Gopher. Once you log on you're ready to start "digging."

Gopher browsers come in many different "species" for different computer environments (DOS, Macintosh, etc.), but most have the same basic features. When you first log on to a Gopher server or "Gopher hole" as they are sometimes called, you are presented with a menu of items to choose from. These items may be text documents, directories, or video or sound files. Figure 2.1 shows a text-based Gopher browsing program. You use the arrow keys to navigate between the entries. The up and down arrows move you vertically through the list. Right and left arrows move between Gopher links. The graphical browser for Windows shown in Figure 2.2 is a useful one because it displays each menu in a separate window. Small icons before each item entry tell the user what the menu choice is linked to. The small folder icons indicate that a menu is linked to a subdirectory, while the page icon indicates a link to a document file. Characters replace icons in a text-based Gopher browser. Gopher information objects (or data types) can be any one of an ever expanding number of items. Gopher associates a number or letter with each information object (Table 2.1). The numbers can be used in Veronica searches as described in Chapter 6.

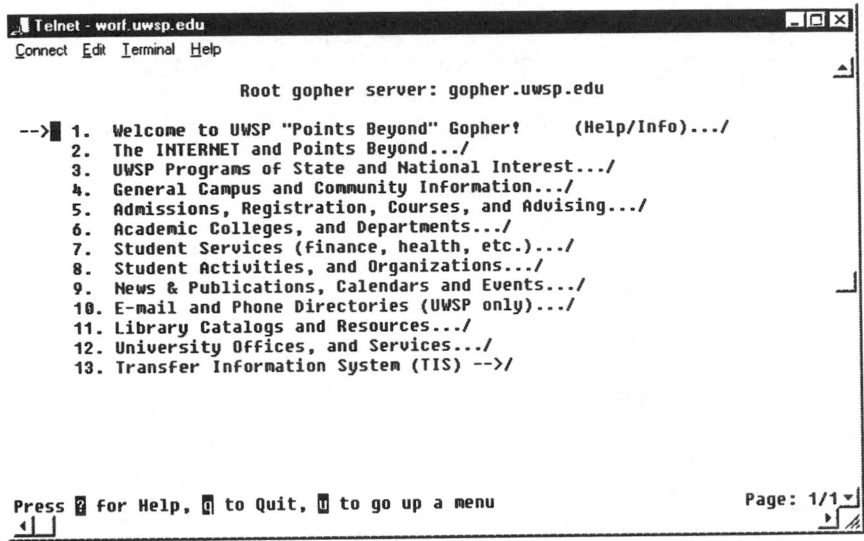

Figure 2.1 Text-based UNIX Gopher browser

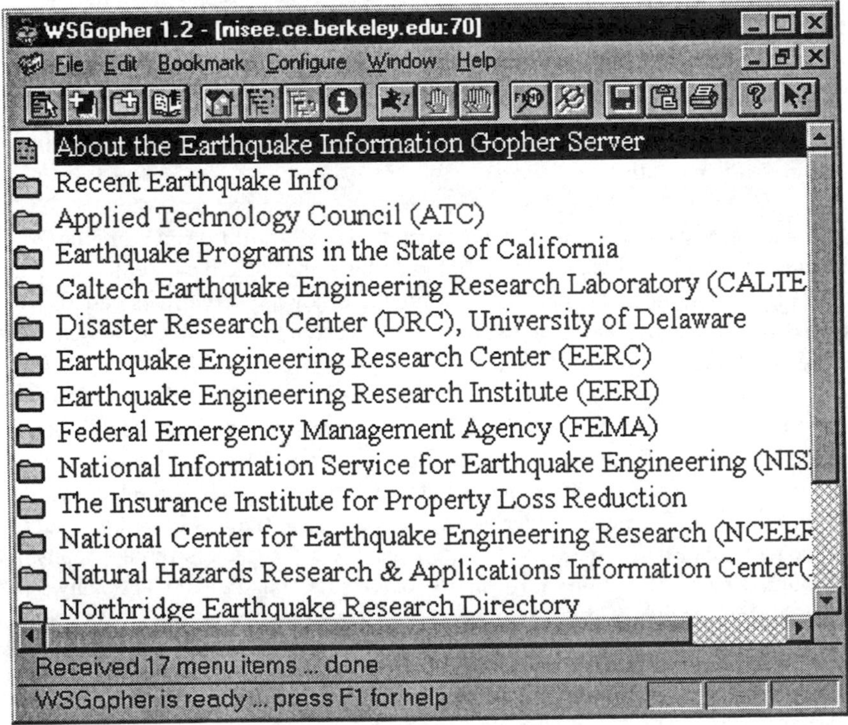

Figure 2.2 Windows-based Gopher browser (WSGOPHER)

Table 2.1 Gopher Data Types

Reference Number	Character Indicator	Information Object (Data Type)
0	.	A text file
1	/	A directory
2	<cso>	A CSO server
3		ERROR
4	<Binhex>	Macintosh BinHex format
5	<PC BIN>	PC binary file
6		Unencoded file
7	<?>	Searchable index
8	<tel>	A Telnet connection
9	<BIN>	A binary
s	<)	Sound file
e		Event (not in v2.06)
I		Image other than GIF
M		MIME
g	<picture>	GIF image
h	<html>	HTML document

It is not that uncommon to lose your way once you have started tunneling through the Internet with Gopher. After the fifteenth or sixteenth site you realize there was some important information you want to look at again eight sites ago, but you have no idea where it is located. Herein lies a major problem with Gopher. You must work down through a hierarchy of menus to get to what you're after. Each time you use Gopher you will march through the same set of menus until you reach your destination. You can't just jump over items to the desired information unless you use bookmarks. *Bookmarks* are address entries in a text file that enable you to mark documents or sites so that you can directly return to them at another time. Most Gopher clients have a bookmark option. On text-based Gopher browsers a bookmark is created by placing the cursor in front of the item and typing the letter "a" to add the item to the bookmark list. Graphical Gopher browsers often have a drop-down menu or button to click for creating bookmarks. Your client software will also let you edit the bookmark file to delete unwanted entries or update addresses. Of course, there's the tried-and-true method of pencil and paper to keep track of those important finds.

Earth Science and Gopher

Gopher service in the past has been a popular way to offer information and data to the Internet community. Yet, much of this information is making its way to the World Wide Web. Several good Gophers for earth scientists still exist, among which is the Earthquake Information Gopher Server (**URL - gopher://nisee.ce.berkeley.edu**). This Gopher hole yields

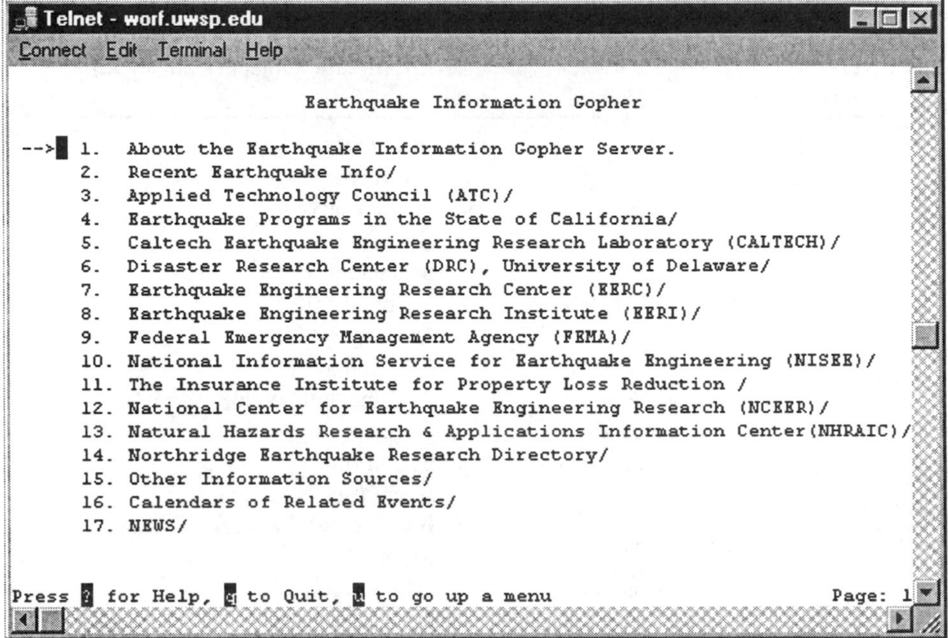

Figure 2.3 Earthquake Information Gopher

a number of useful menus to earth scienctists looking for earthquake information on the Internet.

The Earthquake Information Gopher (Figure 2.3) was created to link together the available online information services in the field of earthquake engineering, earthquake hazard mitigation, and earthquake disaster response. The Gopher document has a long list of online resources, one of which is the Northridge Earthquake Research Directory (Figure 2.4). At this site you'll find information about the Northridge, California earthquake and research that has been done since the disaster. For instance, the "Individuals' Research Projects" menu takes you to abstracts from research relating to the Northridge earthquake and earthquake hazard mitigation.

To learn more about Gopher "burrow" to the home of Gopher (**URL - gopher://gopher.tc.umn.edu**). You'll find information about the program itself, explanations of how to get client software, and a frequently-asked-question file about Gopher.

Navigating the World Wide Web

The World Wide Web is rapidly becoming the most popular part of the Internet. New Web sites are coming online each day. It is no wonder the Web has become so popular with its

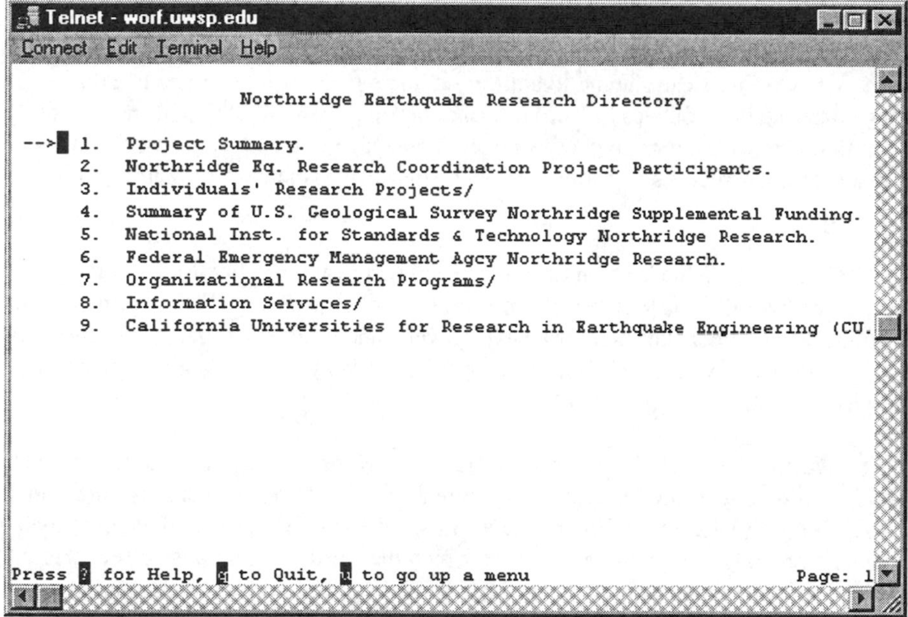
Telnet - worf.uwsp.edu

Connect Edit Terminal Help

```
                     Northridge Earthquake Research Directory

-->  1.  Project Summary.
     2.  Northridge Eq. Research Coordination Project Participants.
     3.  Individuals' Research Projects/
     4.  Summary of U.S. Geological Survey Northridge Supplemental Funding.
     5.  National Inst. for Standards & Technology Northridge Research.
     6.  Federal Emergency Management Agcy Northridge Research.
     7.  Organizational Research Programs/
     8.  Information Services/
     9.  California Universities for Research in Earthquake Engineering (CU.

Press ? for Help, q to Quit, u to go up a menu                     Page: 1
```

Figure 2.4 Northridge Earthquake Research Directory Gopher

ability to display text and full-color graphics, work interactively with remote computers, and carry out video and sound applications, all in a hypermedia environment.

The World Wide Web, the brainchild of Tim Berners-Lee of the Particle Physics Lab in Cern, Switzerland, created a *distributed hypermedia environment* for physicists to share information. A distributed hypermedia environment simply means that the information about a particular subject is distributed on several different computers connected through hypermedia links. World Wide Web servers use a special type of Internet protocol software called HyperText Transfer Protocol (HTTP). HTTP establishes the "rules" by which information is linked and transferred across the World Wide Web. The World Wide Web is not a separate entity, distinct from the Internet. The Web is just another set of computers running HTTP and using the Internet to communicate between them. You link to a World Wide Web server with Web client software called a "browser."

The most popular way of navigating the World Wide Web is with a graphical user interface (GUI). Several graphical interfaces are available, many as shareware or freeware, via FTP, like the National Center for Supercomputing Applications' Mosaic or Netscape's Navigator. These applications are available for the Macintosh, PC-Windows and X-Windows computer environments. After being activated, usually by clicking on a program icon, the browser automatically loads its *home page*. A home page can be many things. It is the top-level document of a Web site. Think of it as the starting page of a site containing links to other pages distributed from the Web site. A home page also is the first page that is loaded by a browser when it is started. Most browsers come preconfigured with a home page, but the user can change to a different home page. A home page is a document created by someone that contains links to information frequently used by that individual. Many users like to create their own customized home page to gain fast access to Internet resources. Chapter 8 shows how to create your own home page to help organize Internet resources.

The World Wide Web environment is a great deal more flexible than any other on the Internet. World Wide Web client software can not only access Web documents, but also connect to Gopher sites, network news servers, and establish Telnet connections and FTP files. Once you've experienced the World Wide Web you'll probably wonder why you need to use any other service.

World Wide Web documents are created in HyperText Markup Language (HTML). HTML documents are really nothing more than ASCII text enclosed by "tags" that tell the Web browser what to do. The user doesn't see the HTML tags when the document appears on-screen. Take the example below, in which the words "greenhouse effect" are a hyperlink to a document that describes the greenhouse effect. The Web browser displays

Desertification is a likely outcome of the greenhouse effect.

But the text in the actual HTML appears as:

Desertification is a likely outcome of the<A HREF = greenhouse.html>
greenhouse effect.</a>

The Web browser decodes the <A HREF> tag as a hyperlink to another document, in this case the greenhouse effect document. The browser underlines the words "greenhouse effect" to tell the user that they are a link to another document.

HTML tags were originally created to process activities, such as telling the browser to retrieve and display a picture on-screen or get a document from another World Wide Web server. Programmers see the document design possibilities of HTML, and new tags are being created to control the formatting of text, the way pictures are displayed, and special actions such as making text blink on and off. Chapter 8 explains HTML in more detail.

The user moves between information by clicking on hyperlinks. Each hyperlink is encoded with a Uniform Resource Locator (URL). The URL tells the Web browser the location of the item that you are linking to. The location includes the type of server the link connects to (Web, Gopher, FTP, etc.), the server's address and directory the file resides in. For example,

http://www.uwsp.edu/acaddept/geog/classes.htm

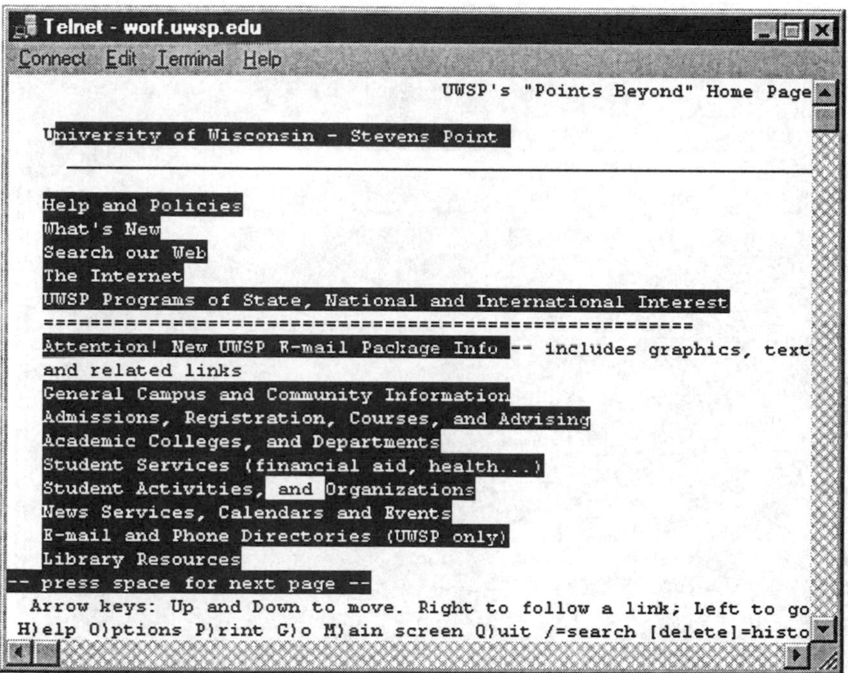

Figure 2.5 LYNX :Text -base browser screen

is the address for a list of geography classes offered by the University of Wisconsin-Stevens Point. The "http" in the URL indicates that the document is located on a World Wide Web server that uses HyperText Transfer Protocol, and "www.uwsp.edu" is the domain name of the server. The remaining portion of the address indicates the subdirectories (acaddept/ geog/) and the name of the file (classes.htm). The extension "htm" indicates that the document is coded in HyperText Markup Language. HTM Language documents also use .html as a file extension.

In the example above, the URL pointed to a Web server given by the http in the address. World Wide Web browsers can connect to other Internet servers as well. When connecting to other servers, the http is replaced with:

gopher	to connect to a Gopher server
ftp	to connect to a FTP site
telnet	to initiate a remote login session
news	to connect to a network news server
wais	to search an Wide Area Information Server

Web browsers come in two different varieties. Text-based browsers like Lynx (Figure 2.5) can only display text information. The links to other documents or files are highlighted

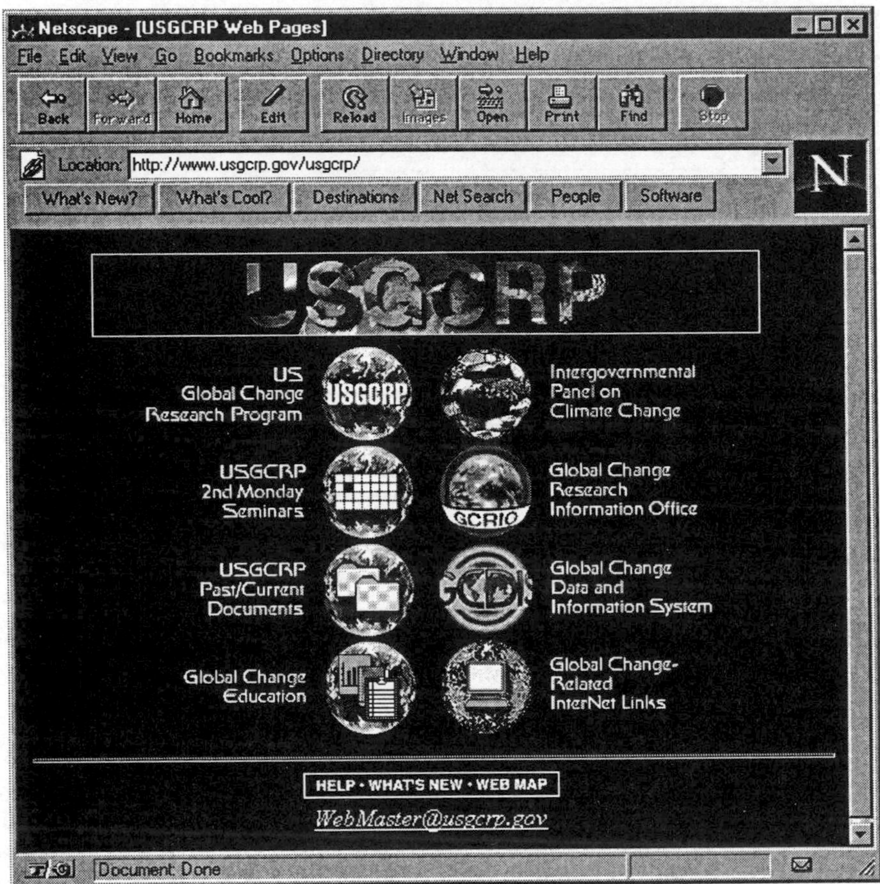

Figure 2.6 Graphical Web Netscape browser screen

in a text-based browser. A user navigates through the World Wide Web using the arrow keys on the keyboard. The up and down arrows move between links on a page while the right arrow moves forward and left arrow back between Web documents. Depressing the enter key over a highlighted link navigates to the site as well. Direct navigation to a site is done by typing the letter "g," entering the URL of the site and then pressing the enter key. Even though graphics are not displayed on screen in a text-based browser, a placeholder can be displayed at the location of a picture or graphic in a document. These usually appear as text inside a bracket.

Most of the popular graphical user interface browsers share common attributes and functions. Figure 2.6 illustrates the popular Netscape Web browser interface. Along the top of the Netscape window is the *title bar,* which tells the user the title of the document being read. Beneath the title bar is the menu bar. Each has a drop-down menu for performing a variety of tasks. The "File" menu lets users load files from their computer, open a URL, or email the document being read. The "Edit" menu lets users copy and paste items from the document or URL location field. A user can reload the present document or view the source code. Viewing a document's HTML code is a good way of learning how to create Web pages, but be aware that not all authors strictly obey good HTML style. The "Go" menu enables users to return to their default home page, navigate forward and back through previously visited documents and view a list of URLs that have been visited during their present online session. The "Bookmark" menu enables users to add and view bookmarks. The "View" menu allows users to edit bookmarks into user-defined subject areas. The "Options" menu permits users to customize the browser. Choices in the "Options" menu permit users to hide or show various menus, toolbars and status bars. Under the "Preferences" choice, users tell the browser what home page to load at start-up, what colors and fonts are available for text and links, what helper applications to use for image, audio and video files accessed from aremote Web site, or whether to simply save such files to disk. The "Directory" menu gives users choices for accessing a variety of Internet search engines, white pages, and browser-specific information. Most browsers include a "Help" menu to answer questions about using the browser and often the World Wide Web. You can access the drop-down menus either by pointing and clicking with a mouse or using the appropriate keystrokes. A toolbar of buttons for quick access to frequently used functions accessed from the drop-down menus also is provided. The toolbar is found directly beneath the menu bar in the Netscape browser shown in Figure 2.6. The URL window or box is found beneath the toolbar in the Netscape browser. The URL field gives you the full address down to the subdirectory and document file name. Most browsers will allow you to type a URL into the box and at the click of the mouse button or tap of the enter key send you off to that URL address. You can copy and paste URLs into this box. This is a handy feature when you come across a URL in a document that isn't already linked or you encounter URLs in an email message.

Earth Online Tip: Most browsers have the ability to turn in-line images off and on. Turn in-line images off to conserve bandwidth unless they're absolutely necessary.

Documents read by the browser are displayed in the document view window. Scroll bars along the side and bottom permit the user to scroll down and across the window to view items that first appear off-screen. Most browsers like Netscape allow you to copy information from the document that is displayed. This is usually done by positioning the mouse at the beginning of the line, clicking and dragging the cursor across the text to highlight it and choosing the copy option. You then switch to the application you want to paste the copied information into and perform the paste function within the application.

Most graphical browsers allow you to distinguish between visited and unvisited links. Visited links are usually underlined and highlighted in a color different from normal text. Once you click on the hyperlink, its color will change, indicating that you have paid a visit to the linked information. Browsers like Netscape permit the user to decide how long the visited hyperlink color should remain before reverting back to the unvisited color.

The beauty of graphical World Wide Web browsers like Netscape, Mosaic, and Internet Explorer from Microsoft is that you can do so many things with them. Chapter 3 shows you how to send electronic mail; downloading files from FTP servers is described in Chapter 4; and initiating Telnet sessions is discussed in Chapter 5.

Earth Science and the World Wide Web

Many earth scientists have recognized the intrinsic value of the World Wide Web as a medium for the delivery of earth science information. The ability to display imagery and its interactivity are noteworthy features that draw earth scientists to the Web. A number of excellent Web sites have appeared at universities and affiliated research institutes, and increasingly on Web servers sponsored by governmental agencies.

A wonderful resource for the study of volcanoes and tectonic activity can be found at Volcano World **(URL - http://volcano.und.nodak.edu/vw.html)** (Figure 2.7). Volcano World brings "modern and near real time volcano information" to the Internet. Volcano World draws on an extensive library of remote sensing images and archival data collections. By following the links

⇒Volcanoes of the World **(URL - http://volcano.und.nodak.edu/volc_of_world.html)**
⇒What's Erupting Now! **(URL - http://volcano.und.nodak.edu/vwdocs/current_volcs/current.html)**

you will get to a world map displaying the locations of current volcanic activity (Figure 2.8). Under the map is a list of the sites. Hot spots on the map, as well as the text links beneath, send the reader off to information about that site. Going to the "Devil's Desk, Alaska Peninsula, Alaska" page **(URL - http://volcano.und.nodak.edu/vwdocs/volc_images/north_america/alaska/devils_desk.html)** brings up a photograph and information about the volcano (Figure 2.9). Additional volcano information and photos are a hyperlink away at the "Alaska Volcano Observatory" **(URL - http://www.avo.alaska.edu/).**

The Alfred Wegener Institute for Polar and Marine Research **(URL - http://www.awi-bremerhaven.de/)** (AWI) is one of sixteen national research centers in Germany. The AWI is primarily financed by the German Federal Ministry for Research. The AWI is charged with undertaking fundamental scientific research in the polar regions, coordinating national polar research projects, and promoting international cooperation in polar and marine research. The AWI Web site is its online gateway to polar research data. A number of meteorological and hydrographic data sets are available from the site. Much of the data requires authorization to access. Visitors, however, can retrieve near-real-time graphs of air

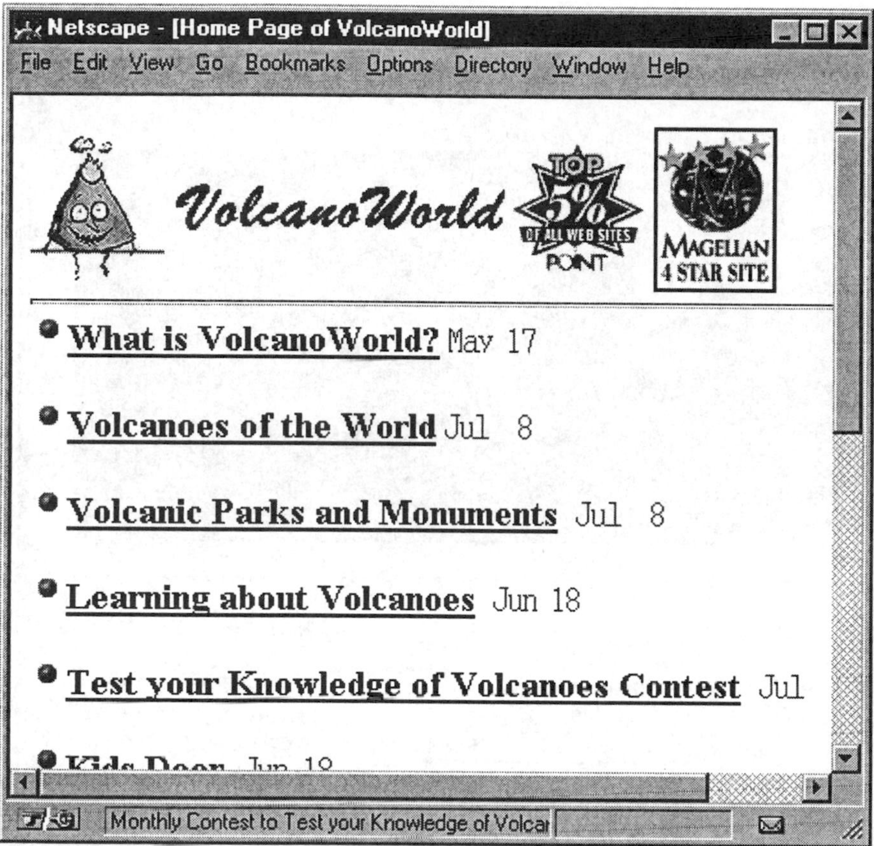

Figure 2.7 Volcano World home page

temperature, precipitation and atmospheric pressure, and mean yearly temperature from 1981 to 1994, as well as a number of other types of data graphs. An online hydrographic atlas of the southern ocean also is available from the AWI Web site. "OCEAN-DATA-VIEW," a software package for the visualization of oceanographic data on a PC, is available for downloading. And data from the World Ocean Circulation Experiment (WOCE) and the NODC World Ocean Atlas, 1974, can be imported directly into the program.

Virtual Field Trips

One of the most valuable professional and educational experiences that any earth scientist can have is taking a field trip. Nothing can substitute for the real, hands-on experience one gets from "mucking about in the field." No book can replace the feeling of looking down from a lofty perch to examine the twists and turns of a river as it erodes its channel into a deep bedrock canyon or the thrill of hiking through a forest examining its various

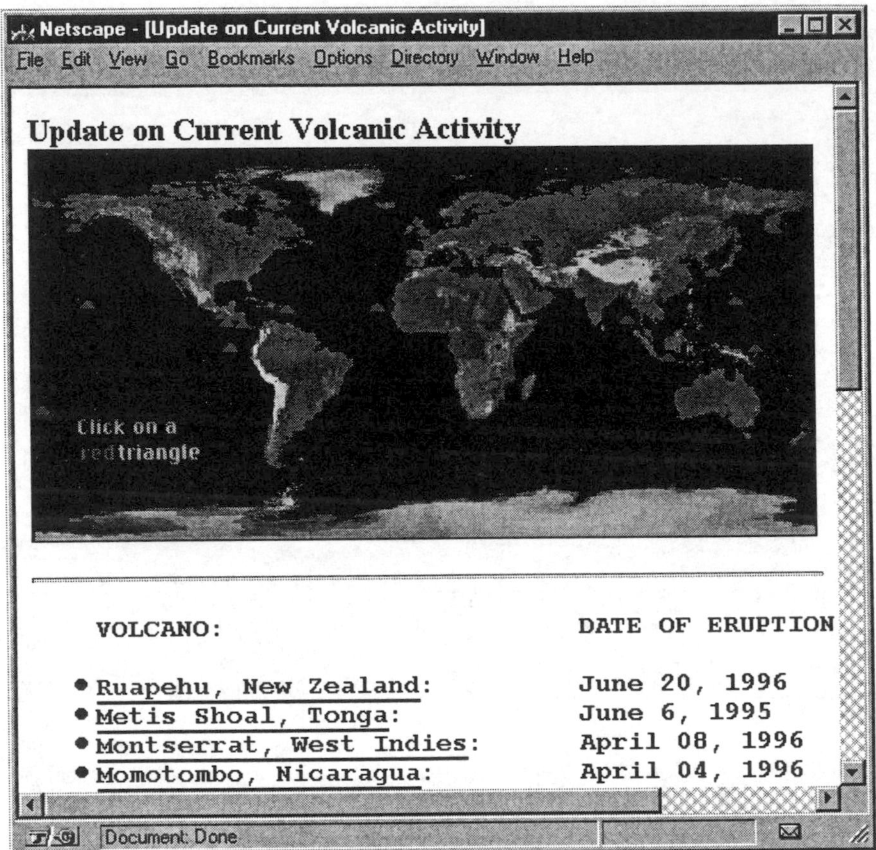

Figure 2.8 Volcano World's "Update on Current Volcanic Activity"

communities of vegetation and animals. However, situations arise when it is impractical, logistically difficult, or physically impossible to get out in the field. Weather may prevent your visit to an educational field site, or a physically disabled student may not be able to navigate a difficult path through a forest. Under these circumstances, virtual field trips may be a reasonable substitute. Virtual field trips are a good pretrip activity. Having students review the trip online prior to conducting prepares them for what they are about to experience.

Virtual field trips utilize computer technology to simulate an excursion to a particular place. Virtual field trips may be "guided" by specific pathways through the landscape as defined by the programmer, or travelers can choose their own way, as one would in a hypermedia environment. Virtual field trips let us see the world from new and unusual perspectives. On a virtual field trip one might switch from ground level to a satellite view of a site at the click of a mouse. The Internet, and specifically the World Wide Web, is the

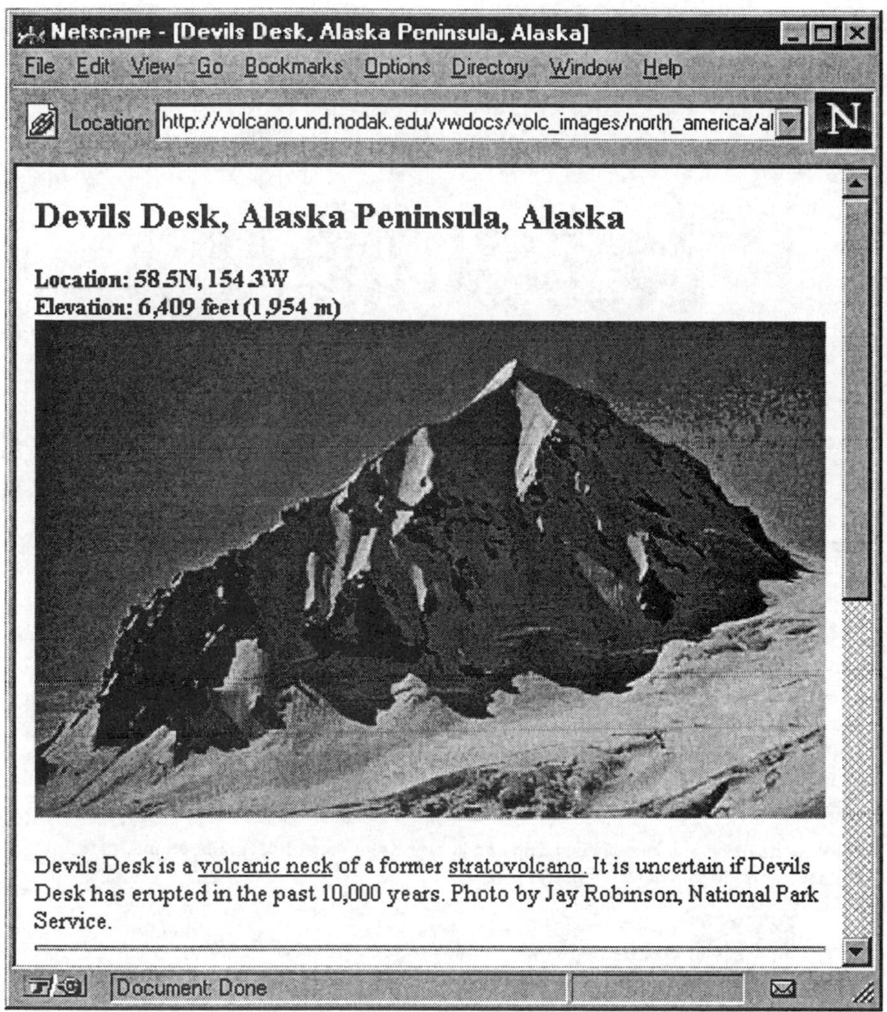

Figure 2.9 Volcano World's "Devil's Desk, Alaska Peninsula, Alaska" page

latest environment for conducting virtual field trips. For instance, the University of Hawaii's Hawaii Virtual Field Trips (**URL - http://www.satlab.hawaii.edu/space/hawaii/virtual.field.trips.html**) are wonderful examples of taking "field trips" over the Internet (Figure 2.10).

The Hawaii Virtual Field Trips home page offers several trips around the islands. For example, you can take a virtual field trip around the Kilauea volcano. From the Kilauea Virtual Field Trips page (**URL - http://www.satlab.hawaii.edu/space/hawaii/vfts/kilauea/kilauea.vfts.html**) you have the choice of examining the volcano from space using a variety

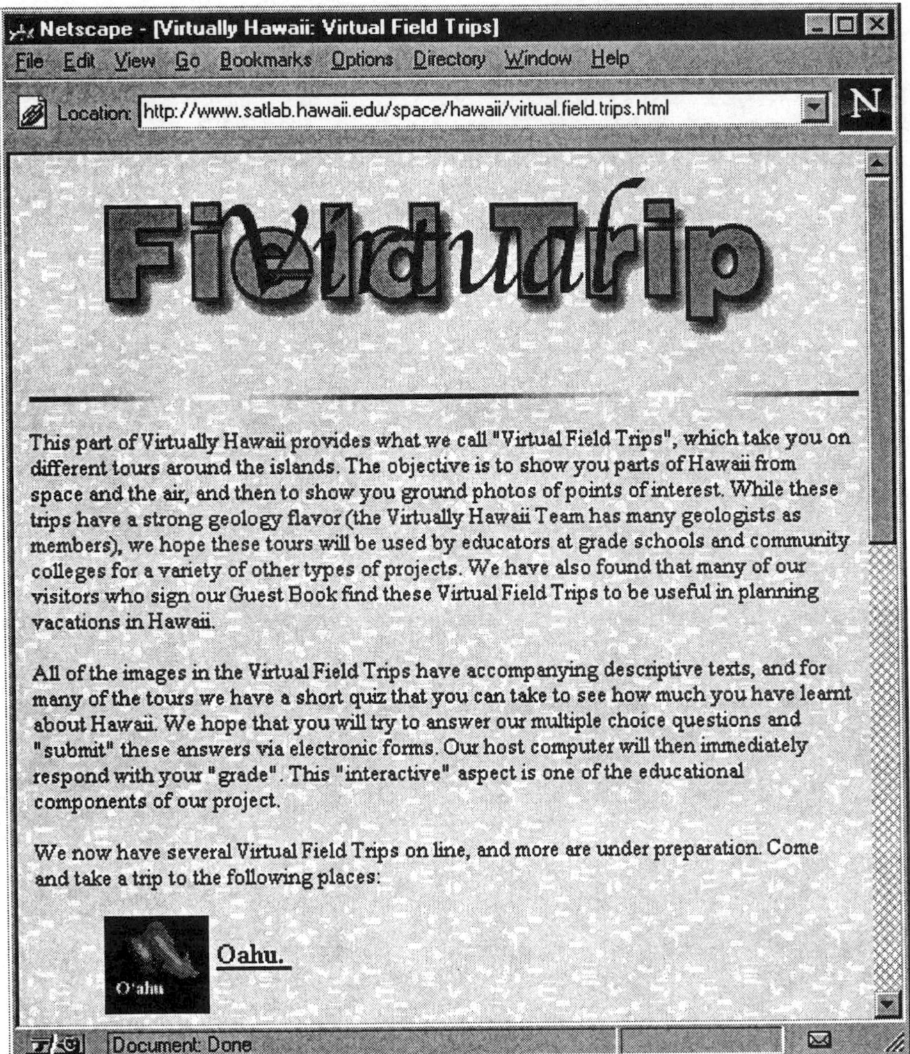

Figure 2.10 Hawaii Virtual Field Trips home page

of satellite and space shuttle photographs or taking a ground-level tour. At the remote sensing page (Figure 2.11) (**URL -http://www.satlab.hawaii.edu/space/hawaii/vfts/kilauea/kilauea.remote.sensing.htm**) a series of reduced-sized photographs from different high-altitude sources are displayed with accompanying descriptive information. Synthetic Aperture Radar, digital elevation models and conventional air photographs make up the collection. When clicked on by a mouse, each smaller photograph will display a larger version of itself. Next, you can get a closer look at the topography by taking a ground-level

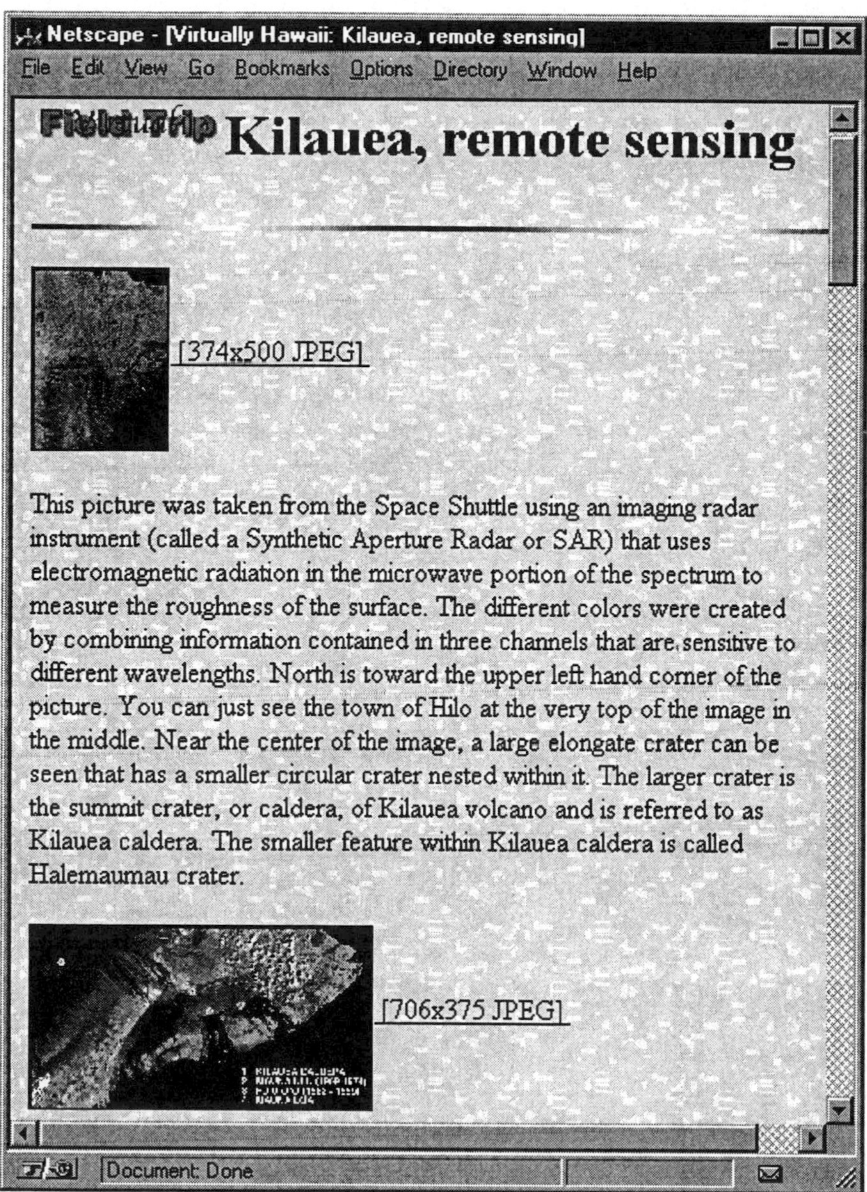

Figure 2.11 Kilauea remote sensing page

tour around the crater. On the ground-level tour page (Figure 2.12) you can "walk" between nine different sites highlighted on a high-altitude photograph of the crater. Each numbered site links to a page that has a photograph and descriptive information about the field site. The user has the option of moving to the next site from this page, returning to the ground

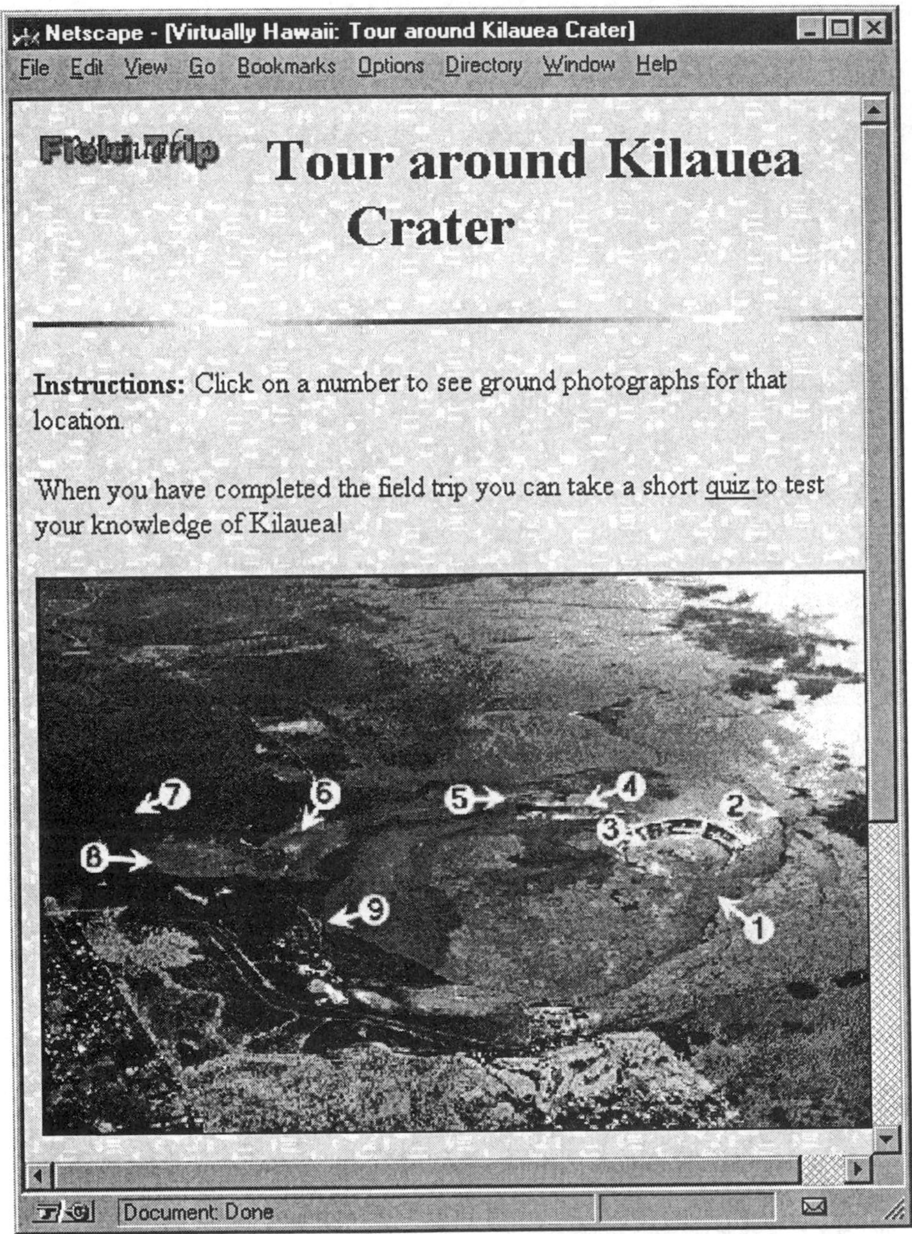

Figure 2.12 Kilauea ground-level tour page

level tour page, or skipping over a few sites. The Hawaii Virtual Field Trip is a great educational resource.

World Wide Web and Earth Science Education

Educators are finding the World Wide Web an extremely useful environment for the delivery of educational materials. Its unique ability to integrate text, graphics, video, and audio make it the kind of multimedia environment suitable for teaching about the complex systems that make up our earth system. Integration of World Wide Web resources into curriculum is occurring at all grade levels in a variety of interesting ways. Delivery of instructional materials may range from a nonhypertext set of lecture outlines to a full, Internet-integrated laboratory exercise.

At the University of Wisconsin-Stevens Point Department of Geography/Geology **(URL - http://www.uwsp.edu/acaddept/geog/geog.htm)** Internet resources are being integrated into all levels of the curriculum. A hypertext version of the introductory physical geography class handbook has been put online **(URL - http://www.uwsp.edu/acaddept/geog/geog101.htm)** for students to access. The handbook contains information about the class, online review questions and an online syllabus. The class uses a variety of Internet resources to illustrate subjects discussed throughout the semester. Links to the resources are provided through the online syllabus. During the first week of the semester, students are given an assignment to log on to the World Wide Web, access the online course guidebook and explore the Web. The intent of the assignment is two-fold: first, to introduce students to Internet technology as applied in geography, and second, to pique their interest in using the Internet for other activities and classes. Their assignment is to navigate to the "Internet Resources for Geography and Geology" page and browse through the links for something that might interest them. They follow the link they have chosen, note what they find and then send an electronic mail message to the instructor as to what they have found. From my experience, students greatly appreciate being introduced to Internet technology early in their academic career and rapidly apply what they have learned about the Internet in other classes. Internet resources are used to supplement daily lecture material and serve as n individualized learning modules. An online hypertext lecture entitled Global Climate Change and the Greenhouse Effect" for an introductory meteorology class is delivered via the World Wide Web. It consists of a hypertext lecture outline with links to resource material located on computers scattered throughout the world. The lesson begins with an audio interview from National Public Radio's "Science Friday" program. By clicking on the program item, the student's Web browser seeks out the program and starts up an audio listening program. After completing the audio portion, students work their way through the outline in a sequential way. Graphics and online digital video punctuate the topics discussed in the lesson. Most of the resources have links to other information, and the students are encouraged to follow these paths if they desire. The Virtual Department Project, underway at the University of Texas-Austin, is bringing online geography curriculum together for educators to use in their classes and is described in Chapter 7.

The Galileo Project is aimed at providing "hypertextual information about Galileo and the science of his time to viewers of all ages and levels of expertise" (Van Helden, 1995). Users explore Galileo's world and influence on science by starting at the "Starting Points

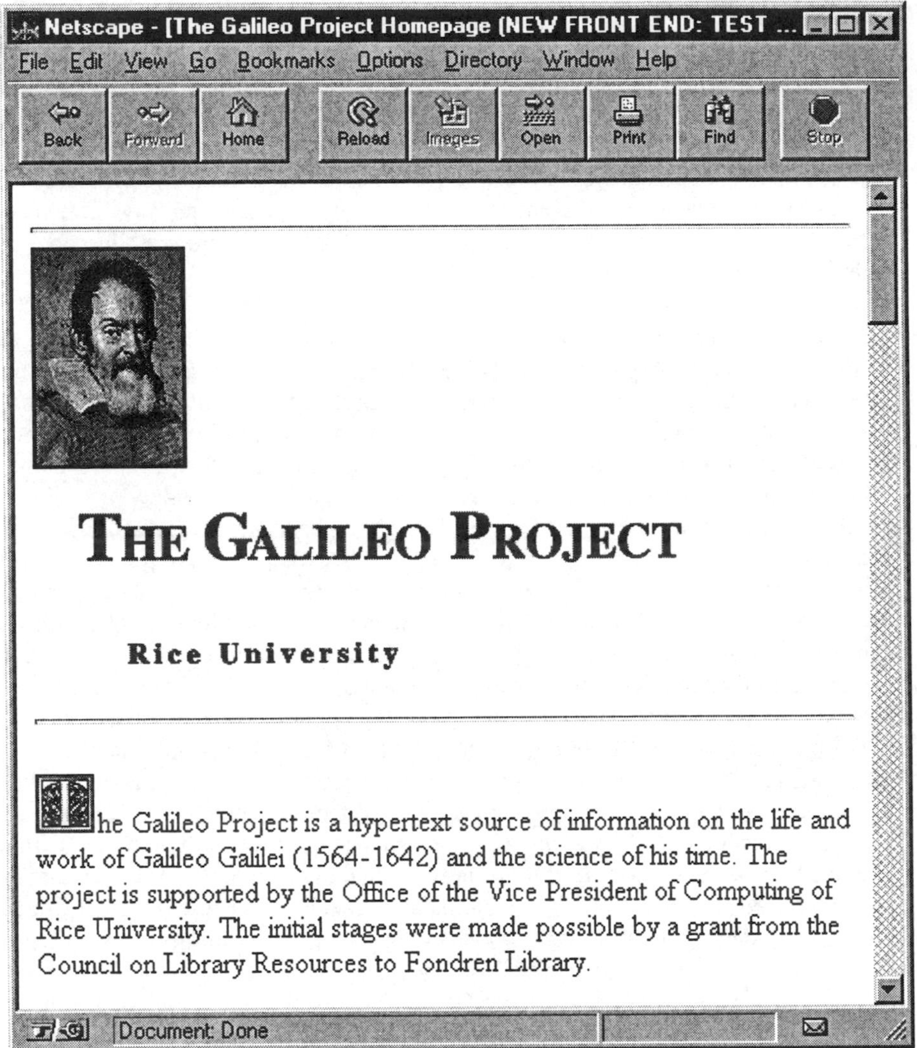

Figure 2.13 Rice University Galileo Project home page

for Exploration Page" **(URL - http://es.rice.edu/ES/humsoc/Galileo/galileo_explore.html)** (Figure 2.13). Readers navigate through Galileo's accomplishments via hyperlinks embedded in maps. A click of the mouse brings up information about Galileo's life and times. The online material created for the Galileo Project is used in a Rice University class "Galileo in Context." A group project dealing with some aspect of Galileo's life is required of all students. The astronomy group's goal was to repeat some of Galileo's astronomical observations. To do this a Galilean telescope and mounting was built by each member of the group. Detailed text and graphic information in a hypermedia format tell how to build an

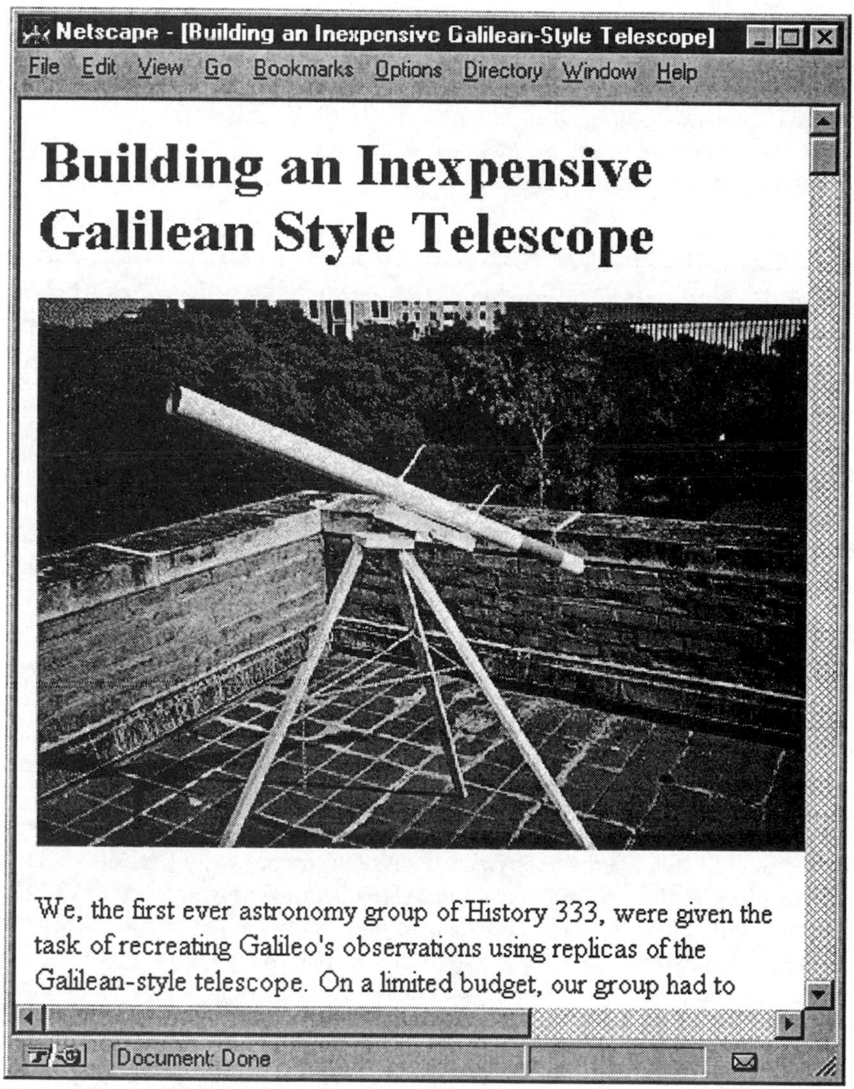

Figure 2.14 Inexpensive Galilean-style telescope

inexpensive Galilean-style telescope **(URL - http://es.rice.edu/ES/humsoc/Galileo/Student_Work/Astronomy95/telescope_design.html)** (Figure 2.14). Each project group creates its own home page to distribute the results of its work. The group pages are linked to the class home page. Progress reports are posted to the class newsgroup.

Geared to the K-12 market, the "Online from Jupiter" project uses the Internet to keep educators and students informed about the Galileo probe mission. Online journal reports give students glimpses into the day-to-day activities of Galileo personnel. Students also can ask questions of the project staff via electronic mail. Online learning resources for educators and a virtual teacher's lounge are available for discussing project activities among teachers. An online photo archive holds images for downloading. This is a wonderful way of bridging the gulf between education and professional astronomy. A personal contact, even in digital form, improves communication and the sharing of ideas between researcher, educator, and student.

➤➤ Focus on the Internet: *Geographic Information Systems and the Internet*

All earth phenomena have some spatial aspect to them, and quite often it varies from one place to another and changes over time. Geoscientists work with spatial data nearly every day. If a geoscientist uses overlays of mapped data to discover spatial or temporal relationships between a set of variables, her or she is using a *geographic information system* (GIS). Computer technology provides the tools necessary to process the data in order to draw conclusions from it. The Internet is another tool for the distribution and analysis of geographic information and spatial data. The Internet provides the geoscientist with:

- with a means of creating a massive distributed archive of spatial data
- an easy and affordable way of moving spatial data files between GIS workers and the public
- a means of providing interactive access to spatial data catalogs
- a forum for the discussion of geographic information methodology and technology

There are a number of publicly accessible data sets available to the GIS professional via the Internet. A noteworthy anonymous FTP site is managed by Lee Moore at Xerox in Rochester, New York (**URL - ftp://spectrum.xerox.com**). Here you can find U.S. Bureau of the Census TIGER files, United States Geological Survey Digital Elevation Models and Digital Line Graphs, and USGS Geographic Names data sets. Central Intelligence Agency world data can be downloaded from this site as well. The source code for reading the data sets is provided too. All the 1:100,000- and 1:2,000,000-scale Digital Line Graph, Land Use/Land Cover and 1:250,000-scale Digital Elevation Model data for the United States are available from the EROS data center FTP site at **URL - ftp://edcftp.cr.usgs.gov**. This site archives Arc/Info coverages and AMLs, along with the source codes for processing the data.

The National Atlas Information Service of Canada (**URL - http://ellesmere.ccm.emr.ca/**) created the NAISMap WWW-GIS home page (**URL - http://ellesmere.ccm.emr.ca/naismap/naismap.html**) for public access to National Atlas spatial data to construct national maps of Canada. The user builds a map by first selecting any number of available data layers to map and submits the choices with a button at the bottom of the page. Base layers include rivers, lakes highways, geological provinces, and low flow and flood flow data. Forest regions, layers, wetlands, and a number of animal species (birds, mammals, reptiles)

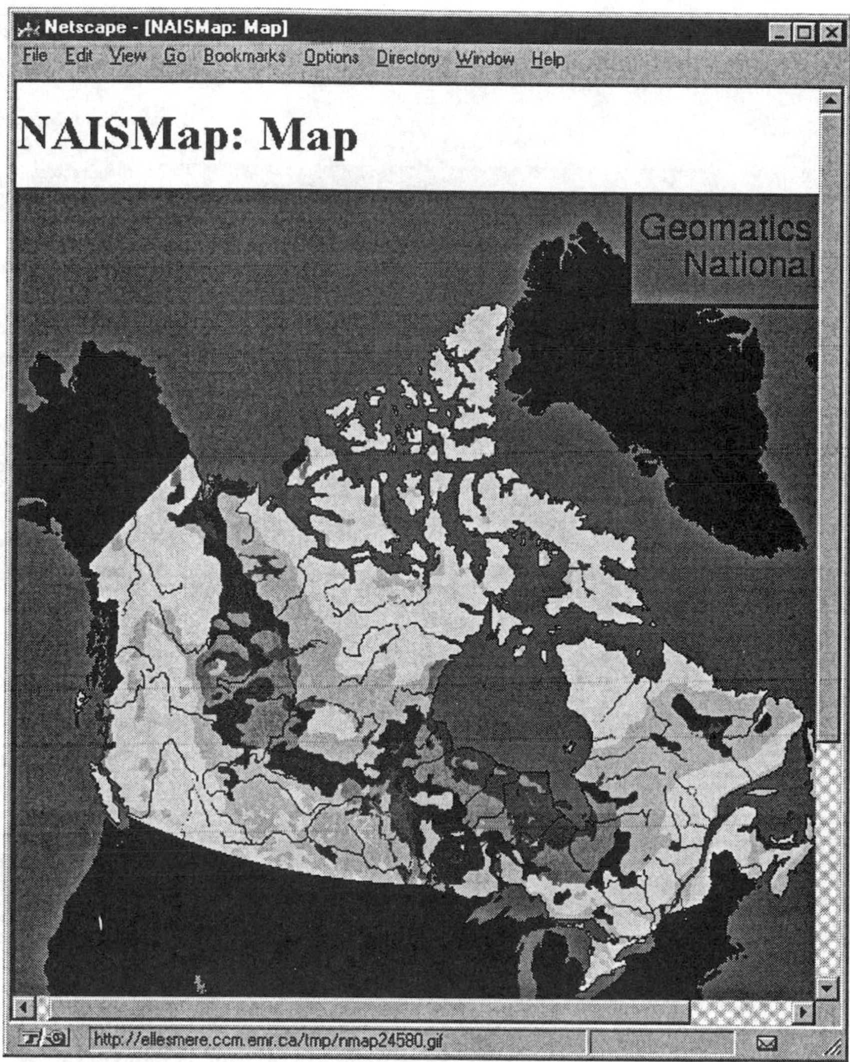

Figure 2.15 Wetlands/rivers/coastline map of Canada: NAISMap Service

can also be extracted and mapped. The subsequent screens verify the list and order of the requested layers, line widths and styles, fill patterns and line colors. After editing, the user submits the choices again, and soon the completed map is downloaded to the screen as a GIF image file. The map in Figure 2.15 was constructed using three layers: wetlands, rivers, and coastlines.

The GeoWeb project (**URL - http://wings.buffalo.edu/geoweb/**) is developing the basic theory and methods necessary for making geographic information available to all who need

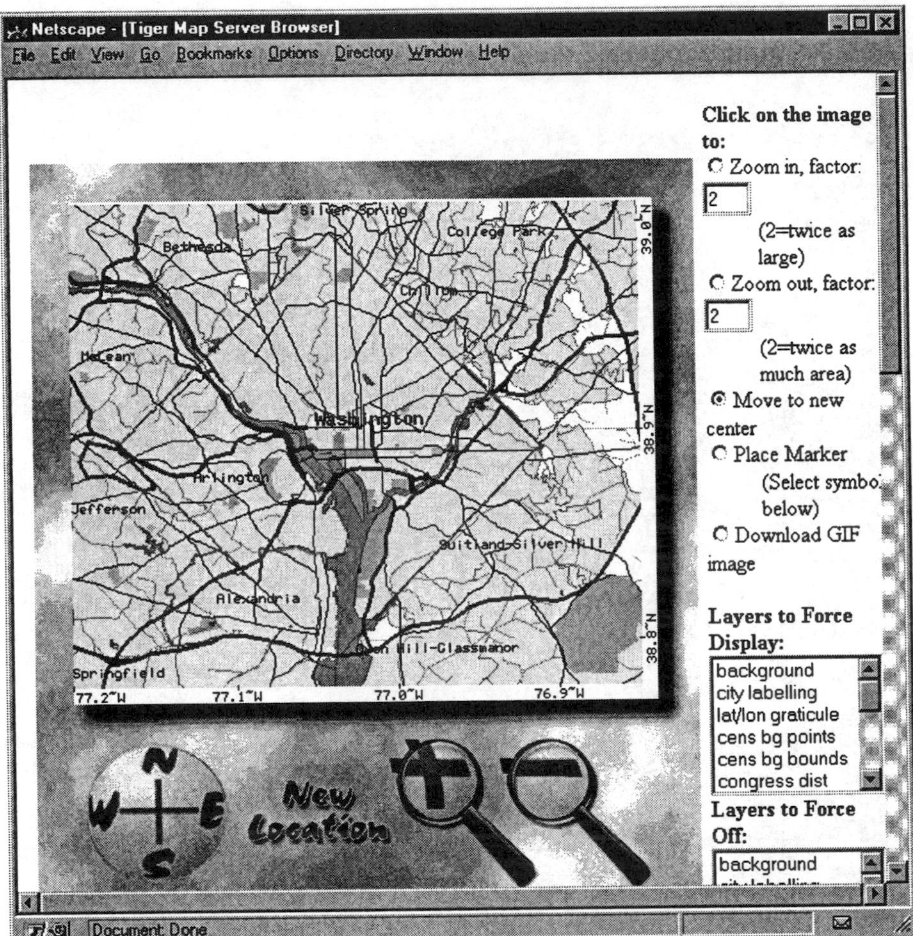

Figure 2.16 Tiger Map Service page

it. GeoWeb is designed to be a comprehensive database of sources for geographic information for the United States. The US Geodat Tiger Map Service page (**URL - http://tiger.census.gov/cgi-bin/mapbrowse-tbl**) is one of many unique links from the GeoWeb page (Figure 2.16). This service permits users to construct maps using the Tiger data sets of any location in the lower 48 states. The user constructs a map by filling in an online data request form. Census overlays containing data such as population density and income from the 1990 census can be added. The user can even place markers with descriptive labels on the map. Once submitted, a program is run on the Geodat server to extract the requested information, create the map, and within seconds deliver it to the desktop. The program takes the data items requested, and creates a unique URL, which can be used to display the map on any HTML document.

Those being introduced to geographic information systems for the first time should stop off at the United States Geological Survey's GIS tutorial located at **URL - http://into.er.usgs.gov/research/gis/title.html**. By using a simple hypertext outline, you can learn the basics of geographic information systems. Here you get information about GIS software, file formats, the way Landsat images can be used to map vegetation, and much more.

The National Center for Geographic Information (**URL - http://www.ncgia.ucsb.edu/ncgia.html**) decided to move its new NCGIA Core Curriculum in GIScience to the World Wide Web (**URL - http://www.ncgia.ucsb.edu/education/curricula/giscc/giscc.html**). The new core curriculum concentrates on providing "fundamental course content assistance for educators—formally as lecture materials, but adaptable for whatever instructional mode each course instructor wishes to use" (Kemp, 1996). The materials are structured much like lecture note outlines. The NCGIA tries not to mandate a particular structure or educational objective, and users are encouraged to pick and choose among the materials best suited to their needs. NCGIA's move to the World Wide Web is a benefit to all. Material dissemination is much easier and more cost-effective over the Web. Editorial changes also are accomplished with minimal cost. And for the end user, the materials are current, easy to acquire and modified for personal use.

What You Have Learned

- Directed, general purpose and serendipitous browsing are ways that people seek out information from the Internet.
- Browsing services fall into two categories: simple, menu-based services like Gopher, and contextual, hypermedia services like the World Wide Web.
- Gopher is an easy-to-use service that navigates the Internet by linking menu choices to directories and files.
- The World Wide Web is a hypermedia environment that navigates the Internet using context-based hyperlinks between documents, images and other forms of electronic media.

Apply It!

In Chapter 1 you were introduced to the Virtual Earth Web site and navigated to the Global Change Master Directory. Let's head back to the GCMD to browse for information about the impact of the greenhouse effect on the hydrological system.

Scroll down the document to "Links to Earth Science, Environmental, Federal, International, and Global Change Servers" (**URL - http://gcmd.gsfc.nasa.gov/cgibin/mduser_dir/pointwais**) (Figure 2.17). Once it has been retrieved I can either use it to conduct an online search or scroll down the document to bring me to a subject table to choose from.

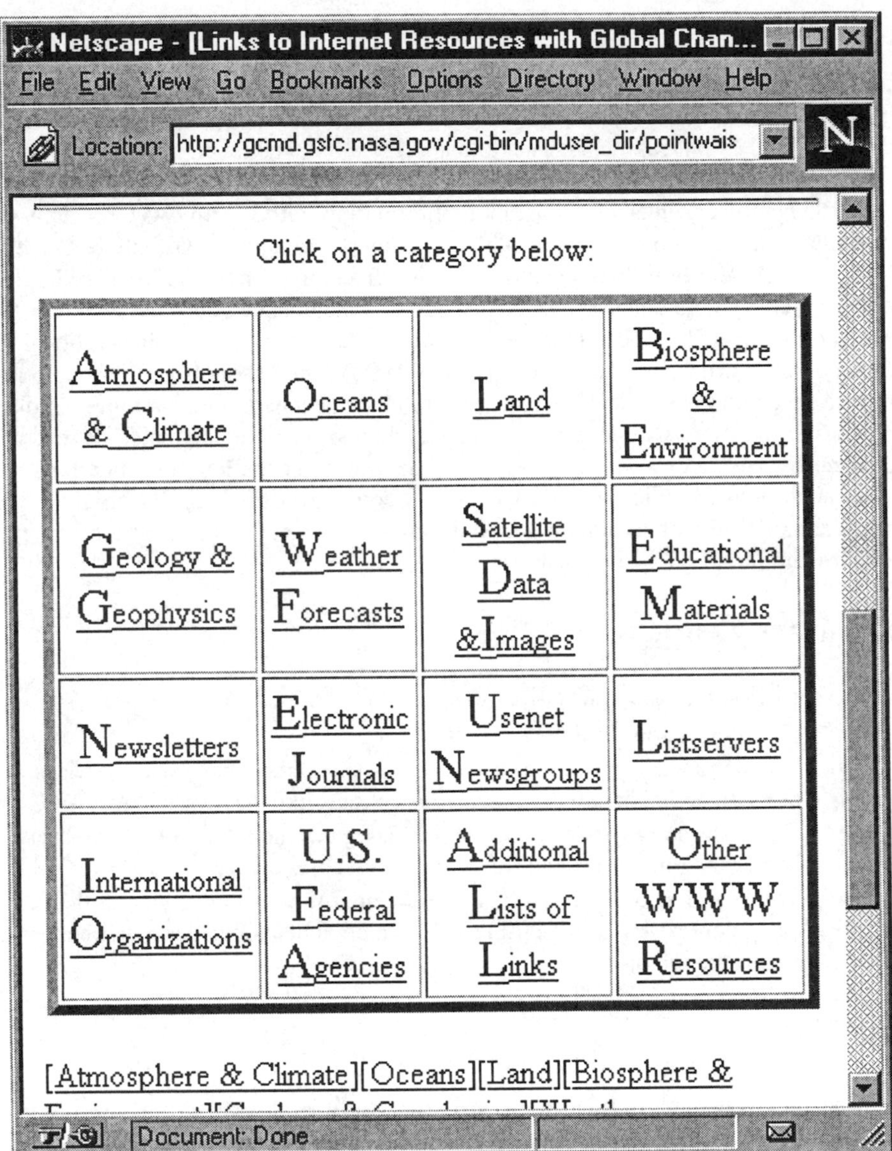

***Figure 2.17** GCMD "Links to Earth Science, Environmental, Federal, International, and Global Change Servers" page*

Clicking on "Atmosphere and Climate" retrieves an extensive listing of Internet sites **(URL - http://gcmd.gsfc.nasa.gov/pointers/meteo.html).** Moving down the list I come to Goddard Institute for Space Studies (NASA/GISS) **(URL - http://www.giss.nasa.gov/),** which is primarily engaged in studies of climate change (Figure 2.18). The GISS home page

Figure 2.18 Goddard Institute for Space Studies home page

is divided into research and information/educational resource areas. Clicking on the "Climate Impacts" button retrieves a background document concerning climate impact research at GISS.

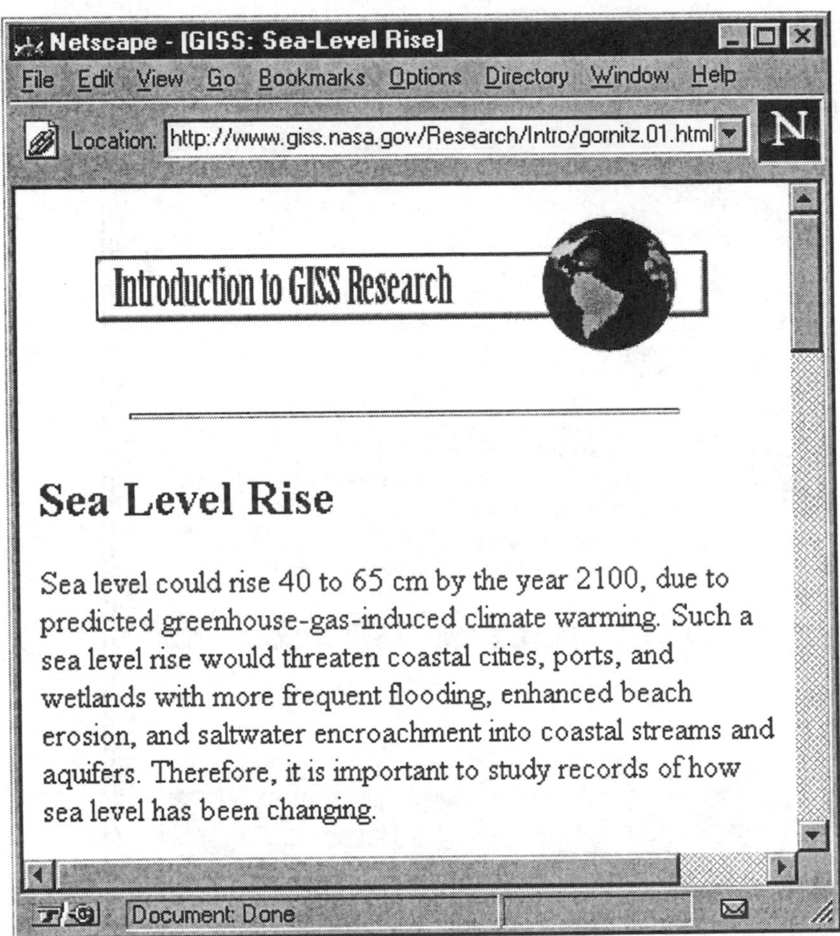

Figure 2.19 Sea level rise research at Goddard Institute of Space Science

At the bottom of the page is a hyperlink to a document about sea level rise research. The sea level rise document (**URL - http://www.giss.nasa.gov/Research/Intro/gornitz.01.html**) briefly describes the evidence for and impact of sea level rises (Figure 2.19).

I'll bookmark this document so I can return to it later. To bookmark an item choose the "Bookmark" menu and then "Add Bookmark."

You're beginning to see why I've described the Internet as a sometimes chaotic and unwieldy journey. Browsing from one Web document to the next is a time- consuming job. You can save yourself some time by connecting to an Internet resource subject list. Chapter 6 discusses searching for information on the Internet, but we can preview a favorite resource site, Yahoo! No, I'm not being overly excited here; Yahoo! is the name of the Web site

Figure 2.20 Yahoo! Internet resources subject listings

(URL - www.yahoo.com/) (Figure 2.20). You can either browse the site via the subject area listings or perform a search by typing a keyword into the field beside the search button and clicking the button. I'll type in "greenhouse effect" to start. Once the search button is clicked, Yahoo! will search through a database of online resources matching my keyword to those in the database. When I conducted my search, Yahoo! returned 66,495 matches containing the words "greenhouse effect. " Now comes the arduous task of going through the "hits" or items returned. The first item on my list is a greenhouse effect visualizer **(URL - http://www.covis.nwu.edu/GEV/GP_3_11_87_0.html).** According to the short annotation the hyperlinked document appears to contain an image showing "Percent of Greenhouse Effect (percent of terrestrial radiation) for November 1987." Clicking on the hyperlink produces a world map showing the fraction of terrestrial radiation retained by the atmosphere (Figure 2.21).

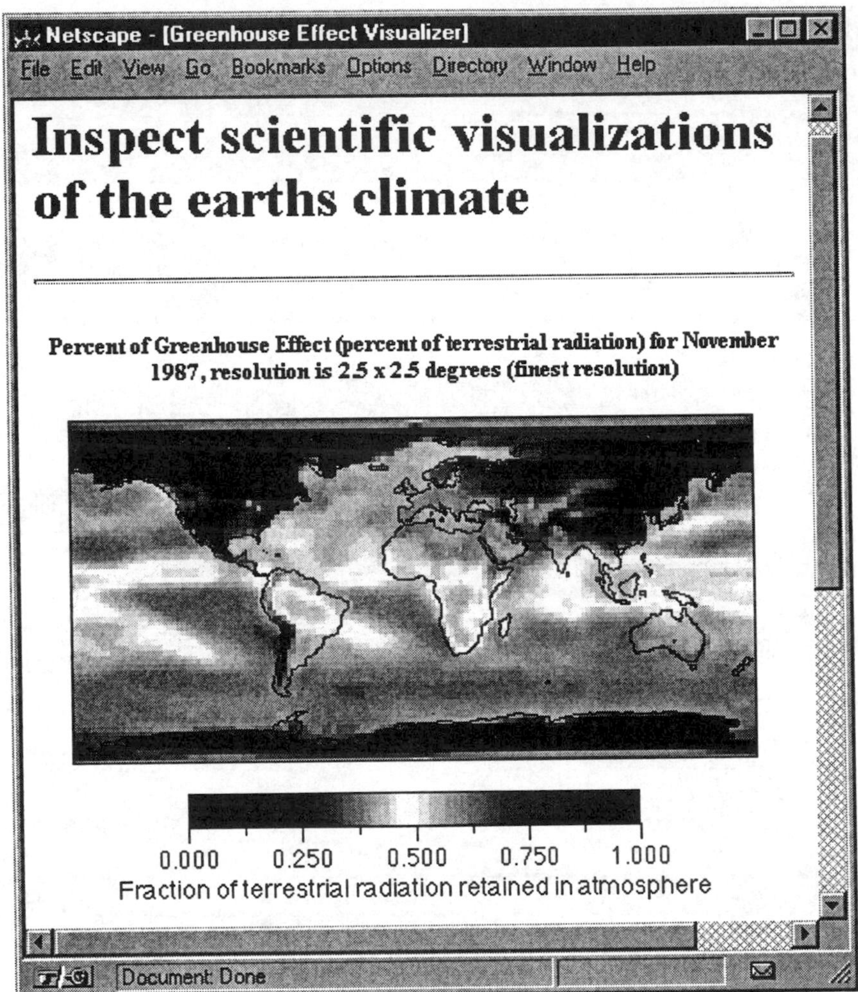

Figure 2.21 COVIS greenhouse effect visualization

At the greenhouse effect visualizer home page **(URL - http://www.covis.nwu.edu/gev.html),** I can create my own visualization based on the same data used in Figure 2.21 (see Figure 2.22). The Greenhouse Effect Visualizer was created by the Learning Through Collaborative Visualization Project centered at Northwestern University and funded by the National Science Foundation. By highlighting the variables, time scale, and resolution and then clicking the "Get Visualization!" button, I can have a map delivered to my desktop in a matter of seconds.

Let's go back to Yahoo! by using either the "Back" button or the "Back" option under the "Go" menu. The last search was pretty broad, so now I'll try one with greenhouse effect

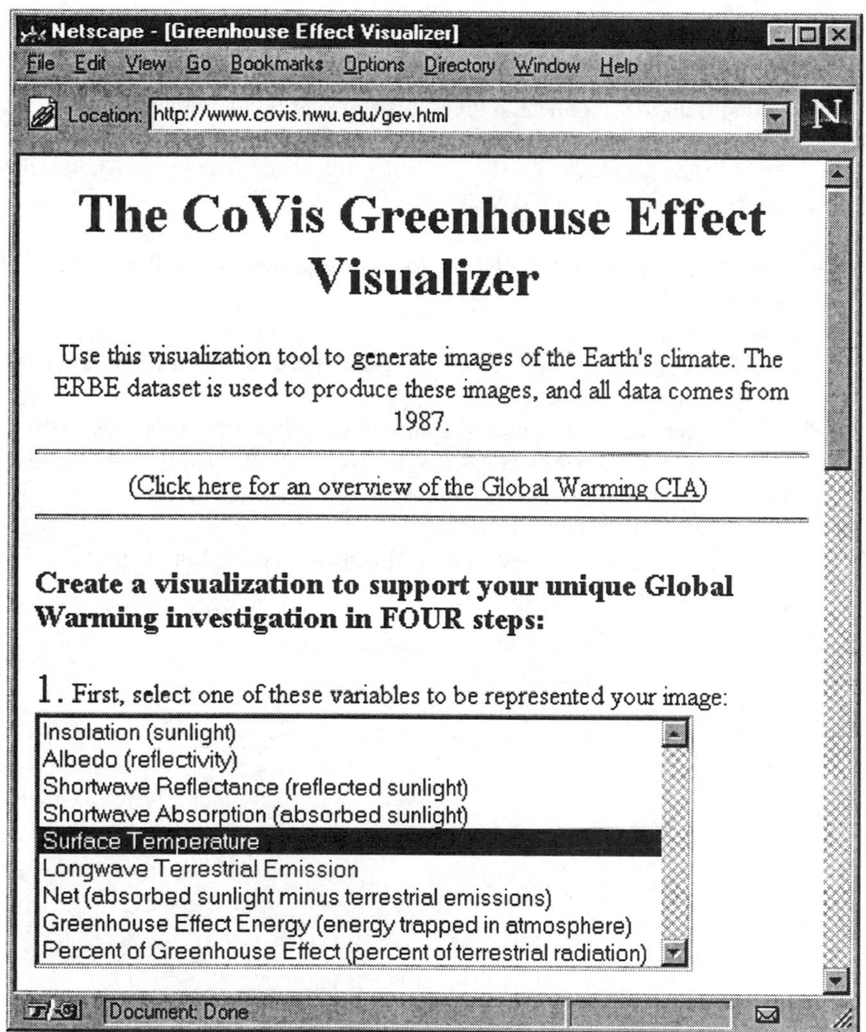

Figure 2.22 COVIS greenhouse effect visualizer tool

and hydrology. I got a different list of resources, one of which is a link to a fact sheet about Vietnam and climate that I'll investigate. Indeed, the document discusses potential impacts of an enhanced greenhouse effect on Vietnam with several references concerning sea level rise and changes in weather patterns. At the bottom of the document is an index button that sends me to the "Index to Climate Change" fact sheets **(URL - http://www.unep.ch/iucc/fs-index.html).** Looks like a gold mine here. The 90-plus fact sheets were put online by the United Nations Environment Program covering the causes, impacts and international response to an enhanced greenhouse effect. These provide excellent background into the issues of global warming and the greenhouse effect.

Try It Out!

1. Take a virtual field trip. Connect to the Hawaii Virtual Field Trip and "walk" around Kilauea volcano. Next stop off at the Cascade Volcano Observatory at **http://vulcan.wr.usgs.gov/** to check out Mount St. Helens. What differences can you see between the Mountt St. Helens and Kilauea volcano sites?

2. Head off to "Volcano World" at **URL - http://volcano.und.nodak.edu/vw.html.** While you're there:

   - Check out the latest volcanic activity. Is any particular part of the world more active than others?
   - Stop by and ask a volcanologist a question about volcanoes at **URL - http://volcano.und.nodak.edu/vwdocs/ask_a.html**. This site also has an extensive hypertext frequently-asked-questions archive.
   - Find a picture of Mount St. Helens.
   - Find out how many times Mount St. Helens has erupted in the past.

CHAPTER 3

Communicating over the Internet: Electronic Mail, Usenet, and Email Interest Groups

Electronic mail may well be the most powerful means of using the Internet. Although the World Wide Web delivers a multimedia-rich electronic world to your desktop, electronic mail connects you to the creator of the online materials. Electronic mail isn't about connecting bits of related information like the Web or Gopher. Electronic mail connects people. Electronic mail, or email, is an enormously popular way to communicate with people across the Internet. Electronic mail is a versatile service that allows you to do a number of things other than just send messages to people. With electronic mail you can attach and send text files, binary objects such as graphic files and "rich text" (word processed files), as well as digital audio and video files. You can use electronic mail to query computer servers to locate and retrieve files. A number of professional and personal activities are supported and enhanced by using electronic mail services. For instance, you can distribute electronic newsletters and magazines and broadcast announcements of upcoming events like conferences and class assignments to large groups of people with ease. Electronic mail is an invaluable way of conducting survey research and virtual seminars. Electronic mail moves you into the world of the paperless classroom where students submit their assignments as an electronic mail attachment for review and grading. Earth scientists are making use of electronic mail by:

- keeping up with colleagues' activities through special interest discussion groups
- participating in online interest groups like GEOED, the email
- discussion list devoted to earth science education
- communicating with students online
- entering into debates over the latest news in geology on the
- sci.geo.geology Usenet group
- keeping up to date on the latest developments in geographic
- information systems through the GIS-L electronic mail interest group
- distributing electronic journals like the Electronic Green Journal to colleagues across the globe

Electronic mail is fast becoming the communication mode of choice, after face-to-face discourse, for the information age. In this chapter we will look at how you send and receive electronic mail and join electronic mail discussions, and how the earth science community is using the Internet to conduct their everyday business.

Why Use Electronic Mail?

Electronic mail's popularity derives from the fact that users can process their communication at their leisure. Like a message machine, your electronic mailbox stores messages that come in at all times of the day and night. You can review and answer messages whenever it is convenient to do so. You eliminate the hassles of "phone tag" and the garbled images that arrive on a fax, and you aren't charged for listening to an answering machine's taped message when calling long distance. Digital media like electronic mail enable us to collect information about the sender of the message. Email messages include the sender's name, location, date of transmission and subject. With your email reader you can filter messages by the information provided, much as a secretary or administrative assistant would, and respond to them as you wish. Being in digital format you can import, copy and paste portions of the message into a word processing program for editing. Messages can be stored for an indefinite period of time, printed or forwarded to another person.

A major attraction to the use of electronic mail is the fact that communication between two people doesn't happen in real time. *Synchronous communication* like a telephone conversation happens in real time with people talking to one another. Unlike a telephone conversation, electronic mail communication between two or more individuals does not happen at the same time. Electronic mail is non-real-time messaging. We call electronic mail an *asynchronous* form of communication. *Asynchronous communication* means that people are not connected to one another with some sort of device at the same time in order to communicate with one another. One person sends a message to another who may or may not be connected to the Internet at that time. The recipient, if connected, may immediately respond, or, if not connected, respond at a later time.

Another advantage of electronic mail's digital format is that duplicate copies can be created almost instantly for wide distribution. Special electronic mail servers called *listservs* can distribute a single electronic mail message to numerous recipients at one time. Listservs are used to distribute messages to electronic mail discussion groups. Listserv discussion groups have become an enormously popular way of keeping up to date with happenings in a topic of interest. Listservs are employed to conduct virtual seminars by professional organizations or in education. Listservs are also used to distribute online newsletters and magazines.

Electronic mail bulletin boards have been created to facilitate communication between individuals using networked communications. Electronic bulletin boards are like a conventional bulletin board where you can post a message for others to read and respond to.

Bulletin board systems like Usenet are an extremely popular way to keep in touch with a large group of people.

There are drawbacks to the use of electronic mail in spite of all the attractions. Electronic mail systems and software come in a variety of styles and types. Some systems may not be compatible with others that you want to communicate with and prevent you from taking full advantage of what electronic mail has to offer. These problems will diminish as open network systems evolve. Electronic mail systems are not 100% secure. Don't send anything that you deem to be of a sensitive nature. Many computer systems have been infiltrated by hackers, and electronic mail tampered with. In spite of these potential problems electronic mail is an extremely useful means of communication.

Using Electronic Mail

Electronic Mail Addresses

Sending and delivering a letter requires a recipient name and address, and electronic mail is no different. In order to send and receive electronic mail you must have an *electronic mail address*. Your electronic mail address uniquely defines the Internet location to which electronic messages are sent. Typically, an electronic mail address has four basic parts, a user name, a mail server name, an organization and a domain. For example, my email address is:

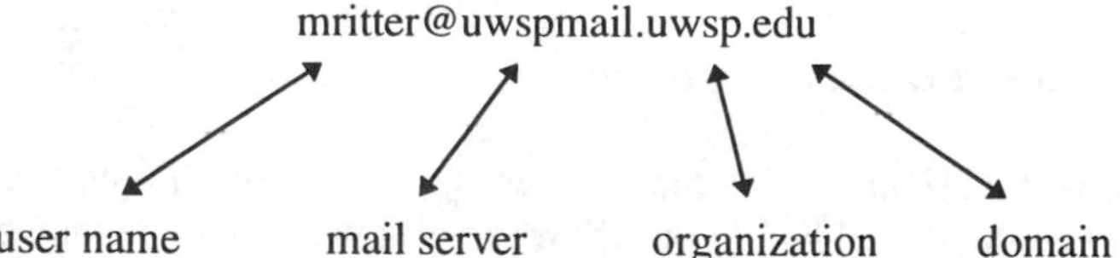

The user name identifies the person. In my electronic mail address, the *user name* is the first letter of my first name followed by, with no spaces, my full last name. Some user names have a sequence of letters and numbers or full names separated by a dash or underscore. User names are defined by computer system administrators to work within the requirements of their particular electronic mail system. The *mail server* is the name of the computer through which your electronic mail passes and is separated from the user name by the "at" sign (@). The third portion of the address is the organization. My organization is "uwsp," which stands for the University of Wisconsin at Stevens Point. The *domain* is the last item in the address. Domains in an electronic mail address are the same as the domains discussed in Chapter 1 concerning addressing computers on the Internet. My domain is an educational institution (edu). The last three components of the address are separated by periods or "dots." One reads the address as "mritter at uwspmail dot uwsp dot edu." The case of a letter in an address is very important to some mail servers. If you capitalize a letter in an

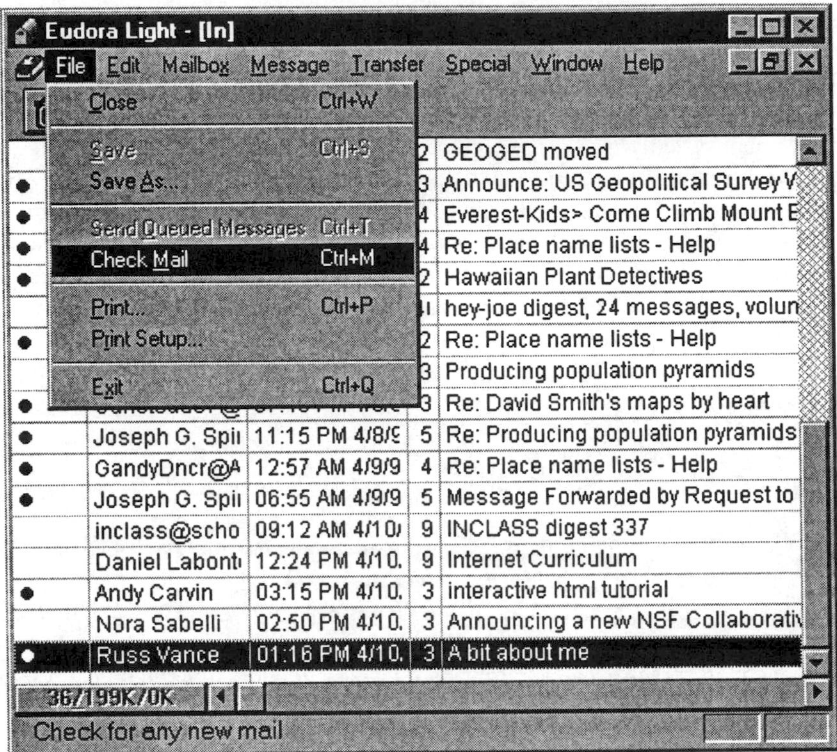

Figure 3.1 Eudora electronic mail program

email address that shouldn't be, the recipient's mail server will interpret it as somebody else's address. In all likelihood you will receive an undeliverable mail error message.

Sending and Receiving Electronic Mail

All electronic mail *client software* enable you to compose, read, receive, and send electronic mail. Email client software is the program you use to connect to your electronic mailbox on your Internet provider's computer server. Once you start the client software it will either automatically transfer or instruct you to manually retrieve any mail in your mailbox. Email programs often use a folder metaphor to identify the location your messages are stored in after they have been composed and saved or received. The "in" folder is used to receive mail, while sent messages are saved in your "out" box.

Creating Electronic Mail Messages

Several programs are available for sending electronic mail over the Internet. The popular Eudora Light mail program for Windows is shown in Figure 3.1. Common drop-down

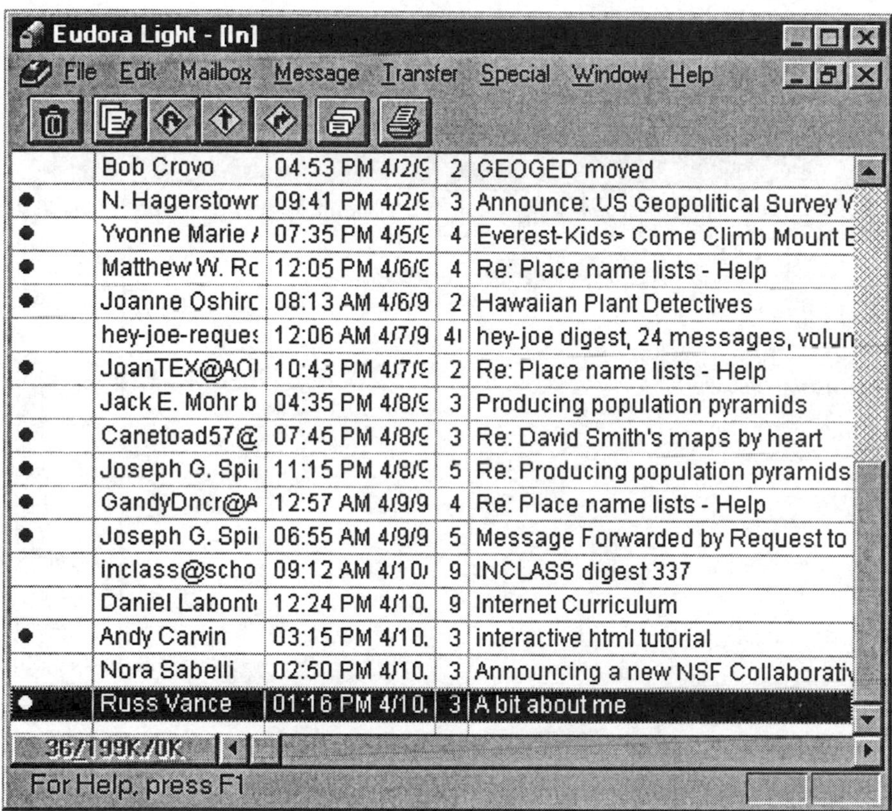

Figure 3.2 Eudora Light inbox

menus are displayed across the top of the window. Drop-down menus are used to send, receive, edit and transfer messages, and utility buttons beneath are used for trashing (deleting) messages, creating new messages, mail forwarding, and so on.

The program window as it appears in Figure 3.2 shows an opened "in box." To open and read a message, simply doubleclick your mouse. Figure 3.3 shows Eudora's electronic mail form for writing messages. Type the subject and the recipient's name in the upper lefthand corner of the window. It is proper netiquette to always include a concise subject description of your message. The body of the message is typed in the large field that occupies much of the center portion of the window. Ideally, the message can be any size, yet some Internet providers, especially commercial ones, have a particular byte size limitation. You should warn recipients at the beginning of the message or in the subject field if you are sending a particularly long message, especially if they are likely to print it. Very long messages can be broken into several messages of smaller length. It's a good idea to indicate in the subject field where a particular message fits in a sequence of several messages. Manuscript-length document files should be compressed and attached to an email message.

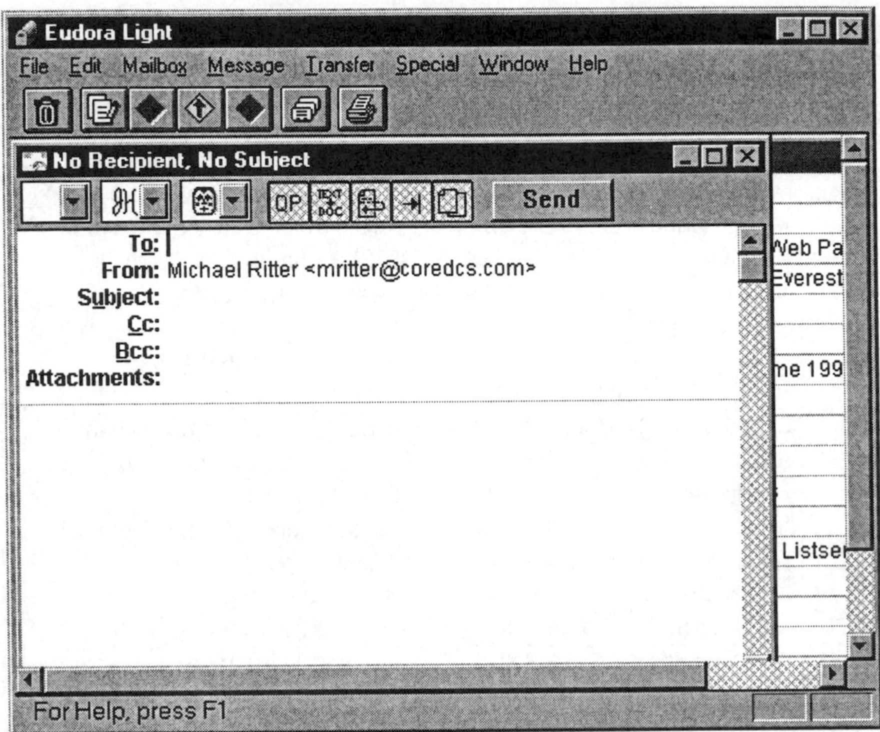

Figure 3.3 Electronic mail form

Recipients can detach the file, uncompress it and import it into their word processing software to read.

Notice that the "From" field is already filled out. This is automatically done by the program when you start a new message. The program will attach an address and time to the message when it is sent. Your email software will likely provide a field for you to send a "carbon" copy of the message to additional recipients, or you can flag it as a "special attention" message. Depending how your program is configured, it may also attach your phone number to the electronic mail header. Use the "Message" menu to send your completed message or click the send button. Some electronic mail programs hold your messages in queue until you tell the program to send it or you check your mail.

An actual electronic mail message is shown in the message display window in Figure 3.4. The two parts of the message can clearly be seen. At the top is the header with the sender's name, date, phone, subject and list of other people the message was sent to. In the center is the body of the message. The drop-down message-handling menu (Figure 3.5) enables the user to answer the sender's message with or without a copy of the original message. Avoid responding to someone's message by including the sender's entire message

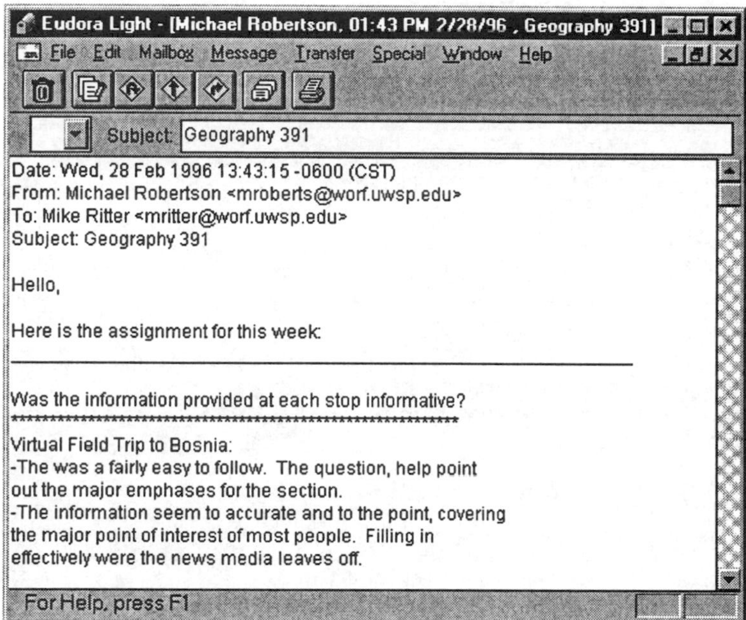

Figure 3.4 Electronic mail message

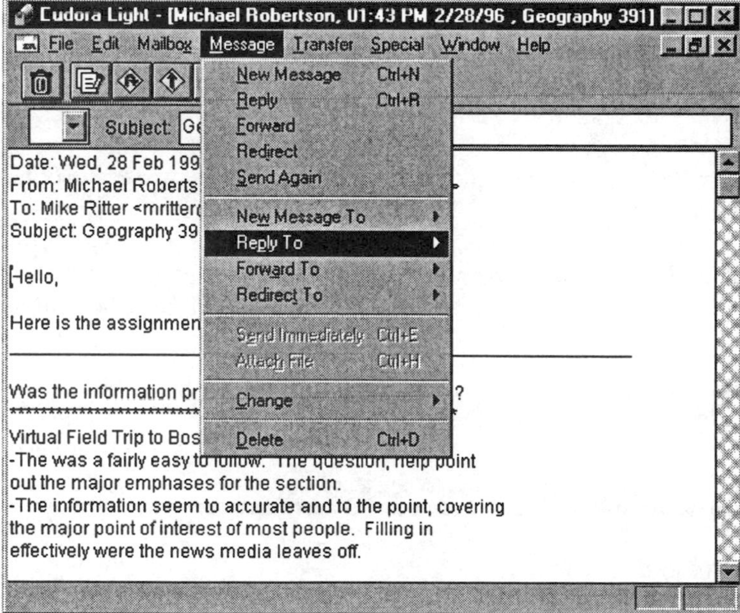

Figure 3.5 Message-handling menu

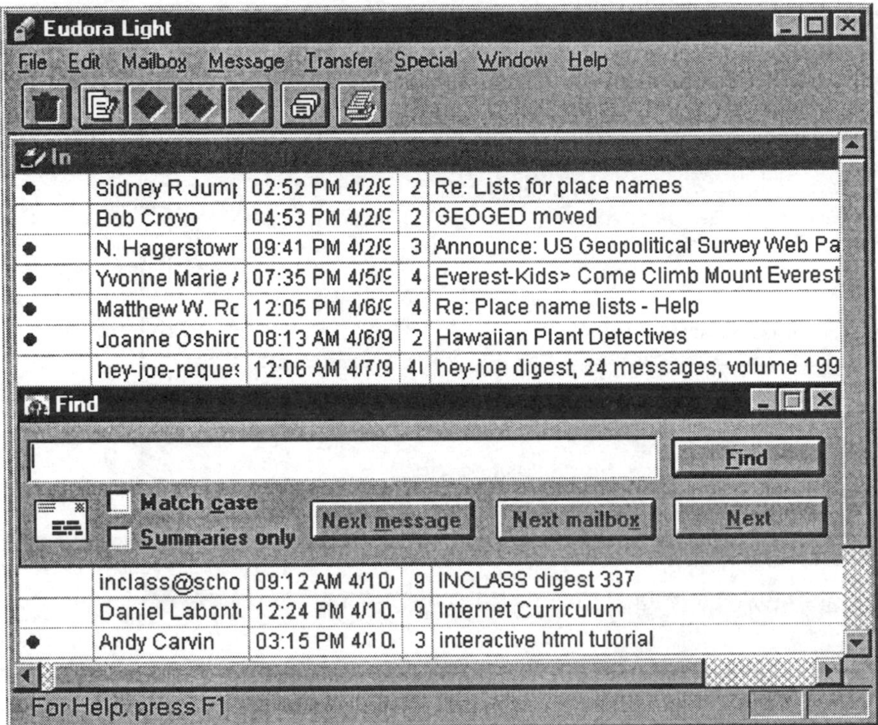

Figure 3.6 Email search option

in the body of your response. It's a waste of bandwidth and storage space to do so. Also avoid copying, and simply refer to the message in the subject field. Even if you feel a need to copy the sender's message, take some time to edit the sender's message to critical phrases that require a response.

The email client in Figure 3.6 permits you to search for text in your messages by filling in a search form and specifying what part of an email message the program will look through.

> ***Earth Online Tip:*** Regularly clean out your electronic mailbox to conserve space on your Internet provider's hard disk. Delete old messages or move them to your hard drive or off to a floppy diskette. Compress messages to conserve disk space.

Emoticons and Acronyms

Face it, email is a pretty emotionless medium unless you add some sort of emphasis to your writing like capitalization or a bold font style. Ever see those funny-looking symbols like

: - (in an email message and wonder what they mean? They are called *emoticons* and are used to indicate an emotion behind your written message. Rotate the page to see that the emoticon in the preceding sentence shows a frown. Here's a few other examples:

: -)	A generic Smiley
: - (	A frown
: - I	Indifferent
% -)	Confused
: - /	Skeptical
: - 0	Surprised

Acronyms are a useful shorthand substitute for text strings or phrases. Some of the common acronyms in use are:

BTW	By the way
BBL	Be back later
CUL8er	See you later
FYI	For your information
F2F	Face to face
<g>	Grin, used like a smiley
IMO	In my opinion
IMHO	In my humble opinion
IOW	In other words
TNX	Thanks

Electronic Mail Communities: Email Discussion Lists and Usenet

The ability to easily distribute the same message to several people at once enables the earth science Internet community to conduct online discussions about topics of common interest to them. Electronic mail listservs and Usenet newsgroups are two Internet services that accomplish this task.

Electronic Mail Listservs

Electronic mail listservs are computer servers running software that enables you to send one message to a group of people at the same time. Email listservs provide the means to engage in electronic mail discussions, also known as *interest groups*. Email interest groups are

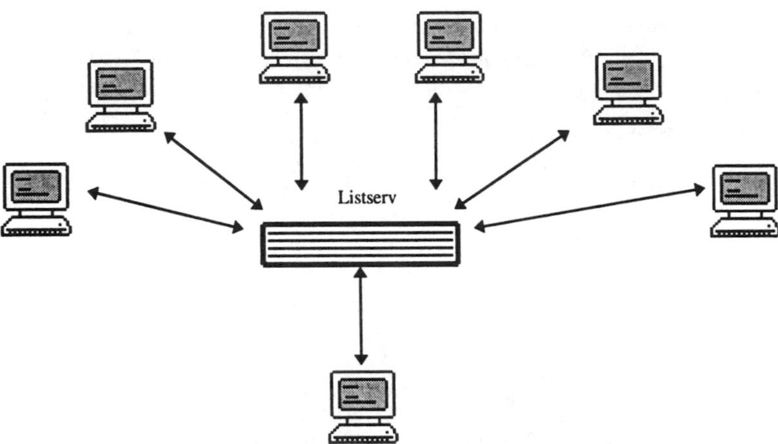

Figure 3.7 Electronic mail routing to a discussion list

composed of people who share a common interest in a particular topic, like geomorphology for example. People discuss the latest developments in their respective fields, ask questions, and share ideas through the interest groups. Hundreds of interest groups have been created over the last few years addressing just about every topic imaginable. You join one of these discussion groups by subscribing to a list. You do this by sending a special subscribe message to the listserv computer. Once your subscription has been accepted you can send messages to the list. When your message arrives at the list address, it is copied and sent out to each member of the discussion list (Figure 3.7). Likewise, you will receive all messages posted by other subscribers to the list. Depending on the listserv used, you will either get each message sent to you individually or receive all the day's postings in digest form. Some discussion lists do not give you a choice in the way messages are delivered. Having them in digest form reduces the clutter in your email in folder.

Electronic mail discussion lists are either moderated or unmoderated. Moderated lists have a person in charge who filters messages that are sent to the list. In theory, the moderator passes along only those messages that pertain to the subject of the list. Profane, obnoxious, or personal messages are filtered out before they get to the subscribers. Unmoderated lists are more freewheeling and may pass along inappropriate messages. Regardless, subscribing to such a list is a good way of getting to know like-minded individuals, discussing topics of common interest, solving problems and discovering new ideas.

To join a listserv you first send an email message to the listserv telling it that you would like to join. Typically this involves sending a subscribe command in the body of the message like:

SUBSCRIBE *<LISTNAME YOUR NAME>*

For example, to subscribe to the Geographic Information Systems Topics electronic mail list known as GIS-L, you send an email message to the listserv at **URL - listserv@ ubvm.cc.buffalo.edu** with the following in the body of the message:

SUBSCRIBE GIS-L Michael Ritter

Shortly after you send your subscription message, the listserv will respond with a confirmation message. Keep a copy of the confirmation message in a safe place. The confirmation message will commonly provide instructions on how to send a message to the list or the administrator of the list, to unsubscribe, and to get other information about the list. To facilitate communication with other subscribers, email messages are sent to the *list address* and not the listserv address. In our example above the listserv address is:

listserv@ubvm.cc.buffalo.edu

but the list address is:

GIS-L@ubvm.cc.buffalo.edu.

If you are new to electronic mail interest groups you'll undoubtedly make a few mistakes along the way. Be careful when responding to a message posted to a special interest group. Posting a response to the entire list rather than the individual who posted the original message is a common mistake. There are some cases when your response may benefit the entire group, so use your best judgment. Don't send personal messages to the entire list either. Remember, your messages ultimately end up on someone else's computer; misdirected messages waste readers' time. Another common mistake is sending an administrative message to the entire mailing list rather than to its moderator or administrator. The last thing that list participants want to receive are people's unsubscribed requests.

There are an extraordinary number of listservs, and their numbers are growing each day. Likewise there are a number of ways to retrieve a "list of lists." You can send an electronic mail message to

listserv@bitnic.bitnet

Leave the subject line blank, and in the body of the message type:

LIST GLOBAL

Beware! This is an extremely large file, on the order of 350 pages or more. The DeSilva List of Lists, which is broken into several smaller parts can be retrieved via File Transfer Protocol **at rtfm.mit.edu/pu/usenet/news.answers/mail/mailing-lists/Part 1.**

Network News and Usenet: The Internet's Electronic Bulletin Board

Electronic mail listservs allow people to join in a discussion about a particular topic by subscribing to each discussion list they are interested in. Electronic bulletin boards let you participate in multiple discussion groups without having to subscribe to any particular one. Instead, you connect to a bulletin board service and peruse the various interest groups available. Then you choose which ones you would like to participate in. Where the listserv automatically sends messages to your mailbox, you must connect to the bulletin board to keep abreast of the discussion.

Bulletin board services share many of the same attributes of conventional information services. Like a conventional bulletin board you can post a message to a group of people. With an electronic bulletin board you can distribute information to a number of subscribers, much the way a newspaper or magazine distributes the same information to its subscribers. Like a newsletter, an electronic bulletin board distributes news and information focused on a particular topic. Like an electronic mail service, electronic bulletin boards send messages quickly and efficiently to large numbers of people. The major electronic bulletin board service on the Internet today is called network news or netnews for short. The netnews system is composed of many newsgroups, each devoted to a particular subject. Articles that look very much like an electronic mail message are posted to a newsgroup for all to see. Like an email message, an article has a header that includes fields for the sender's name, subject of the article and date. The most popular network news service on the Internet today is Usenet.

Usenet is not the Internet; it is an entirely different system. Internet sites can carry Usenet, but many non-Internet computers do too. Because of the multiple ways that network news can find its way to its users, Usenet collectively refers to all sites that participate in the exchange of network news regardless of the network connection or dial-up server (Internet, Bitnet, etc.) they use. Messages sent to an interest group are forwarded to your Internet provider so long as they have a Usenet service feed. Instead of everyone interested in a particular topic receiving individuals messages as an email discussion list, you login to the bulletin board service to see all the messages posted there. You pick and choose the messages to read from the list of archived messages that have come into the Usenet interest groups.

Each newsgroup has a unique name that describes the subject of the group. The name consists of alphabetic character strings separated by periods. The first part of the newsgroup name identifies the type of group followed by the subject of the group and a particular topic within the subject. For instance,

sci.geo.fluids

is a science group (sci.) dealing with geophysical (geo.) fluid dynamics (fluids).

There are seven major news categories:

comp Devoted to computer science-related topics, including information on hardware (e.g., comp.mac) and software systems (e.g., comp.infosystems.gis) and source codes, programming and the like. This is a good place for those in the earth sciences to look for answers to questions concerning software that they are using for education (e.g., courseware) and research (spreadsheets and databases). Questions about discipline-specific software are best directed to subcategories under the sci netnews categories.

misc Includes groups that don't fit any of the other top-level newsgroup categories. Job postings, legal issues, and books fall into this category. This is a good category for recent graduates and those looking to change jobs or occupations (e.g., misc.jobs. offered, misc.jobs.resumes). Job announcements are found in discipline-specific groups too (e.g., sci.geo.geology, sci.geo.meteorology).

news Groups devoted to the news network and news software. Subcategories include announcements of news reader software, new groups, and network news administration issues.

rec Discussions devoted to recreational activities including travel, hiking and skiing. This is not your typical place for the earth scientist, but it might be a good place to make some contacts. Besides, you know how the old saying goes: "All work and no play . . ."

sci Includes groups interested in science, science research, and engineering, excluding the computer sciences. A number of groups of interest to earth scientists are found here (e.g., sci.astronomy, sci.geo.geology, sci.geo.hydrology, sci.geo.meteorology, sci.geo.oceanography, etc.). See Chapter 10 for a complete listing of network newsgroups of interest to the earth scientist.

soc Groups devoted to culture, politics and social issues. Earth and environmental scientists interested in human/environment interactions might look into groups found here.

talk Groups that are a forum for debating controversial topics. Groups like talk.environment are a good place to share opinions and ideas.

Like electronic mail discussion groups, network newsgroups come in moderated and unmoderated flavors. In the moderated groups a person acts as a filter through which articles pass in order to remove articles irrelevant to the subject of the group. Some moderators take their jobs quite seriously while others let most anything pass through to the group.

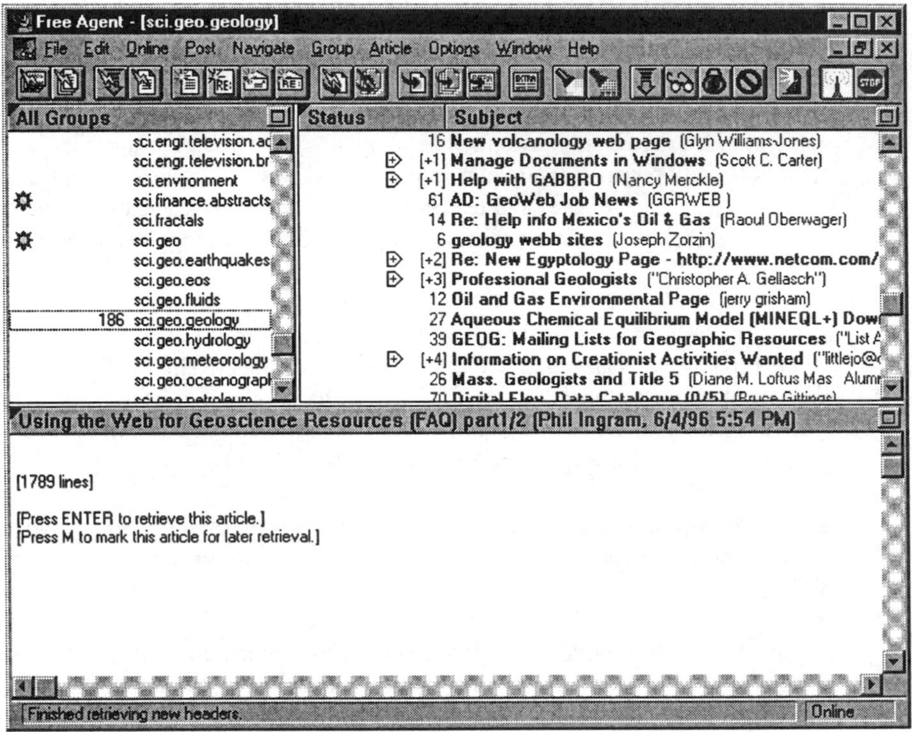

Figure 3.8 Free Agent Usenet news reader software

To read network news you first need to access a computer that participates in a network news service. You'll also need software to decode and read the messages. In most cases your organization or Internet provider obtains a connection to the network news system. Check with your system administrator to see if you have a connection to network news. If not, push to get a connection because network news is an invaluable source of information. News reader programs are available for a variety of computer systems. You can retrieve a shareware news reader from many popular FTP shareware sites. The Free Agent shareware news reader program is shown in Figure 3.8. The program window is split into three smaller windows. On the upper left is the list of newsgroups the news server currently receives. To the upper right is a list of the posting to a particular newsgroup chosen by the user, in this case postings to the sci.geo.geology newsgroups. At the bottom is the message display window. When users click on a message title in the news posting window, it is displayed in the bottom window. See Chapter 10 for sites where news readers are available for downloading. Many World Wide Web browsers like Netscape have built-in network news readers.

Once you connect to a network news server, your news reader program will obtain a listing of all newsgroups available from the news server. The initial processing of available groups could take a while depending on how many groups your network news server has available. Your news reader software will allow you to browse through the titles of groups and subscribe to any number of them. The news reader software saves the subscribed groups' information and uses it to retrieve new articles for future sessions.

Unlike electronic mail discussion groups, Usenet groups do not notify you when new articles are posted to a newsgroup. You must check from time to time on the activity of a group. Once connected to the news server, your news reader software will scan the various groups that the user has been reading and notify you that new articles have been posted to a group. Your news reader program keeps track of previously read articles. Due to the amount of storage space they require, articles are kept on the netnews system for a length of time specified by a computer system administrator. You should check for new articles on a regular basis for this reason alone. Most news reader programs permit you to download messages and save them on your local computer.

A good example of Usenet at work is shown in a portion of a Usenet posting replicated below. An earlier request to the **sci.geo.hydrology** Usenet group asked for information about vegetation and stream sedimentation. The requester graciously compiled the results of the newsgroup query in another posting to share with the newsgroup. The posting is actually from another member who pointed out the value of Usenet for professional growth.

From: John Griffith Evans <John@jgevans.demon.co.uk> Newsgroups: sci.geo.hydrology Subject: Vegetation and its Relationship to Flood Control/Channel Maintenance.

Date: Wed, 27 Dec 95 20:35:47 GMT Organization: Civil Engineer Lines: 74 Message-ID: <820096547snz@jgevans.demon.co.uk> Reply-To: John@jgevans.demon.co.uk X-NNTP-Posting-Host: jgevans.demon.co.uk X-Mail2News-Path: jgevans.demon.co.uk Status: N

The following posting from <gershmanm@ci.boulder.co.us> is a model for conduct on any professional newsgroup - it acknowledges the assistance received and follows by recording the responses so that readers generally may benefit from his enquiry. Thank you 'gershmanm' for setting such a good example of standards.

quote____

I thank all of you who contributed. Here is the information which I received in response to my request.

_____. 1984.Determination of Roughness Coefficients for Streams in Colorado. United States Department of the Interior. US Geological Survey. Water Resources Investigations Report 85-4004.

_____. 1987. How to Control Streambank Erosion. Iowa Department of Natural Resources, USDA Soil Conservation Service. 25pp.

_____. Use of vegetation in civil engineering. 1990 eds. N.J. Coppin, I.G. Richards. Boston. Butterworths xviii, 292 p. : ill. 24 cm.

An excellent starting place for discovering electronic mailing lists is the Clearing House for Subject-Oriented Resource Guides (**URL - http://www.lib.umich.edu/chhome.html**). As the name implies, this World Wide Web site is a clearinghouse of linkages to resource guides developed by the Internet community. These guides contain information about electronic mailing lists, as well as Gopher and World Wide Web resources, and Usenet newsgroups.

Other Uses of Electronic Mail

Electronic mail is much more flexible than one might expect. Electronic mail is a good way to search for files archived on File Transfer Protocol (FTP) servers (described in Chapter 4). A user can interactively query FTP archives by connecting to an Archie server. However, Archie servers are often hard to log on to because of the enormous burden placed on their systems by people looking for programs and files. If you're not in a hurry send an email message to an Archie server to process and it will send the results back via electronic mail (see Chapter 6, "Searching the Internet," for details).

Electronic mail is used to fetch files too. There are two ways to do this; by sending email to an FTPmail server or to a listserv. An *FTPmail server* accepts a request for file transfers via electronic mail, processes the request, and sends the requested file out. To do this, you send the FTPmail server a list of the commands you would otherwise use with an FTP client program. The FTPmail server connects to the FTP archive you're interested in, retrieves the file and sends it to you. You can also use electronic mail to ask a listserv to send you a file located on the server. To retrieve a file send an electronic mail message to the listserv address and in the body of the message type your request. Common requests for the FTPmail servers are of this form:

connect <site>	To open a connection to an FTP server
chdir <directory>	To change to a directory
delete <jobid>	To delete the given job
dir	To obtain a directory listing
help	To obtain help information from FTPmail server
get <filename>	To retrieve a file
quit	To disconnect or end an FTP session

As an example, I'll send an email request to the FTPmail server located at **ftpmail@ftpmail.ramona.vix.com** to retrieve sources.zip, a document describing online sources of weather and climate data. To do so I'll send the following message:

connect vmd.cso.uiuc.edu
chdir wx
get sources.zip
quit

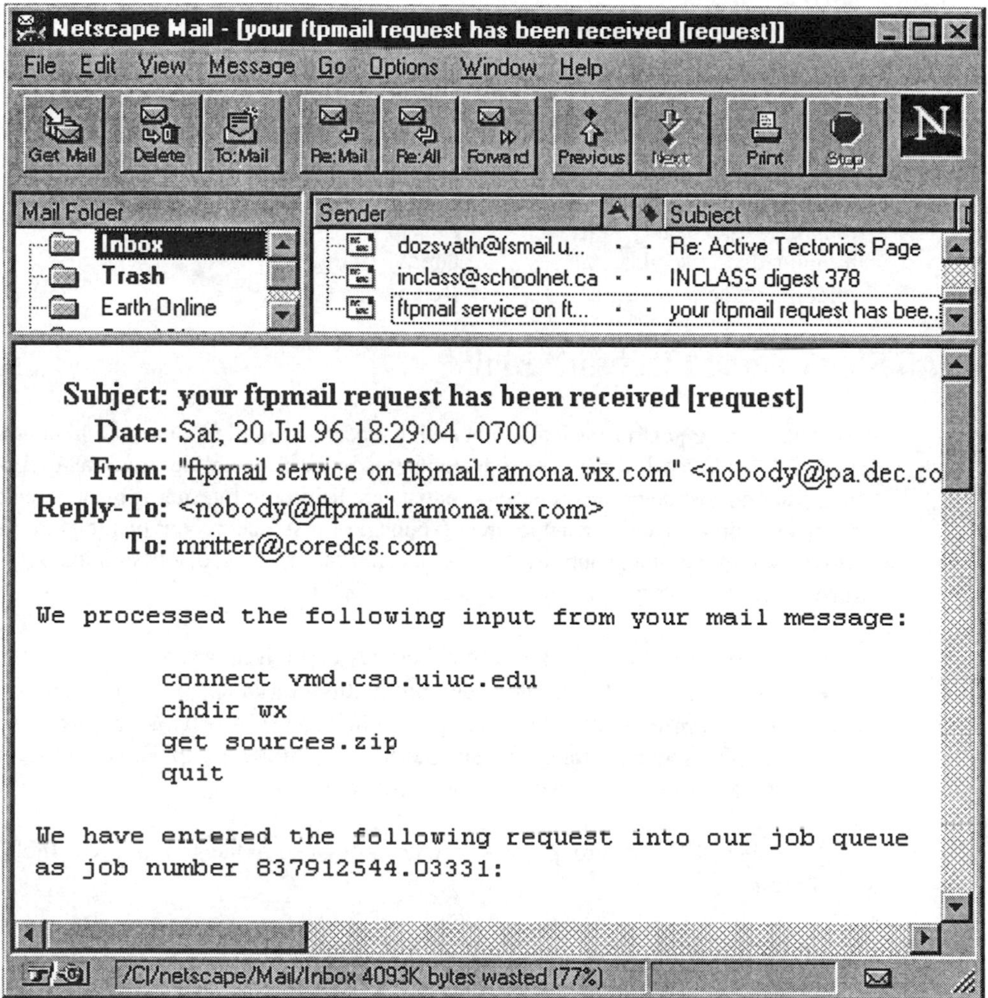

Figure 3.9 Response from FTPmail server

After a short period of time I receive the message from the FTPmail server shown in Figure 3.9. Finally, the request is processed and the requested file is sent.

Several sites on the Internet offer an FTPmail service, and anyone with access to email can use them. Users are requested not to make use of FTPmail services at sites remote from them. Another list of FTPmail servers and links to software can be found at **URL - http://src.doc.ic.ac.uk/ftpmail-servers.html.** Table 3.1 shows a sample of FTPmail servers.

Table 3.1 Sample of FTPmail servers and countries

Address	Country
ftpmail@ftpmail.ramona.vix.com	USA
ftpmail@cs.uow.edu.au	Australia
ftpmail@ftp.uni-stuttgart.de	Germany
ftpmail@grasp.insa-lyon.fr	France
ftpmail@doc.ic.ac.uk	Great Britain
ftpmail@ieunet.ie	Ireland

Earth Science and Electronic Mail

Earth scientists are enthusiastically embracing electronic mail to support and conduct research, keep abreast of the latest developments in their disciplines, and instruct students. One of the most effective ways earth scientists are using the Internet is through electronic mail discussion lists and Usenet interest groups. For instance, recent postings to the **sci.geo.geology** Usenet group reveal several different topics of discussion and requests for information:

- a group member asked how to effectively dry soil samples
- a teacher requested employment information for an upcoming job fair
- a group member asked for help in locating a an EPA software manual, which elicited a quick response by another member of the group who could set up a file transfer of both the manual and the software

A number of Usenet groups have sprung up devoted to the geosciences. Table 3.2 lists a few of these.

University departments are setting up their own network newsgroups to keep their students and faculty informed about the developments in their programs. For example, the Geology Department at Indiana University-Bloomington created the iu.geosci newsgroup to disseminate program information and announcements of upcoming events in their department. (Access to this particular newsgroup is restricted to Indiana University faculty and students, however.)

Electronic mail listservs devoted to earth science are far more numerous because it is much easier to get one started and maintain it. The wide variety of earth science-related listservs is show in Table 3.3.

Earth science teachers are finding electronic mail a good way to keep in contact with their students. Educators have used electronic mail to send and receive class assignments. This is accomplished by setting up a class electronic mail discussion list on a local server. The teacher posts the assignment to the list, which is distributed to all the students. When

Table 3.2 Sample Usenet Interest groups
(compiled from Thoen, 1994; Ramshaw, 1995)

Group	Topic
comp.infosystems.gis	Graphic information systems
sci.geo.eos	NASA's Earth Observation System (EOS)
sci.geo.fluids	Geophysical fluid dynamics
sci.geo.geology	Solid earth sciences
sci.geo.hydrology	Surface and groundwater hydrology
sci.geo.meteorology	Meteorology topics
sci.geo.oceanography	Oceanography and marine science
sci.geo.petroleum	Petroleum exploration, industry, etc.
sci.geo.satellite-nav	Satellite navigation, esp. global positioning systems
sci.image.processing	Scientific image processing and analysis
sci.techniques.mag-resonance	Magnetic resonance imaging and spectroscopy
sci.techniques.microscopy	Discussions of microscopy
sci.techniques.spectroscopy	Spectrum analysis
sci.techniques.xtallography	Discussions of crystallography

the assignment is completed the student emails the paper to the teacher for review and comment. The teacher can import the assignment directly into a word processing program to correct it. After grading the paper the teacher can email the assignment back to the student. Educators are using electronic mailing lists to serve as a virtual seminar "room." Each week a new topic or question is placed on the electronic mailing list, and students have a specific amount of time to respond to the posting. Educators report that participation rates in an electronic discussion, whether required or not, tend to be higher than in discussions attempted during a conventional class. Students who tend not to participate in class feel less intimidated and respond more often. A much larger discussion group is embraced if the class email list is opened up to the entire Internet community.

Electronic mail is a good way for students and teachers to keep in touch. I've found email to be a wonderful way of communicating with students with whom I might never otherwise have had. the opportunity to. Some students feel intimidated by an instructor and won't ask questions during class and occasionally are too embarrassed to come by during office hours for consultation. These students find it easier to send their questions and concerns over email, maintaining some degree of anonymity.

➤➤ Focus on the Internet: *Education and Research with Electronic Mail*

The rapid and flexible exchange of information that electronic mail enables over computer networks is changing the face of education and research at all levels. The earth scientist

Table 3.3 Sample geoscience electronic mail list
(compiled from Thoen, 1994; Ramshaw, 1995)

List	Listserv Address
Arc/Info Support List (ESRI)	listserv@esri.com
Cartography, sci.visualization (Ingrax)	listserv@psuvm.psu.edu
Climatology (CLIMLIST)	listserv@psuvm.psu.edu
Coastal Management and Resources (COASTNET)	lisserv@uriacc.uri.edu
Conservation Biology and GIS (CONSGIS)	listserv@uriacc.bitnet
Computer Modeling in Geosciences (geo-computer-models)	mailbase@mailbase.ac.uk
Dinosaurs (dinosaur)	listproc@lepomis.psych.upenn.edu
Earthquake Preparedness (QUAKE-L)	listserv@nodak.edu
Energy Discussion List (ENERGY-L)	listserv@taunivm.bitnet
Generic Mapping Tools (gmthelp)	listserv@soest.hawaii.edu
Geoscience Information Society (Geonet-L)	listserv@iubvm.ucs.indiana.edu
Geography (GEOGRAPH)	listserv@searn.sunset.se
Geology (GEOLOGY)	listserv@ptearn.bitnet
Geographic Information Systems (GIS-L)	listserv@ubvm.cc.buffalo.edu
Geoscience Information Group (geo-gig)	mailbase@mailbase.ac.uk
GIS, Coastal (COASTGIS)	listserv@irlearn.ucd.ie
GIS, Temporal Subjects (TGIS-L)	listser@ubvm.cc.buffalo.edu
GIS, User Interface Issues (UIGIS-L)	listserv@ubvm.bitnet
GIS, Virtual Worlds Interfaces (VIGIS-L)	listserv@uwavm.bitnet
Global Positioning Satellite systems (GPS-L)	gps-request@tws4.si.com
Groundwater issues (AQUIFER)	listserv@ibacsata.bitnet
Idris Support List (IDRIS-L)	mailserv@toe.towson.edu
Maps and Air Photos (MAPS-L)	listserv@uga.cc.uga.edu
Remotely Sensed Data and Digital Image Processing (IMGRS-L)	listserv@csearn.bitnet
Seismology Discussion (SEISMD-L)	listserv@bingvmb.cc.binghampton.edu
Soils (Soils-l)	listserv@unl.edu
Statistics and Quantitative Methods in Geosciences (STAT-GEO)	LISTSERV@UFRJ.BITNET
Urban Planning (URBAN-L)	listserv@trearn.bitnet
US National Spatial Data Infrastructure (NSDI-L)	listproc@grouse.umesve.maine.edu
Volcano Discussion List (VOLCANO)	AIJHF@ASUACAD.BITNET

Message body syntax: 1) grass lists: <sub firstname lastname> 2) listserv: <sub listname firstname lastname> 3) listproc: <subscribe listname> 4) mailbase: <join listname firstname lastname> 5) majordomo: subscribe listname today has a new research and educational tool in the form of electronic mail. Electronic mail enhances educational and research experiences because:

- it is a more time-saving and cost-effective form of communication
- it provides a flexible way of exchanging information in a variety of different electronic formats (e.g., text graphic, digital sound, etc.)
- it improves communication between people
- it enables you to communicate with a group of people as easily as with one person

Electronic mail can make your research time more effective and productive. During the course of your research you will undoubtedly communicate with colleagues, exchange notes and documents, review written reports, and elicit data and information from people. Electronic mail makes communication with individuals more timely and expedient. An electronic mail message is delivered almost immediately, and the response can be transmitted nearly as fast depending on the reaction time of the recipient.

Electronic mail enhances collaborative review of manuscripts because the text is already in computer-readable form or the software enables the attachment of word processing files for distribution. Recipients need only detach the word processing document, open it in their word processing program, and make the changes they wish. The new version is attached to an electronic mail response and returned to the sender. All of this is done without using paper resources or printer ribbons or incurring postage expenses. Delivery time is much faster than even the speediest courier or conventional mail service.

Electronic mail represents a unique way to conduct survey research, but issues not inherent to conventional mail survey enter into the picture. Tach (1995) synthesized the advantages and disadvantages of using electronic mail for survey research. Conducting a survey via electronic mail is less expensive for the researcher and easier for the participant to return. Being in an electronic format makes editing questions and sorting the data much easier. Questionnaires can be distributed much faster, and lost questionnaires replaced within seconds or minutes. Response rates are 20 to 50% higher for electronic mail surveys than conventional paper questionnaires (Sproull, 1986). Studies also show that people will provide more honest answers to questions submitted by electronic mail than by hard copy or face-to-face interviews. Electronic mail surveys potentially have faster response times and wider audiences. Answers can be generated within minutes of the receipt of the survey, with worldwide coverage.

Conducting surveys by electronic mail presents new challenges to the researcher. Most notable is the demographic limitations on samples. The population and sample of survey respondents is limited to those who have access to electronic mail and an online network connection. The relative insecurity of online networks cannot guaranty confidentiality. As many email systems automatically include one's email address in the header of the message, anonymous surveys are virtually impossible. Additional instructions concerning the use and submission of an electronic mail survey may be required for those unfamiliar with the use of electronic mail. Last but not least is the ever present potential problem of incompatible electronic mail systems.

Today's educational environment is changing in ways that reflect the changes in our modern culture. There are more nontraditional students returning to campuses who, in many cases, have restrictive schedules, making it hard to fit advanced educational experiences in between work and family obligations. A highly competitive work environment is requiring students to equip themselves with many more skills than have been expected of them before. Educational institutions face downsizing of faculty and services as resources become more scarce. Education continually turns toward technology to meet the challenges that face educational institutions, teachers and students. Educators, earth science educators included, see computer-mediated communication as a way of handling some of these problems. Using computer-mediated communication to enhance or deliver instruction provides flexibility in the instructional process. Conducting class discussions over networked communication systems like electronic mail liberates student and teachers from the confines of classroom walls. Neither are required to go to a particular place at a fixed point in time to engage in academic discourse. Instead, the educator can post a question to an electronic mailing list that goes to all members of the class. Students respond at their convenience, whether this is 9:00 in the morning or 12:30 in the evening. Such flexibility relieves the students from the stress of responding immediately to a questioning teacher. Answers can be more carefully examined, researched and communicated. Educators are not constrained by the clock to have topics discussed within the temporal confines of a class period. Having a degree of "anonymity" provided by electronic communication, shy students feel more comfortable responding to questions than with a classroom full of eyes watching.

The ease of sending and receiving electronic mail makes it a good way to introduce students to Internet technology and begin establishing their own professional network of contacts. There is no better way to do this than by having students join an electronic mailing list or keeping track of the postings to a professional Usenet group. Electronic mail interest groups are populated by professionals in their respective fields and serve as a great well of collective knowledge waiting to be tapped. Earth science educators have assigned students to post questions related to a class research project to a Usenet group and monitor the response they received (Butler, 1995).

What You Have Learned

- Electronic mail is a fast and efficient way of communication.
- Electronic messages can be sent to an individual or group at the same time.
- Email's asynchronous form of communication lets you control how and when you respond to messages.
- Electronic mail special interest groups or discussion lists are a useful way of communicating with people who share a common interest in a particular subject.

- Electronic mail is a flexible service and can be used to interact with other systems like Archie, FTP and listserv to query and retrieve files over the Internet.

Apply It!

The strength of the Internet is its electronic mail access to the earth science Internet community. In Chapter 2, the World Wide Web and Gopher provided excellent background information on the greenhouse effect and global climate change. Answers to very specific questions are not easily obtained with the Internet, largely because its chaotic nature and lack of systematic organization. Human experience with the Internet is often the best resource. Those in the Internet community interested in the greenhouse effect discuss their ideas over Usenet newsgroups or electronic mail listservs. You can join in on the discussion by using the Netscape mail facility.

Many World Wide Web browsers have an electronic mail accessibility built into them. However, you must configure the browser to point to your Internet electronic mail server for sending and receiving messages. In Netscape this is done by going through the "Options" menu to the "Mail and News Preference" submenu. Here you'll find fields to enter in the address of your email server. Once these fields have been properly configured you're ready to send electronic mail.

To send an electronic mail message, simply go to the "File" menu and the "New Mail Message" pick, which brings up the message creation window (Figure 3.10). The new message window looks a lot like that of any other electronic mail program, with fields to enter the recipient's name, address, copies of the message to others and subject.

With Netscape Navigator, you can do many of the same things that any other mail program can do. You can attach files, forward messages, defer delivery to a later time, and so on. A great feature of Netscape Navigator's email program is the fact that URLs typed into a message will appear as a hyperlink or icon on the recipient's message. If recipients are using Netscape email, they simply click on the embedded hyperlink to view it in Netscape. Newer electronic mail programs, like Microsoft Exchange, have this hyperlinking function built in.

A few listservs are devoted to, or occasionally discuss, topics of climate change. ATMOSLIST is a moderated electronic mail distribution list for Australian atmospheric scientists and those working in closely related fields. It is used to disseminate information about notices regarding conferences, workshops, data availability, calls for papers, and positions available, as well as requests for information. To subscribe to ATMOSLIST, send an email request to the Internet address:

mailserv@cc.monash.edu.au

The body of the message (not subject line) should contain one line (Figure 3.11):

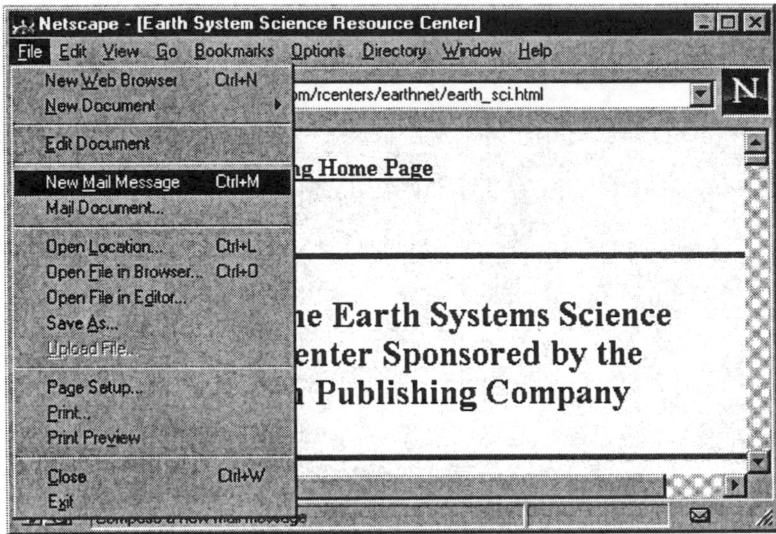

Figure 3.10 Opening a new mail message in Netscape Navigator

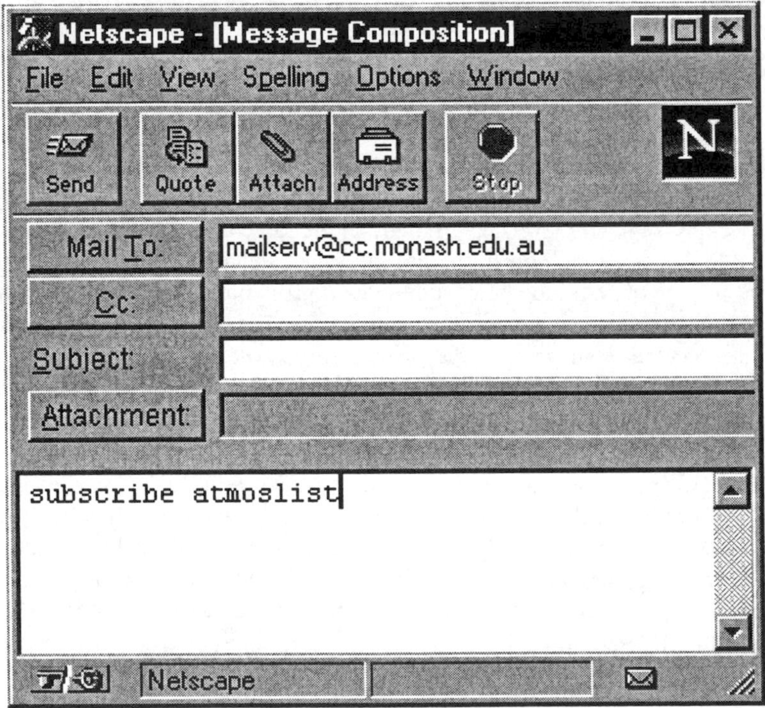

Figure 3.11 Netscape email message composition window

subscribe atmoslist

Like ATMOSLIST, CLIMLIST is a moderated electronic mail distribution list for those working in climatology or a closely related field. Its primary role also is to disseminate notices regarding conferences and workshops, data availability, calls for papers, and positions available, as well as requests for information. It is not intended for "chatting." To subscribe to the list contact:

John Arnfield
Deparment of Geography
Ohio State University
John.Arnfield@osu.edu
John.Arnfield@OHSTMAIL.BITNET

Usenet news is an important source of timely information relating to climate change. A number of newsgroups routinely discuss topics of global change. A few of those are:

bit.listserv.geograph
ca.earthquakes
ca.environment
comp.infosystems.gis
sci.agriculture
sci.bio.conservation
sci.bio.ecology
sci.bio.fisheries
sci.bio.paleontology
sci.environment
sci.geo.earthquakes
sci.geo.eos
sci.geo.fluids
sci.geo.geology
sci.geo.hydrology
sci.geo.meteorology
sci.geo.oceanography
sci.geo.rivers+lakes

To send a message to a Usenet newsgroup from Netscape, you invoke the Netscape news reader by using the "Window" menu and choosing the "Netscape News" menu option. Netscape Navigator's news reader is divided into three windows, one for viewing newsgroups, one for listing newsgroup postings, and one for reading a news posting. The news server window shown in Figure 3.12 displays the news servers and newsgroups you have configured Netscape Navigator to point to. Once you click on a server address, Netscape opens a connection with the server and retrieves the list of available newsgroups. Netscape uses the folder metaphor to collect newsgroups at lower levels in a newsgroup

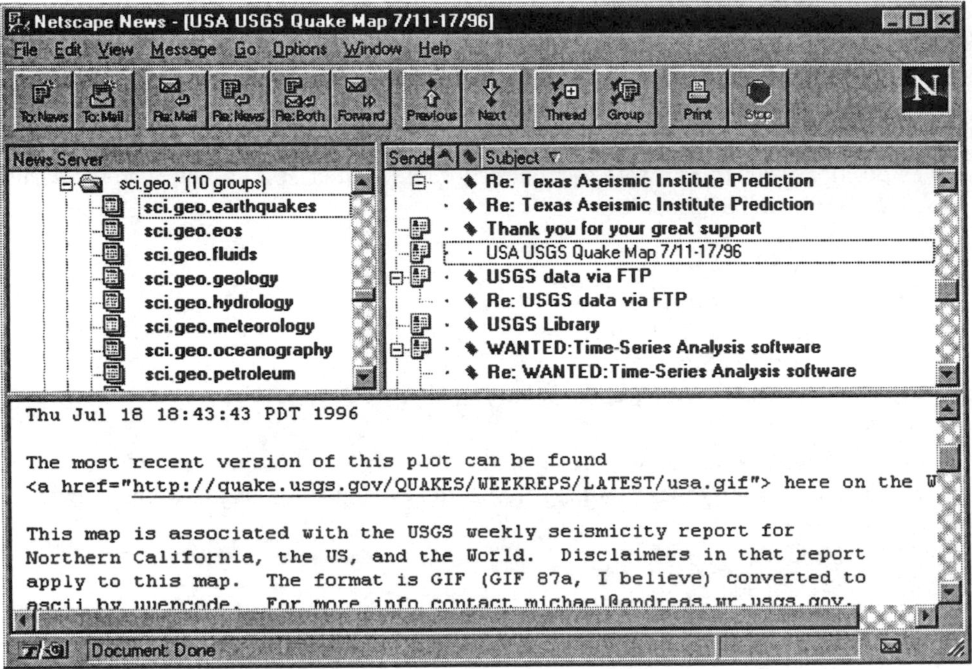

Figure 3.12 Netscape Navigator news reader

hierarchy. Scroll down the list of newsgroups until you reach sci.geo. Most news servers will have the sci.geo.geology newsgroup. Use your mouse to click on a message that appears in the message-listing window.

To send a message to a newsgroup click the "To:Mail" button and the email creation window will appear. Make sure that newsgroups is one of the fields that is displayed above the message creation field. If it's not, go to the "View" menu and choose "Newsgroups" to display the newsgroups field to fill in (Figure 3.13). Type in the name of the newsgroup you want a message posted to. You don't need to fill in the "Mail To:" field. Make sure to include a subject and then click "Send" and its' on its way. You will likely need to wait a day or so to get many responses as Usenet postings disseminate news server to news server.

You have three choices when responding to a newsgroup posting. You may reply to the sender, the newsgroup as a whole or both by clicking any of their respective buttons on the toolbar. Doing so will automatically fill out the appropriate sender and subject fields; you then can type in your message.

Having email capability integrated into a browser simplifies your life online. With this function, there is little need to have separate electronic mail for many users.

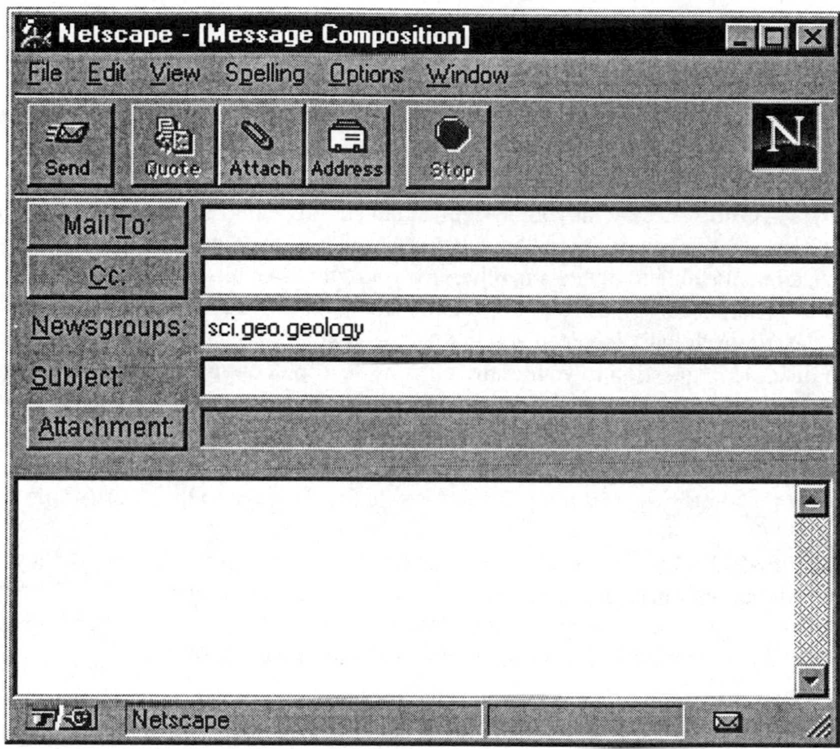

Figure 3.13 Netscape message composition window

Try It Out!

1. Send me an electronic mail message. My email address is:

   mritter@uwsp.edu

   In the subject field type: "***Earth Online*** Email. " Write anything you wish in the body of the message: what you like or dislike about ***Earth Online***, suggestions for changes, new Try It Out! exercises or interesting earth-science-related Internet sites.

2. Join an electronic mail discussion list or Usenet interest group. Scan through Tables 3.2 and 3.3 for a discussion list or group of interest and join. You might want to "lurk around" for a few days to get an idea of the topics that are currently being discussed before sending your first posting. It's nice to introduce yourself to the list or group in your first posting. Let the group know who you are, what you do, and what particular interests you have; maybe ask a question too. Tell the list you found them in ***Earth Online***!

3. Look up a friend or colleague and say hello. See Chapter 5, "Remote Login to the Internet with Telnet," for remote login instructions, and Chapter 6 for details about the Netfind service. In addition to the names of the persons you are trying to contact, you will need to know where they connect to the Internet from and what city and state they live in. Make sure to review the example Netfind search before you do your own.

4. **EDUCATORS**: Check with your system administrator about setting up an electronic mail list. Even though you might not have listserv capabilities on campus, your electronic mail service may be able to create a mailbox for your class. An electronic discussion is a good way to get students "talking" to one another about class material or other matters outside the classroom. It will also keep you in touch with your students. You can post a message or a discussion question to your entire class by "carbon copying" it. Some electronic mail software allows you to create a list of individuals under a single group name. You then address the message to the group name and the message is automatically copied to all members of the list. You can employ this method in your online class discussions. Once a student responds to a question you can forward the message to the class (group).

5. **PROFESSIONALS:** Check into setting up a listserv for a specialty group with your professional organization. Specialty group listservs are a good way to distribute newsletters, give out information about professional meetings, organize paper sessions at an upcoming meeting and just keep in contact with one another.

CHAPTER 4

File Transfer over the Internet: File Transfer Protocol

File Transfer Protocol, or FTP, is the method by which files are moved between computers connected to the Internet. FTP is a popular activity on the Internet because it is interactive and relatively easy to use, and there are literally thousands of programs and data, sound and image files available for you to copy and use. For example:

- The Computer Oriented Geological Society or COGS (**URL - ftp://ftp.csn.org/COGS/**) archive contains a variety of MS DOS and Macintosh programs and source codes. You will find programs related to geochemistry, geophysics, hydrology, LANDSAT imagery, mapping software, and mineralogy, among others.
- The World Paleomagnetic Database archive (**URL - ftp://earth.eps.pitt.edu**) permits you to download databases and programs related to paleomagnetism.

Once you have connected to a few FTP sites you will be amazed at the number of programs and databases that you have access to. A whole new resource for enriching your education and conducting research is at your fingertips.

File Transfer Protocol Servers and Their Resources

One of the original purposes for building the Internet was to provide a means for people to share resources between computers. The Internet was created to permit researchers to archive and send files between each other's computers as a distributed computer system. Within a distributed computing environment, a program that several people use need not be stored on each individual computer. Instead, the program is located on one computer and accessed by several users individually or simultaneously. Users of a distributed system have the flexibility to run a program or examine data on the remote computer or to copy the files to their local workstation when access is needed. Having programs distributed on remote computers negates the need for each person to have large hard drives to store and use the same information.

Like most other Internet services and systems, FTP is built around the client-server paradigm. To send (*upload*) and receive (*download*) files requires an FTP client program running on your local computer. The client program takes the commands issued by your computer, converts them into a "universal" set of commands that the remote FTP server can understand, and requests the server to perform the actions. The server receives the commands, processes the request and returns the items requested.

File transfer is somewhat of a misnomer because you don't transfer the actual file. When you transfer a file you issue a command to the FTP server to read the contents of the file and send a copy of it over the Internet. The local desktop computer listens to the server's communication and puts the file into the local computer's storage banks. Internet network software ensures that no errors or noise interrupt the transfer and destroy the contents of the file. But just as with any kind of technology, problems can occur. Network connections get broken or delayed to the point that your system "times out" before an entire file can be received. This is more likely to occur with large files (one megabyte and larger) or during peak hours of network use.

In many ways, FTP is the complement to Telnet, the topic of Chapter 5. Where Telnet can offer powerful command structures for examining information online, FTP has fewer commands that perform similar though more limited functions. Moreover, Telnet is designed to let you see the information on your computer screen while the information stays on the remote computer. In most cases, FTP requires that you send files to your computer before viewing. Some FTP client programs let you view ASCII text files before transferring to your desktop computer. In contrast to many Telnet-based services, which are organized around a menu structure, FTP systems are organized by directories and subdirectories. This makes finding and navigating the information a little harder. FTP server system administrators often provide an index file listing the files that are contained in a particular directory.

FTP is so popular because the client software is widely available and many File Transfer Protocol servers do not require special accounts and passwords. These servers make their resources available through an *anonymous* FTP accounting system. An anonymous FTP service lets you log on to the server under an anonymous user name and generally without a special password. Most anonymous FTP servers will tell you what to enter as a password, and more often than not, the FTP server will request your electronic mail address as the password. In some cases, restrictions are placed on what directories and files you can access on the anonymous FTP server.

File Transfer Protocol software is efficient and easy to use. There are just a few simple commands that are required to move files between computers. Better yet, the interface has been designed so another computer program can use FTP to automatically send or retrieve files. For example, a program can be written to scan files on a computer once a night and then use FTP to transfer the updated versions to another location. This process would be particularly useful in updating files of information like weather data. A program can be written to scan the data that has been collected from a remote weather observation site and its contents sent by FTP to a main data bank for archiving.

File Transfer Protocol also is flexible, enabling you to transfer any kind of file between different types of computer platforms. The originators of the Internet recognized that people would be using different styles and brands of computers and thus designed FTP, as well as other Internet software protocols, to be "transparent" to computer system design. The client program is written for a specific type of computer like a Macintosh, but it doesn't matter what kind of computer the server you communicate with is. You can transfer files from your Macintosh to a Sun Sparc Station or Pentium server. You can transfer:

- programs either in source or executable form
- ASCII text files, electronic mail messages, documents list, and so on
- graphic images (e.g., BMP, TIF, GIF)
- spreadsheets and databases
- audio, video and multimedia files

Many World Wide Web browsers have the ability to link to an FTP server for downloading files. So why should you use FTP software instead of some other Internet software? FTP software is exclusively designed for transferring files across the Internet. You could attach data files and documents to an electronic mail messages and send them to a remote location. However, if there is incompatibility between the sender's and recipient's email systems, then you might not be able to detach and read the file. Faxing information has become a popular way of distributing information. Faxing involves sending an image or picture of the message between individuals. The main drawback is that the information is difficult to reuse and equally hard to edit. Information that is already in digital form can be easily imported into a text editor or word processing package, read, edited, printed off or exported and sent back to the point of origin in a fast and efficient way. Above all, transferring information over the network using FTP is fast and inexpensive.

> ***Earth Online Tip***: If you download shareware programs, be courteous and send the author(s) the registration fee should you decide to continue to use the program.

Logging on to FTP

You transfer files via FTP with a client program. The client program tells the remote FTP archive what actions to take when you're connected to it. Client programs are either text-based or graphically based interfaces. Web browsers enable you to save files to a local computer but uploading is not available. If you log on to an Internet provider under a shell account you can initiate an FTP session by simply typing "ftp" at the system prompt. Graphical user interface client programs running on your desktop computer are used over SLIP/PPP accounts and direct connections. Next, you'll need the address of the system you want to establish communication with. There are a variety of ways of getting FTP site addresses. You can start by looking in Chapter 10, "Internet Resources for the Earth Sciences." There are a number of other books that publish extensive lists of FTP sites.

People often publish lists of FTP sites in frequently-asked-question files (FAQs). Try sending a message to an electronic mail discussion list or a Usenet group asking for useful FTP sites. Use one of the several Internet search services like Archie, as explained in Chapter 6. Some FTP clients let you save the addresses along with descriptive information into a "hot list" file to make connecting the next time easier.

Once you have the address for an FTP server, you'll need an account, a user ID and an account password for the target FTP system you're connecting to. Most of the time you will be logging on to an anonymous FTP server so a user ID and password is not important. When prompted for a user name you simply enter the word "anonymous." The server will ask you to enter either your full electronic mail address or a tab. It is proper netiquette to enter a correct email address if asked. Many systems like to keep track of the number of users and where they are connecting from. FTP has created more traffic on the Internet than any other application but soon will be replaced by the ever expanding World Wide Web. Most FTP sites limit the number of anonymous logins, so you might encounter difficulty when trying to connect. Have patience and try again later, maybe during off-peak hours.

After you have successfully logged on to the server, you will need to know the names of the files you want and in what directories they reside. Be aware that system administrators delete old or unused files and change subdirectory structures. Be forewarned that the address and directory location you obtain may be out of date or that the file you are looking for has been deleted or moved. You can get a listing of files and directories by entering the "dir" or "ls" command. Some system administrators will leave an index file in a subdirectory explaining what files reside there. You will also need to know the file format and if the file is compressed or uncompressed. Most files are either ASCII or binary. An accurate transfer of the file depends on knowing the file type. FTP does not understand the format or contents of a file. If a user requests FTP to transfer a file using an incorrect format, the resulting copy may be corrupted. The major file types are:

- ASCII: a file that contains text which is only printable characters and assorted punctuation and other characters
- binary: also referred to as an image format; the format used by most programs, spreadsheets, databases, and word processing documents

The File Transfer Protocol default transfer type is usually set to text. Binary transfer works for both ASCII and binary formats. Set the FTP transfer to binary to ensure the transfer of any non-ASCII characters if you're not sure what the file format is. If the file you're transferring is compressed, you will need a decompression program compatible with the format of the compression program used on the file.

A lot of time can be saved if you do a little planning before you start your session. Know the location to store the transferred file to, whether on your hard drive, floppy diskette, or a shared disk space on a local server. It's advisable to place downloaded files into a temporary directory and then move them at some other time. File transfers can take awhile if you have large files or a number of smaller files to transfer. Remember, someone else may be waiting for you to log off so they can get into the system.

After connecting to an FTP server you can obtain a listing of the contents of the directory you have logged into by issuing either of two commands having the same format:

ftp>**dir** <directory-name local-file-name>

or

ftp>**ls** <directory-name local-file name>

Both commands list the files in the given directory on the remote machine. Directory and file name commands are optional. Invoking the directory name command will cause the FTP server to display the contents of the requested directory. If the command is left blank then the contents of the current directory will be displayed. Using the second command (local file name) instructs the server to put the listing into the given file name on your local computer. Omit the command if you want the listing to be displayed on your computer screen. Wild-card characters are permitted with these commands. On most computers, an asterisk (*) is used to display all files with the same name or file extension. For instance, issuing the command

ftp>**dir *.txt**

displays all files with the extension ".txt."

Common FTP Commands

There are several dozen FTP commands for working with and moving files between computers, some of which accomplish the same task. Many are similar to common UNIX commands. Thankfully you only need to know a few of them to get your job done. The more common commands, along with an example, are provided below:

ASCII or text	Set file transfer type to ASCII ftp>**ascii**
binary or image	Set file transfer type to binary ftp>**binary**
bye, close or exit	End FTP session ftp>**close**
cd directory-name	Change working directory on remote system ftp>**cd hydrology**
dir, ls	List directory on remote system ftp>**dir**

get file-name	Transfer copy of file from remote FTP system ftp>**get mydata.dat**
help or ?	Show FTP online help ftp>**help**
lcd	Change working directory on local (your) system ftp>**lcd mydir**
mget	Transfer copies of multiple files from remote system ftp>**mget mydata.dat yourdata.dat**
mput	Transfer copies of multiple files to remote system ftp>**mput mydata.dat yourdata.dat**
open	Open connection to specified remote system ftp>**open ftp.remote.edu**
put	Transfer copy of file to remote system ftp>**put mydata.dat**
pwd	Display working directory on remote system ftp>**pwd**
user	Specify username to remote system ftp>**user**

Now that you have a notion of what File Transfer Protocol is and how it works, let's look at an example session. The example shows the steps and keyboard input through a shell account on a UNIX machine. We will log on to a University of Illinois FTP server with a local client and download a file. There are two ways this can be accomplished. You can start the FTP client first and then use the open command to establish the connection to the FTP server:

%**ftp**
ftp>**open vmd.cso.uiuc.edu**

The alternative way is start the FTP client software and make the connection at the same time:

%**ftp vmd.cso.uiuc.edu**

In either case your client attempts to make the connection:

Connect to vmd.cso.uiuc.edu
220 FTP server at vmd.cso.uiuc.edu, 03:54:38 CDT Wednesday 10/18/95
222 Connection will close if idle for more than 5 minutes
Name (vmd.cso.uiuc.edu:mritter):**anonymous**
331 Send your local userid instead of password for identification, please
Password:

Your password will not appear on screen, even with an anonymous FTP session, when typed. The remote FTP server responds with:

230 Welcome to the University of Illinois anonymous FTP
230
230
ftp>

After reaching the FTP prompt I'll type in the command "dir" to get a directory listing.

ftp>**dir**

200 Port request ok
125 List started ok
read me 80 67 6 2/08/94 10:41:28 anon
wx Notes 77 260 12 2/08/94 10:39:13 anon

The file I'm after is called "sources.zip." It is a FAQ file for meteorology resources that's in compressed format and located in the wx subdirectory. I'll change directories before attempting to download:

ftp>**cd wx**
250 Work directory is wx191 (Read Only)

I'll send another "dir" command to check and see if the sources.zip file is in the subdirectory.

ftp>**dir**

A long list of files is displayed (only the first couple are reprinted here to illustrate what is displayed on screen).

ACUS1 DOC v 75 82 2 1/02/93 16:24:59 wx
AURORA DOC v 77 226 4 4/29/95 9:44:37 wx

Finally, near the bottom of the list we find:

sources zip v 8192 9 17 10/11/95 9:02:45 wx

Now I'll set the file transfer to binary mode and download the file to my hard disk.

ftp>**bin**
200 Representation type is IMAGE

Check the spelling of the file before issuing any transfer commands. Notice that there is a gap between the words "sources" and "zip" in the file listing above. Assume there is a period between the file name (sources) and the extension (zip). Now issue the "get" command with the full file name to transfer the file to your computer.

ftp>**get sources.zip**

200 Port request ok
150 Sending file 'sources.zip'

It will take a short time for the file to be transferred. When the transfer is completed the remote FTP server responds with:

250 Transfer completed successfully.

local:sources.zip remote: sources.zip

66189 bytes received in 5.8e+02 seconds (0.11Kbytes/s)

The file has been successfully downloaded to my hard drive and I'm ready to decompress and examine it. I could have saved the file under a different name by simply typing a new name after the old. FTP will copy, transfer and save the file under the new file name on my desktop computer. For example:

ftp>**get sources.zip metsource.zip**

Transferring files via FTP is much simpler when using a graphical user interface client program like WS_FTP, a PC-Windows software application (Figure 4.1). When users start the program, a session profile window pops up for them to enter information about the FTP server they wish to connect to. Login configuration information can be saved for retrieval during future sessions. After they fill in the required information and click the connect button, the main application window appears. Directories and files on the local computer are presented in windows on the left hand side while the same information for the FTP server is displayed in the right hand side of the application. Users navigate their way through directories by either clicking on the directory title or clicking on the "ChgDir" button and filling in the correct path. Text files can be viewed by highlighting the file and clicking the view button, and soon the files are transferred to the local computer and displayed in a text editor. Buttons to handle making new subdirectories, removing old ones, and deleting and renaming files on either computer are provided. The user defines the type of file transfer by clicking on the appropriate button (ASCII, binary, L8). To transfer a file, the user simply highlights the file and clicks one of the arrow buttons. Clicking on the left arrow button will download a file to the desktop computer, while the right button is used to upload a file to the remote FTP server.

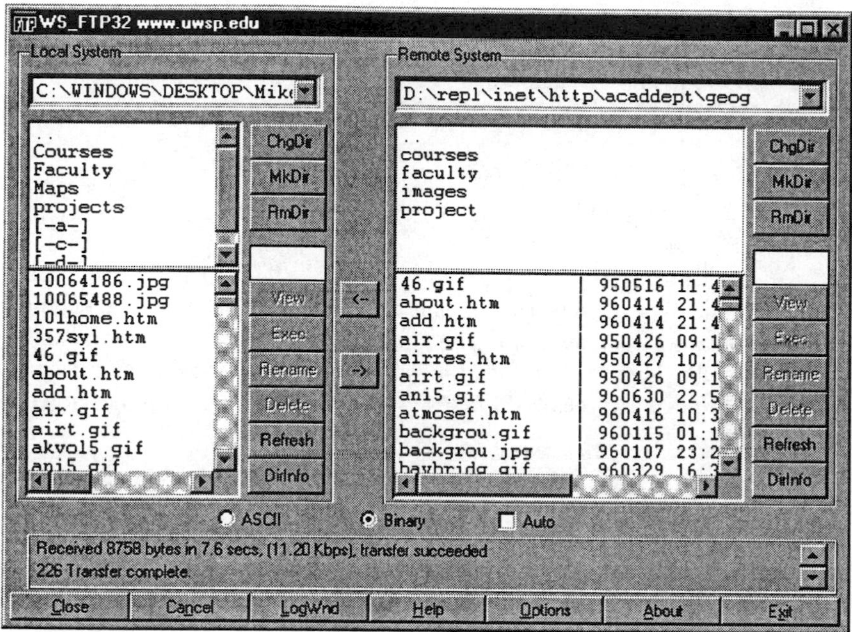

Figure 4.1 WS_FTP PC-Windows client

Files can be transferred via Gopher and World Wide Web browser applications too. For instance, over the World Wide Web you gain access to an FTP server by either clicking on a hyperlink (see Chapter 2) or typing in the FTP server address in the location field of the browser, preceding it with "ftp://" (without the quotes). This tells the browser that you are connecting to an FTP server rather than a World Wide Web server. Once connected the browser displays a list of subdirectories and files (Figure 4.1). Small icons indicate the entries as directories (folders), text files (document), and images (graphic). Additional icons for movies, sounds, and so on are used. Refer to the Apply It! section later in this chapter.

Compressed Files

Most files, like the one I downloaded in the example session above, are compressed to save on storage space. File compression programs scan files to reduce wasted space, duplicate characters, and so on in a file. There are a variety of compression techniques and thus a number of different compression programs available. Files run through on of these programs can be reduced from 30% to 70% in size.

Being smaller than their normal size, compressed files transfer more quickly across the Internet. Compressed files should always be transferred as binary files; to do otherwise is to risk corrupting the file. Compressed files can be identified by their extension. The more common compression utilities are shown in Table 4.1.

Table 4.1 Common compression formats

Compression Program	Decompression Program	File Extension
compress	uncompress	.Z
pack	unpack	.z
Stuffit	unsit	.Sit
PKZIP	PKUNZIP	.Zip

The program you need to use to uncompress the file will depend on the computer you are using and the kind of compression program used. Uncompressing the file may be as simple as typing the program name and file name at the command line. For uncompressing a DOS file that has been compressed with PKZIP and is residing on your desktop computer's hard drive, type

c:**pkunzip.exe source.zip**

PKUNZIP will extract the file to your hard drive and your ready to use it. Consult your local computer systems administrator for the compression/decompression program you might need.

Earth Online Tip: Scan downloaded files for viruses before using them. Unfortunately, the Internet is a major source of computer virus infection.

Earth Science and FTP

Earth scientists are making good use of the opportunities afforded by File Transfer Protocol by making available valuable software and data files for research and educational use. For instance, Florida State University Supercomputer Computations Research Institute makes SciAn, a UNIX-based 3D-visualization package, available for downloading. Several important geoscience FTP servers have come online over the past several years including the Computer Oriented Geological Society or COGS **(URL - ftp://ftp.csn.org/COGS/)** server and the International Association for Mathematical Geology (IAMG) FTP site. The IAMG promotes international cooperation in the application of mathematics in geological research and technology. The IAMG also cooperates with the application of mathematics and statistics to biological and planetary sciences. IAMG's FTP site is an archive for algorithms and source codes of programs that have been published in Computers and Geosciences **(URL - ftp:// www.iamg.org/pub/CG)** and Mathematical Geology **(URL - ftp://www.iamg.org/pub/MG)**. Additional programs are available from Jim Carr's Numerical Analysis for Geological Sciences **(URL - ftp://www.iamg.org/pub/Carr).** The FTP archive is intended to assist IAMG members in acquiring programs and data that have been previously difficult or time-consuming to obtain. Most programs and data have been compressed. Uploading files directly by the public is not possible as it is a "read only" site. However, it is accessible by anonymous FTP. New programs appear after the publication of each issue of Computers and Geosciences. Programs and data from older issues are being uploaded as time permits. Program submission guidelines are provided in the README file found in the /pub subdirectory. IAMG also has created a World Wide Web page interface to its FTP archives, making it much easier to obtain the programs **(URL - http://ftp://images.asc.nasa.gov).** From the FTP Web interface users can click on links to pages that contain the contents of each issue and the available programs and data. Links are provided from the issue pages to the programs available for downloading.

One of the greatest bonanzas for educators is the number of image archives that are linked to the Internet. Nearly 10,000 of NASA's press release photographs from the manned space program are accessible via FTP **(URL - ftp://images.jsc.nasa.gov)**, Gopher **(URL - gopher://images.jsc.nasa.gov/70)** and the World Wide Web **(URL - http://images.jsc.nasa.gov/)**. The digital image collection includes pictures from the Mercury space program to the present. In 1995 some 30,000 earth observation photographs were loaded. For the most part these images are copyright free, like many other images loaded on the Internet by the government, and can be freely used by individuals. The National Geophysical Data Center at Boulder, Colorado, maintains an extensive set of photographs illustrating natural hazards around the world. Each set contains twenty color or black-and-white slides with accompanying background information. The NGDC makes the Earthquakes and the Volcano and Tsunami image sets and captions available for viewing online over the World Wide Web (see Chapter 2 for details about the World Wide Web), yet they are archived on an FTP server. Web pages display scaled-down versions of the photographs along with explanatory captions. Users download the image by clicking on the download link provided at the bottom of the page, which initiates an FTP.

What You Have Learned

- FTP is an interactive means to transfer files of any type between FTP clients (your computer) and remote FTP servers.
- FTP is a fast, efficient, time-saving and cost-effective way of sharing information.
- Anonymous FTP enables anyone to log on and interact with a remote server without the need for an individual account.
- FTP transfers can be done automatically by an external program.
- Only a few commands need be learned to transfer information.

Apply It!

Now that you've been introduced to software that is specifically designed to transfer files across the Internet, let's look at easier ways to do it. Netscape Navigator, like most Web browsers, lets you download files via anonymous FTP transfers. It's quite simple, and you don't need any other helper applications. First , you must tell Netscape to open a session

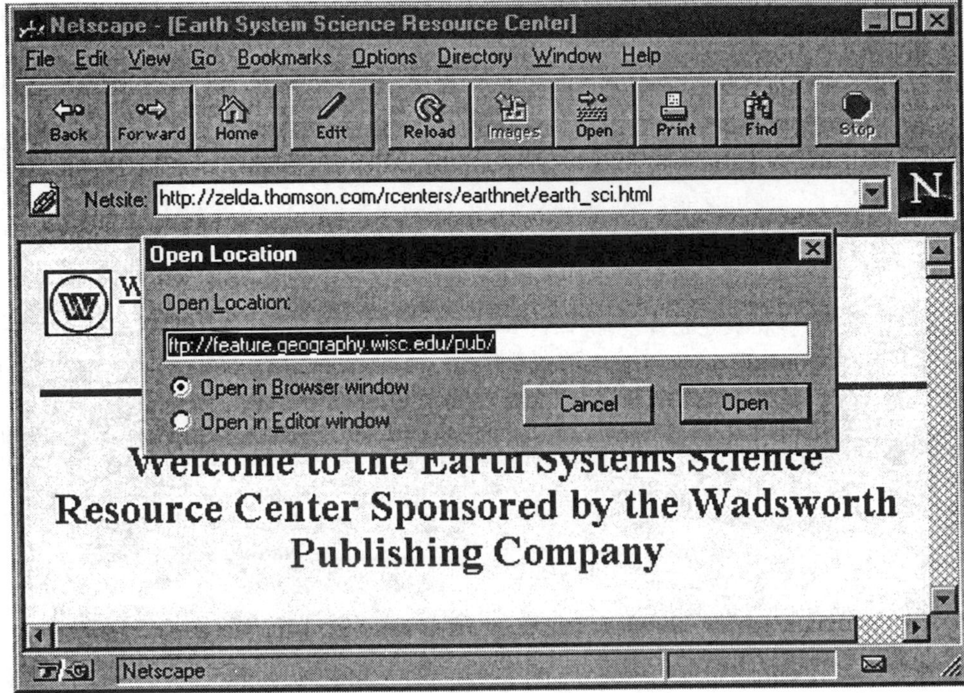

Figure 4.2 Connecting to an FTP site in Netscape

with an FTP site. You do this the same way you open a connection to a World Wide Web site. Go to the "File" menu and choose "Open Location." When the Open Location window appears, type the address of the site into the field and click the "Open" button. You can use the "Open" button on the toolbar to bring up the same window, or simply type the address in the URL Location field and hit the "Enter" key (Figure 4.2).

FTP archives are good places to look for data and graphics. I happened to find out that a graph of carbon dioxide concentrations is available at **feature.geography.wisc.edu in the pub/phys/** subdirectory. I'll open my FTP session by typing the URL into the Open Location window. Recall that the Internet address, **feature.geography.wisc.edu**, is preceded by ftp:// to tell the Netscape browser that I'll be conducting an FTP session and not a Web session (e.g., http://). After clicking the "Open" button, communication is established and the FTP site appears on screen. Figure 4.3 shows the directory structure for the FTP site. Netscape displays icons to represent the contents of a particular item on the list. Each entry on this page has a folder icon beside it indicating that they are all directories (Figure 4.3). I'll choose the "pub/" subdirectory (Figure 4.4); most pub subdirectories are used for general public access. The subdirectory list includes page icons indicating that an item is a text file. The file I'm interested in is the "phys" subdirectory, so I'll click on it to retrieve its directory listing.

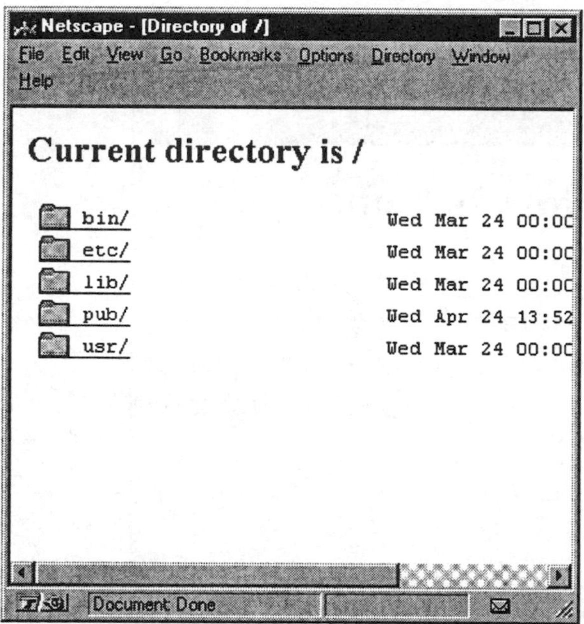

Figure 4.3 Directory structure of feature.geography.wisc.edu

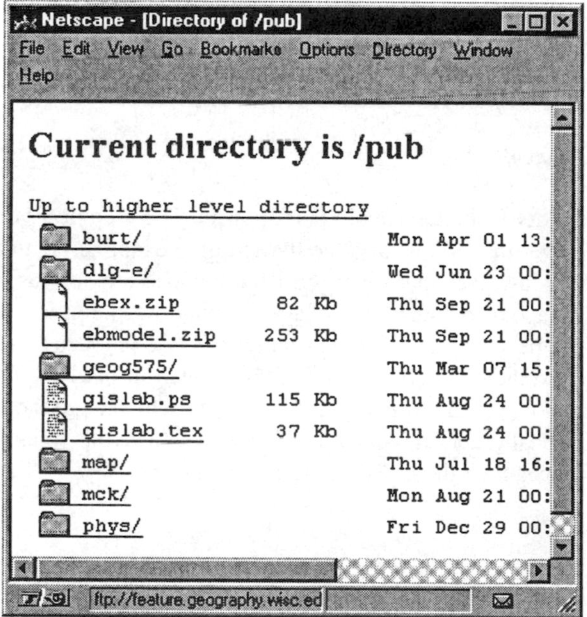

Figure 4.4 Directory structure of feature.geography.wisc.edu pub

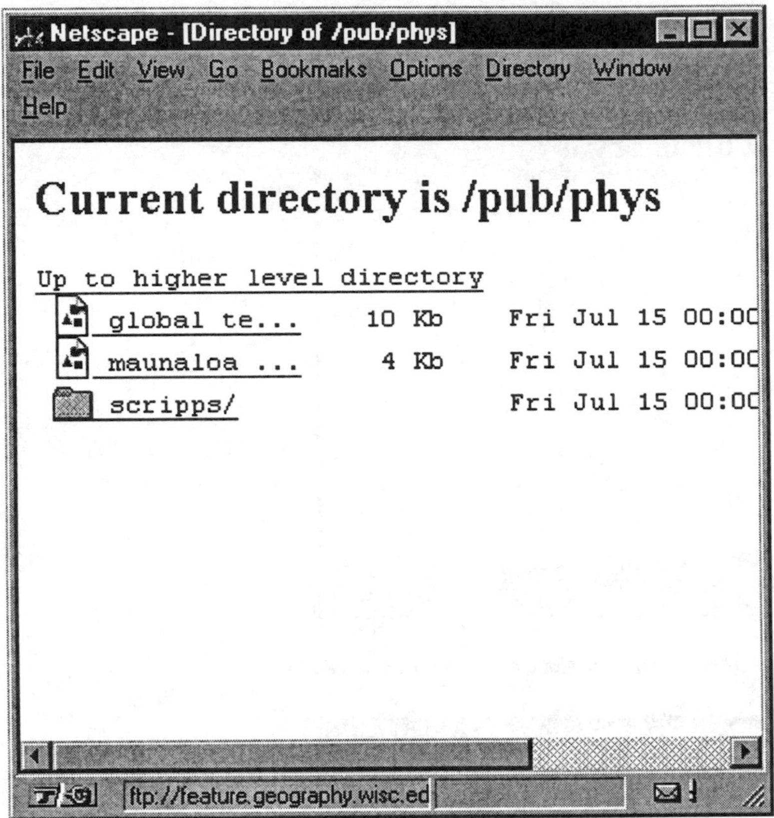

Figure 4.5 Directory structure of /pub/phys

Finally, I'm at the subdirectory I'm interested in (Figure 4.5). The graphic I've been looking for is the maunaloa image file. I'll click on the hyperlink to examine the image on screen first (Figure 4.6). It looks just like what I want so I'll download it by choosing "Save as" from the "File" menu. Netscape responds with a "Save as" window to confirm the file name and location for the file to be saved to. Clicking on the "OK" downloads and saves the file to my desktop computer. It's ready to load into an HTML or word processing document. Because it's in a digital format, I can load it into a graphics program to change the picture's attributes and add text or additional graphics. An alternative way to save this image is to position the cursor over the image, click the right mouse button and choose the "Save image as" option (Figure 4.6).

Try It Out!

1. FTP to the University of Illinois's anonymous FTP server and download a file. This is a busy server so expect some delays. Download the "sources.zip" file if you're interested in

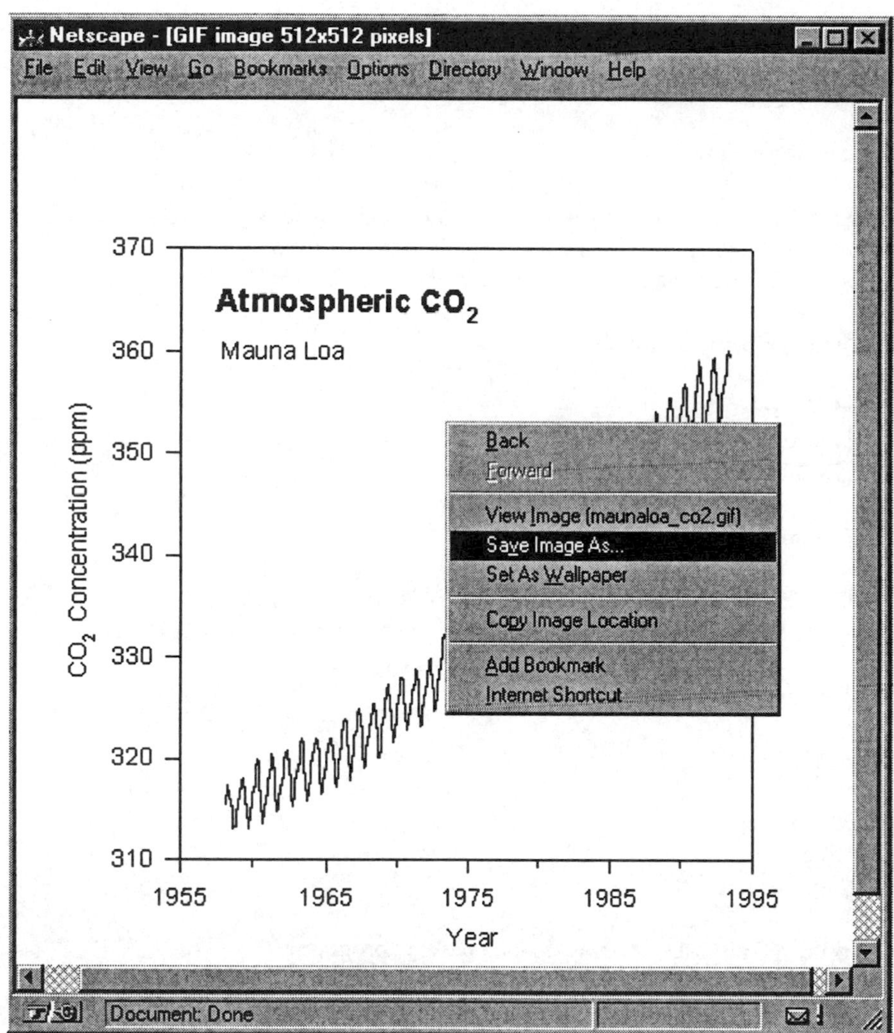

Figure 4.6 Saving the Mauna Loa CO_2 graphic

meteorology and/or climatology. You can follow the example FTP session and substitute your <filenames> for the ones used in it.

2. Try transferring the same file via electronic mail. Use the example for transferring files by electronic mail in the discussion above as a guide.

3. Massive shareware archives are connected to the Internet for people to download test programs. Connect to **URL - ftp://oak.oakland.edu.** Now follow the subdirectories by changing directories (**cd**).

cd SimTel
cd msdos
cd astronomy

to such programs as

astrmt30.zip Astrometric data reduction for CCD images
nalm1995.zip Nautical Almanac Data (hourly) for 1995
sv115. SVGA vector graph. planetary, ephemer. & anim.

For geology software follow

cd SimTel
cd msdos
cd geology

to such programs as

acpl0021.zip Package for analysis & ctrl of pollution (7parts)
np940107.zip NewPet: A geochemical data plotting system

And for mapping information follow:

cd SimTel
cd msdos
cd mapping

to programs like

topov300.zip 3-D topographic map plotting program

There are plenty of programs for other computer platforms too. Another good site to take a look at is **URL - ftp://sunsite.unc.edu**. Check out Chapter 10, "Internet Resources for the Earth Sciences," for other FTP sites.

CHAPTER 5

Remote Login to the Internet with Telnet

Telnet is one of the original Internet applications; it even predates the widely used electronic mail. Though the World Wide Web is stealing the thunder and the attention of most Internet users, Telnet remains a valuable application. Telnet is the remote login application for the Internet. The World Wide Web is primarily designed for information retrieval. But if you want to truly interact with another computer, that is, actually use the resources or software on another computer, you turn to Telnet. Telnet allows you to gain access to a computer system located in another building, across town, or at remote location in another part of the world. Once connected, the Telnet software makes your computer act like a terminal directly connected to the remote computer, giving you the ability to run programs on it. Telnet transmits information in real time, unlike other Internet services that send information in bursts or must download information to your computer before you can use it. This makes Telnet a faster application for interacting with a remote server. Over a Telnet connection you can execute database queries or simulation programs, run Internet software, look through a library online catalog, connect to an electronic bulletin board system, or even talk to people online. You can use Telnet to remotely login to your electronic mail server to read your electronic mail. In many countries that have slow Internet connections, Telnet and electronic mail are the only applications that are available. Those of us in the earth and environmental sciences use Telnet:

- to obtain crustal motion information from the NCEER's Strong Motion Server **(URL - telnet://duke.ldgo.columbia.edu:23)**
- to connect to the Colorado Alliance of Research Libraries **(URL - telnet://pac.carl.org)** to query their system for resources to complete a research paper
- to check in with NASA SpaceLink to get the latest NASA project news and download astronomy-related shareware **(URL - telnet://spacelink.msfc.nasa.gov)**

Telnet and Time-Sharing Computers

Telnet is like the login facility used on a conventional *time-sharing computer system*. Time-sharing computer systems use one large computer to support multiple users at the same time. A user interacts with a time-sharing computer through a *terminal* that includes a keyboard, a video display, and possibly a mouse. A time-sharing computer is accessed with a computer running terminal emulation software, software that makes your computer act like

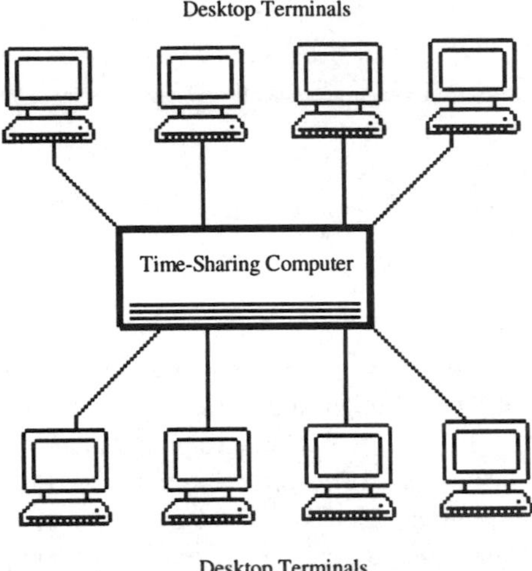

Figure 5.1 Time-sharing computer system

a terminal, too. The terminal connects to the time-sharing computer either directly or over a network line. Multiple terminals can be attached to a time-sharing computer, allowing one user at each terminal to have access to the time-sharing computer's resources (Figure 5.1). The time-sharing computer sets aside a particular part of its resources for each user to run programs with. In so doing, the time-sharing computer's operating system quickly switches between the users to ensure that each person's work proceeds as if he or she were the only person using the system. Users can pick and choose what software they wish to run without interrupting others. Like the personal computer on your desktop, the time-sharing computer responds to your keyboard input almost instantly.

To allocate system resources to authorized users, time-sharing computers require the user to login with a user name and password. The login procedure helps the computer keep track of who is logged in and how many people are using the computer at any one point in time. Even though time-sharing computers permit several people to access its resources at the same time, there are limits to the number of users who have access to it. When you log on to a time-sharing computer it will usually respond by asking you to identify yourself at the login prompt. After I make the initial connection, the time-sharing computer I log onto responds with:

BSDI BSD/386 1.1 (worf) (ttyp3)

login: **mritter**

After I have entered a predetermined login identifier, in this case "mritter," the computer will return with a password prompt.

Password:

To keep passwords secure, they are not displayed while users type them in. Often the remote computer displays a string of asterisks in place of the actual password. If the correctly matched login user name and password are accepted, the computer allows the user into its system and responds with

```
Last login: Sun Dec 17 20:32:44 from dial1.uwsp.edu
Copyright 1992,1993,1994 Berkeley Software Design, Inc.
Copyright (c) 1980,1983,1986,1988,1990,1991 The Regents of
    the University
of California. All rights reserved.

BSDI BSD/386 1.1 Kernel #1: Fri May 27 10:30:57 CDT 1994

You have new mail.
worf-1>
```

Once you are logged in to the system you can gain access to the programs located on your host computer, like Telnet, FTP, electronic mail, or other non-Internet programs. When you start the Telnet program up on the time-sharing computer, your desktop computer is "turned into" a terminal functioning like the terminal described previously. When you type in commands the remote computer excutes them.

Some computer systems permit anonymous login with a shared account name. A number of resources are available through this route for those who can establish a remote login connection with a remote computer. Wide Area Information Servers (WAIS), Archie servers, and Netfind servers are examples of such resources. Accounts have been created with a generic name—often the name of the service. Anonymous Telnet services use the words "anonymous" or "guest" as user names. Anonymous systems either require no password at all or simply ask you to type a <return> to log on to the system.

The Internet Telnet Program: A Closer Look

To use Telnet you need a Telnet client program to connect to a Telnet server, the Internet domain name or IP address of the remote computer you want to connect to and a user ID and password onto the target system. Even though many other Internet services can be accessed with a World Wide Web browser, you cannot directly access a Telnet server. Web browsers and terminal emulation programs like Telnet work quite differently. Terminal emulation programs read and interpret ASCII character sequences as they are transmitted to the client computer. Web browsers focus on displaying multimedia, HTML documents. Because these two functions are quite different, Web browsers call on outside Telnet applications to help them communicate with Telnet servers. The Telnet protocol specifies exactly how a remote login client and remote login server interact. The standard specifies how a client contacts the server, how the client encodes keystrokes and commands for transmission to the server, and how the server encodes output for transmission to the client computer. Telnet is a powerful application that provides general access to the programs residing on a computer without requiring modifications to the programs arising from differences in a user's desktop computer operating system. It doesn't matter if your desktop computer is a DOS, Windows, Macintosh, or UNIX machine; the Telnet protocols let you run any program on the remote computer.

The Telnet program used as an example in this chapter is a command line version typical of the UNIX environment. Telnet has a dozen or so commands that are fairly standard across different versions of Telnet software. You only need a few to establish a Telnet connection. The basic Telnet commands are:

close Close the connection that is presently underway. The close command disconnects you from the remote computer and may close the Telnet program if you specified the host name with the Telnet command.

help Display information about all or specified Telnet commands.

open Make a connection to a remote computer. Most systems will prompt you for a host name (address) if you leave the host name off the open command.

quit Close a Telnet connection and exit the Telnet program.

z Suspend current activity and return to a UNIX shell. You can resume your Telnet session by issuing the fg command on most BSD UNIX systems. Check with your system administrator for more specifics.

Let's look at a sample Telnet session. To start the program you simply type "telnet" at the system prompt:

```
worf-1> telnet
```

The host computer responds with the Telnet prompt:

```
telnet>
```

Next I'll open a connection to the NCEER's Strong Motion server. Once I get a login prompt I need to use "strongmo" as the login and "nceer" as the password (without the quotes). The password is not printed on-screen so it will appear blank.

```
telnet> open duke.ldgo.columbia.edu 23
```

The host computer responds with:

```
Trying 129.236.10.50...
Connected to duke.ldgo.columbia.edu.
Escape character is '^]'.

SunOS UNIX (duke)

login: strongmo
Password:
Last login: Mon Dec 18 12:05:07 from netblazer.ldgo.c
SunOS Release 5.1.3 (DUKE) #7: Thu Jun 30 14:50:13 EDT 1994

***********************************************************

Welcome to Strongmo, the NCEER Strong Motion Data Facility.

***********************************************************
   You have reached the on-line data search utility and bulletin
board at Lamont-Doherty. For now, the menu-driven utility only
works on a vt100 type terminal. Please set your communication
program to emulate one.
   This system will log you off if your terminal has remained
idle for more than 5 minutes.
   New Version 2.0 with additional features and bug fixes:
   1. You can now view time-series data graphically with
Xwindows
   2. Strongmo is now using the Sybase database
   3. You can now revise requests at viewing stage.
   Instructions for these new features are in the help screens
of this NCEER Strongmo Data Facility. See the User's Guide for
Version 1.0 for instructions on reading Help screens. (NCEER-90-
0024)
   To EXIT NOW, type ^C

Please enter name and institution (80 character limit)
```

This is a time-sharing computer. Note the warning about letting the connection lie idle. Most time-sharing computers you connect to will have a specified idle time before closing your connection. You must send some instruction to the computer within the time interval, even if it's just a carriage return. After I enter my name and institution the server responds with its menu:

```
***********************************************************

Welcome to Strongmo, the NCEER Strong Motion Data Facility.

***********************************************************

   You have reached the on-line data search utility and bulletin
board at Lamont-Doherty. For now, the menu-driven utility only
works on a vt100 type terminal. Please set your communication
program to emulate
   NCEER Ground Motion Facility [mainmenu]
```

```
    1. Introduction
    2. Inquire into NCEER Database
    3. NCEER SSA-1 Status Bulletin
    4. Retrieve raw SSA-1 data (passwd required)
    5. Send mail to staff
    6. Quit

    Please make a selection from the menu.

RETURN-select U-Up N-down ^K-exit ?-help NUMBER 1 - 6
```

I've successfully logged onto the Strong Motion site and am ready to use its services.

The Telnet client programs operate in two modes, input mode and command mode. You are in *input mode* once you start the Telnet client software on your desktop computer. Input mode allows you to edit the client program parameters. Once you have successfully logged into a remote site you enter *command mode*. In command mode your desktop computer acts like a terminal to issue commands and interact with the remote computer. You can switch back to input mode by using the Telnet escape character. Most versions of Telnet use the Control-] (control-right-bracket) escape character sequence. You can determine the correct escape character sequence by reading the Telnet documentation that came with your client program. The escape character is usually given to you during the remote login procedure.

> ***Earth Online Tip:*** Download and review instructions for interacting with a remote login site. Stay online long enough to get what you're looking for and then exit. Remember, someone else is probably trying to log on.

A common use of Telnet is to access a Netfind server to information about a person connected to the Internet. A more complete discussion of the Netfind service can be found in Chapter 6. The Netfind service is available at several locations; one of the more popular ones is at the University of Colorado-Boulder. To access it type the following at the system prompt:

```
>telnet bruno.cs.colorado.edu
```

My local host computer makes the connection and the UC- Boulder server later responds with

```
telnet> open bruno.cs.ucboulder.edu
Trying 128.138.243.150...
Connected to bruno.cs.colorado.edu.
Escape character is '^]'.

SunOS UNIX (bruno)

Login as `Netfind' to access Netfind server
```

```
login: Netfind

nsh: Too many Netfind sessions are active. Please try again
later.
   Or, please try one of the Alternate Netfind servers:
archie.au (AARNet, Melbourne, Australia)
bruno.cs.colorado.edu (University of Colorado, Boulder, USA)
dino.conicit.ve (Nat. Council for Techn. & Scien. Research,
   Venezuela)
ds.internic.net (InterNIC Dir & DB Services, S. Plainfield, NJ,
   USA)
eis.calstate.edu (California State University, Fullerton, CA,
   USA)
krnic.net (Korea Network Information Center, Taejon, Korea)
lincoln.technet.sg (Technet Unit, Singapore)
malloco.ing.puc.cl (Catholic University of Chile, Santiago)
monolith.cc.ic.ac.uk (Imperial College, London, England)
mudhoney.micro.umn.edu (University of Minnesota, Minneapolis,
   USA)
Netfind.ee.mcgill.ca (McGill University, Montreal, Quebec,
   Canada)
Netfind.elte.hu (Eotvos Lorand University, Budapest, Hungary)
Netfind.fnet.fr (Association FNET, Le Kremlin-Bicetre, France)
Netfind.icm.edu.pl (Warsaw University, Warsaw, Poland)
Netfind.if.usp.br (University of Sao Paulo, Sao Paulo, Brazil)
Netfind.mgt.ncu.edu.tw (National Central University, Taiwan)
Netfind.sjsu.edu (San Jose State University, San Jose, CA, USA)
Netfind.uni-essen.de (University of Essen, Germany)
Netfind.vslib.cz (Liberec University of Technology, Czech
   Republic)
nic.uakom.sk (Academy of Sciences, Banska Bystrica, Slovakia)

Connection closed by foreign host.
```

Having failed to get onto the UC-Boulder Netfind service I'll try McGill from the list of alternatives.

```
>telnet Netfind.ee.mcgill.ca

login: Netfind
Password:

==============================================

Welcome to the McGill University Netfind server

==============================================
```

The server responds with the same list of Netfind servers as before and sets your terminal display.

```
    I think that your terminal can display 24 lines. If this is
wrong, please enter the "Options" menu and set the correct
number of lines.

    Top level choices:
    1. Help
    2. Search
    3. Seed database lookup
    4. Options
    5. Quit (exit server)
```

I'll choose item 2 to search for myself, and the Netfind server responds by asking me to enter a person's name and the keys, that is, the location. I'll type my last name followed by the location where I work and have an electronic mail address, making sure to leave blank spaces between each search term.

```
    Enter person and keys (blank to exit) --> ritter stevens
point wisconsin
```

I hit the return key and the Netfind server sets off to find my address.

```
    Please select at most 3 of the following domains to search:
    0. uwc.edu (university of wisconsin, centers, stevens point,
wisconsin)
    1. uwsp.edu (university of wisconsin, stevens point)
    2. lib.uwsp.edu (library, university of wisconsin, stevens
point)
    3. me.uwc.edu (mechanical engineering department, university
of wisconsin, centers, stevens point, wisconsin)
    4. me.uwsp.edu (mechanical engineering department, university
of wisconsin, stevens point)
    Enter selection (e.g., 2 0 1) -->
```

The server has responded with several choices from which I'll pick the most likely, as it is the one for the university.

```
Enter selection (e.g., 2 0 1) --> 1
( 1) got nameserver spu1.uwsp.edu
( 1) got nameserver spdns1.uwsp.edu
( 1) SMTP_Finger_Search: checking domain uwsp.edu
( 2) SMTP_Finger_Search: checking nameserver spu1.uwsp.edu
( 3) SMTP_Finger_Search: checking nameserver spdns1.uwsp.edu
( 2) connect timed out
( 2) ask_smtp: Failed to connect to SMTP daemon
( 2) connect timed out
------
Domain search completed. Proceeding to host search.
------
( 2) SMTP_Finger_Search: checking host uwspmail.uwsp.edu
( 5) SMTP_Finger_Search: checking host sis.uwsp.edu
( 1) SMTP_Finger_Search: checking host gbernd.uwsp.edu
( 3) SMTP_Finger_Search: checking host afranz.uwsp.edu
```

```
( 4) SMTP_Finger_Search: checking host ariel.uwsp.edu
( 2) SMTP_Finger_Search: checking host spbsd1.uwsp.edu
( 5) do_connect: Finger service not available on host
sis.uwsp.edu ->
cannot do user lookup
( 5) SMTP_Finger_Search: checking host chasenor.uwsp.edu
SYSTEM: spbsd1.uwsp.edu
    Login: mritter               Name: Mike Ritter
    Directory: /usr/fac/mritter       Shell: /bin/csh
    Office: Geog/Geol, 715-346-4449    Home Phone: n/a
    On since Mon Dec 18 13:22 (CST) on ttyp0 from 143.236.26.121
    No Plan.
```

After several attempts the information is finally found. Netfind returns my login name, office location, office phone, and so on. The "No Plan" entry at the bottom of the user information refers to a "generic" plan file that you can create and make available for reading. As it implies, you describe what you're engaged in. This is a handy little file to use, especially for letting people know if you are going to be away for awhile and difficult to reach.

Hytelnet: Hypertext Meets Telnet

One of the most useful features of remote login is the Hytelnet service. Hytelnet combines the remote access of Telnet with the navigational properties of hypertext. Hypertext is a way to "read" information in a nonlinear way. There is no predetermined way of interacting with the information in a hypertext environment. The path through the information is defined by the user. Hypertext uses "hot" words and icons to link information together. (See Chapter 2, "Browsing the Internet," for an explanation of hypertext and hypermedia.) Navigation occurs by clicking on a word with a mouse or using another keystroke, which sends the user to a linked piece of information. Hytelnet works in conjunction with a large catalog of addresses to login to Telnet-accessible Internet systems like online library card catalogs, Gopher, Freenets, bulletin board systems and Wide Area Information Services. There are a variety of ways to tap into Hytelnet's online resources:

- Running Hytelnet with a direct Internet connection. This is done by downloading the software to your machine and typing a key to make the Telnet connection to the desired resource.
- Using a dial-up connection. The Hytelnet program not only describes the sites provided in its extensive catalog of resources but also the login information required for each one. People with a dial-up connection can browse throughout Hytelnet's catalog, find the sites they want to explore and make a note of the addresses and login procedures. Users start up their Telnet software, provide it with the address to open and, once the connection is made, follow the login procedures provided by Hytelnet.

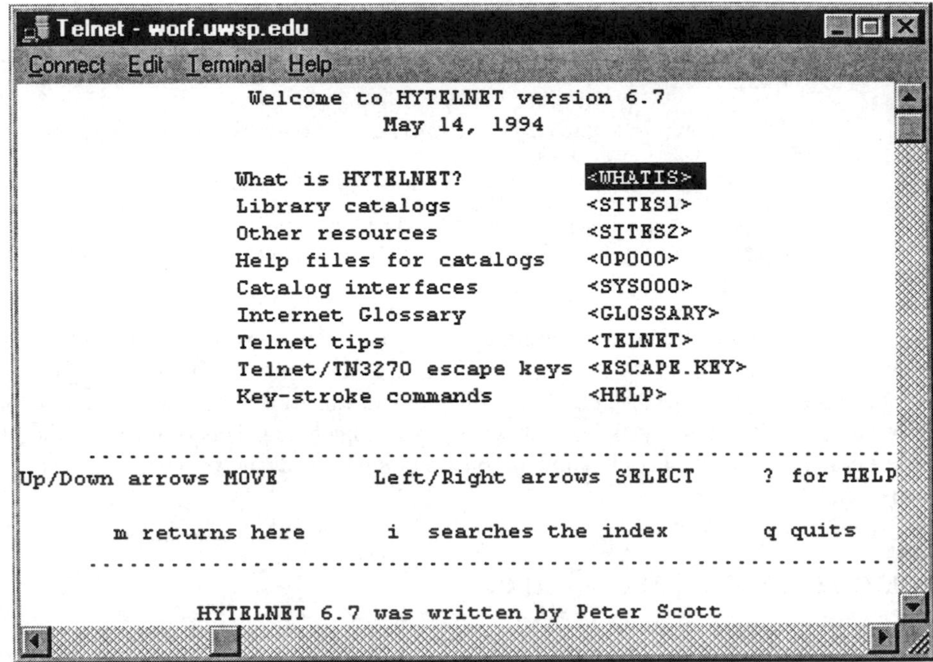

Figure 5.2 Hytelnet main menu screen

- Connecting to Hytelnet through Gopher (see Chapter 2, "Browsing the Internet," for more information about Gopher). Washington and Lee University has made Hytelnet available through its Gopher server. Gopher software has the ability to make Telnet connections so it is natural to combine Gopher and Hytelnet resources.

I'll be using a Telnet session to illustrate how to find earth science information from Hytelnet. First, you'll need to open a connection to a Telnet server. Depending on which Telnet server you connect to, you will login as Hytelnet. Once the login has been completed a menu screen will be displayed (Figure 5.2).

The first menu screen that appears upon startup is a general listing of Hytelnet resources and information. Beside each menu pick is a bracketed abbreviation of the menu <WHATIS>. The bracketed items are highlighted with the cursor indicating that they are links to the information. You use the up, down, right and left arrow keys to navigate through the menus. You can also hit the return key once an item is highlighted to see the next menu of resources. Clicking on the highlighted WHATIS with the enter key or using the right arrow key returns the basic information screen about Hytelnet (Figure 5.3).

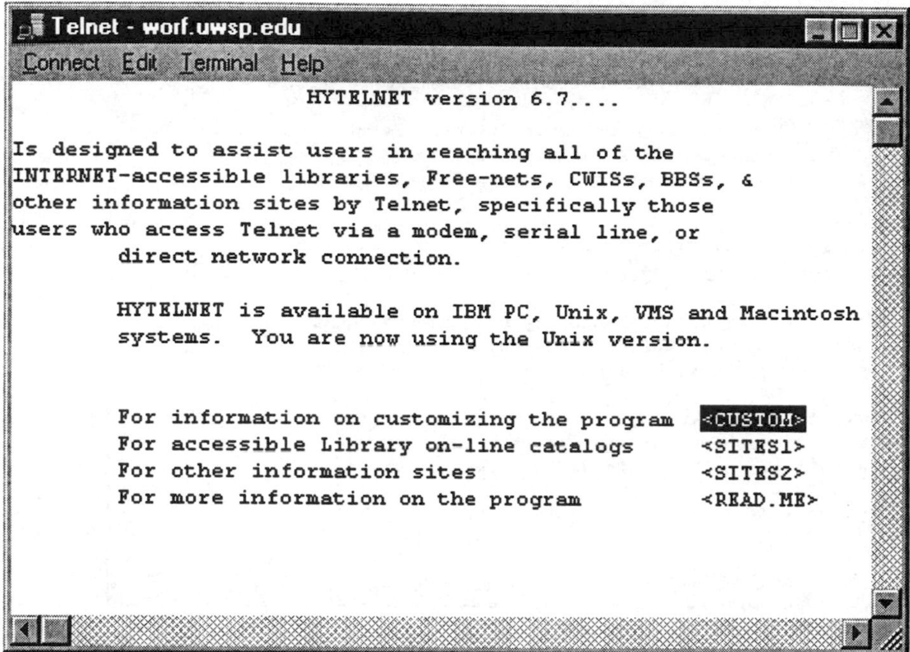

Figure 5.3 Hytelnet "WHAT IS" menu screen

Note that after the brief explanation you are presented with a few menus that will either give you more information about the program or let you go to library and other information systems without having to return to the opening menu screen. To return to the main menu screen you simply use the back arrow key. Although linking to online libraries was one of the reasons for creating Hytelnet and certainly is an important feature, the "Other Resources" menu pick offers a lot, especially to those in the earth science community. Using the down arrow key I'll move to the "Other Resources" menu <SITES2> and then the right arrow key to bring the screen shown in Figure 5.4.

Now we're starting to see how valuable Hytelnet really is as an Internet earth science resource. From the "Other Resources" screen we can access Archie servers to locate files on FTP servers and connect to campuswide information systems to retrieve information about different universities, including links to faculty and possibly student addresses (both surface and electronic mail addresses). A rich source of information can be found under the "Databases and Bibliographies" menu where we connect to, and interact with, a number of government databases. Hytelnet can connect us to distributed file servers like Gopher (see Chapter 2, "Browsing the Internet") or Wide Area Information Services where we can perform an online search of full-text documents (see Chapter 6, "Searching the Internet for Earth Science Resources"). A popular use of the Internet is the distribution of online books accessible from the "Electronic Books" menu pick. Two other menu picks are of particular

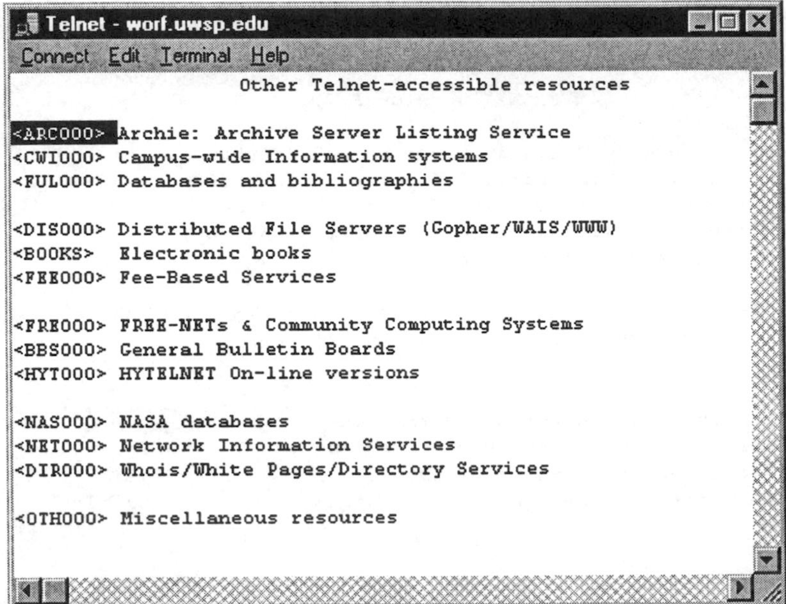

Figure 5.4 Hytelnet "Other Resources" menu screen

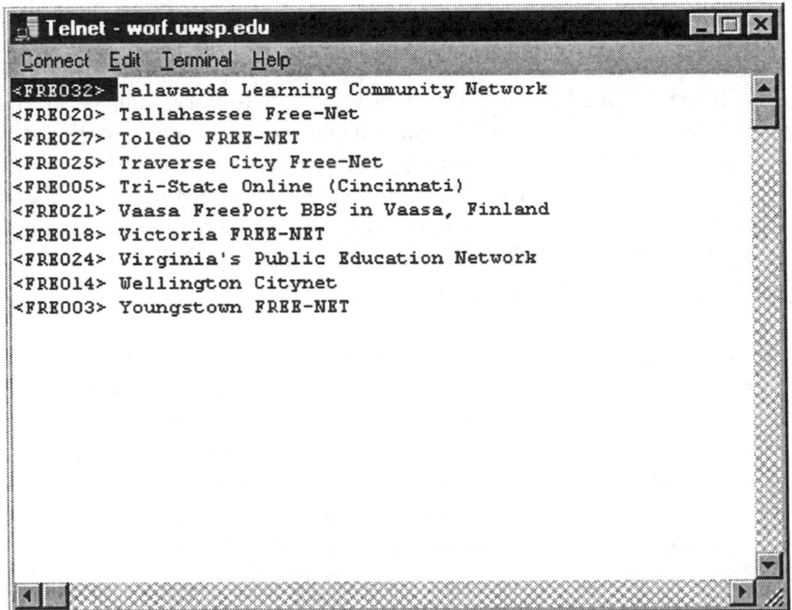

Figure 5.5 Hytelnet screen of Freenets

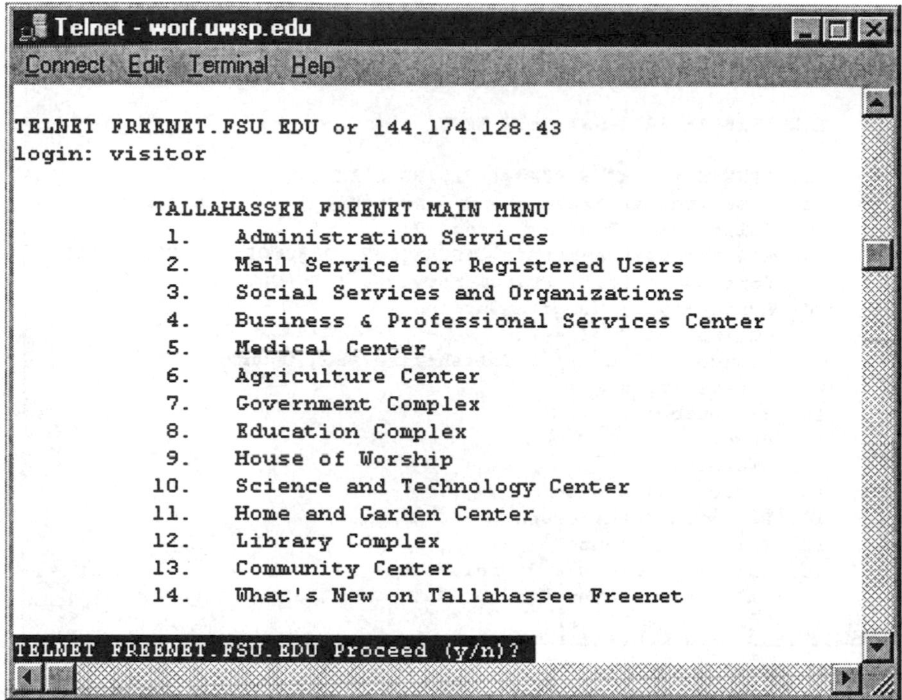

Figure 5.6 Tallahassee Freenet login screen

interest to earth scientists: "FREE-NETs and Community Computing Systems" and "NASA Databases." Freenets are community bulletin boards that offer free access to the local community and a pay service for those logging in from outside the community. However, outsiders can log on as a "guest" and use many of the resources that are available. Choosing the Freenet menu brings you to a screen of Freenet options (Figure 5.5).

Scrolling down and choosing the Tallahassee (Florida) Freenet brings you to a Hytelnet remote login screen (Figure 5.6). The Telnet address and login information are located at the top of the screen and indicate that you can enter the Freenet as a visitor (Figure 5.6). Depressing the enter key brings up the warning highlighted at the bottom of the page. Answering yes initiates a connection with the Talahassee Freenet. After answering several "housekeeping" questions about your terminal emulation and activity, you are presented with a welcome screen and then a main nenu screen with a list of options as depicted in Figure 5.7.

Next I'll choose the "Science and Technology" menu (Figure 5.8). A number of picks of interest to the earth scientist are found on this screen, including links to environmental resources, the National Science Foundation, weather information, the United States

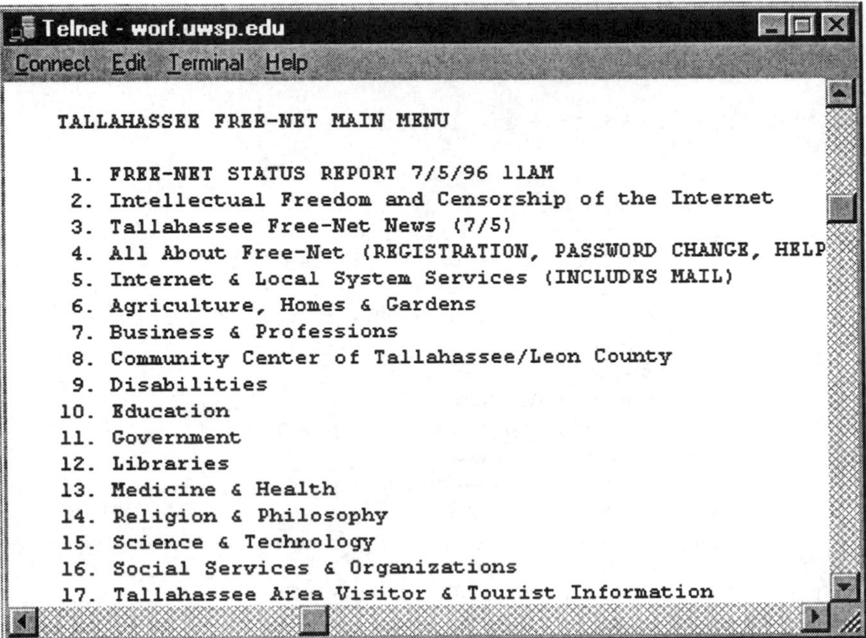

Figure 5.7 Tallahassee main menu screen

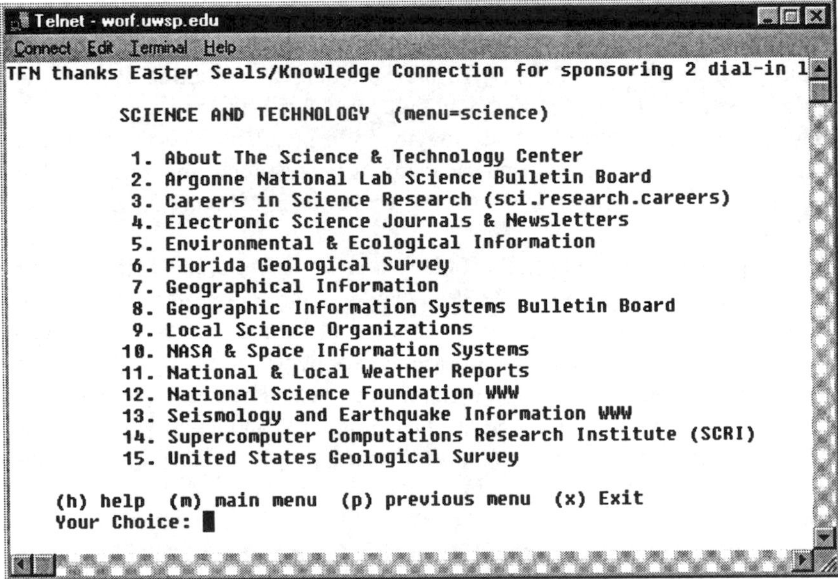

Figure 5.8 Science and technology menu screen

Geological Survey, Geographic Information Systems, and NASA. When you're finished looking at Tallahassee's Freenet use the exit key sequence and you're back to Hytelnet ready for further exploration.

The Hytelnet database is updated on an ongoing basis. Check into the main FTP site for recent updates. You'll find Hytelnet to be a good introduction to the world of hypertext and a source of a wealth of information at your fingertips. Even if you don't use the Hytelnet program, the database itself serves as a great archive of resources. Open it up to find the address of a site to use with other Internet programs like a World Wide Web browser that can access Telnet servers.

Logging into Earth Science with Telnet

There are any number of good examples of the use of remote login to earth science resources with Telnet. As Internet technology continues to evolve, more sites, especially interactive database systems, are turning away from Telnet and toward the World Wide Web environment. However, there are times when it might be easier to Telnet through to these services rather than going through the Web.

The Global Change Master Directory (GCMD) (**URL - telnet:// gcmd.gsfc.nasa.gov**) is a free information system containing descriptions of earth and space science data holdings available to the science community. These include data from the United States Department of Energy, Environmental Protection Agency, National Aeronautics and Space Administration, National Center for Atmospheric Research, National Oceanic and Atmospheric Administration, National Science Foundation and a host of other U.S. government agencies, university data archives and international agency data archives related to global climate change. The directory does not contain the actual data set. Rather it provides pointers to the location of the data set.

The National Space Science Data Center (NSSDC) operates the National On-Line Data and Information Service (NODIS) (**URL - telnet://nssdca.gsfc.nasa.gov**). NODIS is a menu-driven system that provides information on services and data supported by the NSSDC, including Nimbus-7 GRID TOMS data, geophysical models, and the Standards and Technology Information System. NODIS provides links to the NASA Master Directory online search system. The NASA Master Directory provides brief overview information about NASA and many important non-NASA space and earth science data information systems.

The NASA Spacelink Electronic Library is accessible via Telnet (**URL - telnet:// spacelink.msfc.nasa.gov**). This site gives you access to educational services and instructional materials available from NASA and other sources. Aerospace career information and information about NASA programs can be viewed online. From the "Software" menu you can download a number of shareware programs for a variety of computer platforms. Software that you can retrieve includes a gravitation simulation program, star finder programs and sunrise/sunset programs.

Tom Liebert's Geographic Name Server **(URL - telnet:// martini.eecs.umich.edu 3000)** is a useful server to obtain zip codes, population numbers, latitude and longitude and other city statistics from the 1980 United States census. To retrieve information, log on, enter the name of city and press the enter key. Include the state postal code (e.g., Bloomington, IL) or you'll get information on Bloomingtons in every state they are found. Type "quit" to exit the server.

What You Have Learned

- Telnet lets you to remotely login into another computer running Telnet server software to run programs, much as if they were running on your desktop computer.
- Many Internet services are available through Telnet, like Gopher, Archie and WAIS.
- Hytelnet combines a hypertext environment with remote login to easily access databases and bulletin boards across the Internet.

Apply It!

The CARL UnCover database **(URL - telnet://database.carl.org)** is a good place to begin a periodical search for earth science information. The UnCover database is accessible at no charge to the public or by subscription, which provides more functionality and services. Users can search through UnCover's database of journals; its 5,000 current citations are updated each day. You can search by word, topic, or author or browse by journal title.

I'll Telnet from my shell account to log on to CARL UnCover. Type "Telnet" to start a session, then give the "open" command and address to establish contact with CARL UnCover (Figure 5.9).

CARL responds with a terminal type query screen (Figure 5.10). After I give the proper terminal type, option 5 for a VT 100 terminal emulation (a common one), CARL performs more housekeeping duties like checking for a user profile, and finally displays a screen of database choices (Figure 5.11).

Choose item 1, "UnCover–Article access . . ." CARL will check for a user profile, which is not required for using the database over the next few screens. Now we're at the main article database search screen (Figure 5.12).

At the prompt on the bottom of the screen I'll type "w" for performing a search on the keywords "climate, " "change, " and "hydrology. " Entering the keywords at the prompt and

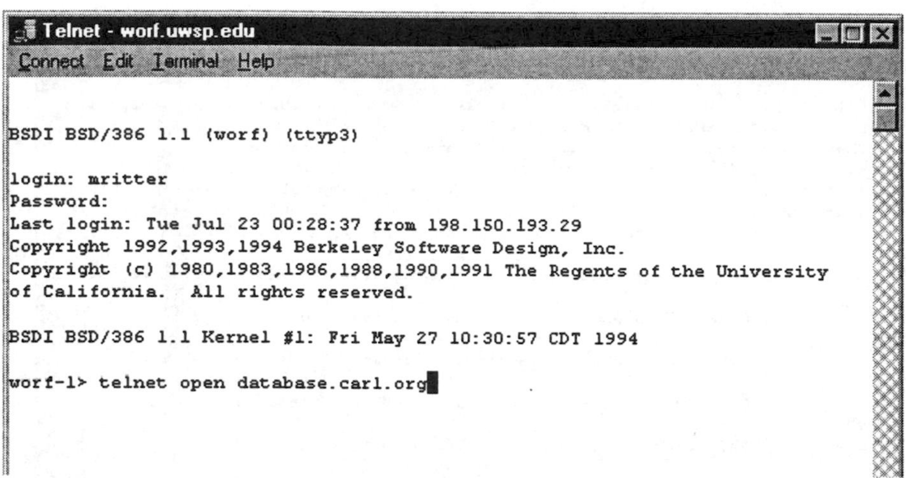

Figure 5.9 Logging onto CARL UnCover via Telnet

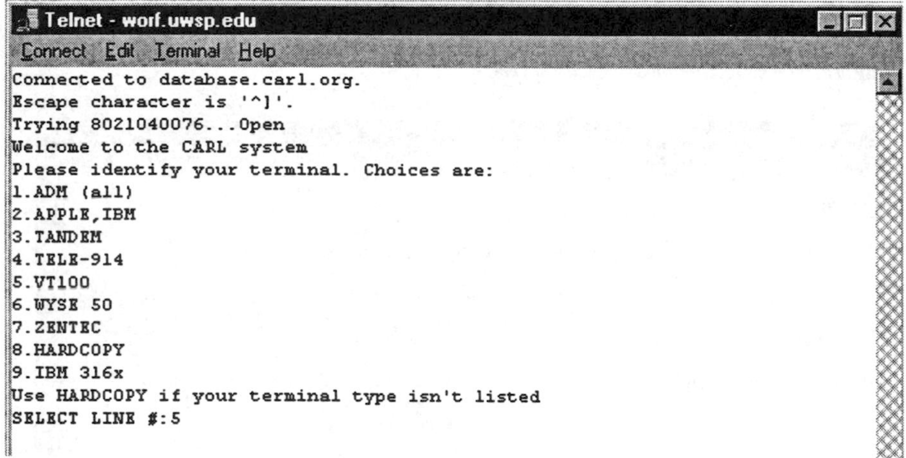

Figure 5.10 CARL UnCover terminal emulation query screen

pressing the enter key initiates my database inquiry. A screen soon appears with the number of "hits" made and the options to display the items found, add a new word and search, or simply quit and start over again. The display screen is a list of the resources uncovered (pardon the pun) by my search, including title, author, publication date, and journal (Figure 5.13).

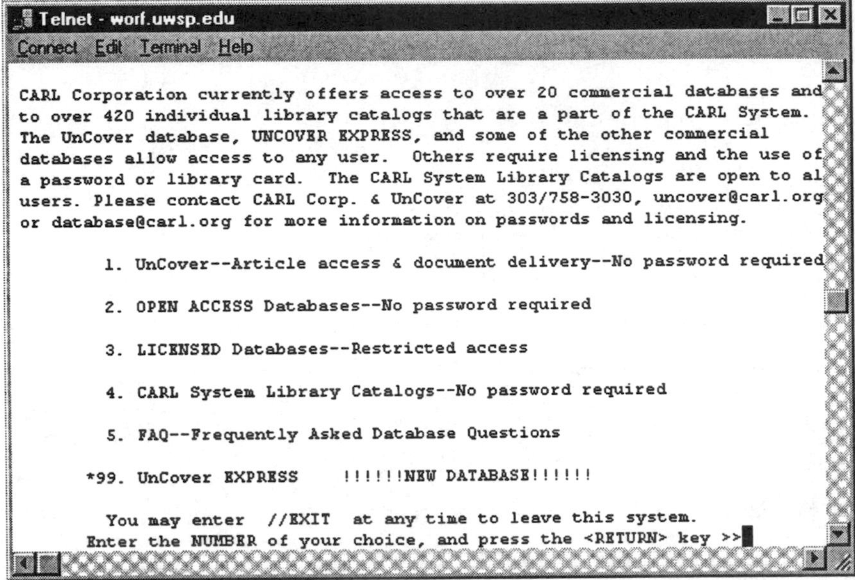

Figure 5.11 CARL database menu screen

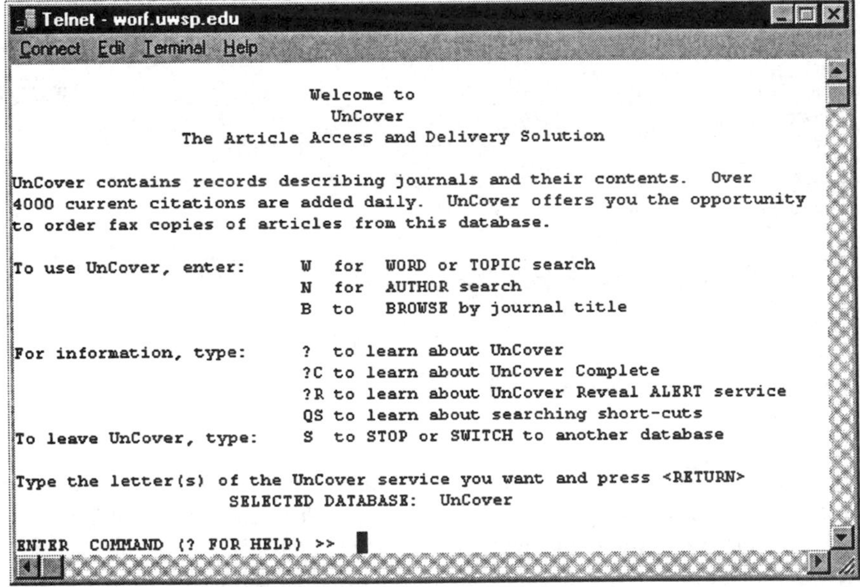

Figure 5.12 CARL UnCover Article Access screen

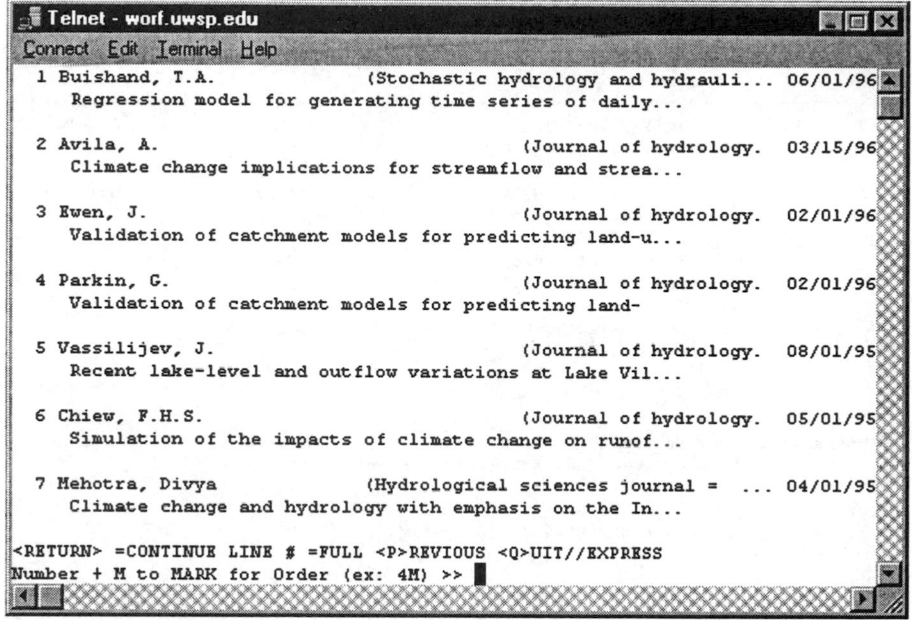

Figure 5.13 CARL UnCover article listing

I simply type the number of the article in at the prompt to retrieve bibliographic information A full display yields a more complete bibliographic entry, as well as the cost of having UnCover fax the article to you (Figure 5.14). I can copy the text from my Telnet client software and paste it into a word processing document for later reference.

Try It Out!

1. Check on the availability of Hytelnet on your Internet provider's system or on whether you can run Hytelnet from your desktop. If you can't do either, Telnet to Hytelnet. Once you have Hytelnet up and running move to:

   Other resources

   Then go to:

   FREE-NETs and Community Computing systems

   Check to see if you have a Freenet in your own or a nearby community. Check out the resources that are available. Many Freenets have a science and technology center or menu of some sort. What kind of earth science resources are available? Check them out!

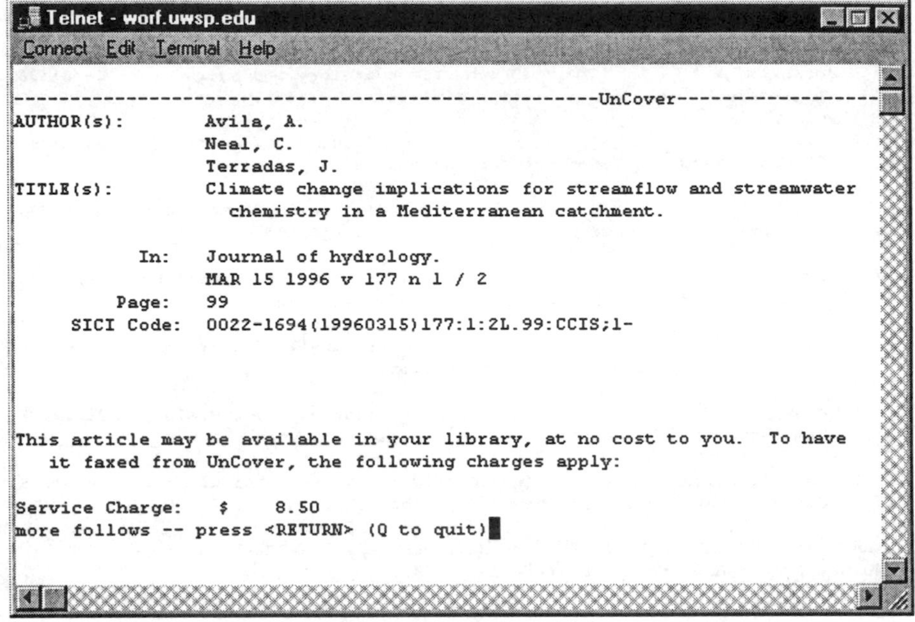

Figure 5.14 CARL UnCover article database record

2. Check on the weather in your local area by opening a Telnet connection to the Weather Underground at **madlab.sprl.umich.edu 3000**. Follow the menu choices to your community or one nearby.

3. Human space exploration is often questioned as a worthwhile scientific endeavor. What benefits were derived from the Apollo lunar space missions? To find out, Telnet to NASA's space link (**URL - telnet://spacelink.msfc.nasa.gov**). Follow the menus:

    NASA.Projects
    Human.Space.Flight
    Apollo.Lunar

CHAPTER 6

Searching the Internet for Earth Science Resources

The Internet is often described as a huge, distributed library of information. A library is an *archive* of information, be it documents, books, video or audio tapes. A distributed library or archive refers to the fact that the information about a particular topic is distributed across several computers rather than being all on the same one. In some ways, you might already use a "distributed library." On many larger campuses the library collection cannot be housed in one building. Instead, books are distributed to smaller libraries scattered around campus. When preparing to do research you might visit several of these branch libraries to get the information you need. You might even find that the information you require is located off-campus. This isn't a problem because you get this information by requesting it through interlibrary loan, and within a few days it arrives at your desk. The problem in maintaining a distributed library system is organizing the location of the resources and providing a way for library patrons to get to the information. The distributed nature of the Internet is no exception. The rapid expansion of the Internet brings megabytes of information on to the Internet each day. This fact makes organizing the location of resources extremely difficult. Not only that, system administrators will move the files to new locations on a server or to a completely different server. Updating new locations becomes a problem too.

From previous chapters you have learned that information may be accessible via different services (Gopher, FTP, the Web). Not all the information located on the Internet can be accessed by one service, with the possible exception of the ever evolving capabilities of World Wide Web browser software. This means that you need to know how to use several kinds of search tools to effectively mine information from the Internet. Not only that, you need to understand a little about how each service searches the Internet. This will help you choose the right place to go to seek out the information you desire. You need patience too, for the explosive growth of Internet users has not kept up with the diffusion of high-speed network connections. The rapidity at which information and data are made available makes updating search tool databases difficult. What you might find today will be different tomorrow. What you find with one tool will be different from another. The fastest way of working yourself into a corner is to limit your searches to a single service.

Choosing the right tools and services for your needs is important to effectively locate information. Before starting a search you should ask yourself several questions. Where do you think your information will be located? Are you looking for a data file? Then FTP searches would be a good place to start. Are you looking for documents about a particular topic? Then a document search engine would be a logical place to start. Maybe the information you need is not online but located in a library. You can still use the Internet to find your information: Telnet to an online library card catalog. How much time do you have to conduct your search? Do you need your information now or do you have time to browse? These are the kinds of questions you need to answer before starting your Internet search. Preparing for your search will make it a more efficient and less frustrating experience.

The purpose of this chapter is to introduce you to several tools available for searching out information on the Internet. It is not intended to be an exhaustive treatment of the development of the tools and or all the ways to use them. There are many good books (e.g., Gilster, 1994) that fully describe Internet search tools and search methodologies. Frequently-asked-question files, Usenet groups and archived help files contain a great deal of useful information about searching the Internet. Instead, I'll pass along the basics of using many of the common search tools and services to get at earth science information in the most efficient way. In this chapter we'll examine the syntax of searching and ways

- to find earth-science-oriented World Wide Web sites using search engines and subject-oriented guides
- to search for files using the Archie service
- to seek out Gopher information using Veronica
- to locate information about people connected the Internet using Netfind, WHOIS and Finger

The Syntax of Searching

Searching the resources of a remote earth science server is much like creating a program. You have to know the syntax for the language that the server's search software speaks. Depending on the search software interface, search engines will accept everything from keyword search terms strung together with Boolean operators to natural language word strings. When searching out resources on the Internet, you have to use the appropriate language syntax for the search engine your using.

Boolean Searching

Most search services recognize Boolean operators for searching their resources. Boolean operators are designed to guide the search engine's method of retrieving information. Various systems and search engines recognize different kinds of Boolean operators. Your search query is interpreted from the right-hand side to the left-hand side of the words entered. Parentheses can be used to force a particular order on to the query. Be aware that some searches are case-sensitive. To minimize unwanted returns or problems, you should check the search system help documentation before creating a search.

The common Boolean operators are AND, OR, NOT and *.

OR Search terms joined with the OR operator represent a logical union between documents. For instance, queries like "rivers OR streams" will return documents with either of the two search terms located in the document. Use the OR operator when combining synonyms or similar concepts.

AND Search terms combined with the Boolean AND operator represent an intersection of those terms. A search query like "rivers AND streams" will turn up every document that contains both search terms. The AND operator is best used when combining dissimilar terms like

astronomy AND education
geology AND journals
climate AND data

If you simply enter two words together, most search engines will recognize it as an "AND" query. For example, if you entered

mississippi river

it would be recognized as "mississippi" AND "river." The restrictions imposed by the AND operator means that fewer "hits" or documents are returned.

NOT The NOT operator is used to exclude documents from a set based on the search terms identified. In this case, using "rivers NOT streams" would exclude all documents in which the search terms are found. The NOT operator works best when you are trying the eliminate a subset of documents from your search. The restrictions imposed by the NOT operator reduce the number of returned documents.

Right-hand truncation (*) Known as *stemming*, right-hand truncation uses an asterisk (*) to create a group of documents containing terms with common roots but different suffixes. The asterisk is used like a wild card when working with directories of files on your system. It does not work within, or to the left of, any characters. For example, the search "geo*" would produce results like geography, geology, and geophysics. The number of documents returned increases, in some cases dramatically, when you use right-hand truncation.

Searching the World Wide Web

The hypertext environment of the World Wide Web makes it both a challenge and a delight to navigate, depending on your immediate need for information and the time you have to find it. Be prepared for some disappointment if you need a quick answer to a question, because the Web can be a tangled place to find it. Organization of information on the Web has come a long way in the last few years. A number of search engines have been created to

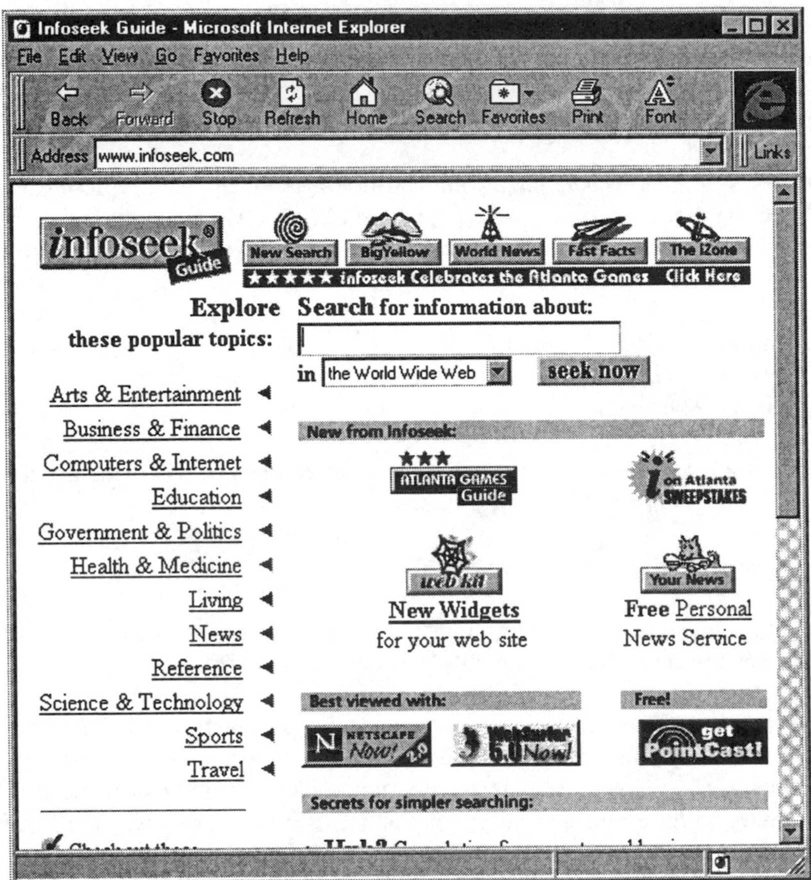

Figure 6.1 The Infoseek Guide search service home page

roam the Internet and seek out online information. Searchable databases of World Wide Web home page resources are coming online, and their holdings, though varying between services, are quite extensive.

How much of the World Wide Web can you search with a Web search service? This depends on what service you choose and how it operates. Archive services for Web pages come as hierarchically organized directories like the popular Yahoo! Web site or searchable Web page databases that use special programs, called "robots and spiders," to search the World Wide Web for home pages.

Either archive service has its advantages and disadvantages. Most search services offer Boolean searching of their Web page databases. Many let you customize your search. Search engines like the Infoseek Guide **(URL - http://www.infoseek.com/)** (Figure 6.1) let

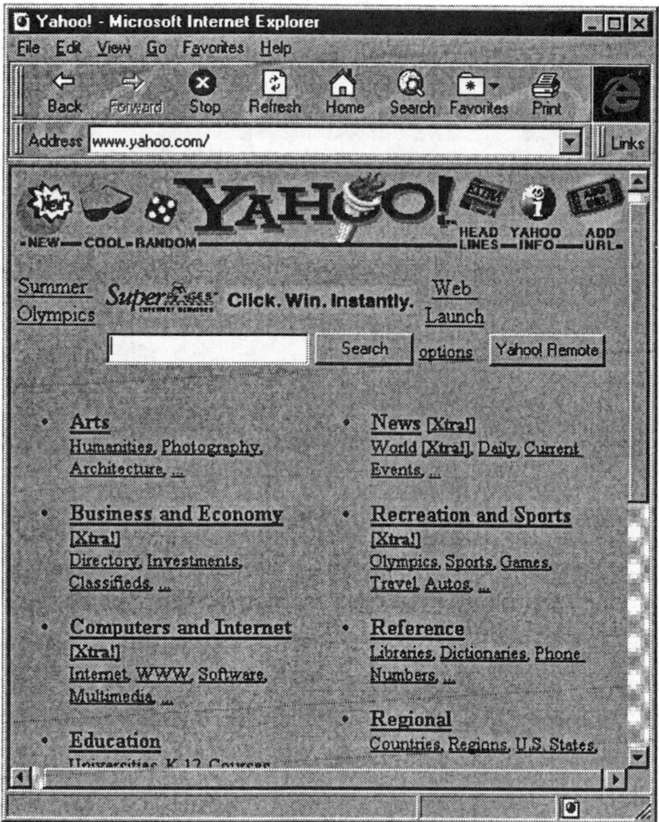

Figure 6.2 Portion of the Yahoo! internet guide

you search through all World Wide Web pages archived in their database. You can limit your search to reviewed Web pages or search through articles posted to Usenet newsgroups. Internet frequently-asked-question files (FAQs) can be searched from Infoseek Guide too. But due to the enormous growth in the popularity of the Web, sites like these are often quite busy.

Best described as a "Web robot," the WebCrawler search engine processes documents one at a time as it navigates the World Wide Web. WebCrawler maintains an index of the Web for searching. WebCrawler creates its index of Web sites by an incomplete first traverse, subsequently relying on auto-navigational mechanisms to fill in the gaps (Pinkerton, 1994). WebCrawler has a second searching component, that of being able to search the Web on demand.

Yahoo! **(URL - http://www.yahoo.com)** is an example of a hierarchically organized directory of Web pages (Figure 6.2). A hierarchical directory is good for those who know

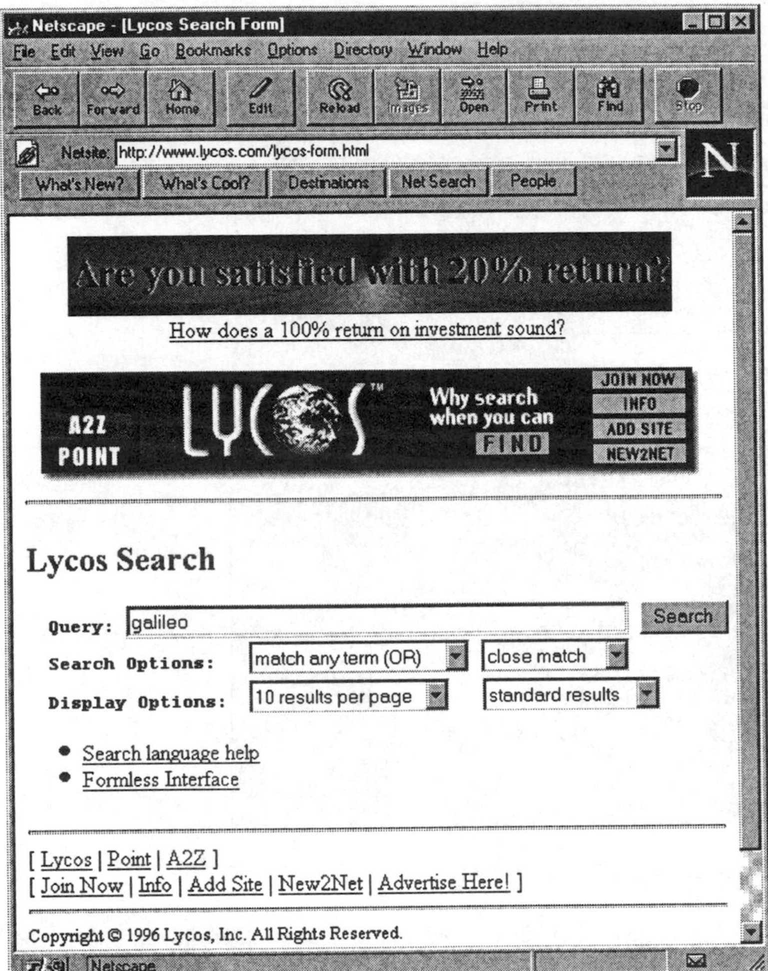

Figure 6.3 Lycos search service

what they're looking for and what category to look for the information in. These kinds of directories generally do not let you view an abstract describing the contents of a Web page. They also require more time to find the information you are looking for by digging through layers of menus and links. Most hierarchical directories permit you to search their holdings too.

If you choose a service that uses robot or spider programs to roam the World Wide Web, your search will likely cover a substantial portion of it. The Lycos **(URL - http://www.lycos.com/)** search service advertises that it encompasses over 95% of the entire World Wide Web (Lycos, 1995) (Figure 6.3). These spider programs are searching not only the

World Wide Web but also Gopher and FTP sites each day, continually adding new resources and updating those that have changed their name or address. The addition of new resources to their site database means that subsequent searches will likely reveal new information. Each address in the database or catalog is associated with information about what the site contains, an outline of the information, and the number of times the site is referenced by other addresses.

A search engine is the software that queries the search service's database of sites and returns a list of "hits." Search services vary in how they search their databases and the Internet. Some allow searching of the entire text of Web documents in their database. Some permit you to search through URLs or titles. I suggest avoiding title searches. Not all Web authors accurately describe the contents of their Web document in the titles, and some titles can be misleading. Search engines like Lycos sort your hits in order of relevance. The Lycos search engine catalogs three kinds of files: HTTP files, Gopher files and FTP files. Information about the file type allows you to find image, full-motion video, sound and other nontext files.

Each search result has a "relevancy" score ranging from 0 to 100. The scores for the search results are determined by the words and phrases that you enter in the search text box; the number of occurrences of the words and phrases on a page determines the score. Common words generate lower scores because they are found on many pages and cannot be easily used to distinguish pages. Uncommon words generate higher scores because the words do not appear on many pages. Higher scores also result from words combined into phrases because the combinations of words are not as common as the individual words. Relevancy scores should be used as a guide. Just because a site ends up with a low relevancy score doesn't mean that it hasn't anything to offer.

I'll use the Lycos search engine to demonstrate a typical search for information on the World Wide Web. One of the big events of 1995 was the *Galileo* visit to Jupiter. To see what I can find out about the project I open a session to Lycos and type the search term "galileo" (without the quotes) into the text field and click the search button beside it. After a few seconds Lycos returns a new screen (Figure 6.4).

The search results indicate that 11,088 documents were found matching my keywords. That is three times as many as I had when running the same search just six months prior. Of these only 83 documents score above a .010 relevancy score. The documents are arranged from highest to lowest score. The underlined words indicate that they are links. If I choose them, Lycos will return a page or more of documents containing the search word I chose. Next I'll scroll down the list of "hits," or documents that Lycos has in its catalog that match my search term (Figure 6.4)

GREAT! I'm shouting (that's what the capitals mean on the Internet). Among the documents is the Project Galileo home page created by NASA's Jet Propulsion Lab. The title is highlighted and underlined, meaning that it is a hot link to the Project Galileo home

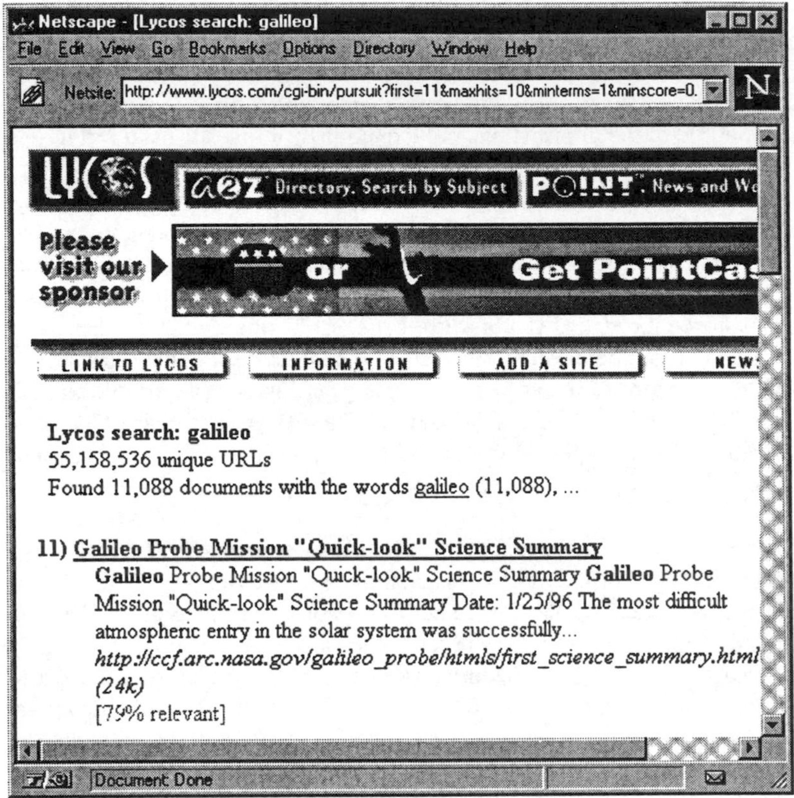

Figure 6.4 Typical Lycos home page abstract

page. The abstract gives me a notion of what the home page is about. I can continue to look through the rest of the hits or go directly to the Project Galileo home page.

There are a number of World Wide Web search engines that you can use. Table 6.1 lists several search engines and their addresses.

Searching for Files with Archie

In Chapter 4, "File Transfer over the Internet," you were introduced to the amazing amount of archived information located on computers connected to the Internet. The inevitable question is, How do I locate a file among the gigabytes of programs and data scattered all across the world? The answer lies with Archie. A play on the word "archive," and not the comic book character, Archie was developed at McGill University in Montreal. Archie servers automatically gather a list of files, along with associated directory information, from public FTP sites and place the list into an indexed database. When you connect to an Archie

Table 6.1 World Wide Web search engines

Service	URL
WebCrawler	URL - http://webcrawler.com
Yahoo	URL - http://www.yahoo.com
Lycos	URL - http://www.lycos.com
InfoSeek	URL - http://www2.infoseek.com
Excite	URL - http://www.excite.com
The Whole Internet Catalog	URL - http://nearnet.gnn.com/gnn/wic/ index.html
TradeWave Galaxy	URL - http://galaxy.einet.net/galaxy.html
Inter-Links	URL - http://www.nova.edu/Inter-Links
The World Wide Web Worm	URL - http://wwww.cs.colorado.edu/home/ mcbryan/WWWW.html
The Clearinghouse for Subject-Oriented Internet Resource Guides	URL - http://www.lib.umich.edu/chhome. html
Special Internet Connections	URL - http://www.uwm.edu/Mirror/inet. services.html
The Awesome Lists	URL - http://www.clark.net/pub/journalism/ awesome.html
Planet Earth Home Page Virtual Library	URL - http://www.nosc.mil/planet_earth/ everything.html
Internet Resources Meta-Map	URL - http://www.ncsa.uiuc.edu/SDG/ Software/Mosaic/Demo/metamap.html
The WWW Virtual Library	URL - http://www.w3.org/hypertext/ DataSources/bySubject/Overview.html

server you can search the database by keywords. The server will return a list of all file names and FTP site locations that match your keyword. Archie does not make a comprehensive sweep across *all* Internet FTP sites. Instead, it targets specific FTP servers whose system administrators have given their permission to search. Within the Archie system, over 230 gigabytes of files are available for searching, and this is only a subset of all the Internet sites that have made their resources available to the public. Archie updates its database by regularly searching through a site's holdings. Be aware that your Archie search may turn up a file that has been removed, or a new file may have been uploaded after the last Archie sweep of a site.

There are several ways to access an Archie service:

- Use Telnet to contact an Archie server. Connect to Archie by issuing the Telnet <server-name> command at your system prompt. The server responds with the Archie prompt, and you're ready to start searching.

- Access Archie via electronic mail. To do this you send your search commands in the body of the message and address the email as archie@<server name>.
- Use an Internet browser like Gopher or a Web client program like Netscape or Mosaic. Archie appears as a menu choice on some Gopher servers. World Wide Web browsers have been specifically engineered to connect to many kinds of server, Archie being one of them.
- Use a client program on your system if one is available. To do this simply type:

  ```
  archie <return>
  ```

  and the Archie program will start up.

Each approach has its own advantages. Archie servers are usually busy places to access. Quite often you will have difficulty logging on to one, especially during prime workday hours. If the Archie server is busy, it will display a list of alternative Archie servers that you can try. Table 6.2 gives you a list of potential Archie sites. If you have access, use your own system's client program. This approach will save you time and network resources. If you're not in a great hurry to get results, then search Archie via electronic mail. Searching via electronic mail may take longer, but a printout of the results is sent to you. You can save the search results in a file for later use.

Accessing Archie Using Electronic Mail

When demand for an Archie service gets too high, consider using electronic mail to conduct your searches. Archie servers usually process interactive logins first, and when demand decreases, will process electronic mail requests. To access Archie through electronic mail, a user must compose an electronic mail message that contains the necessary search commands and send it to an Archie server. If I wanted to search for the popular file decompression program pkunzip.exe, I would compose this message:

From:mritter@uwspmail.uwsp.edu
To:archie@archie.unl.edu
Subject:
Date:October 20, 1995

find pkunzip.exe

Once the message is processed, the Archie server responds by sending a list of sites with subdirectory information to you. There are some guidelines you should follow and restrictions you should note when using electronic mail to search for files with Archie:

- Each command must be on a line of its own.
- Each command should begin in the first column of a line.

Table 6.2 ***Selected Archie servers***

Server Address	Location	Country
ds.internic.net	AT&T InterNic Directory and Database	USA
archie.sura.net	SURAnet, Baltimore, MD	USA
archie.unl.edu	University of Nebraska, Lincoln	USA
archie.rutgers.edu	Rutgers University, N.J.	USA
archie.au	University of Melbourne	Australia
archie.uquam,ca	University of Quebec	Canada
archie.doc.ic.ac.uk	Imperial College, London	United Kingdom
archie.funet.fi	Finnish University and Research Network	Finland
archie.th-darmstadt.de	Technische Hochschule, Darmstadt	Germany
archie.ac.il	Hebrew University of Jerusalem	Israel
archie.unipi.it	University of Pisa	Italy
archie.wide.ad.jp	WIDE Project, Tokyo	Japan
archie.nz	Victoria University, Wellington	New Zealand
archie.luth.se	University of Lulea	Sweden

- Archie servers consider any message with the word "help" in it as a request for help information. As such, the return message will only contain help information.
- Archie servers will ignore all lines that contain an invalid command.
- Archie servers will treat the subject line as part of the body of the message, so it's best to leave it blank. Many electronic mail systems have message length limitations. The Archie software will automatically split a long message into multiple 45-kilobyte-long messages to safeguard against any possible problems with message length.

Accessing Archie with Telnet

Most people access Archie via Telnet. Recall that Telnet is the Internet's interactive remote login service. To perform an Archie search, initiate the Telnet client software and connect to the Archie server. If you are at the system prompt type:

>telnet *<server address>*

For example:

>telnet archie.unl.edu

Or at the Telnet prompt type:

telnet>**open** *<server address>*

telnet>**open archie.unl.edu**

When prompted for a login name, you enter "Archie." No password is required. After login the server sends a few messages about the server and then lets you begin entering commands. At this point you can enter "help" to get information on Archie commands, or you can start searching.

To search for a file type:

archie>**prog** *<filename>*

or

archie>**prog pkunzip.exe**

The server will respond with the status of your search, in particular your position in the queue of other ongoing searches and time to process your request. If your request is successful a list of sites and the subdirectory location will be printed to screen. The list of sites will scroll across your screen at a rapid pace. If you don't have a rollback feature, the previous screens will probably be gone. A good thing to do is to have your results electronically mailed to you by sending the command

archie> **mail** *<email address>*

For example:

archie> **mail mritter@uwspmail.uwsp.edu**

You've undoubtedly noticed that I used both "find" and "prog" as commands to search out files with Archie. The command "prog," standing for program, was used by earlier versions of Archie and now has been replaced by "find." However, many systems still recognize the "prog" command.

The Archie program functions by means of a set of environment parameters that are set up upon loading the program. You can see the default settings by issuing the "show" command:

archie>**show**

You have the opportunity to change several parameters to suit your search by typing

archie> **set** *<parameter>*

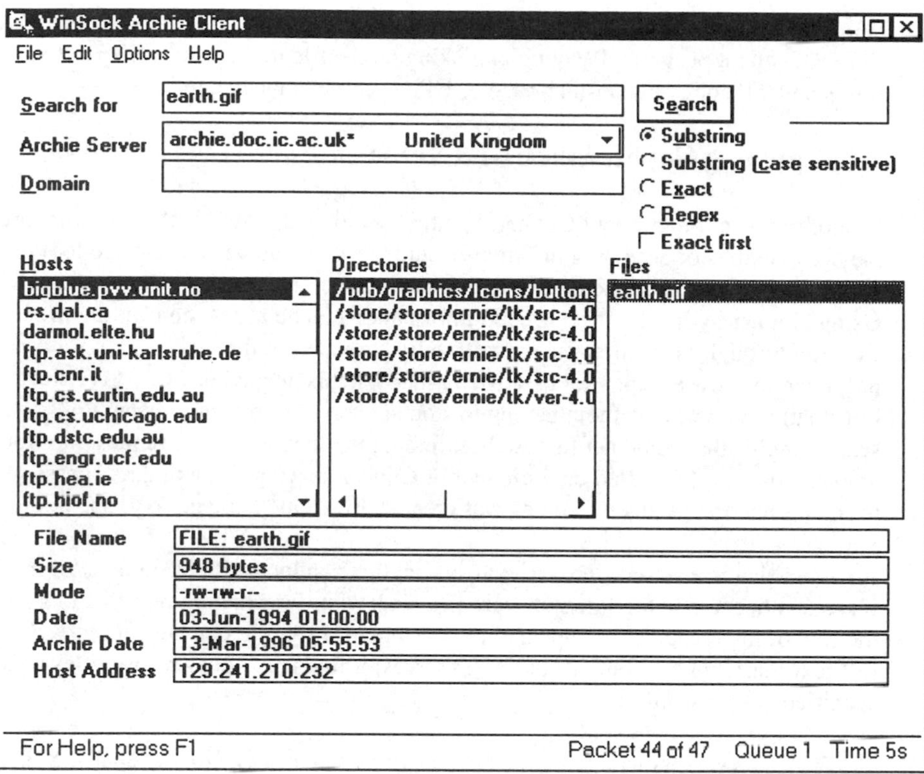

Figure 6.5 WinSock Archie GUI client program

For instance:

archie> **set search sub**

The search will retrieve all files and directory names containing your search term.

Accessing Archie with WinSock Archie

Graphical user interface applications make Archie searches a snap. The WinSock Archie application window is shown in Figure 6.5. A file can be searched for by simply typing the file name in the "Search for" form field, selecting a Archie server and clicking the "Search" button. The search results are displayed in the middle of the window. All FTP servers found to have a file with the same name that I used in my search are displayed in the Hosts box. The location of the file within the directory structure of the server is displayed in the Directories box. The file name is displayed in the Files box. File details (e.g., size, date, Archie date) are retrieved and displayed at the bottom of the application window. The

WinSock Archie client software can be configured to initiate an FTP session with the WS_FTP client program. By double-clicking on the file name, you call up a dialog box that sends an FTP command through to WS_FTP to retrieve the wanted file.

Searching Gopher Space with Veronica

One of the nice things about Gopher, like the World Wide Web, is that the software removes the complexities of accessing information and lets us focus on what we are looking for. The hierarchical menu structure is easy to learn and helps organize information for retrieval. Using Gopher by itself to find needed information can be a time-consuming process of working through menu after menu, only to find yourself at the end of a long journey with not much to show except a lot of wasted time. What is needed is a way to retrieve the information you want without having to stop at every intermediary menu along the way. A search engine that could act like Archie, finding the location of the requested information amongst the barely charted environment of Gopher space and making it accessible to the user, was needed. And so Veronica was created, in Archie's image so to speak.

Veronica is an index and retrieval system that can locate items on most of the Gopher servers connected to the Internet. Veronica finds your information by searching for words in the title of the resource as it appears in the menu of its home Gopher server. It does not do a full-text search of the contents of the resources; it finds resources whose titles contain your specified search word(s).

Veronica servers will give you a choice of how to search Gopher space. You can search Gopher space *by keywords in titles*. This type of search will find all types of Gopher resources (e.g., ASCII documents, image files, Gopher directories, etc.) whose titles contain the search terms specified. You can search Gopher directories only by keywords in titles. This search will return only Gopher directories that contain the search terms requested. You connect to Veronica from a Gopher menu pick; the program will display menu choices (Figure 6.6).

Directory searches are for broad topics, such as geomorphology. If you are looking for something more specific, like dunes, you'll want to search for title words. You can narrow your search by telling Veronica to locate particular types of Gopher resources. You specify the type of resource by adding the "-tX" option to your query, where the X is a letter or number code for the Gopher resource type. It doesn't matter where you place the "-t" flag; it can be in front of or behind the search word. For instance, the query

    ozone -t1

or

    -t1 ozone

will yield the same results.

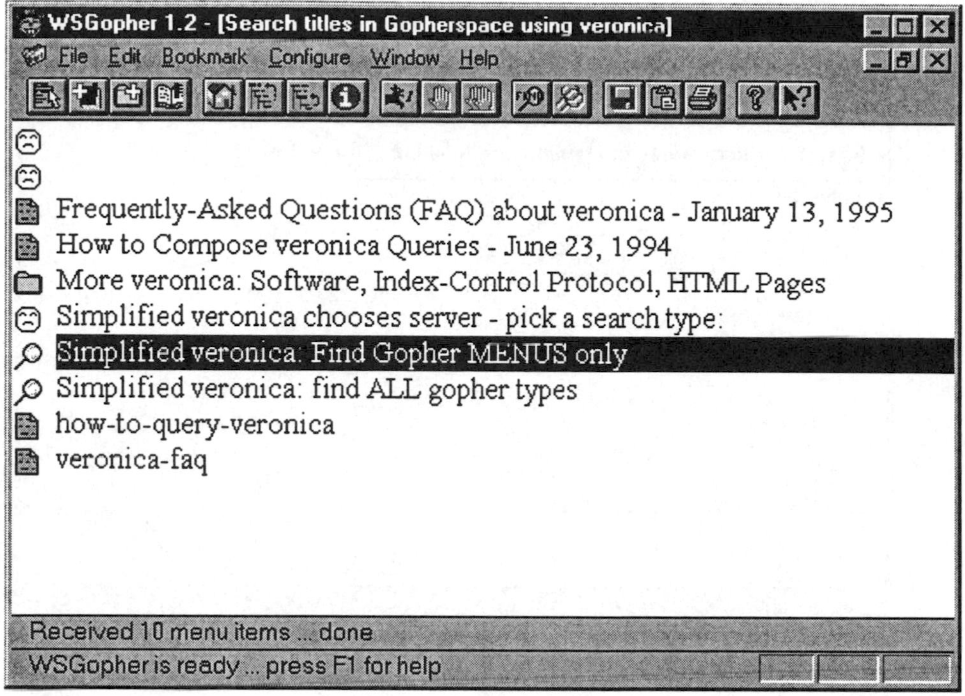

Figure 6.6 Veronica menu

You can specify more than one type in a search. For instance, if you used

Jupiter -t1g

Veronica would return all directory and GIF images with the word "Jupiter" in the titles.

Veronica will permit you to specify the number of items to find (X) by using the "-mX" flag. The "-l" flag is used to create a "log" file of links for the retrieved items. The log file will be displayed as the first "pick" on the Veronica results menu. You must use a single hyphen for each search option. For example:

ozone -t1 -m100

request 100 directory items containing the word "ozone."

Let's look a sample search. I'm going to use "galileo" again as the search term. It is broad enough that I'll search for directories under Galileo. Notice the question marks at the end of all the menus. A question mark indicates that the menu choice is a searchable menu element. I'll move my arrow cursor down to item 8 and use the right arrow to get a box to

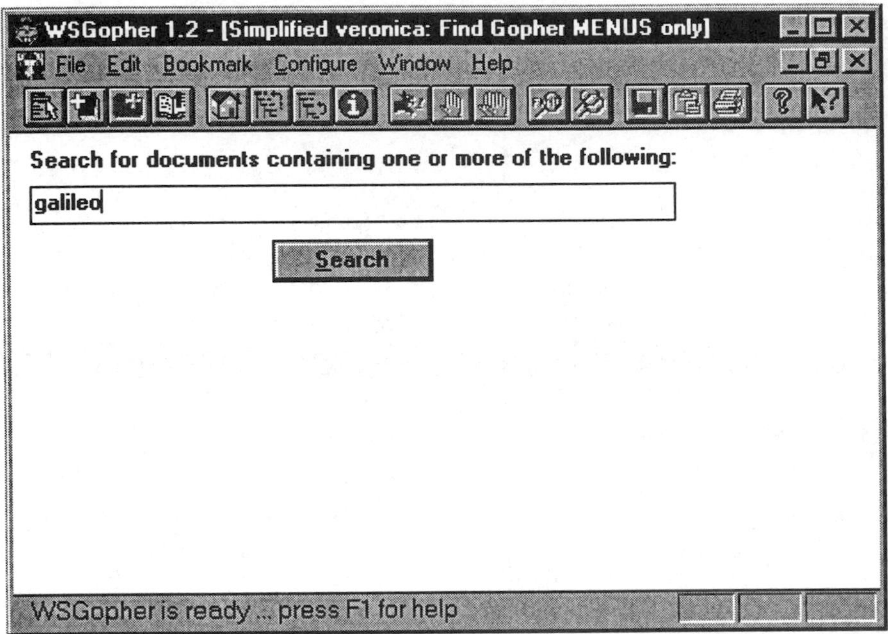

Figure 6.7 Initiating a Gopher search with Veronica

type in the search term. After typing the search term in I press the return key to initiate the query (Figure 6.7).

The query returns another long menu of items (directories) that contain the word "galileo." Notice that some are about the great scientist Galileo, while others are about the NASA *Galileo* project (Figure 6.8).

Wide Area Information Server (WAIS)

Archie and Veronica searches are basically term searches; you are matching keywords to the titles of files or directory menus. They do not search through the text of a document to find your search term. Wide Area Information Server (WAIS, pronounced "ways") enables you to search and retrieve text or multimedia documents stored on the servers. WAIS searches through full text indexes for the information requested and returns a list of documents. You can request WAIS to send a copy of any of the documents found. There are a number of WAIS searchers for nearly 500 databases containing everything from technical documents and bibliographies to newsgroup archives. You can access WAIS in several ways:

- Run a WAIS search in the World Wide Web. This is probably the easiest way.
- Run a WAIS client on your local host computer. This is the most efficient way to do a WAIS search.

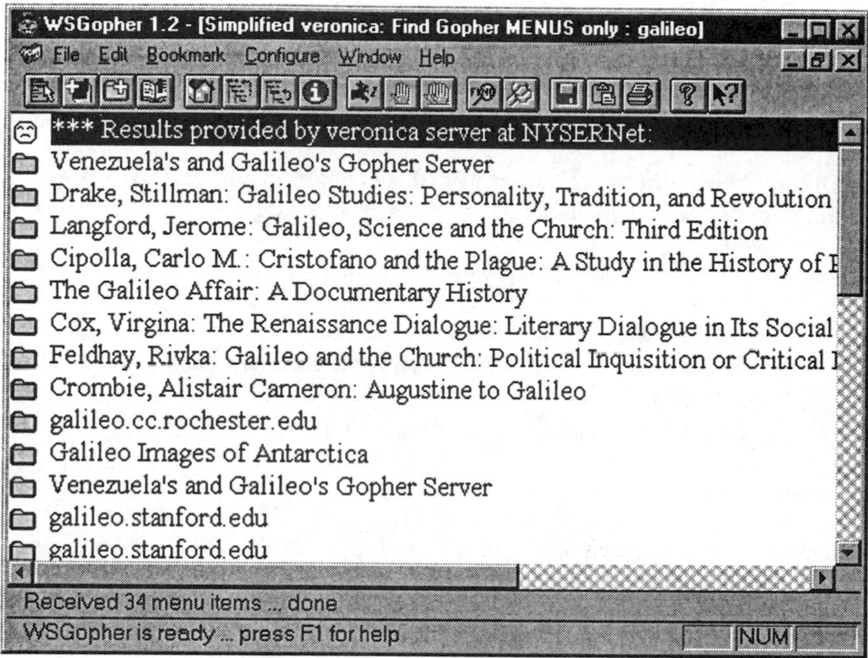

Figure 6.8 Menu of "hits" from Veronica Gopher search

- Telnet to a remote computer that offers access to a public WAIS client. WAIS searching during a Telnet session can be difficult if not impossible. The WAIS interface is complicated and depends on the terminal emulation software you are using.
- Run a WAIS session from a Gopher menu option or via the World Wide Web. The Gopher version of WAIS is easier to use than those accessible via Telnet but still not as easy as a local client. The main drawback to using a Gopher interface to WAIS is that you can only search one database at a time. This provides relevance feedback, which indicates how close a match your search produced. Table 6.3 shows how to access WAIS via the World Wide Web.

Some WAIS searchers specialize in environmental topics, physics, astronomy, and so on. This means that you will have to know where to go to get to the index you wish to

Table 6.3 Sample WAIS sites

WAIS Sites	Login
quake.think.com	WAIS
sunsite.unc.edu	WAIS
WAIS.com	WAIS

search. Because WAIS allows text searching, anything archived on the Internet can be described in a database: Usenet articles, email discussion list archives, binary data. and so on. Programs or images can be downloaded so long as they can be identified by a text descriptor in a WAIS database.

The significant difference between WAIS and other search services is WAIS's ability to respond to search frames in plain English. For instance, you might enter:

```
give me all documents related to the ozone hole
```

Don't think that WAIS can actually understand the entire sentence. What it does is extract individual words to search. WAIS ignores the more common words like "related," "or," "to," and "the" and searches for the less common words like "ozone hole." You can just as easily omit all the unnecessary words and simply type:

```
ozone hole
```

and achieve the same search results as with the longer phrase. Once the search is complete a list of matching items is retrieved. Most WAIS interfaces permit you to retrieve and download the information to your desktop.

Looking for People on the Internet

WHOIS

WHOIS enables you to search out people connected to the Internet. Like other search services, WHOIS searches a database of names. Given that there are as many as 20 million people connected to the Internet, there is no way that WHOIS can find any particular person. The typical WHOIS server lets you search a database of names within your own organization. You can move between organizations and their WHOIS servers with relative ease. However, before you get started you need to know some information about the person you're trying to find. You should know the name of course, the organization the person is affiliated with (e.g., a company, university, or government agency) and the city of residence. WHOIS servers can be accessed by:

- opening a Telnet connection to a WHOIS server with the command

  telnet *<server name>*

- using a local WHOIS client
- sending an electronic mail WHOIS search to **mailserv@ds.internic.net**

WHOIS databases can be searched by name, handle (a unique identifier), or mailbox. Table 6.4 lists the addresses and locations of selected WHOIS servers.

Table 6.4 Selected WHOIS servers

Address	Location
whois.pacbell.com	Pacific Bell (US)
whois.sunquest.com	Sunquest Information Systems (US)
zippy.telcom.arizona.edu	University of Arizona (US)
whois.bates.edu	Bates College (US)
whois.berkeley.edu	University of California at Berkeley (US)
whois.cwru.edu	Case Western Reserve University (US)
whois.dfci.harvard.edu	Dana-Farber Cancer Institute (US)
whois.messiah.edu	Messiah College (US)
whois.msstate.edu	Mississippi State University (US)
whois.ncsu.edu	North Carolina State University (US)
whois.oxy.edu	Occidental College (US)
whois.cc.rochester.edu	University of Rochester (US)
whois.sdsu.edu	San Diego State University (US)
whois.slac.stanford.edu	Stanford Linear Accelerator Center (US)
whois.bcm.tmc.edu	Baylor College of Medicine (US)
whois.ubalt.edu	University of Baltimore (US)

Earth Online Tip: WHOIS servers are for queries about specific information. Extended queries intended to obtain large sections of the directory represent not only an excessive use of server resources and bandwidth but also an unfair use of directory information that belongs to individuals.

Netfind

Netfind is like the white pages of your telephone directory. Give Netfind a person's name and description of where he or she works, and it will attempt to locate the telephone number and electronic mailbox information. Recall that to conduct a WHOIS search you need to know the right server to search on. With Netfind you can log on to any Netfind server and provide it with the person's name and work location, and it will conduct a search over many servers. Once supplied, Netfind searches its seed database to find Internet domains that match the specified keywords. If there is more than one matching domain, Netfind displays the list of matching domains and asks you to select up to three to search.

When the search is completed, Netfind returns a summary of problems encountered during the search through remote domains, information about the most promising electronic mail address for the person being sought (if available), and information about when the person most recently logged on to the Internet (if available). If more than one person is

Table 6.5 Netfind servers

Host Address	Country
bruno.cs.colorado.edu	USA
ds.internic.net	USA
eis.calstate.edu	USA
krnic.net	Korea
monolith.cc.ic.ac.uk	England
mudhoney.micro.umn.edu	USA
netfind.anu.edu.au	Australia
netfind.ee.mcgill.ca	Canada
netfind.if.usp.br	Brazil

located by a search, the summary does not include information about email targets and most recent/current logins.

There are two ways to run a Netfind search:

- Use a client program on your system. Type "netfind" at your system prompt to see if you have access to Netfind.
- Connect to a Netfind server via remote login with Telnet. Telnet to **bruno.cs.colorado.edu.**

You can use the Netfind software at your site, or you can Telnet to one of the hosts listed in Table 6.5.

Netfind requires the name of a person, with keywords to indicate where that person works. I'll Telnet into the University of Colorado Netfind service and search for information about myself. After I log on to my Internet service provider I'll type:

```
telnet> open bruno.cs.colorado.edu
Trying 128.138.243.150...
Connected to bruno.cs.colorado.edu.
Escape character is '^]'.

SunOS UNIX (bruno)

Login as 'netfind' to access netfind server
```

At the login prompt I'll do as the server instructs and type:

```
login: netfind
```

```
=====================================================

Welcome to the University of Colorado Netfind server.

=====================================================
```

A long list of alternatives sites are given in case the present Netfind server is too busy.

```
Alternate Netfind servers:
   archie.au (AARNet, Melbourne, Australia)
   bruno.cs.colorado.edu (University of Colorado, Boulder, USA)
```

I think that your terminal can display 24 lines. If this is wrong, please enter the "Options" menu and set the correct number of lines.

```
Top level choices:
   1. Help
   2. Search
   3. Seed database lookup
   4. Options
   5. Quit (exit server)
```

I'll choose 2 to search for myself:

```
Enter person and keys (blank to exit) --> ritter uwsp
```

The Netfind server finds three potential domains to look for my profile.

```
Please select at most 3 of the following domains to search:
   0. uwsp.edu (university of wisconsin, stevens point)
   1. lib.uwsp.edu (library, university of wisconsin, stevens
        point)
   2. me.uwsp.edu (mechanical engineering department,
        university of wisconsin, stevens point)
Enter selection (e.g., 2 0 1) -->
```

If there are more than 100 matching domains, Netfind will list some of the matching domains/organizations and ask you to form a more specific search. You can use any of the parts of an organization's name (or any of the components of its domain name) as keywords in searches. Using more than one keyword implies the logical AND of the keywords. Specifying too many keywords may cause searches to fail.

Item "0 uwsp.edu" looks like a reasonable choice. Netfind returns with:

```
Enter selection (e.g., 2 0 1) --> 0
( 1) got nameserver spu1.uwsp.edu
( 1) got nameserver spdns1.uwsp.edu
( 1) SMTP_Finger_Search: checking domain uwsp.edu
( 1) do_connect: Finger service not available on host uwsp.edu->
cannot do user lookup
```

```
------
Domain search completed. Proceeding to host search.
------
( 1) SMTP_Finger_Search: checking host uwspmail.uwsp.edu
( 2) SMTP_Finger_Search: checking host sknapp.uwsp.edu
( 3) SMTP_Finger_Search: checking host sis.uwsp.edu
( 4) SMTP_Finger_Search: checking host gbernd.uwsp.edu
( 5) SMTP_Finger_Search: checking host afranz.uwsp.edu
( 3) do_connect: Finger service not available on host
sis.uwsp.edu -> cannot do user lookup
( 3) SMTP_Finger_Search: checking host ariel.uwsp.edu
( 1) SMTP_Finger_Search: checking host worf.uwsp.edu
SYSTEM: worf.uwsp.edu
   Login: mritter                      Name: Mike Ritter
   Directory: /usr/fac/mritter         Shell: /bin/csh
   Office: Geog/Geol, 715-346-4449     Home Phone: n/a
   Last login Sun Mar 10 13:38 (CST) on ttyp0 from
          198.150.193.52
   No Plan.
   Login: critter                      Name: Christoph Ritter
   Directory: /usr/stu/critter         Shell: /bin/csh
   Office: Magdeburg Project, 715-346-4127 Home Phone: n/a
   Last login Fri Mar 15 06:00 (CST) on ttyp1 from 141.44.27.16
   No Plan.
```

Two hits were made, and mine is the first one.

Finger

The Finger program is used to retrieve a file or information about a person by using an electronic mail address. To use Finger you simply type "finger" at your system prompt and enter the electronic mail address:

```
worf-6> finger mritter@uwspmail.uwsp.edu
Login: mritter                          Name: Mike Ritter
Directory: /usr/fac/mritter             Shell: /bin/csh
Office: Geog/Geol, 715-346-4449         Home Phone: n/a
On since Mon Dec 18 13:22 (CST) on ttyp0 from 143.236.26.121
Plan:
Geography/Geology World Wide Web Page
```

Basically the same information has been retrieved in a much shorter time and with less hassle than the Netfind service. However, Netfind can use much less specific information to run a search than Finger. Finger can also be used to retrieve other files. For instance, to retrieve an update in earthquake activity you can Finger to **quake@geophys.washington.edu**.

```
worf-8> finger quake@geophys.washington.edu

[geophys.washington.edu]
Login name: quake        In real life: Earthquake Information
Directory: /u0/quake     Shell: /u0/quake/run_quake
Last login Mon Dec 18 10:47 on ttyp6 from 164.157.206.13
```

```
Mail last read Mon Oct 23 03:46:40 1995
Plan:
The following catalog is for earthquakes (M>2) in Washington and
Oregon produced by the Pacific Northwest Seismograph Network, a
member of the Council of the National Seismic System. PNSN
support comes from the US Geological Survey, Department of
Energy, and Washington State.
Catalogs for various regions of the country can be obtained by
using the program 'finger quake@machine' where the following are
machines for different regions.
gldfs.cr.usgs.gov (USGS NEIC/NEIS world-wide),
andreas.wr.usgs.gov (Northern Cal.),
scec.gps.caltech.edu (Southern Cal.),
fm.gi.alaska.edu (Alaska),
seismo.unr.edu (Nevada),
mbmgsun.mtech.edu (Montana),
eqinfo.seis.utah.edu (Utah),
sisyphus.idbsu.edu (Idaho),
slueas.slu.edu (Central US),
tako.wr.usgs.gov (Hawaii)

Additional catalogs and information for the PNSN (as well as
other networks) are available on the World-Wide-Web at URL:
'http://www.geophys.washington.edu/'
DATE-TIME is in Universal Time (UTC) which is PST + 8 hours.
Magnitudes are reported as local magnitude (Ml). QUAL is
location quality A-good, D-poor,
Z-from automatic system and may be in error.
DATE-(UTC)-TIME LAT(N) LON(W) DEP MAG QUAL COMMENTS
yy/mm/dd hh:mm:ss deg. deg. km Ml
95/11/16 18:08:06 45.00N 122.58W 26.2 2.1 C 25.6 km SE of
Woodburn, OR
95/11/21 03:01:05 47.71N 120.30W 5.6 2.8 B 8.7 km NW of Entiat
95/11/28 14:42:53 49.18N 123.60W 10.0 2.3 C 40.4 km W of
Vancouver,BC
95/12/09 17:32:53 48.40N 122.21W 0.0 2.1 B 9.0 km E of Mount
Vernon
95/12/17 15:01:47 47.58N 120.21W 12.4 3.1 B 7.4 km S of Entiat
```

Notice that the earthquake information contained in the report is a part of the "Plan" file. The report delivered to our desktop provides us with a wealth of information. The document points us to other possibilities to finger for information in different parts of North America and on other kinds of servers that such information can be obtained from. At the document is the information we are looking for: dates, times, magnitudes, and locations of earthquake activity in northwestern North America.

You can keep up to date with NASA by "fingering" NASA News at **nasanews@space.mit.edu** (Figure 6.9). Users can retrieve the latest information on such things as the schedule for upcoming space shuttle missions, including the crew's activity schedule for that day.

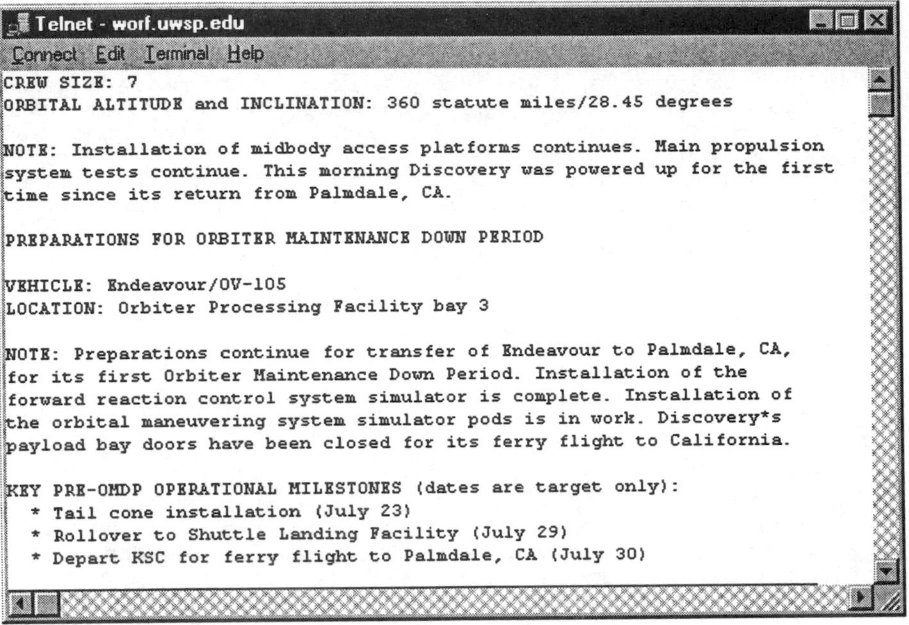


```
CREW SIZE: 7
ORBITAL ALTITUDE and INCLINATION: 360 statute miles/28.45 degrees

NOTE: Installation of midbody access platforms continues. Main propulsion
system tests continue. This morning Discovery was powered up for the first
time since its return from Palmdale, CA.

PREPARATIONS FOR ORBITER MAINTENANCE DOWN PERIOD

VEHICLE: Endeavour/OV-105
LOCATION: Orbiter Processing Facility bay 3

NOTE: Preparations continue for transfer of Endeavour to Palmdale, CA,
for its first Orbiter Maintenance Down Period. Installation of the
forward reaction control system simulator is complete. Installation of
the orbital maneuvering system simulator pods is in work. Discovery*s
payload bay doors have been closed for its ferry flight to California.

KEY PRE-OMDP OPERATIONAL MILESTONES (dates are target only):
  * Tail cone installation (July 23)
  * Rollover to Shuttle Landing Facility (July 29)
  * Depart KSC for ferry flight to Palmdale, CA (July 30)
```

Figure 6.9 Finger response from NASA News

What You Have Learned

- Search engines use Boolean operators to frame a query for their database.
- Database and network searches can be accomplished with robot-like programs that scour the Internet for resources.
- Subject-oriented database services permit a user to look for information by navigating through a hierarchy of menus.
- Archie is used to search for the location of a particular file on the Internet.
- Veronica is employed to search Gopher space for menu titles and directories.
- WAIS is a database index search engine for archives.
- WHOIS, Finger and Netfind are used to search for information about Internet users.

Apply It!

Searching for resources on the Internet can be a time-consuming job. In previous Apply It! sections, we have relied on knowing the address of a site to start our pursuit of climate change Internet resources. We turn to the search services discussed in this chapter when we need more help finding our way.

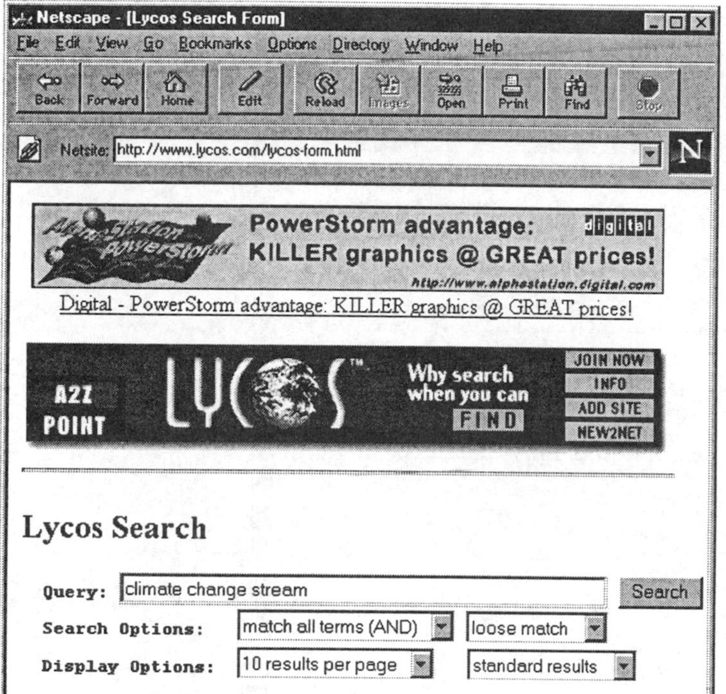

Figure 6.10 Starting an "advanced" Lycos search

In this Apply It! section I'm going to search for information related to the impact of climate change on stream flow. Earlier in this chapter we examined the Lycos search engine. Let's return to Lycos to conduct our new search. This time I'm going to use the advanced features of Lycos, which enable me to decide how matches are executed and what type and amount of information will be returned to me about my query. First, I'll connect to the Lycos search form at **URL - http://www.lycos.com/lycos-form.html** (Figure 6.10). The search form provides the usual keyword field and search button to initiate the query. Below these items are additional options to shape my search. First is the "Search Options," the default of which is to use the OR Boolean operator. The OR operator will search out all documents that contain any of the terms. The drop-down "Search Options" list box lets me use a Boolean AND operator to match various combinations of terms in my search list. This is especially handy if you're unsure of the spelling of one your keywords. For instance, say you wanted to search for information about Shishaldin volcano in Alaska but were unsure of its spelling. In the Query field you might enter "Shisaldin Shisalden Alaska." Lycos searches through its holdings to match both of the spellings to Alaska. In this way you are sure to find the right one. (Hopefully *one* of the search terms is spelled correctly!) The Lycos search lets me determine the selectivity of the match as well. Lycos will use its relevancy score to determine the strength of the match and whether to return the match to you. The stronger the match, the fewer returns I'll receive, but this also eliminates irrelevant

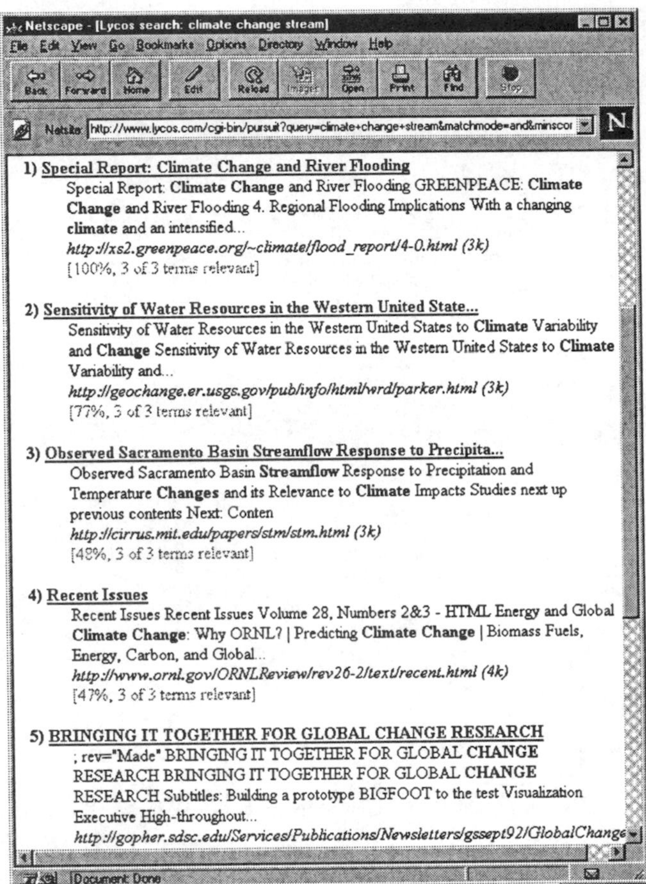

Figure 6.11 Lycos advanced search query results

documents. To save yourself some time, use a strong match for common keywords and a loose match for less common ones.

Lycos lets you determine how your query results are displayed. Two options are given, one for the number of results ("hits") displayed on a page and one for the amount of information returned. There are three levels of detail: standard (the default), summary (the minimum amount of information is displayed) and detailed (all information is displayed).

To begin my search I'll enter the keywords "climate change stream" (Figure 6.10). I purposely left the word "stream" in singular form because Lycos might match "stream" to larger words like "streamflow. " I'll set the Search Options to "match all terms (AND)" first but keep the selectivity at "loose." My query is started by clicking the "Search" button.

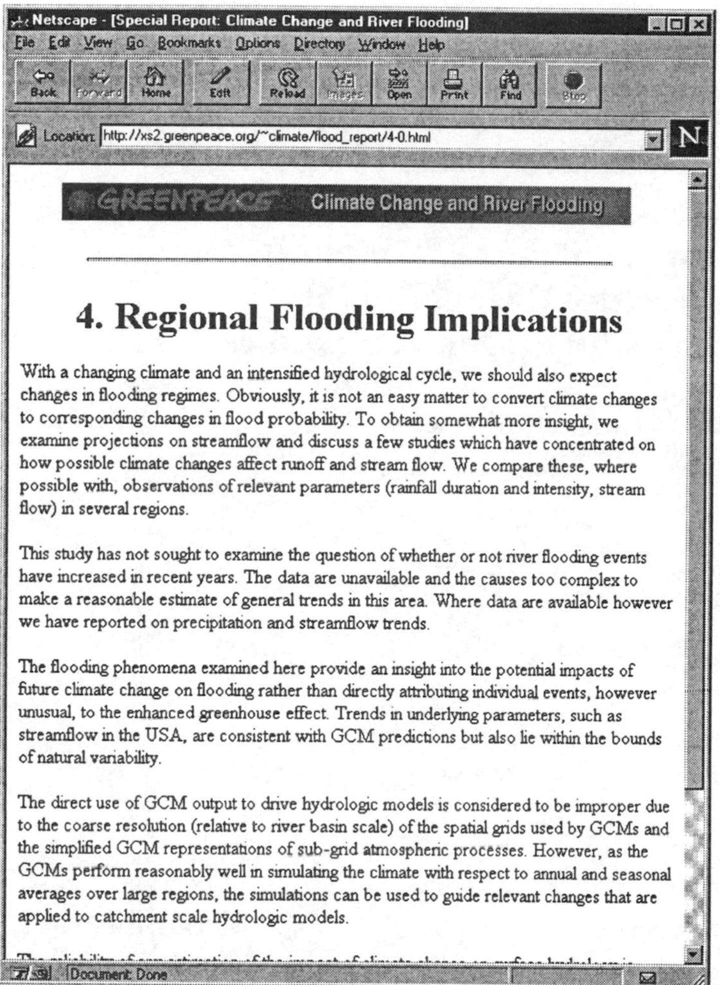

4. Regional Flooding Implications

With a changing climate and an intensified hydrological cycle, we should also expect changes in flooding regimes. Obviously, it is not an easy matter to convert climate changes to corresponding changes in flood probability. To obtain somewhat more insight, we examine projections on streamflow and discuss a few studies which have concentrated on how possible climate changes affect runoff and stream flow. We compare these, where possible with, observations of relevant parameters (rainfall duration and intensity, stream flow) in several regions.

This study has not sought to examine the question of whether or not river flooding events have increased in recent years. The data are unavailable and the causes too complex to make a reasonable estimate of general trends in this area. Where data are available however we have reported on precipitation and streamflow trends.

The flooding phenomena examined here provide an insight into the potential impacts of future climate change on flooding rather than directly attributing individual events, however unusual, to the enhanced greenhouse effect. Trends in underlying parameters, such as streamflow in the USA, are consistent with GCM predictions but also lie within the bounds of natural variability.

The direct use of GCM output to drive hydrologic models is considered to be improper due to the coarse resolution (relative to river basin scale) of the spatial grids used by GCMs and the simplified GCM representations of sub-grid atmospheric processes. However, as the GCMs perform reasonably well in simulating the climate with respect to annual and seasonal averages over large regions, the simulations can be used to guide relevant changes that are applied to catchment scale hydrologic models.

Figure 6.12 Greenpeace page on Regional Flooding Implications and climate change

The results of my search, shown in Figure 6.11, contain some good prospects, particularly the first document from the environmental organization Greenpeace, which has a relevancy score of 100%. Organizations like Greenpeace contribute an enormous amount of material to the online community.

This page discusses the validity of general circulation models to forecast regional flooding due to changes in climate (Figure 6.12). It is a portion of a special report furnished by Greenpeace focusing on climate change and river flooding (**URL - http://xs2.greenpeace.org/~climate/flood_report/**). It's a good addition to my growing list of resources so I'll bookmark it for later reference.

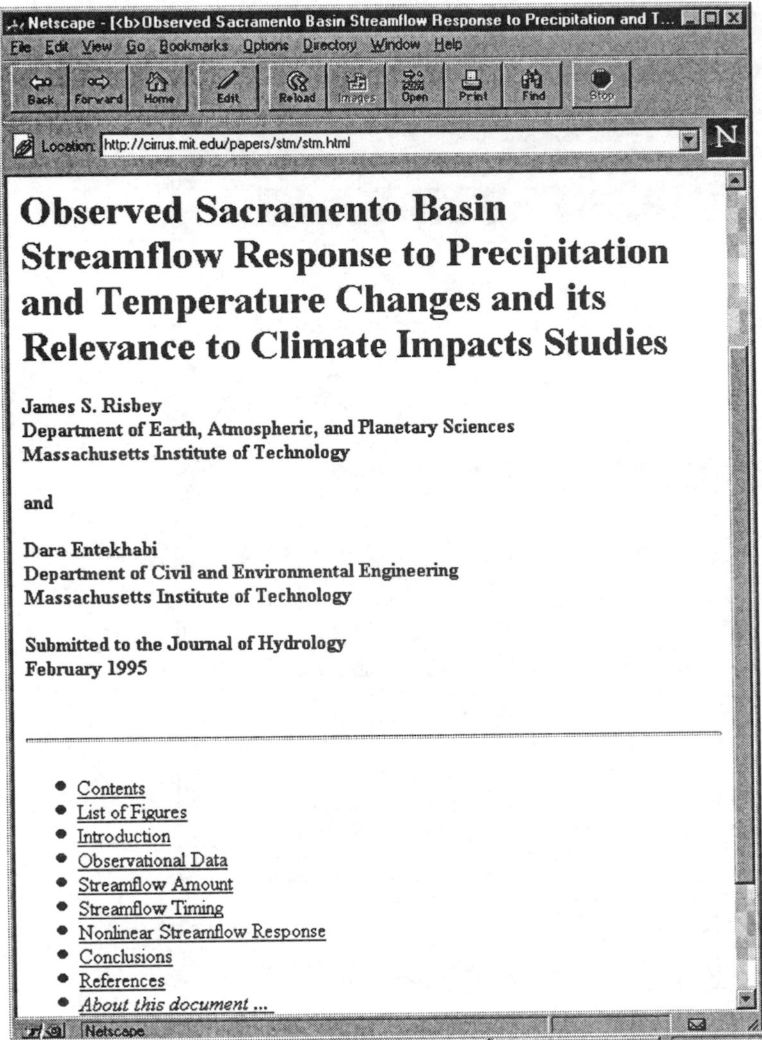

Figure 6.13 Research paper about the streamflow response to climate change

Returning to my search results I'll scroll down to item 3, "Observed Sacramento Basin Streamflow Response to Precipitation," and click on it to see how useful it is. It has a low relevancy score, 48% but it did match the three terms. This is another good find (Figure 6.13) as it is an actual research paper investigating "streamflow response from the historical record rather than from hydrological models of the basin, and [comparing] observational results with model results" (**URL - http://cirrus.mit.edu/papers/stm/stm.html).** Note that the paper was submitted to a professional journal and so at this time has not undergone peer review of its research methods or results. Nevertheless, useful information is provided.

This Apply It! has generated a few new materials to add to our climate change resource list. Be aware that if you apply this same search you'll probably end up with different results because Lycos, like other Internet search services, is adding new resources every day. The search I make tomorrow may yield different results than the one I ran yesterday. It can be frustrating to keep up with, but the addition of new, up-to-date online materials is worth it.

Try It Out!

1. Each of the following items can be found on the Internet. Use the appropriate search service to locate the resources below. How many can you find?

    - CIA World Factbook
    - world maps
    - Roget's Thesaurus
    - periodic table of the elements
    - geographic name server
    - an image of Jupiter
    - the weather forecast for Minneapolis, Minnesota
    - a weather map of Europe

2. Finger the latest earthquakes at **quake@gldfs.cr.usgs.gov**. Plot the location of the earthquakes on a base map of the world. Where do most of the reported earthquakes originate? Is there any pattern? Compare the location of the earthquakes to a tectonic map of the earth. What were the most recent earthquakes to strike the northwestern portion of the United States?

3. Find out what the author's latest plans are by fingering him at **mritter@uwsp.edu**.

CHAPTER 7

Educational and Professional Activities on the Internet

The Internet provides the professional earth scientist, educator and student with a number of tools to conduct their daily activities in new and effective ways. For instance, one can distribute and share data as soon as it becomes available over the Internet. One can either distribute small sets as attachments to electronic mail or archive the data for downloading by individuals logging into one's server. Interactive technologies and software allow researchers to login to a computer server and query the contents of databases. Data in tabular or graphical form can be made instantly available over the Internet to users from archival sources. Administrating correspondence between faculty, students and work groups separated by great geographical distances is easily accomplished with Internet electronic mail. Earth science educators at all levels of instruction are recognizing the potential of the Internet as a teaching and learning resource. Educators are enriching their classroom activities with Internet resources such as virtual field trips, online exercises, and multimedia presentations. The Internet has opened a whole new realm in the world of publishing. Electronic journals are an exciting way of communicating research results to a global community of readers. Professional organizations use the Internet to inform their members and the public of organizational activities and resources. Career information is literally at your fingertips on the Internet. In this chapter we'll take a look at how the Internet is being used to accomplish these activities and how you can employ them too. In doing so we'll explore a few representative sites for these activities.

Earth Science Education on the Internet

The Internet's extensive digital library-like holdings make it a rich environment for learning earth science. Students will find resources as up-to-date as yesterday's earthquakes, today's weather and the future outlook for El Niño. You can tap into the vast resources of the best libraries in the world like the Library of Congress, or search through extensive online article databases like the Colorado Alliance of Research Library's CARL UnCover. Archives of image, sound and digital video files await use in research projects and enhance your knowledge of earth processes. Educators will find teaching and learning resources ready to download virtually free of charge. Educators have the means to invoke new ways of communicating with their students, encouraging them to become active learners in the information society. Educators find in the Internet a means of communicating and sharing ideas with colleagues scattered throughout the world. The Internet, if used wisely, can radically change the way we teach and learn earth science. In this section you will find out

- how earth scientists are delivering classroom materials over the Internet
- what educational online earth science resources are provided by the government and professional organizations
- how to keep in contact with students and conduct virtual seminars on the Internet
- how to promote collaborative learning with the Internet

Many of the activities that will be discussed in this chapter do not require the use of the Internet per se. You can send electronic mail to a student over a local area network or you can load a class outline on a local server for students to review without the need to connect to the Internet. However, our learning environment is greatly enhanced when the digital resources of the Internet are brought into the picture. By offering your educational materials over the Internet you not only provide increased benefits to your students but also open up those resources to a potentially larger audience who will benefit from them. The spirit of cooperation and sharing with the global community has been a guiding force behind the expanding resources of the Internet.

Computer-Mediated Communication

Computer-mediated communication, or CMC for short, is the use of a computer network to discover information and share ideas. Ellsworth (1995) defines three modes of computer-mediated communication:

- *Human-to-human using a computer.* This form of CMC involves person-to-person communication with a computer using services like electronic mail and computer conferencing with listservs and Usenet.
- *Human-to-computer for information maintenance and retrieval.* This type of communication involves the use of computers to access, search and retrieve files from archival sources for text, images, video and sound files, and so on using services like File Transfer Protocol.
- *Human-to-computer for process assistance.* Interactivity between humans and computers for process assistance utilizes a computer to facilitate instruction and learning. This has typically been described as computer-based or computer-assisted instruction or learning. A computer presents choices or encourages a user to explore pathways to information.

Communication and learning over regional and global networks bestows a number of benefits on students and changes the way in which teachers interact with students. Computer-mediated communication encourages students to explore information and become active educational workers. CMC promotes self-discipline and requires students to take responsibility for their own learning. Networked computers have greater potential in education than the stand-alone, knowledge-server computers used by many schools today. Knowledge-server computers utilize preprogrammed educational software or "interactive" educational games. Knowledge-server computers limit students to the information resources loaded on the machine or to peripheral hardware and software (i.e., materials located on a CD-ROM or laser video disk). On a knowledge-server-type computer, exploration and interactivity is limited by the way software authors or teachers control the structuring of and linkages between material. This form of computer-mediated learning confines the student to the local learning environment of the desktop computer. The active learning environment provided by a computer with access to local, national and international networks increases interaction and communication among students, teachers, peers, parents, and other members of the world community. New and different points of view are discovered. Learners have new freedom to explore additional pathways to information.

Computer-mediated communication empowers learners to seek out information on their own terms. The greatest benefit of computer-mediated communication is its ability to liberate instruction from the constraints of time and distance. By initiating a variety of activities, both online and offline, facilitators can encourage an active, challenging learning environment. Time and location no longer play a role in learning. Learning under the lecture discourse model of teaching requires students to assemble in a particular location at a predetermined time to receive instruction. The computer-mediated communication learning model enables a student to receive instruction independent of location and time. So long as the student has access to a computer equipped with a modem and a phone line, or more recently coaxial cable lines, instruction and learning are available at the discretion of the student. Such independent self-instruction permits students to spend as much time as they need to learn a particular subject. It likewise frees educators from the same restrictions that the lecture discourse model places on students. Educators have greater flexibility in determining how they teach. Computer-networked technology places more control in the hands of the student to learn and frees the educator to explore new pathways to knowledge (for example, see Figure 7.1).

Empowering learners with potent tools and resources like the Internet creates a new student-teacher relationship. Teachers replace their role as a dispenser of information with a new role of facilitator of information. Students create or find their own path to information while teachers help clear the way. Within this paradigm, educators help create the milieu of learning while the students take more control over how they interact with the subject material. Instead of following a specific learning pathway defined by the teacher, students are encouraged to strike off on their own. That is, a basic structure of information can be provided to the student, the main objectives of a lesson so to speak. However, information related to the topic of the lesson can be linked for students to explore and get a more fully developed understanding of the topic.

Earth science educators are using computer-mediated communication over the Internet to enrich their classes with new online materials. Educators are turning to the Internet as a means of delivering their entire classes, permitting students to achieve their academic goals

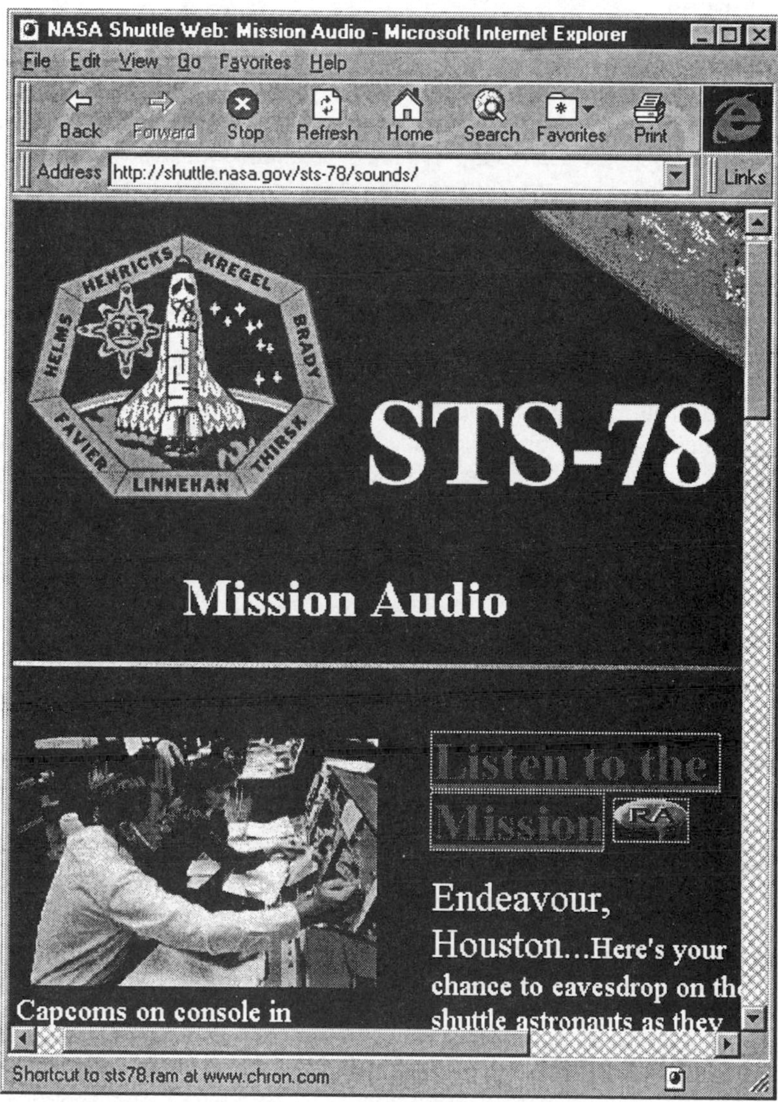

Figure 7.1 NASA's Mission Audio site: live mission audio over the World Wide Web

at their own pace and usually in shorter periods of time. Educators employ the Internet to post syllabi, class notes, grades and assignments online for students to keep abreast of class activities. Electronic mail is used to disseminate announcements and keep in contact with students. Many of these activities are efficiently integrated into hypertext documents and loaded on to World Wide Web servers. By pointing and clicking, students can call up their next reading assignment, ask the teacher a question, work collaboratively with other students, review exam questions and take exams online.

Getting the Word Out: Administering Your Class Online

Educators are finding the Internet an effective means of administering the daily and semester-long activities of their classes. One of the easiest ways of keeping students abreast of the ongoing activities is with an *online syllabus*. An online syllabus can be as simple as a text document loaded on a server for students to read or as complex as a hypertext document with links to the instructor's electronic mailbox and online course materials. There are several advantages to having a hypertext class syllabus online. The syllabus can serve as a jump-off point to readings located on the Internet. Students bring up the class syllabus, scroll down a list of required readings and click, and the reading appears on-screen. HTML lets students create hyperlinks between online lecture notes, the syllabus and online review lessons. Teachers can make corrections or updates to the syllabus as the semester proceeds. Additional information can be inserted or information revised to reflect changes in the scheduling of lectures and discussions or changes in the timing of exams. Having a permanent record of the syllabus available online enables students to download and print off additional copies if their original printed copy is misplaced or lost. Documents composed in HTML are device independent and can exist on a local or global networked server for students to access any time. If they are working at a computer terminal they always have the online class materials available at their fingertips. With the ever expanding number of computers on campus these days, online resources are readily available.

Moving the syllabus into a hypermedia environment greatly enhances its utility, especially to the student. Supplemental resources can be linked to keywords and phrases in the syllabus. For instance, Figure 7.2 illustrates a hypertext introductory physical geography course guidebook that I created. Conventionally the guidebook has been duplicated and given to students (at a substantial cost to the department!). The online guidebook has pertinent information about the class schedule, grading, the department's learning labs, exam review sheets, and links to resources on the Internet. At the bottom of the page is my electronic mail address. The electronic mail address is coded such that when students choose it (and if their Web browser permits it) they will initiate an electronic mail session to send me a message. Having this option does not require students to start up their electronic mail program separately or to remember my electronic mail address. It is a good practice to include your email address at the bottom of your Web documents anyway, especially if they include educational materials like lecture notes, exam review sheets or exercises. Having your electronic mail address available gives students an efficient means of contacting you no matter what time of day or night it is.

The class syllabus can be accessed from the guidebook home page (Figure 7.3). The syllabus has the typical information, but a new dimension has been added. My electronic mail address is an active link so that students can contact me from this page. Farther down the page is the list of lecture topics, readings and Internet assignments. The Internet assignments are used to supplement material discussed in class. These items are all active links, so all students have to do is point and click on the item and soon the material will be brought to their desktop. Included in the assignments are several virtual field trips. The

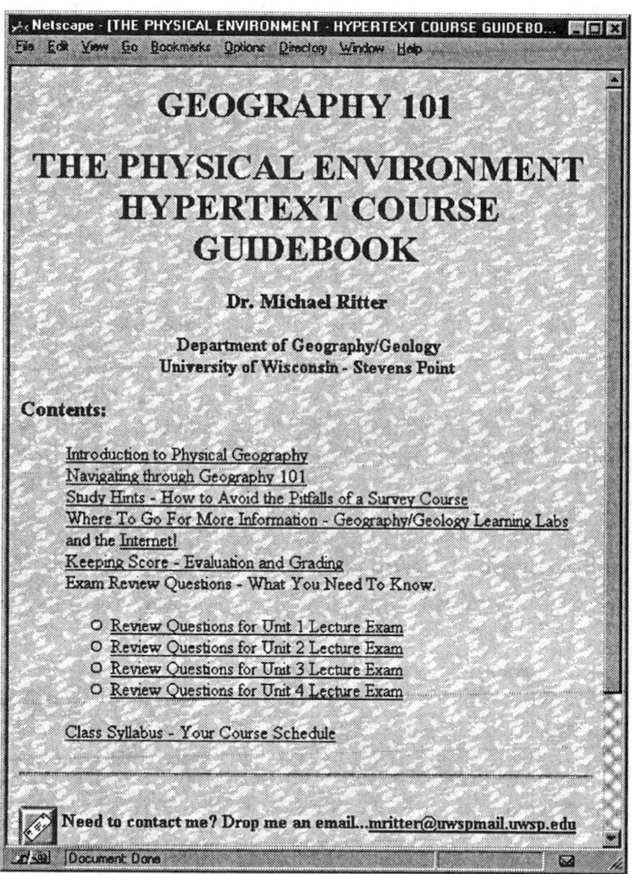

Figure 7.2 Online course guidebook

Internet can bring far off places to students' desktops—to take a virtual trip through a rain forest or along the Hudson River Valley of New York.

As an educator I believe that it is crucial to keep in close contact with my students; however, busy schedules do not permit the accessibility that is desired. To remedy this situation many educators, myself included, are using electronic mailing lists to keep students abreast of the latest developments in their classes. An electronic mailing list, like those operated over electronic mail listservs or mailing groups, is used to distribute announcements of class cancellations, changes in the class schedule, notification of the posting of grades, and posting of discussion questions and exam review notes. Students can post to the electronic mail list as well. I encourage students to share their experiences and announcements of upcoming events that pertain to the class that other students might benefit from. A class announcement page is hyperlinked to the class home page, giving students another means of keeping up with class activities.

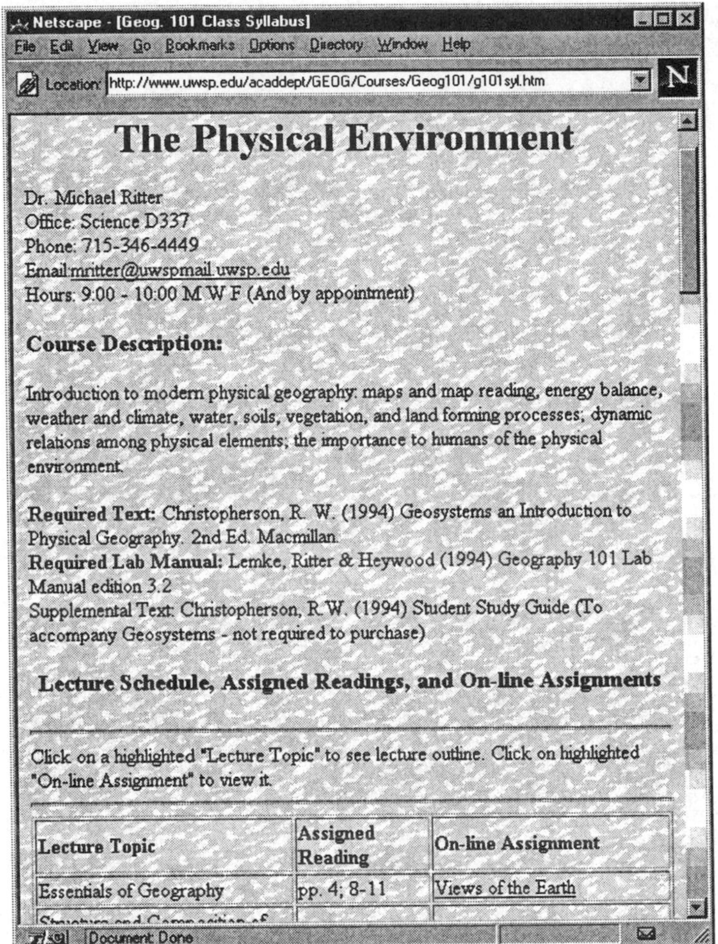
Netscape - [Geog. 101 Class Syllabus]

File Edit View Go Bookmarks Options Directory Window Help

Location: http://www.uwsp.edu/acaddept/GEOG/Courses/Geog101/g101syl.htm

The Physical Environment

Dr. Michael Ritter
Office: Science D337
Phone: 715-346-4449
Email:mritter@uwspmail.uwsp.edu
Hours: 9:00 - 10:00 M W F (And by appointment)

Course Description:

Introduction to modern physical geography: maps and map reading, energy balance, weather and climate, water, soils, vegetation, and land forming processes; dynamic relations among physical elements; the importance to humans of the physical environment.

Required Text: Christopherson, R. W. (1994) Geosystems an Introduction to Physical Geography. 2nd Ed. Macmillan.
Required Lab Manual: Lemke, Ritter & Heywood (1994) Geography 101 Lab Manual edition 3.2
Supplemental Text: Christopherson, R.W. (1994) Student Study Guide (To accompany Geosystems - not required to purchase)

Lecture Schedule, Assigned Readings, and On-line Assignments

Click on a highlighted "Lecture Topic" to see lecture outline. Click on highlighted "On-line Assignment" to view it.

Lecture Topic	Assigned Reading	On-line Assignment
Essentials of Geography	pp. 4; 8-11	Views of the Earth

Document: Done

Figure 7.3 Online class syllabus

Online Class Materials

Educators increasingly are turning to the Internet to deliver class material to their students. There are several advantages to placing materials on the Internet rather than, or in addition to, putting them in the library or giving them out to students as hard copies. Libraries close; the Internet doesn't. Class materials are always available on the Internet no matter what time of day or what day it is. As long as students can get to a networked computer they can have access to the information. One copy of the material placed on the networked computer server can be read by as many people as need be. Copying twenty-page documents for 100 students can get very costly. Placing materials on a server enables students to either read the documents online or download them to their desktop. Here they can also annotate them with

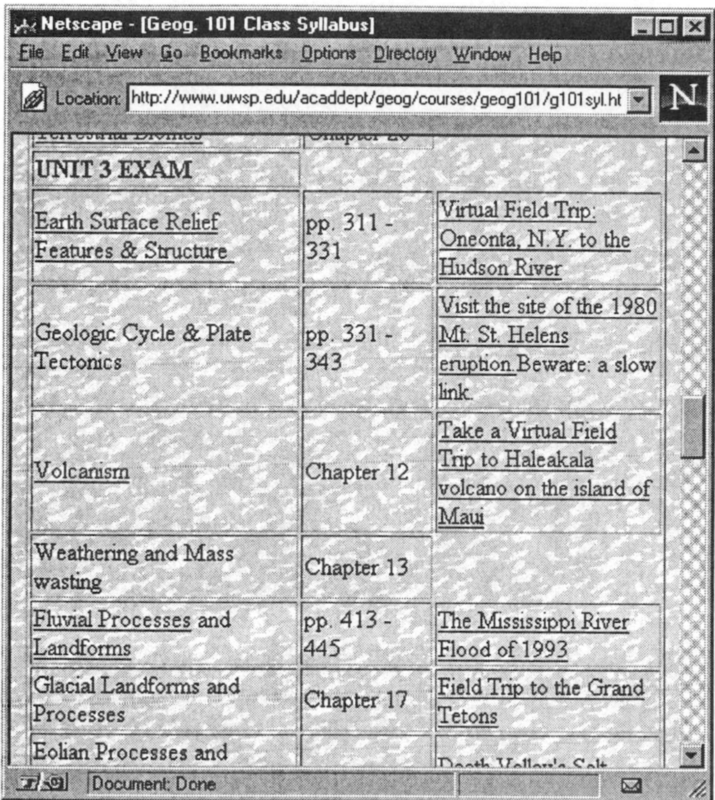

Figure 7.4 Online course syllabus

their own notes. They can highlight important elements of the text in a word processor and copy and paste passages into their own papers, being careful to cite the source of the passage, of course. Materials in digital form are much easier to revise as well. A single copy can be edited at any time and is immediately ready for "duplication" or reading by the whole class after uploading to a networked computer.

Getting started with online class materials can be very easy. A lecture outline in ASCII text format can be placed on a server for students to access in a variety of ways. The easiest is to place the class notes or outline on a World Wide Web server as a preformatted text file, where students can view the outline with a browser like Netscape or Mosaic. Students can save the document to their desktop computer or copy particular pieces of text with the Web browser. Formatting your lecture outline as a hypertext document is the most effective way of delivering lecture outlines. With HTML, illustrations used in class can be placed in the document or hyperlinks to image files can be embedded in the text. Document hyperlinks can be made to subjects covered in related lectures that have been placed on line or to reference material located elsewhere on the Internet (Figure 7.4).

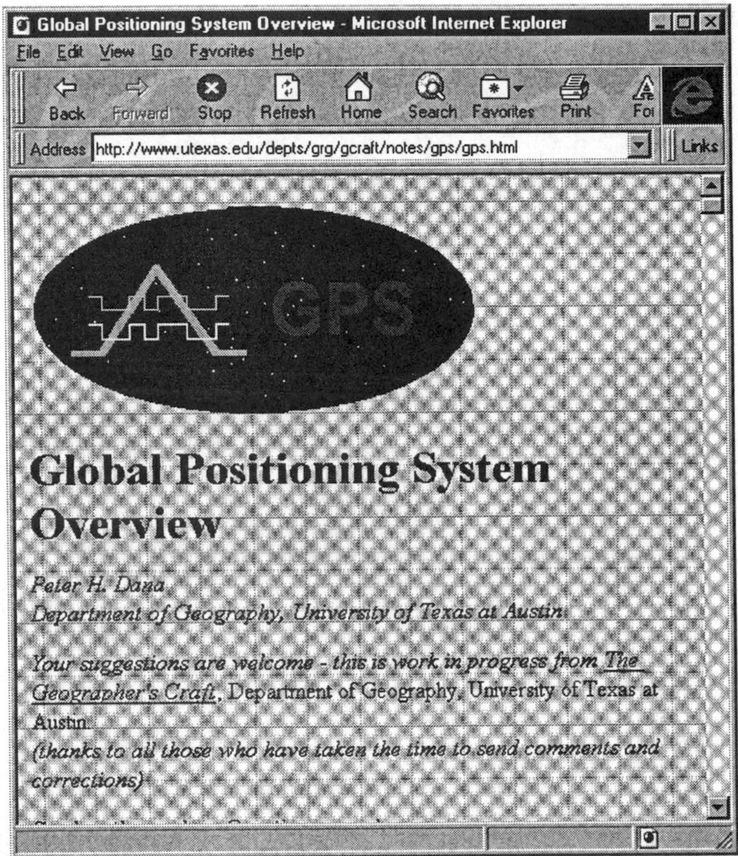

Figure 7.5 The Geographer's Craft: Global Positioning System Overview lesson

A good example of using the World Wide Web to distribute online class material is the Geographer's Craft, a geography class taught at the University of Texas-Austin. The Geographer's Craft project (**URL - http://wwwhost.cc.utexas.edu/ftp/pub/grg/gcraft/contents.html**) is a teaching initiative under development by the Department of Geography at the University of Texas-Austin to improve the teaching of geographical techniques. Funded by a National Science Foundation grant, the Geographer's Craft is a two-semester introductory-level class employing active-learning, problem-solving methods of instruction in a hypermedia environment and using the Internet to deliver many of the course materials.

The class takes an integrated, problem-oriented approach to teaching geographical techniques, drawing on cartography, geographic information systems, spatial analysis, remote sensing and field methods. Though the class meets for a conventional lecture, many of the supporting course materials are being developed as an online electronic textbook in the World Wide Web (Figure 7.5). Class lecture notes and study material can be accessed

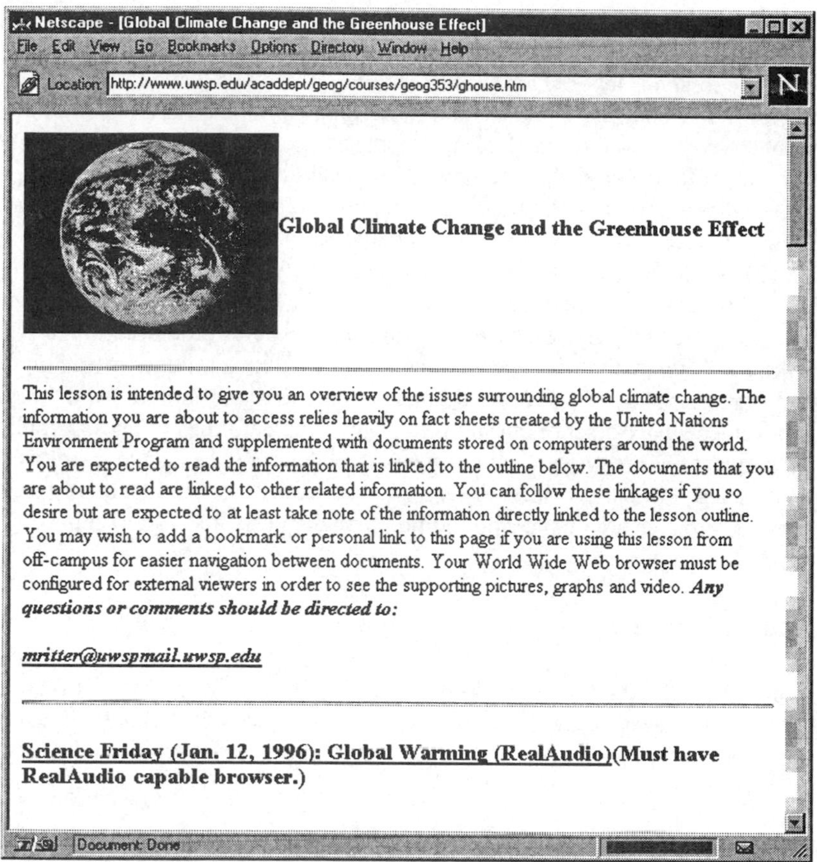
This lesson is intended to give you an overview of the issues surrounding global climate change. The information you are about to access relies heavily on fact sheets created by the United Nations Environment Program and supplemented with documents stored on computers around the world. You are expected to read the information that is linked to the outline below. The documents that you are about to read are linked to other related information. You can follow these linkages if you so desire but are expected to at least take note of the information directly linked to the lesson outline. You may wish to add a bookmark or personal link to this page if you are using this lesson from off-campus for easier navigation between documents. Your World Wide Web browser must be configured for external viewers in order to see the supporting pictures, graphs and video. ***Any questions or comments should be directed to:***

mritter@uwspmail.uwsp.edu

Science Friday (Jan. 12, 1996): Global Warming (RealAudio)(Must have RealAudio capable browser.)

Figure 7.6 Online Global Climate Change and the Greenhouse Effect lesson

from the "Notes and Study Materials" **page (URL - http://wwwhost.cc.utexas.edu/ftp/pub/grg/gcraft/notes/notes.html**). Students are provided with online warm-up exercises **(URL - http://wwwhost.cc.utexas.edu/ftp/pub/grg/gcraft/warmup/contents.html)** as well. These are designed to introduce students to various technologies employed throughout the course (electronic mail, the World Wide Web, Geographic Information Systems software, etc.). For instance, a 3D modeling exercise of Greytown, Nicaragua, is used to familiarize students with 3D modeling techniques, camera views and flyby animation using MicroStation. After a brief description of the site, with an accompanying full-color map of the region, step-by-step instructions on how to create various 3D renderings and flyby animation are given. All materials from the Geographer's Craft project are free to copy and use for educational purposes so long as the source of the material is credited.

In some cases, earth science educators use online instruction to replace lectures that were conventionally delivered in a classroom setting. The home page of a "Global Climate

Change and Greenhouse Effect" "lecture" is shown in Figure 7.6. The lecture was typically delivered over two 50-minute sessions, but now it is left to students to complete on their own time. The lesson is laid out in outline form. First, students listen to a debate over the issue of global warming and climate change, originally broadcast as a National Public Radio program and now archived on the Internet. Students navigate through the material by clicking on an outline element and retrieving the material from the Internet. A great majority of the material that makes up the lesson is contained in fact sheets provided by the United Nations Environment Program, while additional sources scattered throughout the world have been linked in. Students are required to read and study the material that is directly linked to a particular outline element. In many cases the retrieved information contains hyperlinks to related information. Even though students are not required to read the second-order links and beyond, they are encouraged to do so. The natural inclination on the part of most students is to follow the additional links out of curiosity, if nothing else. At the end of the lesson students have a set of questions to answer and activities to perform online. Answers to questions are written online and electronically mailed to the instructor. For my classes I read and grade the written assignments within my electronic mail program and send them back to students. Papers don't pile up on the desk, and I can keep a copy of all assignments turned in to me.

Online Field Trips

The online world of the Internet breaks down the barriers of distance to permit us to "go" to places that we may never have the chance to visit. As described in Chapter 2, earth scientists are using the Internet to electronically travel to distant places to learn about their world. Virtual field trips

- can be taken at any time and in any weather, as many times as one likes
- can be linked together to provide comparisons
- overcome the impediment of physical space and let the user examine the landscape in ways not otherwise possible
- enable site information to be linked with reference or related materials at some other location to provide greater depth of learning and exploration
- allow activities similar to a real field trip to be built into or simulated with a virtual field trip

The Indian Peaks virtual field trip "walks" the user through a portion of the Indian Peaks section of the Colorado Front range (**URL - http://www.uwsp.edu/acaddept/geog/project/gravft/1pvft/index.htm**) (Figure 7.7). Users begin their journey by first gaining some background knowledge of the physical setting of the region prior to starting the field trip. Users navigate by clicking numbered site "hot spots" on a map, which links them to stops along the way. From a site page, users either navigate directly to the next stop or return to the field trip map to jump to other sites.

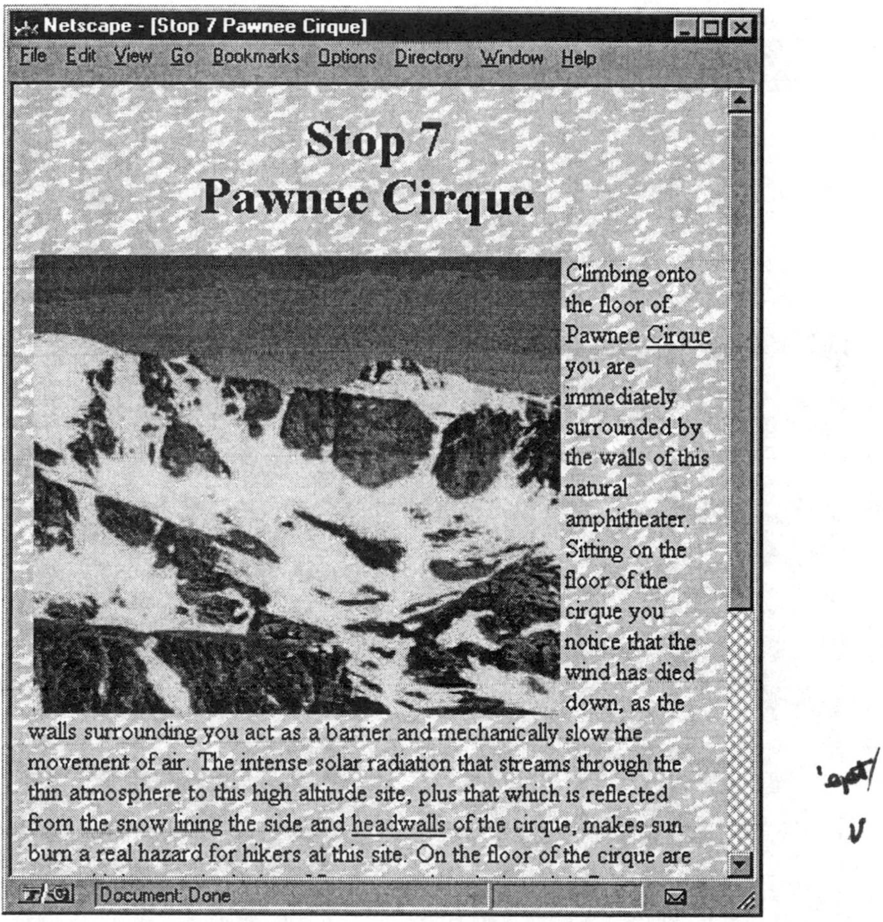

Figure 7.7 Pawnee Cirque stop along the Indian Peaks virtual field trip

A site field trip site page contains a brief description of the physical environment at that stop. Hyperlinks to more in-depth information are provided. Clicking the "cirque" hyperlink in Figure 7.7 retrieves the document shown in Figure 7.8. A color air photograph shows Pawnee Cirque from a different visual perspective, one not available on an actual field trip. At the bottom of the site page is a text field for notes and answers to questions asked about the site. The notes are submitted and archived to a log file. The electronic field journal can be printed out or emailed to the user or to a teacher for grading. If you don't have access to a field site such as this, you can still produce a virtual field trip from resources located on the Internet. There are numerous image archives scattered throughout the Net to draw on. NASA, the USGS, and NOAA are good starting points to find images. A virtual field trip to the northwestern United States can be assembled by linking resources at such sites as the Volcano Observatory, LTER's HJ Andrews Web site, and Web resources provided by

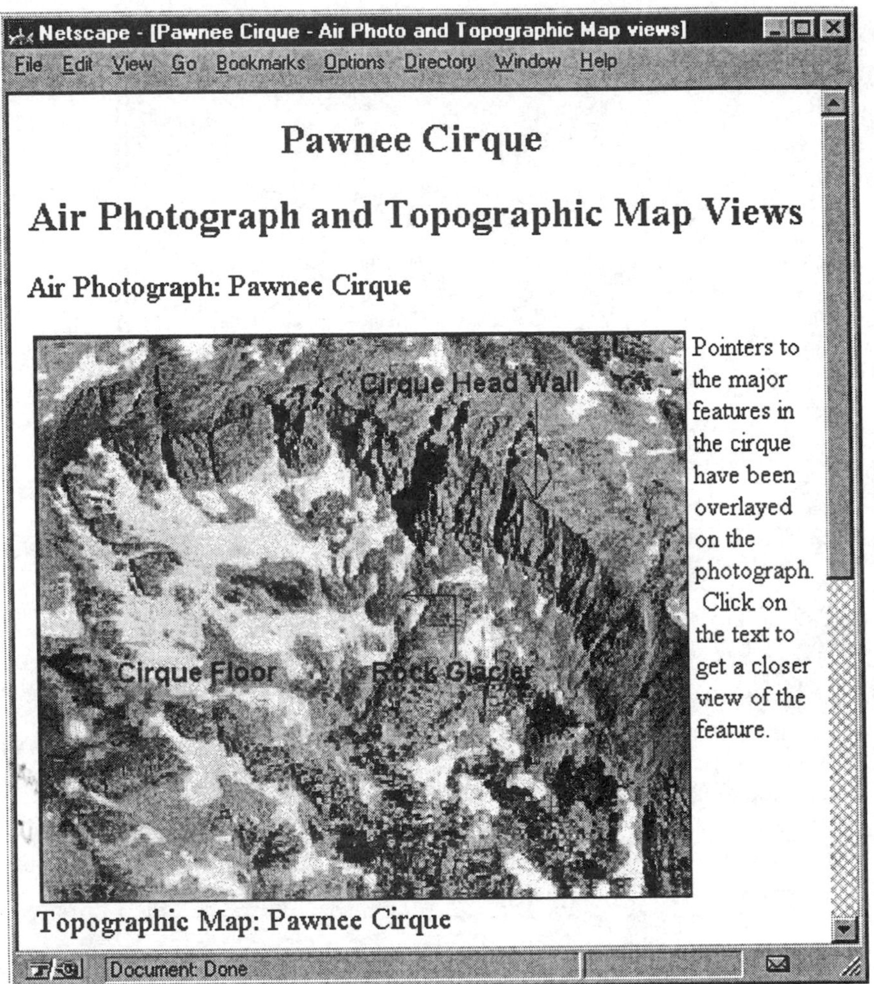

Figure 7.8 Aerial view of Pawnee Cirque

particular states in the region. You do have to rely on others for the availability of materials presented in this way. Your materials might disappear unexpectedly, so try to secure the right to download images to your own server to mount your field trip.

Collaborative Learning

Educators find the Internet a useful tool for collaborative learning. Collaborative learning on the Internet takes several different forms. Electronic mail discussion groups are used to exchange and debate ideas related to course content. Instructors post a weekly discussion topic on the class email list for all to respond to. The mail list can be private for class participants or open to the general public. The advantage of opening to the general public is the addition of points of view from outside the group. Other students or professionals working in the discipline can be drawn into the discussion, enriching the learning environment. The disadvantage is the potential for crank messages totally unrelated to the discussion.

Group projects have another route of communication between members with electronic mail. The successful completion of a group project requires discussion and exchange of ideas about group member roles and contributions to the project. Students often have difficulty finding time when all members can meet to work on their project. The asynchronous nature of electronic mail communication, discussed in Chapter 3, enables students to keep in closer contact. Members meet online to discuss issues by electronic mail. Group members can share portions of their project documentation for examination and critique by attaching it to an email message.

Geographers at Radford University combine electronic mail, the World Wide Web and other Internet resources in learning about international environmental issues. During the semester students work on a group project that follows an environmental problem from its proximate causes to its extended consequences and possible solutions. Students search the Internet to find information relevant to their topic and place hyperlinks to them on a group Web page. Students from other groups are required to read the information provided on the page and submit three questions that the group can address during its final presentation.

Professional Activities and the Internet Earth Science Community

Information Discovery and Data Archive Resources

One of the most important uses of the Internet is sharing data. Researchers in the Internet community are creating interactive Internet resource sites that enable users to extract and manipulate their data online. A perfect example of this is the Cornell Middle East and North Africa Project **(URL - http://www.geo.cornell.edu/geology/me_na/main.html)**. The researchers' objective has been to collect and organize all available seismological, geophysical, and geological data sets for the Middle East and North Africa into a digital information system that is accessible via the Internet. At their Profile Maker Web site **(URL - http://www.geo.cornell.edu/geology/me_na/profile_maker/profile_maker.html)** users extract data and generate cross-section maps by filling out an online data configuration form (Figure 7.9). Drop-down lists guide the user through the data types and format. The data sets are available for download too.

After the configuration form is submitted, the profile is displayed on screen (Figure 7.10). Options for retrieval of the plot in postscript or GIF format are available, as is elevation and depth data for three variables: topography elevation, basement depth, and moho depth.

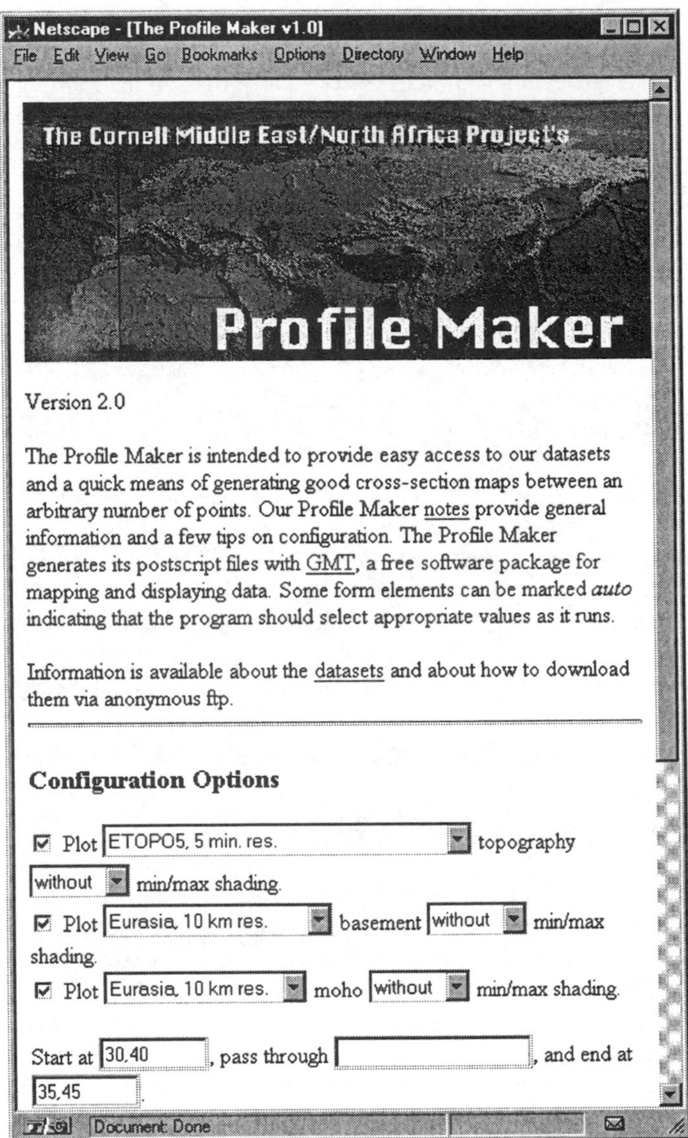

Figure 7.9 Middle East and North Africa Project Profile Maker data access form

Grant Writing Information

Grant writing is an important task for many professional earth scientists. Organizations like the National Science Foundation (NSF) are using the Internet to help you along in this process. NSF's World Wide Web home page (**URL - http://www.nsf.gov/**) is a compendium

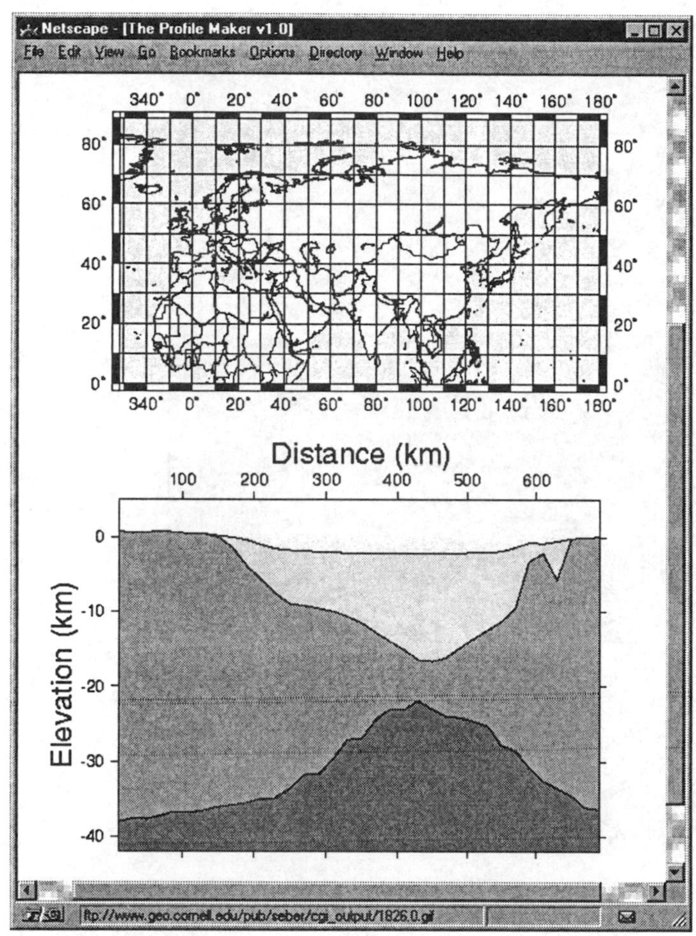

Figure 7.10 Output from Middle East and North Africa Project Profile Maker

of online resources for the grant writer (Figure 7.11). Information on programs, grant deadlines and recent grant awards is available. Manuals and reference guides for writing NSF grants can be read online. There are even grant forms (e.g., summary budget sheets, project descriptions, biographical sketches) that can be completed online. You can download a forms kit in Word for Windows format for offline completion too.

Most government agencies provide access to grant information from their World Wide Web home pages or Gopher sites. The U.S. Environmental Protection Agency **(URL - http://www.epa.gov/OER/)** provides a variety of online information about funding opportunities for academics, small businesses, and professional geoscientists. Information on contact phone numbers, email addresses, application procedures and submission deadlines is available online.

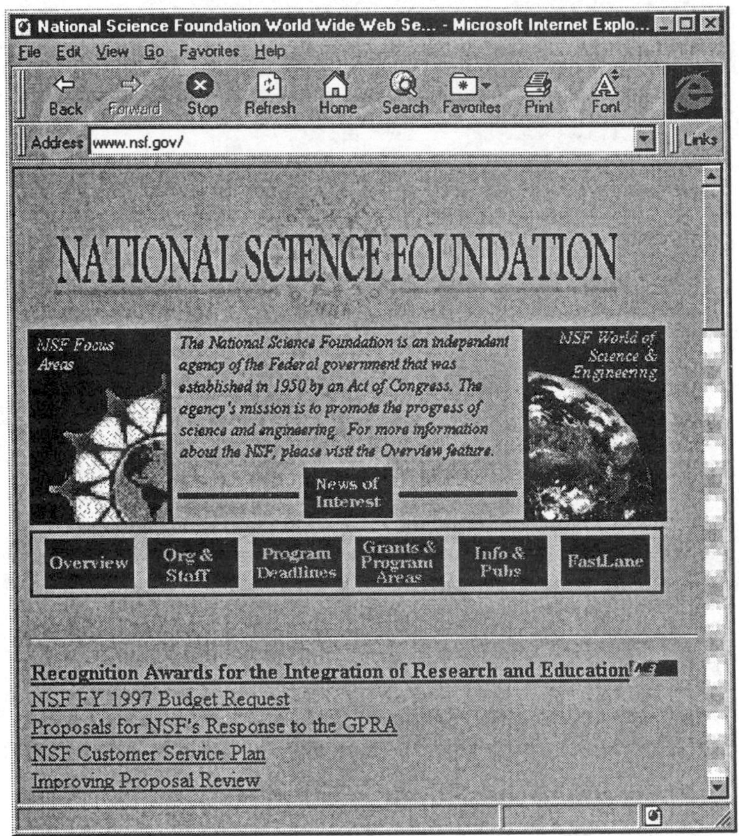

Figure 7.11 National Science Foundation home page

The Grants Web (**URL - http://infoserv.rttonet.psu.edu/gweb.htm**) home page links users to a variety of funding sources and agencies. Links to agency grant and researcher guides are particularly useful. Grants Web links you to grant databases like the National Science Foundation.

The Community of Science Web server (**URL - http://cos.gdb.org/**) helps you identify research contacts and funding opportunities and provides links to several funding agencies. The Community of Science maintains a database of 50,000 first-person expertise descriptions, a 5,000-record database of inventions, and a 2,000-record database of facilities records for you to search.

Professional Organization Home Pages and Gophers

Professional organizations find the Internet a useful way of keeping their members abreast of the latest developments in their field. Professional societies like the Geological Society of

Figure 7.12 Geobyte home page of the American Association of Petroleum Geologists

America (**URL - http://www.aescon.com/geosociety/index.htm**) or the American Meteorological Society (**URL - http://atm.geo.nsf.gov:80/AMS/**) employ the Internet to:

- distribute information about the organization
- solicit new members
- distribute information about upcoming organization meetings
- distribute online abstracts and papers from conference proceedings
- conduct virtual conferences online
- distribute employment information
- make learning resources available to the education community
- provide links to Internet resources of interest to their members

The American Association of Petroleum Geologists has posted the "Geobyte" home page (**URL - http://www.geobyte.com/**) for its members and others interested in petroleum exploration geology (Figure 7.12). Under the AAPG "Infoservices" hyperlink, Geobyte

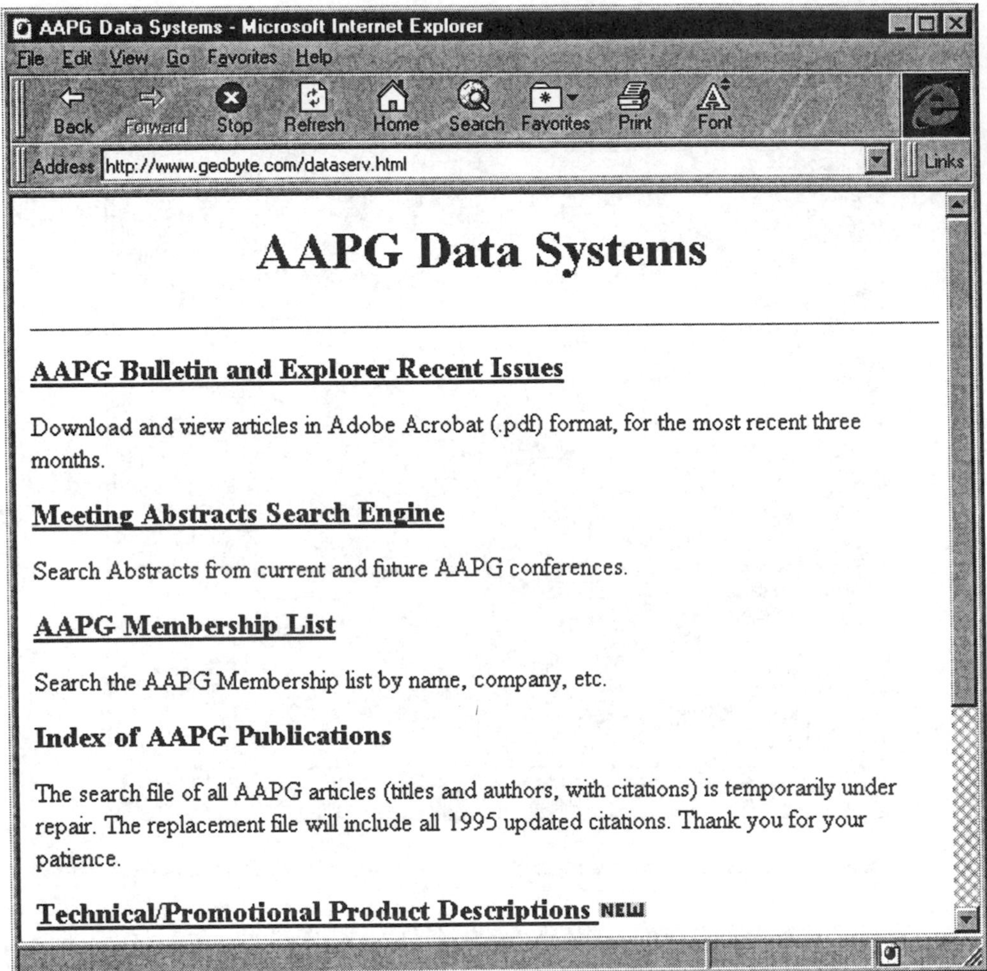

Figure 7.13 Geobyte Data Systems page

provides connections to information about the association and its activities, members and leadership. The "Data Systems" link provides access to data resources and services. Like most good sites, Geobyte offers a link to other Internet sites of interest to members of the exploration community. Choosing the "Data Systems" pick brings to screen a wealth of hyperlinks to AAPG information (Figure 7.13). At the top of the list is a link to the association's two journals, the Bulletin and Explorer. Pointing and clicking on the Bulletin and Explorer link brings up a page of links to recent editions of the journals. Clicking on the April 1996 Bulletin and Explorer link retrieves a page that lists full-text versions of the articles published in the journals (Figure 7.14). The April 1996 page lists each article by title and file name. Each of the files has a PDF extension telling us that it is in Portable

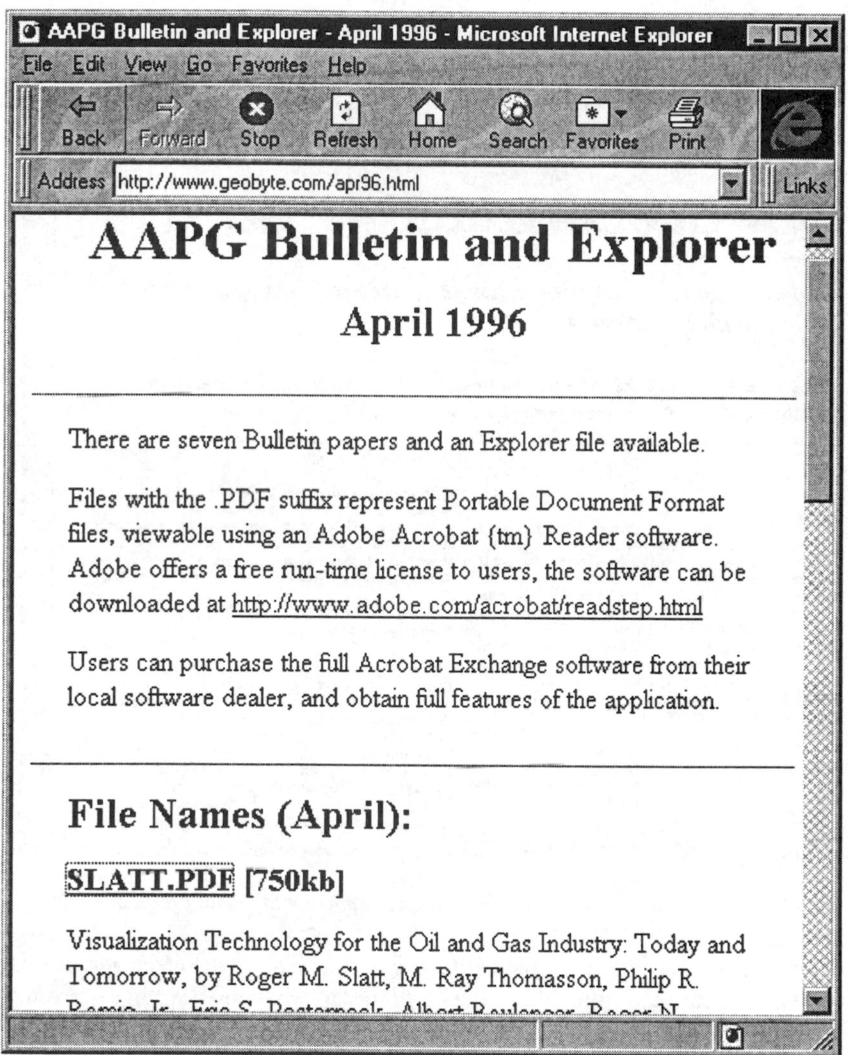

Figure 7.14 Geobyte AAPG Bulletin and Explorer page

Document File format and is meant to be read with the Adobe Acrobat reader. Adobe Acrobat is an electronic publishing program that permits the publisher to format the article much like a conventional print magazine, with graphics incorporated within the text. Many sites that use files in the Adobe Acrobat format will provide a link to download the program so you can view the files as noted on the AAPG Bulletin and Explorer page shown in Figure 7.14. Otherwise you can retrieve a copy of Adobe Acrobat from **URL - http://www.adobe.com/Software.html**. When I click on the highlighted KELLEY.PDF link, my browser downloads the file to my desktop computer and starts up the Adobe Acrobat reader

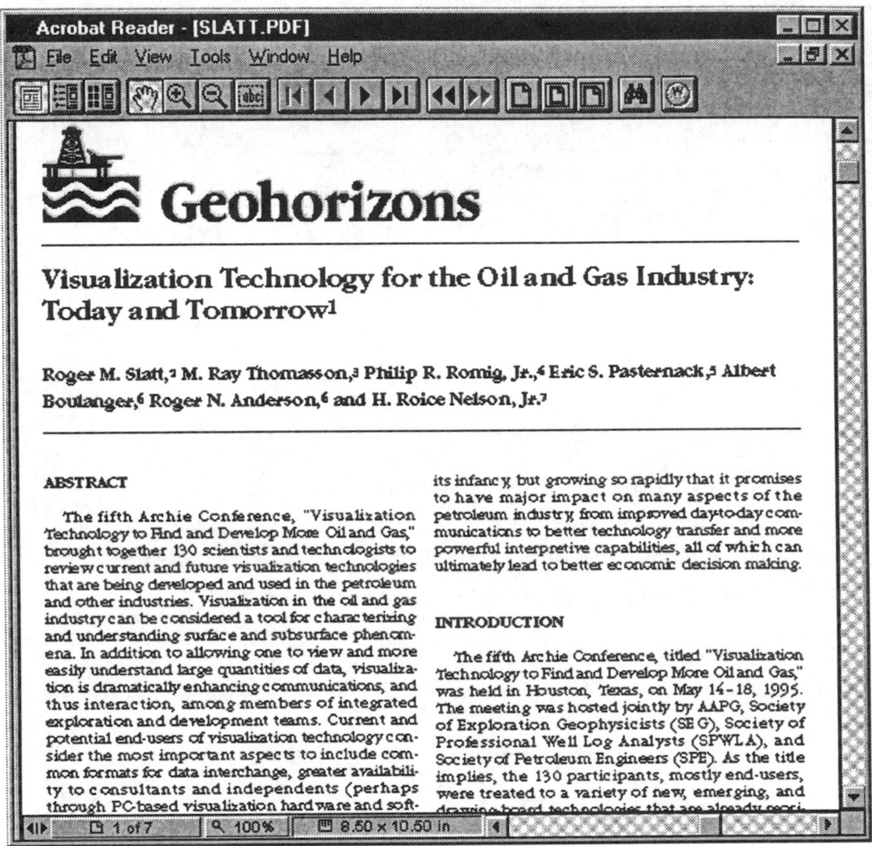

Geohorizons

Visualization Technology for the Oil and Gas Industry: Today and Tomorrow[1]

Roger M. Slatt,[2] M. Ray Thomasson,[3] Philip R. Romig, Jr.,[4] Eric S. Pasternack,[5] Albert Boulanger,[6] Roger N. Anderson,[6] and H. Roice Nelson, Jr.[7]

ABSTRACT

The fifth Archie Conference, "Visualization Technology to Find and Develop More Oil and Gas," brought together 130 scientists and technologists to review current and future visualization technologies that are being developed and used in the petroleum and other industries. Visualization in the oil and gas industry can be considered a tool for characterizing and understanding surface and subsurface phenomena. In addition to allowing one to view and more easily understand large quantities of data, visualization is dramatically enhancing communications, and thus interaction, among members of integrated exploration and development teams. Current and potential end-users of visualization technology consider the most important aspects to include common formats for data interchange, greater availability to consultants and independents (perhaps through PC-based visualization hardware and software) is in its infancy, but growing so rapidly that it promises to have major impact on many aspects of the petroleum industry, from improved day-to-day communications to better technology transfer and more powerful interpretive capabilities, all of which can ultimately lead to better economic decision making.

INTRODUCTION

The fifth Archie Conference, titled "Visualization Technology to Find and Develop More Oil and Gas," was held in Houston, Texas, on May 14-18, 1995. The meeting was hosted jointly by AAPG, Society of Exploration Geophysicists (SEG), Society of Professional Well Log Analysts (SPWLA), and Society of Petroleum Engineers (SPE). As the title implies, the 130 participants, mostly end-users, were treated to a variety of new, emerging, and

Figure 7.15 AAPG Explorer article viewed with Adobe Acrobat reader program

program, which loads the file for viewing. Figure 7.15 shows the electronic format of the article, with figures and figure descriptions similar to what you have in a conventional print-style journal. Adobe Acrobat preserves the formatting of the original text and figure placement and description.

Professional Conferences

Chapter 3, "Communicating over the Internet," demonstrated how efficient and effective communication can be over the Internet. The Internet is recognized by professional organizations and their members as a time-saving and cost-effective way to organize and conduct conferences and workshops. Organizing these activities is a time-consuming process, from the announcement of a conference to the convening of participants. Internet services like email, listservs, Usenet groups, and the Web expedite the organizational process.

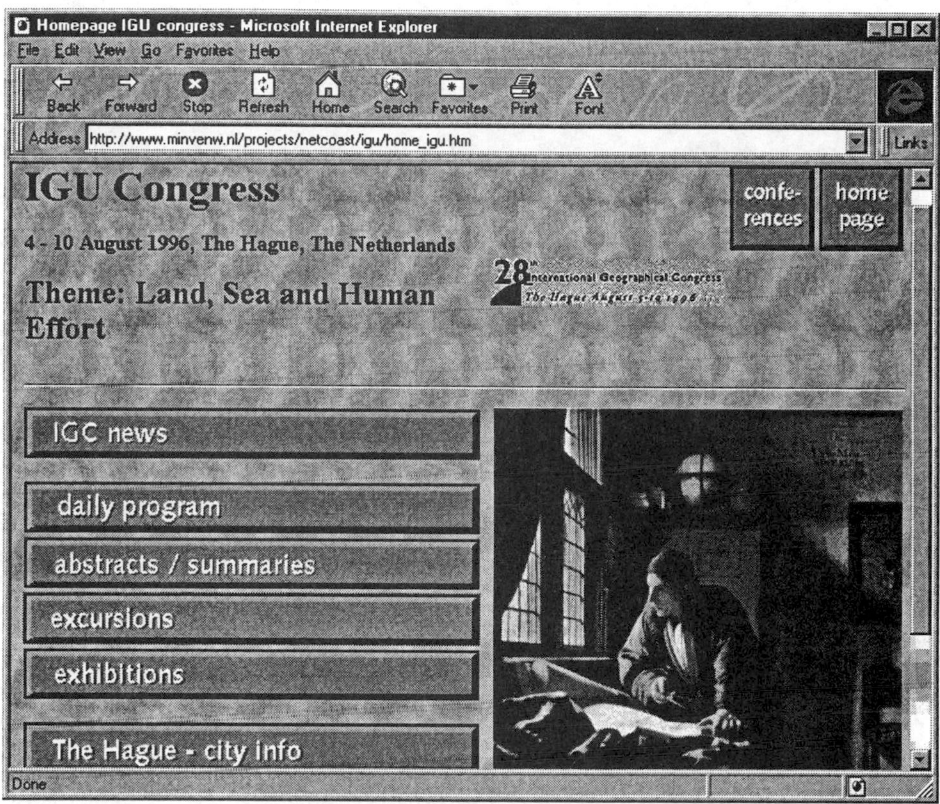

Figure 7.16 International Geographical Union home page

Because announcing a conference or workshop in published advertisements or mailing circulars to interested parties is expensive, professional organizations have turned to email listservs and Usenet groups as a way of getting the word out. Email listservs and Usenet groups target particular audiences that are interested in the theme of a conference. Electronic mail makes it easy to cross-post one message to several groups for conferences or workshops that garner interest from diverse groups of professionals like earth scientists. Email announcement of conferences should always include an email *and* surface mail contact address. Conference participation forms can be included as a part of the posting or as an attached file. Announcing a conference via the World Wide Web can be particularly effective. The International Geographical Union home page (**URL - http://www. anaximander.nl/igucge.htm**) is a noteworthy example (Figure 7.16).

The IGU provides links to all important conference information like the daily program, list of sessions, registration procedures and social events. Conference abstracts and summaries are available for downloading, and participants can register for field excursions online.

The American Geophysical Union, like many other organizations, provides electronic fill-in participation forms. The program participant simply fills in the required information in online form fields and clicks a button at the bottom of the page to send it off to the central office for processing. Some users do not have forms-compatible software, so it's a good idea to give participants the option of a form that can be printed off, with the information filled in manually and sent by surface mail.

Many conference organizers now are asking participants to submit their conference abstracts in digital form on computer diskette. Abstracts in digital form are easily attached to email messages, avoiding the expense of mailing diskettes and possibly losing them in the mail. The digital form also benefits those who procrastinate in turning in abstracts. Having abstracts in digital form enables the conference organizers to archive them on a World Wide Web or Gopher server for participants to review before or after the conference. For those participating in specially organized paper sessions, the session organizer can send copies of the abstracts to the other participants for review and possibly revision prior to delivery at the conference. These Internet tools open a communication line to many more individuals, a global community, that cannot be accomplished through conventional ways.

Professional organizations are providing abstracts or an electronic version of conference proceedings for viewing by the public like that found at the Geobyte home page discussed earlier. Hypertext Web documents of abstracts or the presented paper have many advantages over a conventional paper-bound copy. Hypertext linkages to video or sound files to embellish the presentation are possible. Embedded electronic mail links enable readers to send comments directly to the author(s) without having to use other software or modes of communication to create and send their message. Linkages to other relevant research or to bibliographic citations are possible as well.

The "virtual conference" is gaining favor as a way of convening a conference to exchange ideas without having to bring attendees to a central location. Imagine no more rushing to overheated conference rooms with poor lighting and inefficient audio/video capabilities. The fact that paper presentations can be visited at any time, on any day, is a major advantage to conducting a conference on the Internet. Shrinking budgets are making it more difficult for professionals to keep abreast of current research in their chosen fields or to attend meetings. Virtual conferences eliminate housing and transportation expenses (and lost luggage!). Virtual conferences have been mounted using a variety of Internet services and technology. The World Wide Web and electronic mail are two services that have been effectively employed to conduct a virtual conference. Virtual conferences conducted over the Internet cast a much wider net (pardon the pun) over those who can participate and interact. Multimedia paper presentations often require various hardware devices like videotape, laser discs, and CD-ROM with large screen displays for adequate viewing. Control over the pacing of the material is set by the presenter, who is under a time limitation in a conventional paper presentation. And poorly designed graphics can be difficult to read from the back of the room. But Web documents can link still images, video clips, sound files and so on to the document for readers to control at their own pace. Professional organizations are mounting virtual conferences using the World Wide Web as the means of delivering papers. Authors submit papers and other media files with instructions for hyperlinking to the organizers who created the hypermedia documents. Papers submitted in ASCII text format can be easily converted to hypertext. As noted in the previous paragraph, Web documents are an effective way of delivering conference papers because they can include embedded links to media that may not be particularly easy to use in a conventional setting. Virtual conference "attendees" pay a registration fee for the conference, which permits them to join in an email discussion list for the conference. Electronic mail discussion lists prove valuable because they can potentially draw in many more people than is possible during a conventional paper session. Even "timid" conference attendees are more likely to post a message to the list or at least to the author of the paper than they would be if they were in a conventional session. Nonregistered attendees are not permitted access to the discussion list but can still view the research papers.

University Departments on the Internet

Earth-science-related university departments are using the Internet to conduct their business. A department's business goes beyond that of educating its students. An academic department provides special services to the rest of the academic community, such as offering consulting services or housing special library collections. It must keep its university community, and especially its administration, aware of activities going on in the department. In today's world of budget de-allocations and entrenchment departments must demonstrate their significance to the mission of their institution. Departments provide outlets for the publication of professional research papers prepared by their faculty. Publishing an occasional paper series is a means of sharing the results of research projects with colleagues. For example, the University College of London geography department has uploaded several papers to their Gopher server for students, faculty and others to download and read.

Faculty members must advise students as to how they can meet their academic and professional goals. Students must be kept apprised of their academic progress and informed of the requirements of the job market once they graduate. In addition, the vitality of an academic program requires a constant influx of students to replace those who are graduating. New majors conventionally come to a program by word of mouth or through promotional seminars or brochures. Earth science departments and those of related disciplines are using the Internet to attract students to their programs and advise them. These online educators realize the population of students that the Internet can reach and will increasingly do so. Posting information on the Internet about your program can get your message out to students on your campus and campuses scattered throughout the world and increasingly to high school students and guidance counselors.

There are a number of notable examples of how earth science and earth-science-related departments use the Internet for the various activities outlined above. A good starting point is at the University of Wisconsin-Stevens Point's Department of Geography and Geology

Figure 7.17 University of Wisconsin-Stevens Poing Geography/Geology home page

(Figure 7.17). The department uses its World Wide Web page to further most of the activities listed above. From the "Department" home page you can get information about the department and its programs. You can get a listing of faculty members with a description of their specialization from the "Faculty" page, which includes electronic mail connectivity from hyperlinks embedded in the page (Figure 7.18).

A particularly useful part of the department's Web page offerings is its program information pages. Information about the core classes for each major and links to the individual areas of concentration within the department are provided. Choosing the "Core

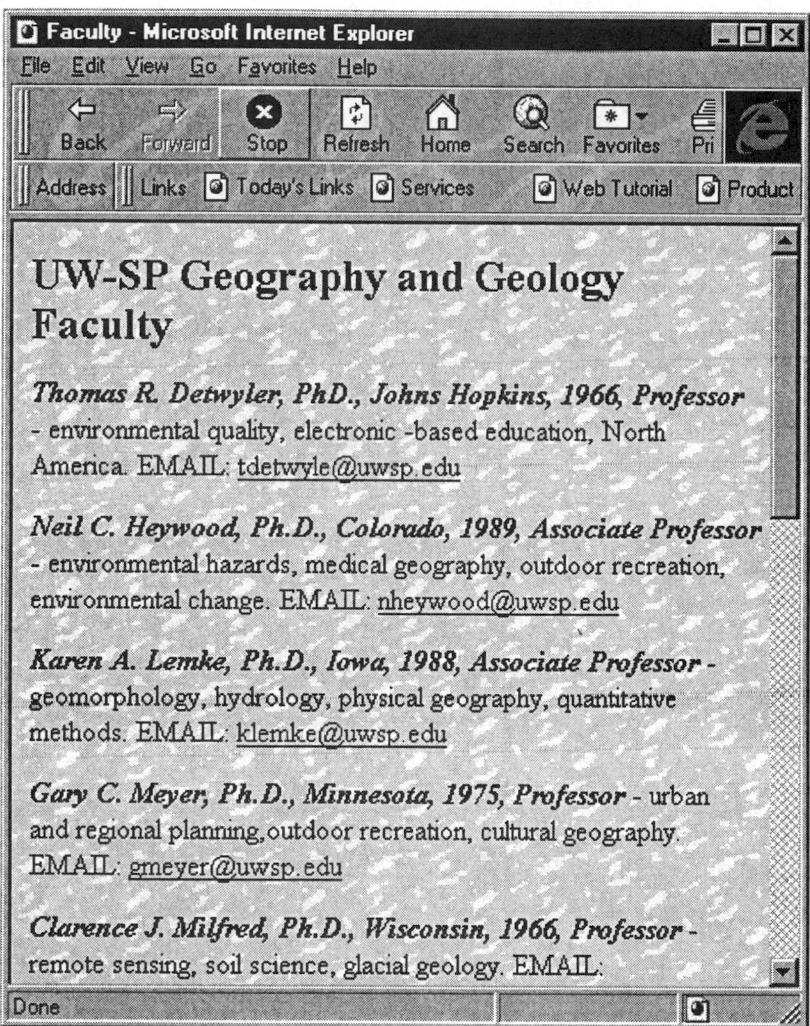

Figure 7.18 Online faculty directory

Courses" link on the programs page brings up a suggested academic plan for completion of the classes (Figure 7.19). Each of the classes listed is linked to a class description located on another hypertext document. When the class link is chosen the class description page is read into the browser and the class description is located and brought to the top of the screen for viewing. If there is a prerequisite class it's also linked to the appropriate class description.

Most departments like to keep their colleagues informed as to the goings-on in their department. Many departments use a "News" page to let the public know what's been happening in the department. Announcements of publications, paper presentations and

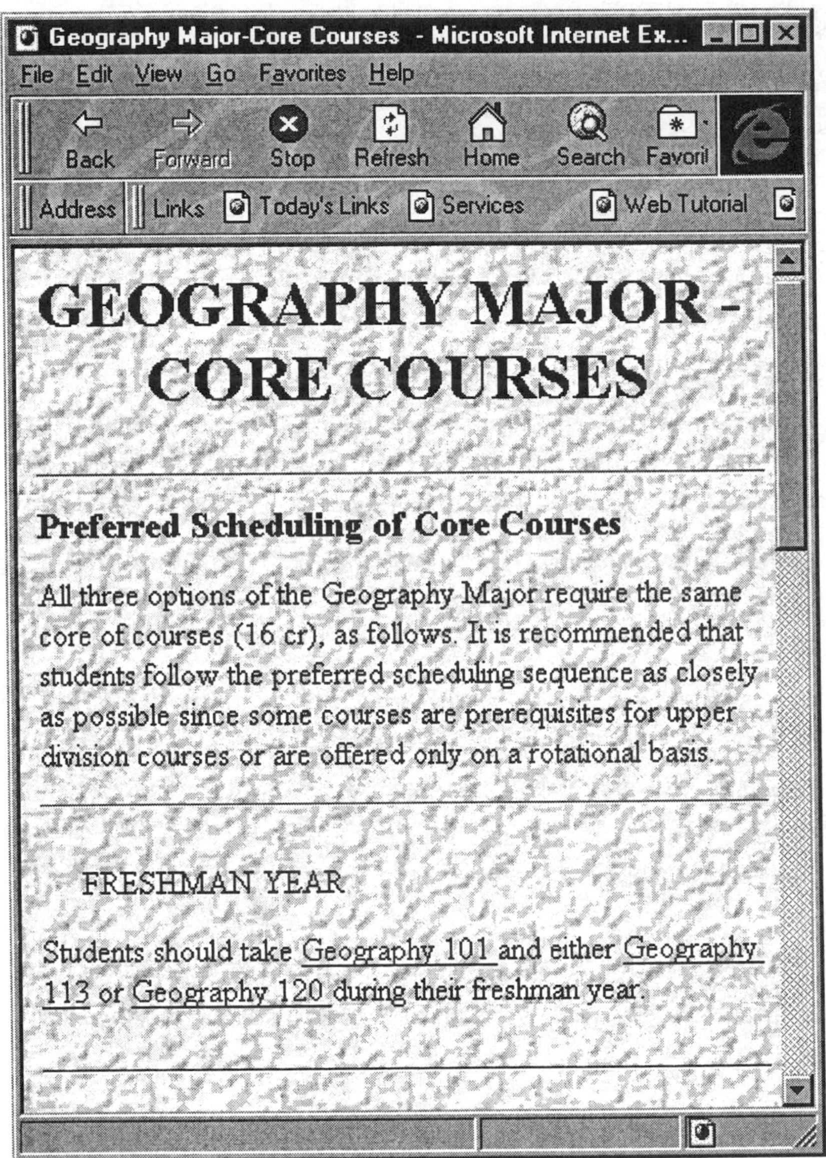

Figure 7.19 UW-SP Core Courses page

awards are made online. Names of the faculty published on the "News" page are hyperlinked back to the "Faculty" page if people are interested in finding out more about particular individuals and communicating with them via electronic mail. When announcing their participation in a conference, several members load copies of their paper abstracts online so that users can find out what the papers are about.

Collaborative Research and Information Dissemination over the Internet

The main reason for creating the World Wide Web, and the Internet itself, was to have a means for the scientific community to collaborate on research activities. The collision of the Shoemaker-Levey comet with the planet Jupiter serves as a fine example of how the Internet can be used for collaborative research. When the Shoemaker-Levy comet struck the surface of Jupiter the Internet was used to bridge the distance between remote observatories, research teams and laboratories (Beatty, 1994). Scientists at the University of Maryland were ready with a special electronic mail system that instantaneously distributed highlights from one researcher's observations to hundreds of anxiously awaiting scientists. The Comet-Impact Network Experiment, composed of researchers from the University of Arizona located at nine different observatories around the earth, continuously covered the event and used the Internet to keep its widely dispersed teams in constant contact with one another. In the winter darkness of Antarctica, the South Pole Infrared Explorer (SPIREX) had an ideal view of Jupiter's surface. A satellite-aided link to the Internet enabled the observing station to instantly transmit pictures back to the University of Illinois. By July 27, approximately two million images had been downloaded over the Internet from the Space Telescope Institute at NASA's Goddard Space Flight Center, the Jet Propulsion Laboratory and the European Southern Observatory in Germany by both ordinary citizens and scientists.

Career Information and Job Hunting

So you want to work in an earth-science-related field? The Internet can help you with that too. It won't get you the job, but at least it will make you aware of potential jobs and how to apply for them. Many government agencies, like the Earth System Science Division of NASA **(URL - http://wwwghcc.msfc.nasa.gov:5678/),** routinely put links to job announcements on their home pages. Companies are using the Internet to advertise upcoming job fairs and even sponsoring online job fairs. At these sites, companies provide employment opportunity information, corporate biographies, and contact information for those who can't be on-site visitors to actual job fairs. University home pages often contain links to job announcements and placement services. CareerMosaic **(URL - http://www.careermosaic.com/infoseek.html)** is a clearinghouse for job announcements on the Internet. Clearinghouses like these offer resume advising services, and some archive your resume in searchable databases.

How do you find out about a job without cruising all over the Internet? You can enter keywords into a search engine or use one of many career-related resource sites. For example, I queried the Lycos search engine with "employment earth science" and immediately found the announcement on the Earth System Science page described above. Usenet newsgroups and electronic mail discussion lists are another good place to look for job announcements. Look in discipline-specific groups as well as those devoted to announcing jobs. Don't hesitate to make your presence known on a newsgroup or discussion list. There may be someone out there looking for a person like you.

The Internet is a great place to post your resume, especially as a Web document. A lot of people are creating online resumes as a part of their personal home pages. Online World Wide Web resumes can include embedded pictures, sound and links to your references if they have electronic mail addresses. Publications and abstracts from professional presentations can be made available to potential employers. Don't forget to include your own electronic mail address as a part of your resume!

Managing Day-to-Day Duties with the Internet

Computer technology, we are told, holds the promise to seamlessly integrate and manage our day-to-day activities. The advent of computer software suites or software packages that integrate word processing, spreadsheet, database, personal information management and desktop publishing software was the first step in this process. These suites permit information to be shared, copied and pasted between programs as an integrated whole. Now the connectivity of computers over local, regional and global communications networks moves this process a giant step forward to permit sharing and integration of information between not just computer programs, but whole computer systems. This means that analog information transfer by hard copy (printed material or fax) can be supplanted by digital information transfer.

Digital Integration and the Paperless Office

The bane of many a professional's life is the ever increasing accumulation of paper in the form of newsletters, memoranda, student papers, research reports, and so on. Digital technology is helping to relieve this problem. As personal computers continue to appear in our offices and classrooms and networked computing grows, there are fewer reasons to communicate information in hard copy form. There are many more advantages to working in a paperless, digital environment than an analog one. Distribution of digital information is as quick and as reliable, for the most part, as conventional means of information distribution. Information in digital form can be easily searched, retrieved, edited and reproduced.

To see how digital information and the Internet can affect the way you conduct your business, consider some of your daily activities. As an academic my day usually begins with reviewing messages that have accumulated prior to my arriving at the office in the morning. Messages most likely were delivered through voice mail, interoffice mail, the postal service, fax or electronic mail. I must sift through them to prioritize them in the order I wish to respond. Voice mail requires that I listen to each message individually, not knowing the origin of the message prior to listening to it. If it originated from a faculty colleague with voice mail on my campus, the message might be preceded with a message header to alert me to its author. Interoffice memos usually have a header from which I can tell if they're important or not. Mail delivered by post has to be opened to view its contents and ascertain its significance. Electronic mail, however, has all this information provided up front and can be tagged by the author as a "special attention" message in need of a prompt reading and reply.

Each message I receive will probably require a response. Having access to digital technology and a computer network makes answering many of these messages much easier. Electronic mail messages can be easily sorted by importance (special attention messages), date and time, subject and so on based on the header information. The message is read online and responded to immediately from within the electronic mail program. After I type the response it is immediately forwarded to the recipient. No delay due to mailing or expense of postage is incurred. If the message gets lost, I have a digital copy that can be immediately re-sent. I can copy portions of the original message I received into my response to specifically address key points. If the message needs to be forwarded to other people, I can do so at the touch of a few keys or buttons. No paper is exchanged or left to accumulate on my desk. Electronic messages can be archived on diskette, taking up much less physical space than a folder of paper in a file cabinet.

Inevitably during the day memos concerning departmental matters or reminders of upcoming meetings must be sent to colleagues. Prior to the digital revolution a secretary or I had to type the memo, copy it, and deliver it for mailing. Now much of this correspondence can be done through electronic mail. Rather than typing this correspondence and sending out hard copies, wasting paper and money on copying, I open up my electronic mail program, create the memo and send it off to the required recipients. If special formatting of a document is required that can't be handled by email software, a word processing document can be attached to an email message. Recipients simply detach the document and load it into their compatible word processor. Mass mailings of information can be accomplished with electronic mail as well. Many email programs let you create special lists, or groups of people (actually their addresses) under one address. When you send a message to the group, the software recognizes the group name (address), looks up the addresses in the list, and mails the message to each member of the group.

Keeping in contact with students is important, from both an administrative and a personal standpoint. I like students to have as much interaction with me as possible, whether they are discussing problems with the class, asking for advice about their academic career, or simply wanting to discuss a point of interest having to do with earth science. Inevitably, my schedule and those of my students do not coincide with one another. I have made it a practice to introduce electronic mail and the Internet to all my students, be they freshman or senior. In so doing, I not only open their lives up to the online environment but also give them an additional means of keeping in contact with me. I create class electronic mail lists for posting announcements concerning changes to the class schedule, canceled classes, assignments, exam information, and exam grades. Students post messages to the list about upcoming events that are relevant to the class, such as seminars and speakers who are coming to campus, or recent news events dealing with topics discussed in class. I've created World Wide Web pages for each of my classes that include the class syllabus, supplemental online resources, and announcement pages. There is purposeful redundancy in the announcements placed in electronic mail as well as the Web pages. Most students check their email on a regular basis, so class announcements get to their mailboxes the day I create them. However, there is the possibility they may be deleted or delayed due to mail server problems. Having announcements archived on a class home page provides a "permanent" record of them for students to refer to.

Online submission of class assignments also is possible with digital technology and networked computers. Students who prepare written assignments with word processing software can save their work and attach it to an electronic mail message addressed to the instructor. The instructor detaches the assignment, imports it into a word processor, and reviews the assignment. The instructor can insert comments directly into the text of the assignment. Incorrect answers or suggested changes to the assignment can be highlighted in the document. Once the instructor grades the assignment it is attached to an electronic mail message and sent back to the student. The instructor can save the original document for comparison with any revised copy. Class worksheets and assignments can be set up as a form in a HTML document and kept on a Web server. The student uses a forms-readable Web browser to fill in the answer fields for each question. Upon completion of the answer sheet, the student clicks on a submit button and the answer sheet can be sent to the instructor's electronic mail address.

Publishing on the Internet

Professional and commercial organizations are recognizing that the Internet is an ideal place to publish online journals and books. Publishing on the Internet has many advantages over conventional print media. First is the timeliness of information. Print journals have a relatively long lag time between submission of an article and final publication. Article text and supporting graphic material are routinely created and submitted for publication in digital form to conventional print journals. With publication material already in digital form, it is easy to publish electronic journals. A major savings in paper, ink, and labor is incurred by publishing in digital form as well. The greatest benefit to all who publish is the potential global audience that can read and react to the published work.

Mounting publications on the World Wide Web is best because of the inherent advantages Web documents have. HyperText Markup Language has evolved to the point that there is little distinction between HTML and electronic publishing programs. Some versions of HTML support sophisticated formatting of graphics, text wrapping around images, a number of font styles, and equation formatting. Web documents can have decorative borders and backgrounds. Superimposed on all this are the navigation properties of hypertext and hypermedia. Multimedia capabilities offered by the Web permit authors to enrich their publications with visually stimulating graphics, as well as sound and video, which are not available with print media. Hyperlinking encourages exploration and enrichment of the material. Table 7.1 lists several earth science publications that distribute articles or abstracts over the Internet.

Table 7.1 Selected earth science publications with online abstracts and article titles

With Abstracts:	Geophysics (current) http://sepwww.stanford.edu/seg/GEOPHYSICS.html Journal of Seismic Exploration (1992-1995) gopher://jse.tn.tudelft.nl/11/JSE
With Article Titles:	Annales Geophysicae (1994) gopher://trick.ntp.springer.de/11/TOC/585/ Applied Spectroscopy Journal (January 1994-present) http://esther.la.asu.edu/sas/journal.html Bulletin Geodesique (1994) gopher://trick.ntp.springer.de:70/11/TOC/190/190-94 Bulletin of Volcanology (1994) gopher://trick.ntp.springer.de/11/TOC/445/ Geological Society of America Bulletin (current) http://www.aescon.com/geosociety/pubs/bulletin.htm Geology (current) http://www.aescon.com/geosociety/pubs/geology.htm Geotimes (current) gopher://jei.umd.edu:71/11/Geotimes/ Journal of Metamorphic Geology (current) http://www.gly.bris.ac.uk/www/jmg/press.html

Electronic publication on the Internet takes several forms. They can be published and disseminated over electronic mail, be published as Web or Gopher documents, or be available for download and offline reading. There are several good examples of earth-science-related electronic publications on the Internet. For example, EarthWorks **(URL - http://www.utexas.edu/depts/grg/eworks/eworks.html)** is a refereed journal that focuses on the concerns of contemporary geography (Figure 7.20). Manuscripts can be found in all areas of the discipline, particularly those that stress relationships between people and the environment in ecological and historical perspective. EarthWorks is an excellent example of an online journal that takes full advantage of the World Wide Web's hypermedia capabilities. Being a Web publication, the journal can include black-and-white and full-color illustrations, diagrams and maps, as well as sound clips, video clips and animation. Articles may link to other documents and data sources located on the Internet and Web.

The Electronic Green Journal **(URL - http://drseuss.lib.uidaho.edu:70/docs/egj.html)** (Figure 7.21) gets to a large audience by utilizing many different Internet services. The Electronic Green Journal is provided over the World Wide Web **(URL - http://www.lib.uidaho.edu/docs/egj.html)** through Gopher **(URL - gopher://gopher.uidaho.edu/11/UI_gopher/library/egj)** and by FTP **(URL - ftp://www.lib.uidaho.edu /pub/egj/)**. You

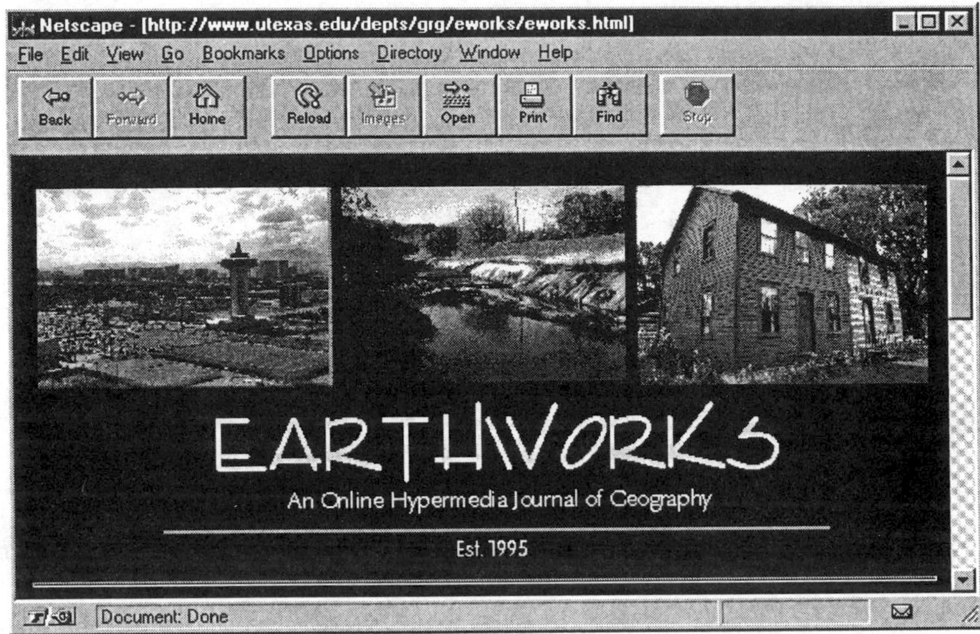

Figure 7.20 EarthWorks online journal

can subscribe to the journal via email by sending a message to **majordomo@uidaho.edu** with the following included in the body of the message:

subscribe egj <*Your email address.*>

Electronic publication raises professional development issues, however. Questions remain as to how peer-reviewed electronic publications compare to conventional peer-reviewed publications in the eyes of administrators when used for determining professional advancement. Not all administrators view them as equal, especially the technologically less inclined administrator. However, this will have to change as the digital information society permeates through our culture.

Each day new academic and professional uses are being implemented on the Internet. The use of the Internet by earth scientists is restricted only by our imagination. It is difficult at best to keep up with new additions to our online set of tools. Stop by the ***Earth Online*** Web site to help keep yourself informed of the ever changing online environment of the earth science internet community.

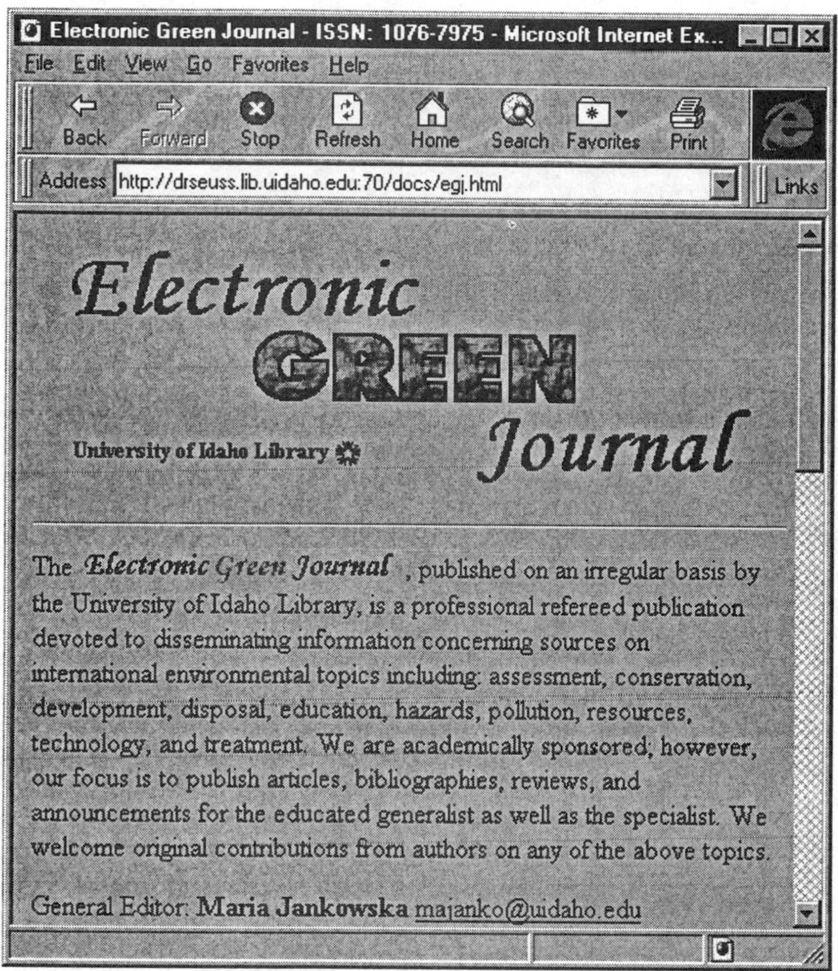

Figure 7.21 Electronic Green Journal home page

➤➤ Focus on the Internet: *The Virtual Geography Department*

A fine example of the use of the Internet for education and professional development is the Virtual Geography Department project "located" at the University of Texas-Austin. Among the goals of the Virtual Geography Department is to gather curricular materials for the classroom and the laboratory that can be used across the Internet and the World Wide Web by geography students and faculty at any university. The Virtual Geography Department project seeks to develop new types of online instruction and publications that promote collaborative research. The Virtual Geography Department uses the distributed nature of the

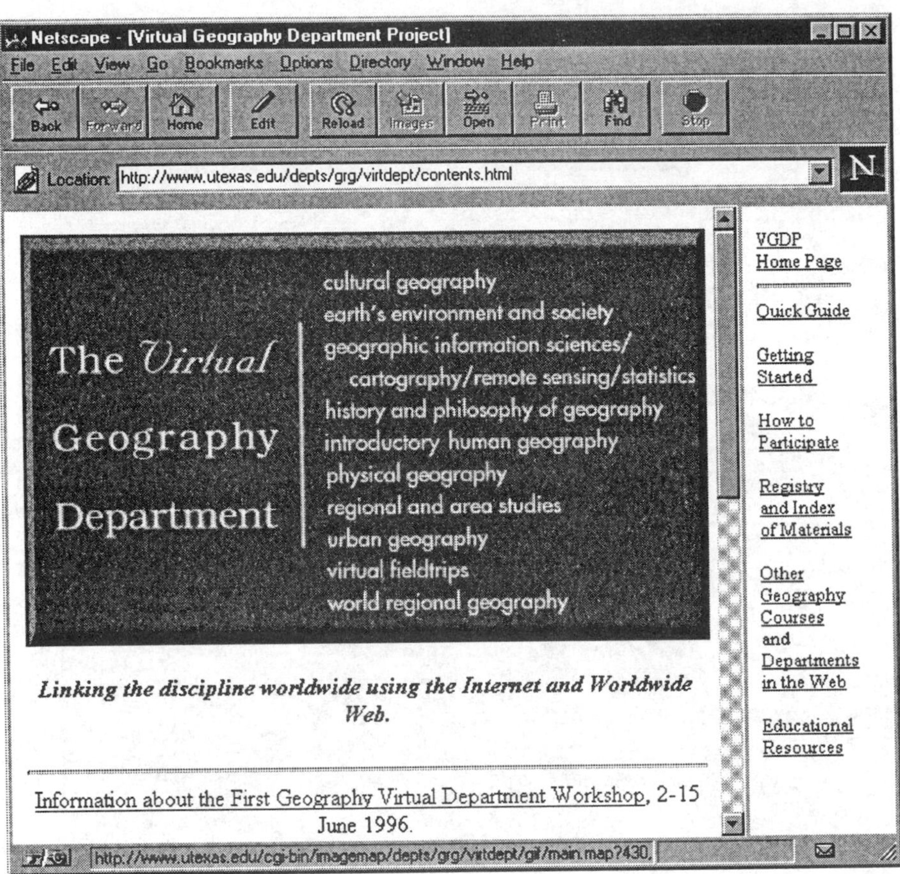

Figure 7.21 Virtual Geography Department home page

Internet to provide access to a wide variety of materials to geographers and nongeographers alike. The Virtual Geography Department project is a virtual "clearinghouse" of geographic materials. The project does not archive materials at a central location. Rather, users obtain access to the materials from Virtual Geography Department home pages. The various project pages serve as links to information located on other servers scattered throughout the world. Project materials have been created by the Virtual Department project team and provided by nonproject contributors.

The project team has taken great strides toward meeting its objectives. Those opening up the Virtual Geography Department home page (**URL - http://www.utexas.edu/depts/grg/virtdept/contents.html**) (Figure 7.22) will find a number of links to resources for teaching, learning and conducting geographic research. For instance, a stop at the "Departments" page gives you access to numerous home pages and Gopher sites for geography departments around the world. The "Online Course" page (**URL - http://www.utexas.edu/depts/grg/**

virtdept/courses/courselist.html) provides links to online class materials mounted by geographers around the world. The various online classes offer everything from lecture notes, sample exam questions, and exercises to virtual field trips. For, example, EarthWorks, which was cited earlier, recently debuted as a refereed journal addressing contemporary issues in geography. Articles cover areas of geography with special emphasis on people-environment relationships in an ecological or historical context. Feature sections in the journal include:

- The Gallery, where potential uses of hypermedia are demonstrated
- Lecture Hall, which emphasizes the application of hypermedia in education
- In Conference, which features papers from conferences and conference proceedings
- Web in Review, which critiques online resources
- Looking Ahead, which features articles and commentary on future applications of hypermedia, the Internet, and the World Wide Web in geography

The Geography Virtual Department is a good start toward integrating hypermedia technologies into geography. As virtual departments like these grow, their connectivity via the Internet will greatly enhance the sharing of ideas and information for understanding the dynamics of the earth system.

What You Have Learned

- Computer-mediated communication and learning is an effective way for delivering educational material
- Online learning is active learning.
- Electronic communication is a valuable way to stay in contact with students and colleagues. Electronic mail is a useful tool for the submission of class assignments and online discussions.
- Online class information is a good way to keep students informed.
- The Internet is a useful tool for professional organizations to keep in contact with their members and distribute materials (conference information, journal publications, newsletters) to them.
- Career information abounds on the Internet. The Internet can be an effective way to link employers with potential employees (e.g., online job announcements and job fairs, online resumes).

Apply It!

The Internet was created for the purpose of transferring and providing access to archived information. The most complete source of information about our earth lies in the hands, or computers, of a number of government agencies. Government agencies under the direction

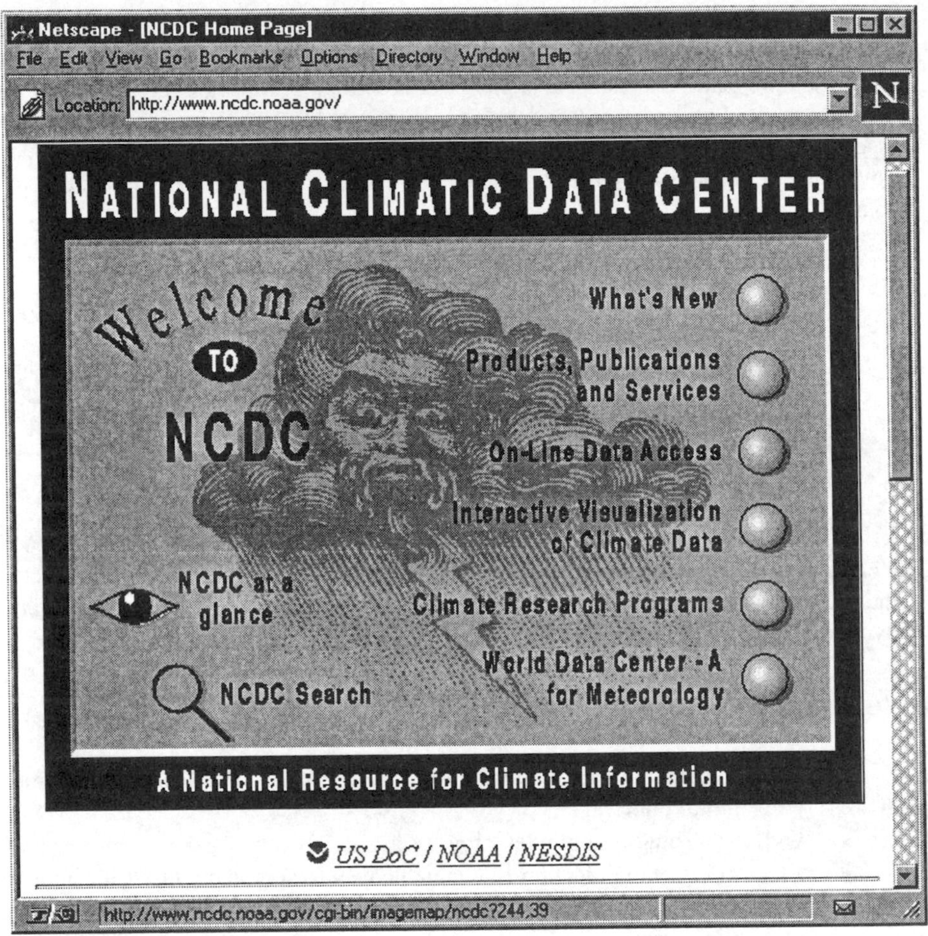

Figure 7.23 National Climate Data Center home page

of the United States Congress and the president are making their storehouses of data available in digital form. Sites whose purpose is to interactively dispense information are turning to the World Wide Web as their main interface with the public. In this section we will look at how climate change data is being disseminated across the Internet.

The National Climatic Data Center (**URL - http://www.ncdc.noaa.gov/**) is a key data management department within the NOAA charged with acquiring and archiving data in support of programs involved in remotely sensed and in situ meteorological and climatological research (Figure 7.23). The NCDC provides online access to a wealth of information (data, software, and publications) for the public and research communities. It maintains an "Interactive Visualization of Climate Data" page (**URL - http://www.ncdc.noaa.gov/homepg/interprod.html**). At this page users choose between the Global Climate

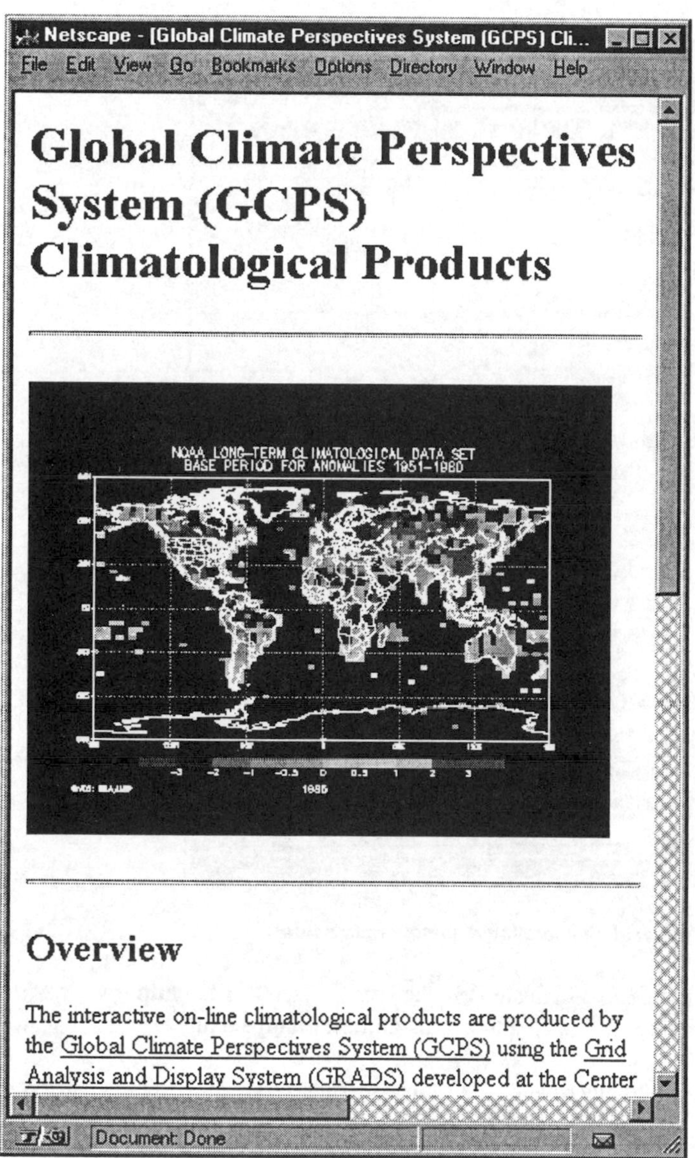

Figure 7.24 NCDC Global Climate Perspectives System online products

Perspectives System (Figure 7.24), which provides access to interactive visualization of gridded data sets, or Climate Visualization (CLIMVIS) interactive visualization of varied-point data. With CLIMVIS time series, contour and vector visualizations can be constructed from Global Summary of the Day, First Order Summary of the Day, and the Climate Division Drought data. Some records date back to the 1860s.

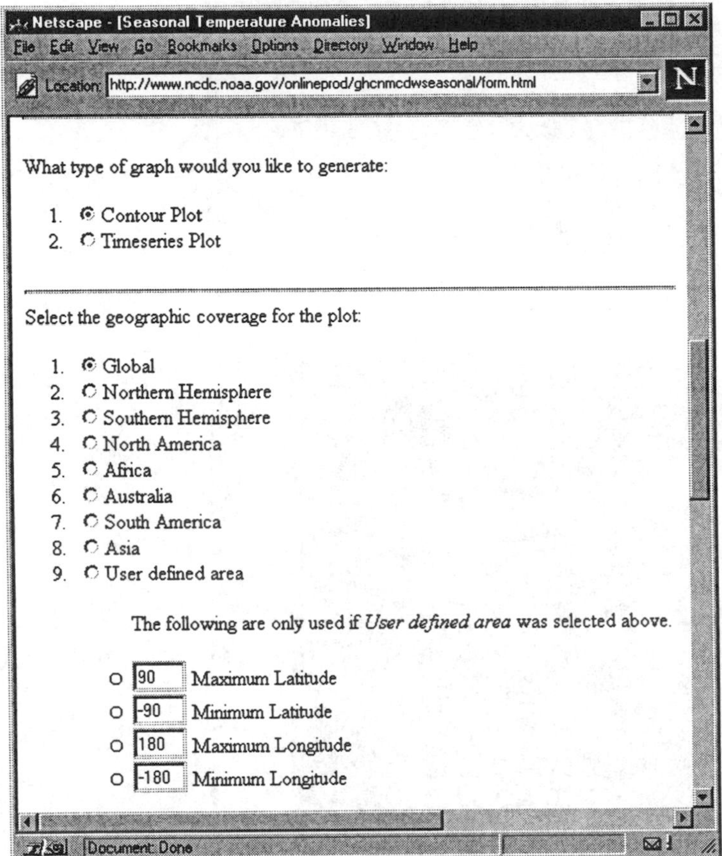
Netscape - [Seasonal Temperature Anomalies]

File Edit View Go Bookmarks Options Directory Window Help

Location: http://www.ncdc.noaa.gov/onlineprod/ghcnmcdwseasonal/form.html

What type of graph would you like to generate:

1. Contour Plot
2. Timeseries Plot

Select the geographic coverage for the plot:

1. Global
2. Northern Hemisphere
3. Southern Hemisphere
4. North America
5. Africa
6. Australia
7. South America
8. Asia
9. User defined area

The following are only used if *User defined area* was selected above.

- 90 Maximum Latitude
- -90 Minimum Latitude
- 180 Maximum Longitude
- -180 Minimum Longitude

Document: Done

Figure 7.25 NCDC Seasonal Temperature Anomalies page form

I'm choosing the Global Climate Perspectives System (**URL - http://www.ncdc.noaa.gov/onlineprod/prod.html**) link first to access climate change data.

Scrolling down the page reveals the following data sets:

NOAA Baseline Climatological Dataset
Seasonal and Annual Temperature Data
Monthly Temperature Data
Seasonal and Annual Precipitation Data
Monthly Precipitation Data
Microwave Sounding Unit (MSU) Lower Tropospheric Data

At the "Seasonal Temperature Anomalies" page **(URL - http://www.ncdc.noaa.gov/onlineprod/ghcnmcdwseasonal/form.html)** (Figure 7.25) I'm able to create time series plots

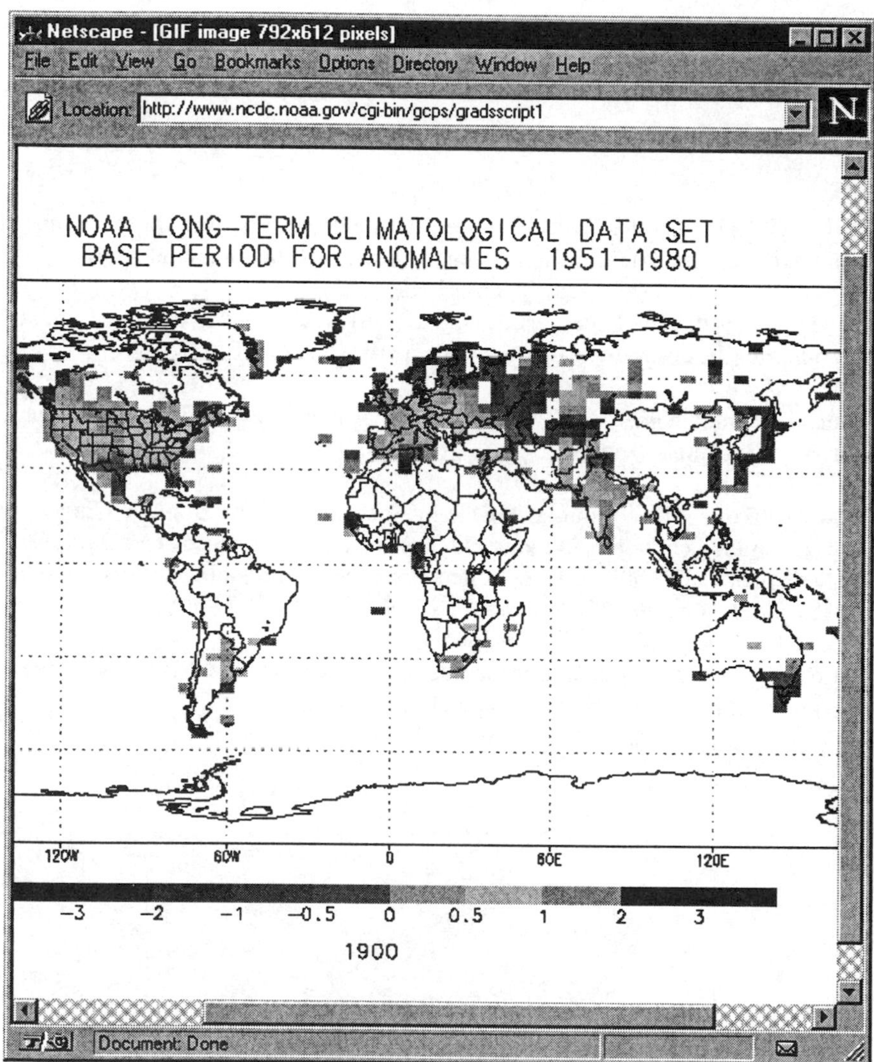

Figure 7.26 Temperature anomaly plot from NCDC

or maps of global temperature anomalies by filling out the online data request form. I define the geographical coverage of the plot, the time range over which a plot is generated (1900 to 1995), the season, and the output format. Clicking the "Submit" button at the bottom of the page sends the data request to the server and within seconds the data plot is delivered to the desktop (Figure 7.26). I left the default (starting) values for all the settings except for the output. I set the background for my contour plot to white and the output format as a GIF file. Downloading the file as a GIF lets me put it right in a Web page or edit it in just about any graphics program. To save the plot, I'll position my cursor over the image and click the right mouse button. A window appears with one option to "Save Image As." By choosing this one I'll be prompted by my computer to tell it where to save the image to. Once this is done the image is instantly transferred to my hard drive.

Try It Out!

1. **EDUCATORS:** Visit the "World Lecture Hall" and check out the various online classes. You might get some ideas for implementing your own class materials online.

2. **STUDENTS**: Visit the Lycos search engine **(URL-http://www.lycos.com)** and search for job opportunities in your chosen field of expertise. GOOD LUCK!

3. Visit a university home page by linking to the "Universities on the Internet" home page. Maybe you're already online.

4. Visit the "Earth Science Journals on the Internet" page from Columbia University (**URL - http://www.ldeo.columbia.edu/journal.html**) and look at an electronic. Or "travel" to the University of California-Berkeley collection of electronic **journals (URL - gopher:// ucsbuxa.ucsb.edu:3001/11/.Journals**).

5. Looking for a project that uses the Internet? Check out the NSF online to see if it has any grant programs that might be suited to your project.

CHAPTER 8

Putting the Internet to Work

The Internet can be a bottomless well of information, or it can be a frustratingly chaotic journey through cyberspace. The seemingly haphazard evolution of the Internet poses a challenge to those wanting to effectively use it for locating information, rather than just "surfing" through it. Many attempts have been made to systematically organize, catalog, and reference the location of materials on the Internet. Chapter 6, "Searching the Internet for Earth Science Resources," illustrated several search engines that attempt to do so. Each method, however, covers a particular service on the Internet: Veronica for Gopher space, Archie for FTP, and so on. There are few comprehensive catalogs of the Internet.

No matter what our job is, we require and thrive on information. There is certainly no lack of information on the Internet. What most of us are faced with is how to get at the information we need while filtering out that which we don't. A little know-how and the right tools will determine how effective our time will be online. Make sure that you familiarize yourself with the tools before trying to use them. Take a little time to read the documentation or "readme" files that come with the software. It is tempting to jump right into the software and try to use it. But doing this on the Internet may turn out to be a real time waster.

It is incumbent on users to examine why they are using Internet technology to achieve their goals. By examining what you want to accomplish with the Internet, you can create an *Internet methodology*. Methodology means that a defined set of steps is employed to achieve a goal. Developing an Internet methodology entails defining a set of steps, or a strategy, for using the Internet to attain your goals. The methodology you adopt will vary depending on what your goal is. If your goal is communication of information, then electronic mail or Usenet is the appropriate tool. If you're looking for data to complete a research project, then tools that interact with online databases will be employed. If computer-mediated learning is your goal, then the World Wide Web may be the place to start. If your goal is obtaining information about a subject pertaining to earth science—say, the volcanic history of North America—you might employ several different Internet tools and services and look to specialized sites and databases.

Throughout this book you have learned that the Internet creates several new opportunities to conduct your work. In Chapters 1 and 7, the Internet was described as a framework upon which we can conduct our daily activities. Of late, the World Wide Web has presented the most favorable environment within which to do this. Web documents created with HTML successfully integrate many of the tools that we use in our day-to-day activities. Advanced browsers permit us to communicate with our colleagues on the floor beneath us or halfway around the world. Hyperlinks embedded in Internet resource pages organize and provide access to earth science information located on different computer servers.

In this chapter we'll put together what we have learned up to this point to provide an integrated approach to using the Internet. This includes:

- defining your task and goals for using the Internet
- defining your methodology for bringing all the Internet resource tools together to find and organize information on the Internet
- showing you how to create simple HTML documents to organize your daily information needs and implement electronic mail through your Web browser
- examining shareware available on the Internet that will help get these tasks accomplished

Goals and Tasks

Defining your goals and assessing the tasks required to meet them are the first steps toward the execution of any project. Your immediate task will fall into one of several categories depending on the desired outcome. *Closed tasks* have a specific goal or answer and often include subgoals. Suppose you require information about the effects of ozone depletion for a term paper. You identify several subgoals, among which is to find resources explaining how ozone depletion affects the marine ecosystem. In this case, you have a definite goal in mind and will require a much more directed search for information. *Open tasks* are more subject-oriented and less specifically defined. Browsing can satisfy the requirements of either an open or closed task depending on what browsing method you adopt. Once you have established a definitive picture of your desired goals, you proceed to defining your methodology.

Defining Your Methodology: Asking a Few Questions

Developing your approach to using globally networked information resources is not much different than the way you search for information without the Internet. You employ many of the same techniques that you use when doing conventional library research. You define your topic, suggest key terms related to your topic, and then proceed to pertinent library resources (e.g., card catalogs, printed or electronically accessed CD-ROM databases, etc.). While in the library you probably use any number of different search procedures and resources. A similar approach can be adopted when using the Internet as a digital library. Keep in mind that the way you approach using the Internet today will be entirely different in a year or two. The rapidity with which new Internet software and hardware is introduced forces users to reexamine how they interact with the Net.

From earlier chapters you have learned that the kind of access you have to the Internet determines what Internet services are available and how you interact with them. Dial-up access is often slow, and some services like the World Wide Web can't be efficiently accessed unless you have a SLIP/PPP account. The various Internet services offer access to different kinds of information and interact with that information quite differently from one another. Recall that the Gopher service is a menu-based service that is basically limited to displaying text material on-screen. One must often "burrow" through countless menus before coming to the information desired. On the other hand, HyperText Markup Language and World Wide Web browsers embed context-sensitive linkages to related information and easily access a variety of media. Web browsers provide uniform access to many Internet services too, while Gopher is restricted to a few. New versions of Web browsers, like Netscape Navigator 2.0 and Microsoft Explorer 2.0, have the capability to "plug in" other applications to run programs like Macromedia director files. This capability permits the full use of hypermedia and navigation that you would have if running the presentation software itself, only now with linkages to globally networked resources too. Both the World Wide Web and Gopher permit you to search for information. Yet search engines on the Web often come up with vastly different results due to their database linkages and method of searching. Because of the numerous possibilities for accessing information, you should carefully take these things into consideration prior to starting your Internet excursion.

At the beginning of the book I described the Internet as both a digital library and an environment in which to conduct your daily activities. The digital library metaphor implies an impersonal archive of information. There are any number of earth science information servers awaiting your digital input. The Internet as an environment is a dynamic and ever evolving system, changing as the inputs and outputs of human and technical resources are employed in its development. The dynamism evoked in electronic interest groups and the hyperlinking of resources on the World Wide Web draw us into an interactive world inhabited by people wanting to share information and finding the best ways to do it. This is borne out each day in earth-science-related Usenet groups and through exciting Web sites like those at NASA, introducing us to the space science community and all it has to offer.

First, stop and ask yourself if the Internet is the right place to be or begin with. What is it that you are likely to need from the Internet? Is the information you're looking for likely to be online or offline? This may be a difficult question to answer. If you're looking for information of a historical nature or research publications that predate the last few years, the Internet may not be the best place to go. Traditional sources of information like libraries are still a good place to start when looking for information. Does the library have an online card catalog? If so, then the Internet is an efficient way to proceed. The library catalog may be accessible via the World Wide Web, Gopher, or Telnet. Are you looking for information in a digital format? If so, then the Internet may well be the place to look. Even if the information is not archived on the Internet, you might be directed to the offline source of such data.

The type of information you're looking for will determine the Internet service you'll use. If you are looking for documents, a good place to start is a document search engine.

Which one? I prefer starting with the World Wide Web for a couple of reasons. It's the fastest growing segment of the Internet and is the preferred place to make information available. Web documents embed graphical information, sound and video, making the Web an attractive place to mount information. If the material is relatively new—say, three years old—the Web is the best place to check first. Otherwise, using Veronica to check Gopher space is advised. If you're looking for a particular file, turn to Archie to search through FTP servers. Use a couple of different FTP servers to scan as their databases may not be contain the same information.

If you're trying to make contact with someone, then electronic mail is the place to start. Is there someone in particular you are trying to contact for information? If you have their electronic mail address, then you can get right to work. However, turn to a Netfind server if you need to search for it. You can always use the telephone to call the person you need to get an electronic mail address from. This might seem a little silly at first, but using electronic mail for subsequent contacts and conversation will save you much time and expense. If you are seeking out information from specialists in a particular field, try a Usenet newsgroup. Posting a question on a newsgroup will likely put you in contact with a person who can help you find what you're looking for. Posting to a newsgroup is likely to pay off larger benefits as Usenet newsgroups do not require users to subscribe to them, unlike electronic mail discussion lists. You can easily cross-post your message to Usenet newsgroups too. Here's a good example of what can happen. A woman from my local community was given 500 rock and mineral samples to be donated to a school in our sister city in Poland. She was in need of an English-to-Polish scientific dictionary to translate the names before sending them to Poland. I sent a request for information to the sci.geog. geology Usenet group and within a few days had over a dozen suggestions from subscribers to the newsgroup from all over the world.

Sitting Down to Work

Now that you have decided that the Internet is the right place to be to conduct your work, you can get down to the activity of sorting through the various services available to you.

Write down all the keywords or -phrases that describe the information you are seeking. Once you write them down, review and refine them. Can they be split into smaller phrases or more specific keywords? A prime determiner of the efficiency and success in using the Internet is how carefully you formulate the central problem and related questions that surround the task at hand. This is particularly important when dealing with the millions of gigabytes worth of information ready to be seized upon in an Internet search. A too broadly defined question will yield an avalanche of articles, books, and other assorted references that could take days to go through. Try breaking your topic or question down into subtopics or smaller questions. If you can do this, then your original topic was too broadly defined. Narrowly defined keywords will yield more manageable search results. However, searches using too narrowly defined keywords may not turn up anything at all either. Pay attention to case-sensitive items; this will be important with some search engines.

Search the World Wide Web with one of the many search engines available (see Chapter 6, "Searching the Internet for Earth Science Resources") using your keywords. I start with the World Wide Web because it is the fastest growing part of the Internet and most people and organizations are adopting the Web to distribute information. The latest information and data are posted on the World Wide Web or archived at an FTP site. You can still get to FTP archives from the Web with your Web client software. Multifunction browser software makes it easy for you to extract information once it is located. HTML documents can be read on-screen, downloaded and saved or printed off as hard copy. Online forms give you control over requesting particular bits of information from large databases. Use the appropriate Boolean operator to limit or expand your search results.

Review your results and refine the search. After you have the first round of potential sources, size up the results and refine the keywords you used in the initial search. If you received too many hits, try limiting the number of returns by setting a specific number of items to return or adding words to the original search term. Adding an additional search term and using the AND Boolean operator is a start toward refining your search.

Bookmark items that look promising. Bookmarking is the electronic equivalent of those little sticky tabs used to mark pages in a book. Bookmarks enable you to retrieve information quickly without having to retrace your steps through Web site after Web site. A bookmark file is like a "database" file of references. Most bookmark files are ASCII text files. The entries can be copied and pasted into a bibliography database for fast sorting and retrieval at a later date or into your word processing document bibliography. Some Web browsers allow you to add annotations and descriptions of the bookmarked site.

Search various subject-oriented guides like Yahoo! or the Clearing House for Subject-Oriented Guides for pointers to information. Many of the online guides have special categories set up for earth science, astronomy, geography, geology and the like. Most subject-oriented guides lead you through a series of resource pages, each page containing more specific information. Subject-oriented resources like these are good place for nondirected browsing as well as searching. They do not have as extensive resources as other search engines do, however.

Locate and choose a few electronic mail lists or Usenet newsgroups to join. These are places for utilizing your earth science Internet community directly. To cast a rather narrow net, choose an electronic mail discussion list. Email listservs must be joined by individuals, and audience size is restricted on the basis of the narrowness of the discussion list subject matter. Usenet newsgroup membership is in a constant state of flux because one can drop in on any number of newsgroups without having to subscribe. The two methods of communication can get the word out and distribute a question to a very large and diverse audience of professional and amateur scientists. They will have pointers to offline information as well as online. An email response from the earth science Internet community may be able to point you in the right direction quicker that an Internet search service.

Investigate frequently-asked-question files archived by Usenet groups and email discussion lists. These often have good pointers to information on many different Internet services. Some provide electronic mail addresses of specialists who have created online resources in their respective earth science fields. Frequently-asked-question files can be archived at or linked from many of the popular subject-oriented guides. Updated frequently-asked-question files are often distributed via Usenet newsgroups and electronic mail listservs. Ask the interest group if there is an FAQ file available for downloading after subscribing to an email listserv or when you first log on to a Usenet newsgroup. Archive the FAQ file on your computer so you can have quick access to it.

Use WAIS to search WAIS databases. This step presupposes that you can find a database covering the topic you're interested in looking for. Remember, WAIS does not look at the data you're requesting; it looks through an index of resources. The likelihood of your finding what you're interested in thus is correlated with the thoroughness with which the index was created.

Use Telnet to connect and search remote libraries for resources with applications like Hytelnet. This will be a time-consuming process because you will have to browse around different libraries and online resources to find what you're after. Leave this option for last.

Once you've completed the steps above, sit down and review your results. Determine which services/steps provided the best results. Sift through and organize your search results. Have you obtained the information you're looking for in specific enough detail to meet your needs? If not, determine how to revise your search topics to focus in on your information needs. Return to the search engines for the World Wide Web and more narrowly define the search with restrictive Boolean operators. Don't forget online colleagues. They are a great source of information to help you accomplish your goals.

Citations for Online Resources

The advent of the Internet as a source of published information creates new questions concerning the use of those materials by the rest of the Internet community. What rights do we have in using someone else's documents that have been published on the World Wide Web? Can I download an image that I find and use it on my Web page? What is the proper way to cite Internet information sources that I use in a research report? Unfortunately, there are no clear-cut answers to many of these questions. The Internet is so new and different from other media that these issues will take time to sort out. However, a few caveats concerning intellectual property rights can be observed.

There are a number of style manuals that suggest the proper way to cite materials that you have used in a piece of creative work like a research paper or book. Likewise, several citation style formats have been suggested for online materials. The Alliance for Computers and Writing has endorsed the MLA-style format of Walker (1995). Walker provides citation styles for most Internet services and protocols.

World Wide Web, Gopher and Telnet Sites

To cite resources on the World Wide Web, give the author's name, title of the work enclosed in quotations marks, the title of the complete work (if applicable) in italics, the full URL, and the date of the visit in parentheses.

Example:

> Wells, L., "Geoarchaeological Investigations at Tell Abu Duwari" http://geogweb.berkeley.edu/PersonalPages/lwells/TABD.html (25 June 1996)

For material from changeable resources like an online journal, the American Psychological Association (APA) and the Modern Language Association (MLA) suggest that the date of publication follow the journal name and the number of paragraphs or pages be included.

Example:

> Crampton, J. "Networked Education," *EarthWorks* (1996):13 par. http://www.utexas.edu/depts/grg/eworks/wir/crampton/v1no1.html (25 June 1996)

Electronic Mail, Listservs and Netnews

To cite electronic mail correspondence or postings to listservs and netnews, give the author's name, subject of the correspondence in quotation marks, address of the listserv or netnews group, and the date of the posting. Addresses may be omitted from personal electronic mail.

Example:

> Ritter, M., "Holocene Glaciation," sci.geo.geology (2 Aug. 1995)

File Transfer Protocol (FTP) Resources

Citations for files downloaded from an FTP archive include the full title of the paper in quotation marks, the full Internet address of the paper, and the date of access.

Example:

> Ritter, M. "Going Digital: The Geography Department in the Information Age" geodept1.uwsp.edu pub/ritter/papers/ (22 July 1996)

Citation Information on the Internet

Several Web sites have excellent information about citing electronic sources:

MLA Citation Guide
URL - http://www.cas.usf.edu/english/walker/mla.html

Citing Computer Documents
URL - http://neal.ctstateu.edu/history/cite.html

Williams College Library Web
URL - http://www.williams.edu:803/library/library.www/cite.html

Becoming an Active Participant in the Internet Earth Science Community

How can you become an active participant in the earth science Internet community? First, GET CONNECTED! Next, learn how to effectively employ the multitude of tools and resources available from the Internet. No, you don't need to become an expert at everything, but there are ways that you can integrate the tools easily into your work and education. Even though the Internet is described as a chaotic environment in which to work, software tools are helping to harness its potential. Many Internet browsers have built-in or "plug-in" functions to simplify downloading files, finding reference information, or browsing the latest network news in your particular area of earth science. Becoming an active participant in the earth science Internet community is a two-way street. The Internet is certainly a good place to get information, but it is also a good place to give back. That is, providing information to the earth science Internet community is a way for you to make a contribution. This could range from offering help to someone over an electronic mail list to creating and sharing information over the World Wide Web. Creating materials for the Internet and especially the World Wide Web has never been easier. Developing materials for the Internet places you in control of how information is organized and how others have access to it. For instance, learning HyperText Markup Language is a simple way to harness many of the resources that you use on the Internet. A thorough review of HTML is beyond the scope of this book. But the discussion below will help you get started. I suggest you check any of the numerous HTML books out on the market today to expand your knowledge of creating documents for the earth science Internet community. Looking at others' work is an enormous help. Most browsers enable you to view the source code of an HTML document. Use these as examples and guides for your own work. Be careful though; not everyone conforms to the rules, and errors in their coding may cause you problems.

Harnessing the World Wide Web for Work and Education

One of the easiest ways to become a creative force in the development of the earth science Internet community is through the creation of World Wide Web documents. A knowledge of HyperText Markup Language is required to create and disseminate materials over the World Wide Web. HTML has evolved over the years into a flexible means of designing digital documents that closely resemble their analog equivalents. Many of the same capabilities for formatting text, placing graphics, and linking information can be done with HTML. But don't be left with the impression that you'll be able to do all the same things your word processor can do. As the demand for more control over document formatting rises, HTML designers will provide the means to do so. The following discussion will give you a general understanding of what HTML is and some simple instructions on how to code Web documents.

Creating a Successful Web Page

A successful Web document or set of documents will greatly benefit from a little prior planning. Try employing the following steps in writing your Web page; modified from Lemay (1995):

- Decide on the purpose of your Web page
- Decide how your audience should use your Web page(s)
- Break up your content into main topics
- Design a navigation scheme
- Storyboard the structure
- Create documents
- Test the page
- Edit the structure and text

Before you actually sit down to program your Web page, stop and consider the purpose and audience for your Web document. If the document you're about to create is a personal Web page, then the structure can be laid out according to your own specialized needs. You program navigation methods that suit your own style and level of Internet expertise. Information linkages will address your daily work or educational requirements. If your document is for a broader audience, then more control over the navigation should be turned over to the user. Documents created for larger audiences must take into account varying levels of Internet expertise. Online help may be needed to provide Internet novices with information to access special features or files from your Web page. For instance, if you include audio or video clips in your page, a reminder to have the user's browser properly configured for the audio or video format needs to be included. Sometimes special HTML codes will need to be used to overcome differences between browsers that people will access your page or document with. Text-based browsers "look and feel" different than graphical browsers. How will the user navigate through your Web document? Will it be like a conventional book, starting at the first page and moving sequentially page by page? Or will users be encouraged to explore online resources for themselves, using your Web page or document as a launching pad? Whatever your goal, there are a few caveats that should be followed for designing useful Web pages. Once these questions are answered you can decide on how you structure the presentation of information contained in your documents.

Several possible structures can be employed for your Web pages. A *hierarchical structure* is the easiest for most users to follow. Navigation through a hierarchical structure is bidirectional. The user moves up for more general information or down toward more specific information. A *linear structure* is one in which the reader moves from page to page in a sequential pattern. A linear structure is bidirectional as well. Information is accessed by moving back and forth between pages, much the same way one reads a book. A linear structure imposes rigidity and limits on both the freedom that your users have to explore information and the way you can present information. Linear structures are useful for delivering tutorials, when the user must move through a process in a sequential fashion. Linear structure with alternative paths is a variation on the linear structure theme. It permits users to take alternatives paths to information; readers start from a main page and branch out to explore information.

Linear and hierarchical structures can be combined for documents that need to be both highly structured and linear. An author using a linear-hierarchical structure must provide context-sensitive clues to positions and paths for the reader. Navigation can be forward and backward and up and down, making it easy for the reader to get lost in a series of documents.

Finally, a *web structure* provides little or no overall structure to a set of information. The only thing that ties each page together is a hyperlink. Readers move from one document to the next following their own chosen path. Each page in a Web structure stands alone. The content of the message you are delivering is basically contained on the page. Contextual links are placed in the body of a page, which links to related information elsewhere on the Internet. The linked information is not critical to understanding the concepts embodied in the originating document. For instance, a discussion of the atmosphere of Jupiter makes reference to the *Viking Explorer* mission, and a link to the *Viking* mission home page is included in the document. It is not crucial that the reader know all about the *Viking* mission to understand the nature of Jupiter's atmosphere.

The disadvantage of a web-structured environment is that it is easy for a user to get lost traversing from one link after another. Unless the path from and back to the originating link is easily discerned, users can become frustrated in retracing their steps. Some Web document authors request their readers to bookmark their starting page for easy navigation back. Placing a "Back to home"-type icon on your document is the best way to help your reader find a way back.

After you have decided on a structure for your document, the next step is to determine what information goes in it and how each page relates to one another. *Storyboarding* is a good way to help you organize your information for a Web presentation. Storyboarding is a design technique used in filmmaking where the author sketches out the key concepts that are included on each page of the document. One approach is to sketch out key topics and concepts that will appear on each page on separate cards or pieces of paper. The concept boards are then arranged in the order the information is to flow. Storyboarding helps an author decide on how bits of information relate to one another and how the user navigates between them.

Now we're ready to start coding. While there are many tools available that help you create HTML documents, no special software is required to make them. A simple text editor and a list of HTML markup tags are all you need to begin creating your Web documents. It doesn't matter what kind of computer processor you're working with either. The browser that you use on your Macintosh, MS-Windows, OS/2 or UNIX machine will be able to read the HTML. Be forewarned though: earlier versions of some browsers may not be able to decode new tags added to the HTML. Originally, HTML was created to describe the structure of Web documents. That is, HTML was used to describe the various parts or elements of a document, like the document head, body, paragraphs, lists and the like. These elements are defined in terms of tags. HTML markup tags are the "code" used to tell the Web browser how to display information for the user. HTML tags tell the browser where to place an image, how to format a paragraph or an individual piece of text and how to link to information for retrieval and display. Tags are text surrounded by angle bracket (< >) characters (e.g., <EMPHASIS>). Beginning and ending tags are used to define the action on a particular piece of text or graphic. Ending tags use a slash to distinguish them from beginning tags. For example, to code a piece of the text "Earth Science Internet Resources" as a first-order heading, I use the <H1> beginning tag and </H1> ending tag:

<H1>Earth Science Internet Resources</H1>

HTML tags are not case-sensitive, but they stand out on the coded document better if you capitalize them.

Some elements or tags have *attributes*. An attribute tells the browser what an element is or how to handle it. For instance, all HTML documents are composed of a body element <body>. The body may contain a background image over which the document text is displayed. For instance,

<body background="weave.gif">

The portion of the body tag background="weave.gif" is the attribute of the body.

Although there are many standard HTML tags, several new ones are proposed from time to time. Tags included in the HTML Level 2 and most Level 3 specifications are implemented in all browsers today. Software vendors like Netscape and Microsoft have suggested, and use, HTML tags specific to their browsers. It's advisable to stick with the HTML specifications that have been accepted to reach the largest audience for your Web documents. Put a warning on your document specifying whether you have constructed your document to be used with a particular browser or HTML specification. If you do, it is nice to provide a link to a site that can provide a browser for which you have designed your document.

In this chapter I'll use a table of contents page to demonstrate how to create a simple document for the World Wide Web. The table of contents page can serve as either a resource page for online information or as a personal home page. The document will contain a:

- document title
- graphic
- text explanation
- contents listing
- author reference and email address

All Web documents contain a particular set of HTML tags that defines the formatting of the document, the title and content of the document. To begin creating an HTML document, you need to provide some information to tell programs how to decode your document. This first line in your document will be the DOCTYPE tag. The DOCTYPE tag informs a program of markup language used to create your document and what document type definition (DTD) must be used to decode it.

If you are using HTML Level 3 tags, the DOCTYPE tag would take this form:

```
<!DOCTYPE HTML PUBLIC "-//IETF/DTD HTML//EN">
```

Following the DOCTYPE tag are the HTML begin and end tags (<HTML> and </HTML>), which enclose the rest of the document and define it as HTML-formatted text. Our initial document now contains:

```
<!DOCTYPE HTML PUBLIC "-//IETF/DTD HTML//EN">
<HTML>
</HTML>
```

Now we can begin adding meat to the document. First, we place beginning and ending HEAD tags between the HTML tags. Title bar information falls between the HEAD tags and is displayed in the title bar of a Windows-style browser (Figure 8.1). The title of my document is "Earth Science Internet Resources Home Page," so the document is coded:

```
<!DOCTYPE HTML PUBLIC "-//IETF/DTD HTML//EN">
<HTML>
<HEAD>
<TITLE>Earth Science Internet Resources Home Page</TITLE>
</HEAD>
</HTML>
```

The body of the document follows the head and is contained between body tags of the form:

```
<!DOCTYPE HTML PUBLIC "-//IETF/DTD HTML//EN">
<HTML>
```

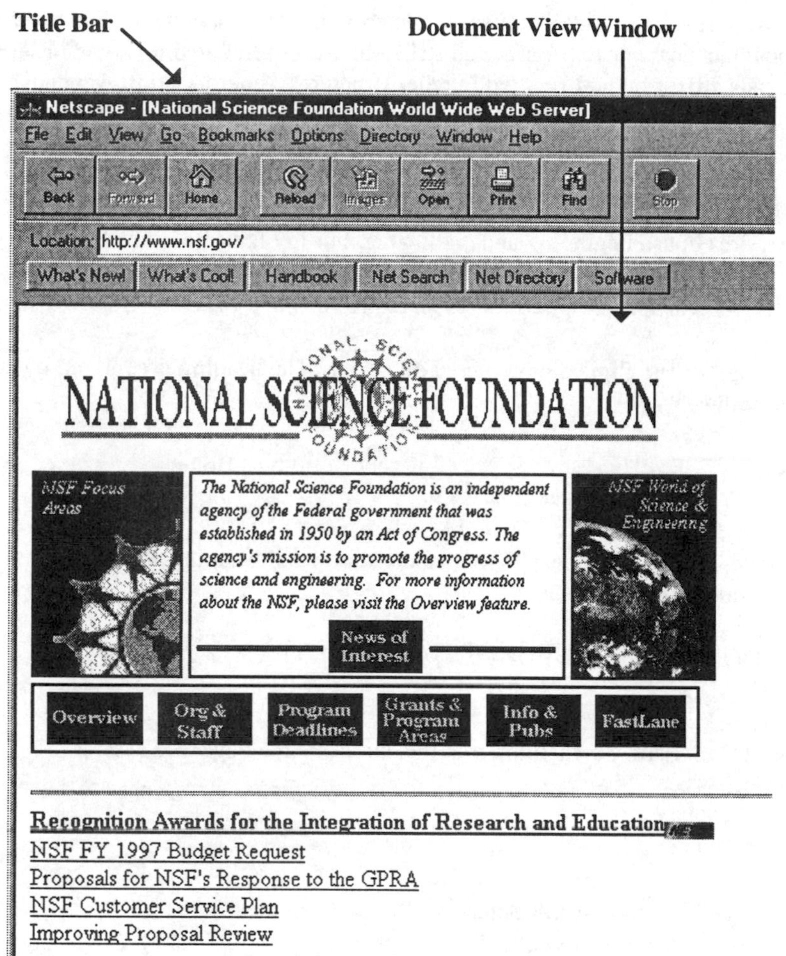

Figure 8.1 World Wide Web browser

```
<HEAD>
<TITLE>Earth Science Internet Resources Home Page</TITLE>
</HEAD>
<BODY>
------- Body of document here --------

</BODY>

</HTML>
```

Now we're ready to add the content to our evolving Web document. The body of an HTML document contains text formatted as headings, preformatted text, and ordered or unordered lists. Text can be formatted in other structures as described in Appendix 2, "Common HTML Tags." My document will begin with its title and a short piece of introductory text. To draw attention to the title of the page I'll format it as a first-order heading. The latest version of HTML provides for six levels of headings distinguished by font size; first-order headings are the largest, sixth-order headings the smallest. Defining a heading requires both a beginning and ending tag. For my first-order heading

```
<H1>Earth Science Internet Resources Home Page</H1>
```

text can be right or left aligned or centered on a page. The heading is centered by enclosing it with *center* tags:

```
<CENTER><H1>Earth Science Internet Resources Home
        Page</H1></CENTER>
```

Let's take a look at the entire HTML source code and what the document looks like. The source code is:

```
<!DOCTYPE HTML PUBLIC "-//IETF/DTD HTML//EN">
<HTML>
<HEAD>
<TITLE>Earth Science Internet Resources Home Page</TITLE>
</HEAD>

<<BODY>>

<CENTER><H1>Earth Science Internet Resources Home
        Page</H1></CENTER>

</BODY>
</HTML>
```

Let's add some explanatory text now. I want my user to know what the document is about and how to use it, so I'll add the following text:

Welcome to the
Earth Science Internet Resources Home Page.

This home page is your gateway to earth science resources on the Internet.

This page is under continual construction, so visit often.

Choose a topic below:

1. Astronomy
2. Climatology
3. Education
4. Environmental Science
5. Geographic Information Systems
6. Geography: Physical Geography
7. Geology
8. Government
9. Internet
10. Meteorology
11. Oceanography

Created by Michael Ritter.

My document is cast in a hierarchical web structure. Each page in the document contains links that progressively relate to more specific information on a particular topic. Yet each page in the document has links to permit lateral and backward navigation to related information.

I bring the attention of the reader to the title of my Web document by placing it in the center of the screen and emphasizing the document title. I start with a salutation, "Welcome to," as a second-order heading. A second-order heading is displayed in a smaller font size than a first-order heading so as to not detract from the title of the page but still draw the attention of the reader. Next comes the title, defined as a first-order heading, enclosed with <H1></H1> tags. Additional emphasis is gained by formatting the title in bold (<B> </B>) and italics (<I></I>. To give the page a little pizzazz, we'll add an image of the earth from space. This is a NASA image I retrieved via FTP. I enclose the image file name, "earth2.gif," with the <img src> tag. This tag tells the browser that an image (img) is to be displayed, and the file (src) will be displayed in the document. The image file will reside in the same directory as the HTML document. If it resides in another directory, I'll have to let the browser know what directory it is in. Be aware that the actual screen layout is controlled by a user's browser configuration. Your formatting may well look different in other users' Web browsers. For example:

```
<center><H2>Welcome to</H2>

<img src="earth2.gif">

<H2>Earth Science Internet Resources Home Page.</H2>
```

```
This home page is your gateway to earth science resources on the Internet.
</H2></center>

<center><H3>This page is under continual construction so visit often.
</H3></center>
<HR>
<H2>Choose a topic below:</H2>
```

Horizontal dividers are placed on a page to separate the document into component parts using the <HR>, "Hard Rule," tag. I've placed a hard rule between the title information and the contents listing.

Earth Science Internet Resources Home Page's table of contents is an alphabetical listing of links to earth science resources. I prompt the reader to gain access to the home page's resources by having them "Choose a topic. . . ." The available choices are arrayed in an indented column. I used the *ordered list* tags, <OL></OL>, to accomplish this.

```
<OL>
<LI><a href="astro.htm">Astronomy</a>
<LI><a href="climate.htm">Climatology</a>
<LI><a href="education.htm">Education</a>
<LI><a href="environ.htm">Environmental Science</a>
<LI><a href="gis.htm">Geographic Information Systems</a>
<LI><a href="physgeo.htm">Geography: Physical Geography</a>
<LI><a href="geology.htm">Geology</a>
<LI><a href="gov.htm">Government</a>
<LI><a href="internet.htm">Internet</a>
<LI><a href="meteor.htm">Meteorology</a>
<LI><a href="ocean.htm">Oceanography</a>
</OL>
```

The <LI> tag before each entry tells the browser that the rest of the line of code is a list item. Seeing an ordered list, the browser will place a number before each line. Enclosing each entry in the contents listing of links are the <A HREF=". . ."></A> tags. The Uniform Resource Locator for the linked information falls between the quotation marks after the equals sign. Text placed between the end angle bracket on the beginning tag and the ending tag will be highlighted and underlined by your browser to indicate a link. We're just about through now. I'll separate the listing from the rest of the page with a hard rule and "sign" the page with a link to my electronic mail account. A "mailto" reference is used to tell your Web browser to initiate an email session after clicking on the linked text. For example:

```
<HR>
<center>Created by <a href="mailto:mritter@uwsp.edu">Michael
Ritter</a>mritter@uwsp.edu</center>
```

Let's take a look at the full code:

```
<!DOCTYPE HTML PUBLIC "-//IETF/DTD HTML//EN">
<HTML>
<HEAD>
<TITLE>Earth Online</TITLE>
</HEAD>

<body>

<center><H2>Welcome to</H2></center>
<center><H1><I><B>Earth Online</B></I></H1></center>
<center><img src="earth2.gif"></center>

<center><H2>An Internet Guide for Earth Science<BR></center>

<center><I><B>Earth Online</B></I>is your gateway to earth science resources
        on the Internet.</H2></center>

<center><H3>This page is under continual construction so visit often.
        </H3></center>

<HR>

<H2>Choose a topic below:</H2>
<OL>
<a href="astro.htm">Astronomy</a><br>
<a href="climate.htm">Climatology</a><br>
<a href="education.htm">Education</a><br>
<a href="environ.htm">Environmental Science</a><br>
<a href="gis.htm">Geographic Information Systems</a><br>
<a href="physgeo.htm">Geography: Physical Geography</a><br>
<a href="geology.htm">Geology</a><br>
<a href="gov.htm">Government</a><br>
<a href="internet.htm">Internet</a><br>
<a href="meteor.htm">Meteorology</a><br>
<a href="ocean.htm">Oceanography</a><br>
</OL>

<HR>
<B><I> Earth Online </I></B> is maintained by <a href="mailto:mritter@fsmail.
        uwsp.edu">Michael Ritter</a>

</body>

</html>
```

Figure 8.2 Sample home page displayed in Netscape Navigator

Save the file and read it into your browser to check for errors. Then transfer it to your Internet provider's Web server and load it into your browser. Figure 8.2 shows how this file would look with Netscape Navigator.

➤➤ Focus on the Internet: *The Earth System Science Community*

The Earth System Science Community (ESSC) project (**URL - http://www.circles.org/ESSC/home.html**) is a good example of how the Internet is bringing together professional

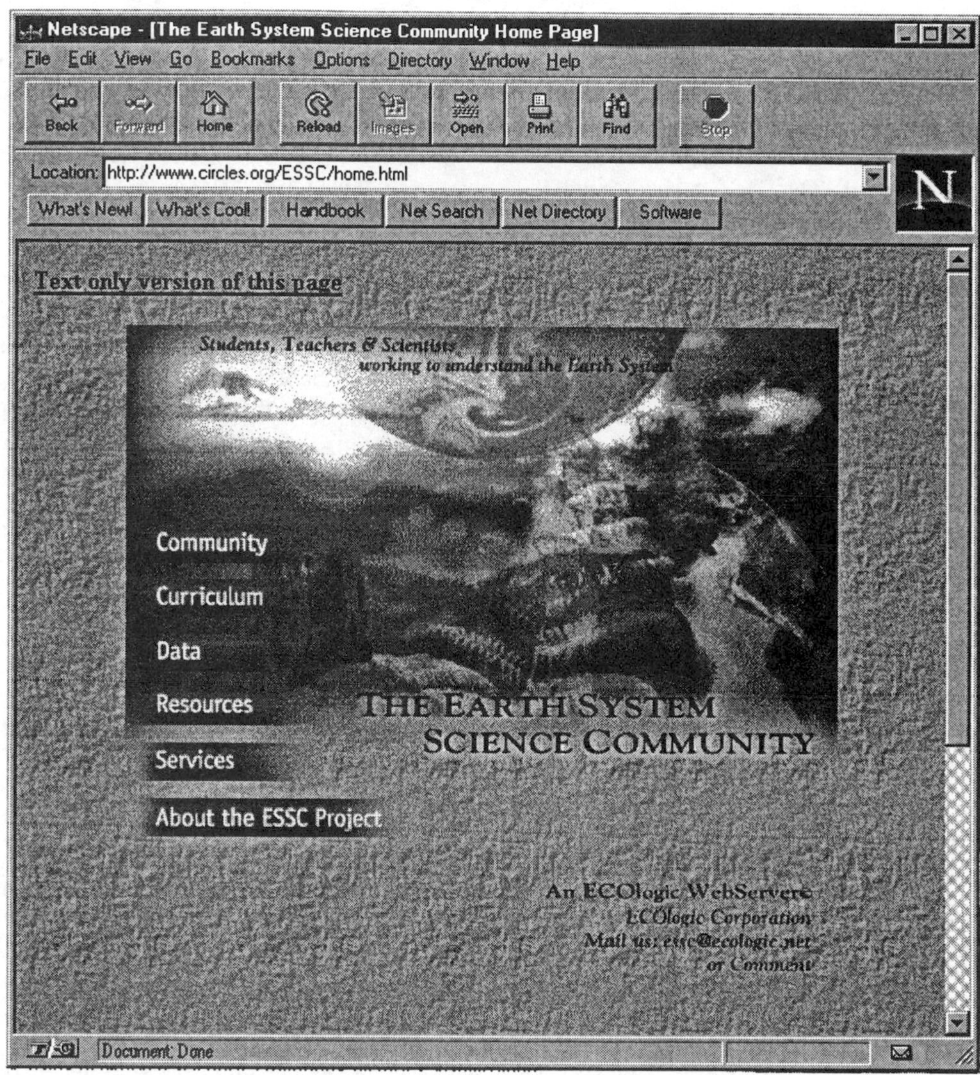

Figure 8.3 Earth System Science Community home page

earth scientists, university and secondary educators and high school students to more effectively teach and learn about earth system science. The ESSC is developing an online community and curriculum for high school earth system science. Funded by a grant from NASA in 1994, the ECOlogic Corp. is creating an ESSC curriculum test bed that will include twelve high schools and six universities around the country. The goal of the test bed project is to "enable any teacher, student, or school connected to the Internet to begin investigating the Earth system quickly, easily, and inexpensively" (Figure 8.3).

Earth systems science is a holistic approach to the study of the earth. In order to explain earth dynamics and change, ESS stresses the investigation of the interaction between the various components that make up the earth system. The ESS model is interdisciplinary, using networked scientific computing facilities, and visualization and modeling tools and drawing on a community of like-minded researchers to study the underlying processes of the earth. The ESSC project realizes that science students rarely have access to the tools and techniques for visualizing and analyzing earth system information. The World Wide Web is seen as a way to bring resources distributed on far-flung computing systems together for students to access.

By providing a mechanism to support ongoing collaboration between educators, students and professional earth scientists, the ESSC enables students and teachers to investigate and develop a holistic understanding of the earth system. This is accomplished by helping students to learn process thinking, employ the scientific method through collaborative problem solving, build models and use modern, scientific communication. Finally the ESSC is developing an earth system science curriculum and support system over the Internet.

To meet the objectives of the program, the project has already designed a summer immersion workshop during which ESSC participants develop an understanding of the earth's dynamic processes. During the first summer workshop in 1995 educators investigated the hydrologic cycle and provided the background necessary to enable students to conduct investigations. Participants developed skills to analyze systems, to tap remotely sensed data and visualization tools and to use HTML to publish their results.

The ESSC program curriculum consists of several team projects and integrates widely distributed information and digital communications networks in support of classroom activities. Projects focusing on investigating and defining the earth as a system are supported by other projects categorized by earth subsystems (e.g., hydrosphere, lithosphere, etc.). Special themes have been identified (El Niño) that cross system boundaries and require a systems approach and that complement the curriculum. Technology is a tool used to do work and to communicate the results of that work. The earth systems science curriculum is dynamic and requires the use of tools that can effectively integrate disparate sources of information into a unified understanding of earth processes. To utilize the talents of many individuals scattered across the United States, the program uses distributed information technologies like the Internet to collaborate on the creation of the curriculum.

Students work collaboratively in teams, relying on peer education as a means of learning. Team investigations require background research, hypothesis formulation, qualitative and quantitative modeling and scientific communication of results on the World Wide Web. Online access to data relevant to the investigation of earth systems is provided. For example, temperature distribution data to support ESSC investigations is extracted from the GEDEX CD-ROM of World Monthly Surface Station Climatology data sets. ESSC uses resources located on other Web sites to serve participants. ESSC draws on the CoVis project server to provide access to earth energy budget visualizations. The fruits of these investigations are being borne as many interesting student projects are being distributed over the World Wide Web (**URL - http://www.circles.org/ESSC/resources/samples.html**).

What You Have Learned

- Putting the Internet to work in an efficient way requires an Internet methodology.
- Multiple approaches to information discovery must be applied to the fluid medium that is the Internet.
- Linear, linear-hierarchical, and web structures are all methods by which individuals can navigate a Web site.
- Hypertext documents are easy to create for simple hypertext Web pages.

Apply It!

Earlier in the chapter you were introduced to HTML programming and the way to create a World Wide Web document. Throughout Chapters 1–7 you encountered many different resources that address the climate change problem. Let's put our experience together to organize the online resources we have collected into a Web resource page for climate change. As mentioned earlier, you don't need special software to create the document. Open up the text editor and follow along. Make sure to save your file as a text file with either the htm or html extension, depending on your system.

I want to build a resource page for people to access information about climate change. The first thing to do is sort through the resources I'm interested in and assign them to groups or categories. These groups are:

Organizations and resource servers

- Global Change Master Directory
- Geological Survey
- Goddard Institute for Space Studies
- National Climatic Data Center

Hot lists

- The Virtual Earth

Online documents and publications

- Sea Level Change Web Document
- United Nations Environment Program Fact Sheets

Searching

- Lycos
- Yahoo!

Visualizations and images

- Greenhouse Effect Visualizations
- Interactive Visualizations (from NCDC)

The document structure will reflect the organization laid out above. The page will consist of unordered lists of sites for each category. Each list item is a hyperlink back to the original source. The document will include a graphic, my electronic mail address, and the creation date at the bottom of the document.

Define the document first as an HTML document and define a title for the browser title bar. Recall that all the text of an HTML document is enclosed in the <HTML></HTML> tags and the title is placed within the HEAD element.

```
<HTML>
<HEAD>
<TITLE>Online Climate Change Resources</TITLE>
</HEAD>
-------
-------
</HTML>
```

(The dashed lines between </HEAD> and </HTML> mean that other text will be located here.) Next we'll add the body of the document. I'll format the document title as a first-order heading centered on the page:

```
<HTML>
<HEAD>
<TITLE>Online Climate Change Resources</TITLE>
</HEAD>
<BODY>
<CENTER>Online Climate Change Resources</CENTER>
-------
-------
</HTML>
```

Now I'm ready to create my lists and hyperlinks. When I define the link this time I'm going to specify the entire address for a hyperlink. The example given earlier in the chapter didn't specify the absolute URL for the link because the hyperlinked documents resided in the same directory as the originating HTML document. The categories will be formatted as second-order headings, and each list item <LI> will be preceded by a bullet. Let's see what the first set of resources would look like in HTML:

```
<HTML>
<HEAD>
```

```
<TITLE>Online Climate Change Resources</TITLE>
</HEAD>
<BODY>
<CENTER><H1>Online Climate Change Resources</H1></CENTER>
<H2>Organizations and resource servers</H2>
<UL>
<LI><a href=“http://gcmd.gsfc.nasa.gov/”>Global Change Master Directory</a>
<LI><a href=“http://www.usgs.gov/”>United States Geological Survey</a>
<LI><a href=“http://WWW.giss.nasa.gov/”>Goddard Institute for Space
        Studies</a>
<LI><a href=“http://www.ncdc.noaa.gov/”>National Climatic Data Center</a>
</UL>
-------
-------
</HTML>
```

Let’s add the rest of the resources now. There are some UNEP facts that I want to go straight to, so I’ll embed another unordered list within the “Online Documents and Publications” list:

```
<HTML>
<HEAD>
<TITLE>Online Climate Change Resources</TITLE>
</HEAD>
<BODY>
<CENTER><H1>Online Climate Change Resources</H1></CENTER>

<H2>Organizations and resource servers</H2>
<UL>
<LI><a href=“http://gcmd.gsfc.nasa.gov/”>Global Change Master Directory</a>
<LI><a href=“http://www.usgs.gov/”>United States Geological Survey</a>
<LI><a href=“http://WWW.giss.nasa.gov/”>Goddard Institute for Space
        Studies</a>
<LI><a href=“http://www.ncdc.noaa.gov/”>National Climatic Data Center</a>
</UL>

<H2>Hot lists</H2>
<UL>
<LI><a href=“http://atlas.es.mq.edu.au/users/pingram/v_earth.html”>The Virtual
        Earth</a>
</UL>

<H2>Online documents and publications</H2>
<UL>
```

```
<LI><a href="http://www.giss.nasa.gov/Research/Intro/gornitz.01.html">Sea
        Level Change</a> (Gornitz, V. 1996)
<LI><a href="http://www.unep.ch/iucc/fs-index.html">United Nations
        Environment Program Fact Sheets</a>
<UL>
<LI><a href="http://www.unep.ch/iucc/fs003.html">An introduction to the
        climate system (UNEP)</a>
<LI><a href="http://www.unep.ch/iucc/fs001.html">An introduction to the
        science of man-made climate change.</a>
<LI><a href="http://www.unep.ch/iucc/fs009.html">Why "climate change" and
        "global warming" are not the same thing.</a>
<LI><a href="http://www.unep.ch/iucc/fs104.html">The impact of climate change
        on water resources</a>
<LI><a href="http://www.unep.ch/iucc/fs237.html">The debate over allocating
        responsibility for climate change</a>
</UL>
</UL>

<H2> Searching</H2>
<UL>
<LI><a href="http://www.lycos.com">Lycos</a>
<LI><a href="http://ww.yahoo.com">Yahoo</a>
</UL>

<H2>Visualizations and Images</H2>
<LI><a href="http://www.covis.nwu.edu/gev.html"> COVIS Greenhouse Effect
        Visualizations</a>
<LI><a href="http://www.ncdc.noaa.gov/homepg/interprod.html">Interactive
        Visualizations of Climate Data (from NCDC)</a>

<hr>
Created by <a href="mailto:mritter@uwsp.edu">Michael Ritter,
mritter@uwsp.edu</a>. Last revised July 21, 1996. MER
</HTML>
```

At the bottom of the page I put an author reference, my email address using the "mailto" tag and the revision date. Let's take a look at what we have (Figure 8.4). Save the document as "cchange.htm" (use the html extension if you can). Now open the file in Netscape by using the "File" menu and the "Open file in Browser" menu pick.

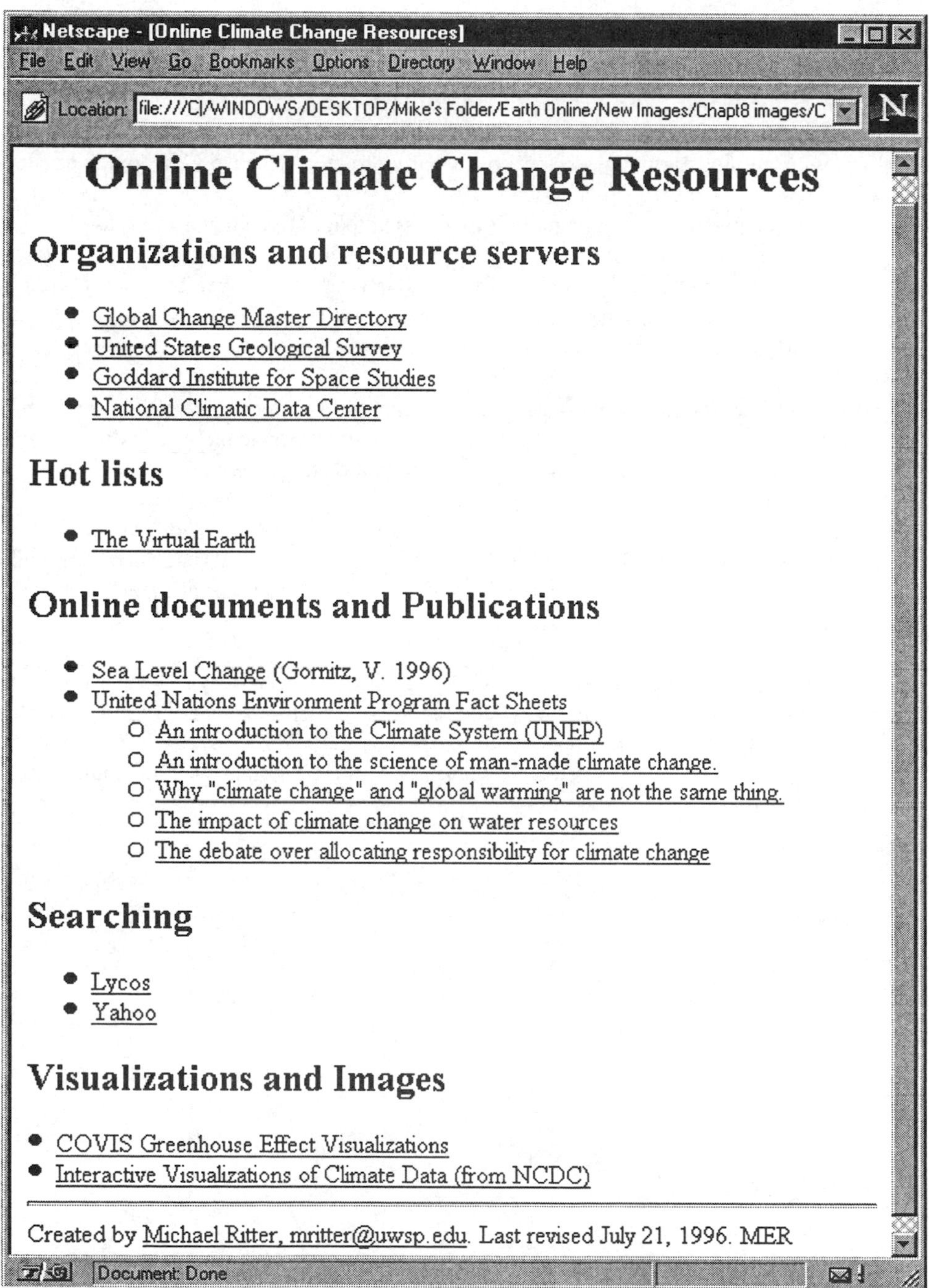

Figure 8.4 Personal online climate change resources page

Try It Out!

1. Use the World Wide Web to connect to "Introduction to HTML and URLs" at **http://www.utirc.utoronto.ca/HTMLdocs/NewHTML/intro.html**. This Web document is an excellent starting place for those wanting to create their own Web documents.

2. Build a personal home page. Follow the example in the chapter to build your home page. Take a look around at other home pages to get ideas as to how you might create your own. Use the "View Source" option on your World Wide Web browser to see how others created their home pages. Provide hyperlinks to favorite software sites and eliminate the need to use FTP software.

3. **STUDENTS**: Instead of writing a traditional term paper for your class, write a hypermedia version. Term papers constructed in hypermedia let you draw on many more resources than you can with a conventional hard copy version.

4. Create a hypermedia resume. Resumes posted on the World Wide Web attract a potentially larger audience than one can expect to address through conventional dissemination methods. Provide hyperlinks research or other original work in digital form stored at your Web site.

5. **EDUCATORS:** Create a class home page. This is a good way to keep your class up to date and informed. A digital syllabus can draw together science resources scattered across the Internet to support your classroom activities. Convert your lecture notes to hypertext outlines. Hyperlink key terms to digitized images or other supporting graphics.

CHAPTER 9

Where to Go from Here

Keeping Up with the Internet

You undoubtedly realize by now that the Internet is an ever changing environment in which to learn and work. Keeping up with changes in the Internet is like try to hit a moving target. New resources are constantly coming online, client software is enhanced with new features and continually rolled out tried-and-true services give way to new and exciting ways to tap into networked resources. How can you stay abreast of all the changes? Staying current with the Internet requires some of the same strategies you use to find information on the Internet. There is no one site on the Internet that will keep you up to date with new online resources. Instead, your approach will be from a variety of different angles and sources of information. In this chapter we'll investigate how to keep current with changes in the Internet and pose some ideas as to what lies ahead for the earth science Internet community.

What's New and Sites of the Week

When returning to your favorite earth science site, or any site for that matter, check for a "What's New" page. A "What's New" page runs down the most recent changes to the Web site. A good Web site administrator will always alert visitors to additions to their resources by placing either a "What's New" icon or an image beside the link and connecting you to a "What's New" page. Many World Wide Web browsers provide some means to tap into a "What's New" site directly from their browser toolbar or menu system. A "What's New" site usually is a general-purpose site, containing many links unrelated to the earth sciences. Sometimes, however, an earth-science-related link shows up in these documents. The hyperlinks change on a periodic basis depending on the source of the "What's New" document. You will have to check in often to keep up with any changes.

The Earth Science Site of the Week (**URL- http://agcwww.bio.ns.ca/misc/geores/sotw/sotw.html**), brought to you by the Geological Society of Canada, is a good place to check on what's happening in the earth science Internet community. Each week or so, a notable earth science site is featured. A small summary of the featured site is provided with a link to the site's home page. An archive of past Earth Science Sites of the Week is also provided.

Online Resource Centers and Subject Guides

Online resource centers are Internet sites that serve as a clearinghouse of linkages to online resources. The primary function of these sites is to offer, as best they can, a "one-stop shopping center" for digital information. Many such sites exist. For instance, in Chapter 6, "Searching the Internet," online subject guides are discussed as a place to search for Internet resources. These sites serve as a good place to keep up with changes going on with the Internet. One of the most popular, Yahoo! (**URL - http://www.yahoo.com/**), is a great starting place, as is EINet's Galaxy (**URL - http://galaxy.einet.net/galaxy.html**).

Publications

The Internet doesn't seem to have hurt print media too much, as the number of books and magazines devoted to the Internet has multiplied as fast as the Internet itself. Many excellent resource guides have been produced, although few specifically for earth-science-related disciplines. These guides are often alphabetical listings of Internet resources sorted by subject. Often there are sections devoted to earth science, geology, meteorology and the like. The main disadvantage with any conventional print book is that it is often out of date by the time it makes it to print. Internet sites come and go, directory structures and addresses change, and software upgrades change program capabilities. Most Internet- or computer-oriented magazines now include a section on Internet resources. Professional newsletters keep their members up to date with Internet resources of interest to them by publishing regular columns devoted to the Internet. The most recent "printed" information comes in the form of digital, online publications.

Netsurfer Digest (**URL - http://www.netsurf.com/nsd/index.html**) is a free, general-purpose online publication of news and information about the Internet. Netsurf Digest is delivered by electronic mail each week, providing the reader with electronic snippets about Internet resources. The digest is delivered in either plain ASCII or HTML format. The HTML-formatted version can be saved or read into your Web browser, giving you immediate access to hyperlinked sites. The Netsurfer Focus special issues, which delve into specific topics in more depth, are occasionally published.

Current Cites is the monthly publication of the UC Berkeley library covering various areas of information technology. Citations include electronic publications as well as conventional print books and articles dealing with Internet-related sources and topics. The publication is available via electronic mail by sending a subscription message to **listserv@library.berkely.edu** with the following in the body of the message:

sub cites <*your name*>

Electronic Newsletters like the Internet Scout Report, published weekly by the Internet Information Center (InterNic), are distributed via electronic mail and on InterNic's World Wide Web site (**URL - http://rs.internic.net/scout_report-index.html**). This report publishes information about new Internet sites on the World Wide Web, Gopher, and many other Internet resources and services.

Electronic Discussions

Services like electronic mail discussion lists or Usenet newsgroups provide you with the most up-to-date information. Interest groups and general-purpose Internet groups keep you abreast of the latest developments on the Internet. Service-specific groups are where you turn to find out the latest goings-on in the World Wide Web, Gopher, or other Internet services. Turn to hardware- or software-product-specific groups to discuss the latest developments and changes to a particular browser, or to a program like ArcView for geographic information systems research. Some sites distribute newsletters to keep you informed about new online resources or changes in old ones.

"Net-happenings" keeps you informed as to what's new and happening on the Internet. Subscribe to the list by sending the message

subscribe *<your email address>*

to **majordomo@dsmail.internic.net**.

NEW-LIST is an email list created to announce new electronic mail lists. To subscribe send the message "SUB NEW-LIST <your name>" and mail to **listserv@vm1.nodak.edu**.

NEWNIR-L announces new international Internet resources. To subscribe send the message "SUB NEWNIR-L <your name>" and mail to **listserv@itocsivm.csi.it**.

Usenet newsgroups are particularly helpful in keeping you up to date with the goings-on of the Internet. Some newsgroups are devoted strictly to announcing new developments while others are devoted to discussing the use of particular Internet services. For instance, the "comp.internet.net-happenings" newsgroup is used to announce new Internet sites like the Forest Health page **(URL - http://www.dnr.state.mi.us/www/fmd/pest/forheal.html)**, which reports on the health of Michigan forests. Internet users are also alerted to the publishing of new electronic journals and shareware and freeware sites. The "comp. infosystems.www.announce" is devoted to announcements specifically pertaining to the World Wide Web, while the "comp.infosystems.www.advocacy" newsgroup discusses issues surrounding the use of the Web and materials published on it. The "comp.infosystems.www. authoring.html" is a good place to turn for questions related to authoring documents for the World Wide Web.

To keep up to date with the goings-on in geoscience, you can turn to the Web for the "Geoscience Resources FAQ" file compiled by Phillip Ingram. The FAQ file is posted on a monthly basis to a number of earth-science-related Usenet newsgroups. You can obtain the most recent version of this information from the sci.answers, comp.answers or news.answers newsgroups. You can also send an electronic mail message to **mail-server@rtfm.mit.edu** with the following line in the body of the message:

send usenet/news.answers/geology-faq/geosci-resources/part1

Replace the part 1 with part 2, part 3, or part 4 for the remainder of the files. You can retrieve the same files via anonymous FTP by logging on to

rtfm.mit.edu/pub/usenet/news.answers/geology-faq/geosci-resources/part1

again replacing part 1 with the appropriate file name. A hypertext version of the FAQ file is accessible from The Virtual Earth (**URL - http://atlas.es.mq.edu.au/users/pingram/v_earth.html**) and The Soft Earth (**URL - http://atlas.es.mq.edu.au/users/pingram/s_earth.html**) Web sites.

Here, and on the Horizon: The Real and Virtual Earth

The Internet is evolving from a digital archive to an interactive environment beneath our fingertips. Interenetworking provides a means for the interactivity between humans and other humans, between humans and computers, and between computers and other computers. Many new and exciting innovations have come online recently and are slated to become more widespread in the near future. Data visualization, virtual reality, real-time audio and video are relatively new technologies that are being distributed over the Internet that will benefit the earth science community.

In Real Time: "Being There"

The desire and need for information on demand has spurred many in the earth science community to turn to the Internet as a way to receive information in real time, or as it happens. In the past, computer users were content with Gophering to a news site to read the daily or weekly postings or dropping into a government Web site to download the latest weekly or monthly data report. Now, we can receive information on demand, and in real time. Internet technology permits scientists and the general public to watch and even participate in scientific research as it happens. For instance, during the controlled flooding project on the Colorado River in 1996, the U.S. Geological Survey used satellite telemetry to distribute real-time streamflow data over the World Wide Web. On March 26, 1996, the Bureau of Reclamation opened the Glen Canyon Dam and released about 45,000 cubic feet of water for a one-week period. Four streamflow-gauging stations along the river below the Glen Canyon Dan were equipped with satellite telemetry. The USGS gave public access to the streamflow data and permitted people to follow the events of the controlled flood experiment through the **Web (URL - http://wwwdaztcn.wr.usgs.gov/floodpr.html**). The USGS provides access to real-time hydrologic data for the United States (**URL - http://h2o.usgs.gov/public/realtime.html**), furnishing instantaneous streamflow data in a graphical format over week-long periods (Figure 9.1).

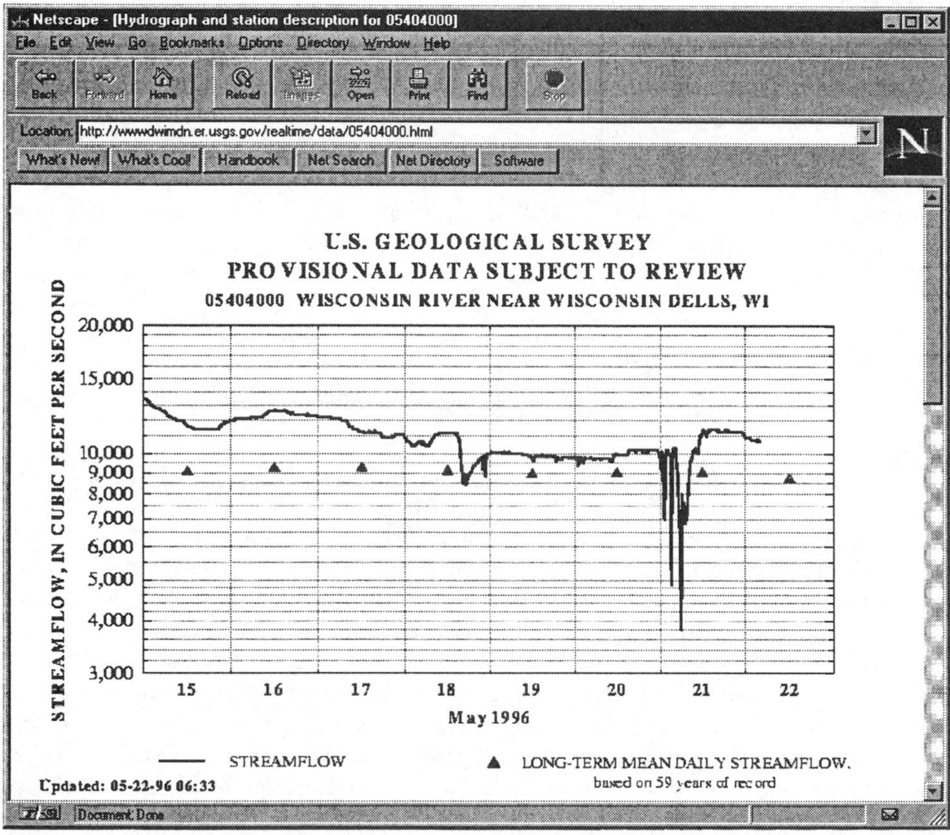

Figure 9.1 Hydrograph from USGS real-time hydrologic data site

The notion of real-time data delivery is a relative one. Although not truly in real time, many sites provide very up-to-date information or data about their projects. A case in point is the 1996 South African Everest expedition. This was the first "high tech" trek to the highest point in the world. Equipped with laptop computers and satellite telephony, the world community for the first time could experience the climb as it happened. The public had access to the climbers via Internet electronic mail. Pictures shot at the various base camps were sent via satellite uplink for distribution over the World Wide Web. Visitors to the Web site can download the first virtual reality scenes from Mt. Everest. You can almost imagine yourself walking the ice-covered slopes of Mt. Everest as you navigate around the panoramic view of base camp 2.

During the writing of this book, NASA and the *Houston Chronicle* took an exciting step toward delivering real-time information over the World Wide Web by providing live audio and video access to space shuttle mission STS 77. From the mission home page, a visitor could listen in on discussions conducted between NASA personnel and astronauts in space. Live pictures showing the shuttle's orbit and Mission Control were broadcast each minute. A chat-back link was provided to discuss the shuttle mission and its activities. A visitor to the site now can branch off to a rich source of online space exploration via the "Space Links" **page (URL - http://www.chron.com/content/interactive/space/links.html)**.

A fun and unique distribution of real-time information over the Internet is the broadcast of live video camera views of what's happening around the world. Internet users are connecting cameras to the Internet and at predetermined time increments are snapping pictures and "instantly" distributing them across the Net. For example, KCNC Television of Denver, Colorado, distributes pictures of the mountains west of Denver from its "Mountain Cam" **(URL-http://www.kcncnews4.com/cgi-bin/citycam.exe?6)**.

Virtual Reality: Just Like Being There?

Virtual field trips were examined in Chapter 7 as a means for people to explore places without having to physically be at the location. In most cases virtual field trips are created around a series of still photographs, and the participant maneuvers through the landscape by linking from one image to another. However, over the last several years, computer programmers have created three-dimensional worlds within computers. Virtual reality "is a computer environment in which a user is immersed and can experience simulated visual, auditory and force sensations" (Ostler, 1994). Virtual worlds are "constructed" in computers; hence programmers can design these new environments in whatever fashion they like. Most virtual worlds to this point have been artificial drawings of the environment. Now, earth scientists and computer programmers are teaming up to produce realistic environments in which scientists and students alike can explore and learn about the earth. Many World Wide Web browsers now support the viewing of virtual reality modeling language files or will spawn an external viewer when a VRML file has been downloaded. A user can navigate through the virtual world. By the time this book comes to print there will be many more exciting uses of virtual reality. However, the internet earth science community is using virtual reality in a couple of different ways. First, virtual reality is used to visualize three-dimensional space. This was VR's intended purpose. Second, virtual reality is used as an interface to information. Three-dimensional models can be navigated to reveal or provide access to hyperlinked data.

NASA Intelligent Mechanisms Group personnel are providing VRML models of mission hardware and sites. Visitors can "walk" through the terrain of Kilauea volcano or examine a three-dimensional model of the Marsokhod Planetary Rover. Hyperlinks are encoded into the models at particular places. For instance, hyperlinks to online technical specifications are encoded into the components of the rover model. Clicking on a component brings up information.

The SkyView project **(URL - http://skyview.gsfc.nasa.gov/skyview.html)** from the High Energy Astrophysics Science Archive Research Center **(URL - http://heasarc.gsfc.nasa.gov/docs/HEASARC_HOME_PAGE.html)** has designed a "Virtual Observatory" where users can retrieve images of any part of the sky at wavelengths from radio to gamma rays. Both basic and advanced interfaces to the SkyView databases over the Web are used to send a request to the SkyView server. An interactive interface for X-Windows is available too. Users define the center of the field to be retrieved, a data survey to use (e.g., digitized sky, IRAS Sky Survey Atlas, etc.), coordinates, projection, brightness, and so on. An image is processed and displayed online after the request has been submitted.

VRML Topographic Map Generator (**URL - http://evlweb.eecs.uic.edu/pape/vrml/etopo/**) is an interactive program that generates virtual reality model language topographic maps on the fly. Brought to you by the SeaWiFS project, maps are created from NOAA NGDC ETOPO-5 topographic data set for the entire earth's surface. An online fill-in form to specify the latitude and longitude, size of map in degrees, grid resolution, elevation exaggeration and map texture resolution lets you generate the desired map. The VRML map is sent down to your desktop VRML browser for viewing. You can move about the terrain as desired within the VRML browser.

The ALB Crystallography home page (**URL - http://fluo.univ-lemans.fr:8001/**) brings you the 3D Crystal Structures in the VRML **site (URL - http://fluo.univ-lemans.fr:8001/vrml/vrml.html**), where virtual reality is used to examine inorganic crystal structures with a VRML plugin to your World Wide Web browser. Users walk around, look at and move through various crystal structures. The benefits of virtual reality technology are easily apparent when looking at this site. Visualizing structures like these is extremely difficult from a static, two-dimensional photograph. Three-dimensional models are useful in learning the configuration of crystal structures. But having the ability to manipulate them—that is, turn them over, look at them in different perspective and even get inside them—gives the user (student) a whole new way of learning.

Multimedia: Audio and Video on the World Wide Web

Although audio and video have been available over the Internet for some time, users have had to download the entire file prior to viewing it in a "helper application" running outside their Web browser. Now streaming technologies are bringing real-time audio and video to our desktops. Although video feeds can be delivered over a modem with as slow a speed as 28.8 baud, much faster modems are required to get anything approaching full motion. At lower speeds, video is choppy and audio often out of sync. However, delivering audio over the Internet has come a long way. Now, reasonably good-quality audio can be achieved at modem speeds as low as 14.4 baud. A number of audio streaming technologies have been developed, and numerous sites around the world are adopting them to add a fuller dimension to the content of their World Wide Web sites. Distribution of radio programs is a natural for the Internet. Several radio programs are being regularly archived on the Internet. National Public Radio archives its "All Things Considered, " "Morning Show" and "Science Friday. "

Multimedia presentation software enables users to create dynamic presentations through the electronic melding of text, sound, images and video in digital form. Software companies are now trying to develop ways for presentation authors to distribute their creations over the Internet. Multimedia developers are enabling the distribution of their products over the Internet by "plugging into" existing Internet browser programs. Plugins enabling the full functionality of the original multimedia presentation have been developed for macromedia products like Director and Asymetrix's Toolbook. Microsoft's Power Point can be configured to export presentations as HTML documents.

➤➤ Focus on the Internet: *Computer Oriented Geological Society*

The Computer Oriented Geological Society (**URL - http://www.csn.net/~tbrez/cogs/index.html**), otherwise known as COGS, was founded in 1982 and is dedicated to helping geologists and other geoscientists using computers. COGS provides a forum for geologists to exchange ideas and experiences with colleagues about their use of computers for research and education. COGS functions as a clearinghouse, providing information about software, hardware and data sets via the COGS bulletin board service (COGSnet) and a newsletter (COGSletter) and participates in larger computer information networks like GeoInfoNet (Bresnahan, 1994). COGS uses the World Wide Web to distribute information about the society and provide an interface to its various functions and services. COGS information and data can be retrieved from its FTP file server through conventional mail order services.

The COGSletter keeps members of the society up to date with developments such as geological data, data sets distributed on CD-ROM and book reviews. Back issues of COGSletter can be read online. Advertisements by commercial software and hardware vendors are also included.

COGS and the Society for Mining Metallurgy and Exploration (SME) cooperatively sponsor the computer bulletin board COGSnet. COGSnet is a stand-alone system accessible by telephone lines through a modem. You do not have to be a member of the society to access the message area and software downloads. Nonmembers have more restricted file access and more limited connect time than do members of COGS or SME. The message areas are a good place to drop in for conversation with like-minded geoscientists. The chat areas are a good place to extend your professional network and keep up to date with the latest happenings in the geosciences. COGSnet maintains an extensive field archive for its members. Nonmembers have limited access to the archived files. Data sets, games, computer utilities and other public domain programs also are available, as is an index to files archived by the COGSnet site.

What You Have Learned

- You can keep up with changes with the Internet by employing a multiple resources strategy.
- The most up-to-date information on the Internet can be obtained from electronic newsgroups and online publications.
- The Internet is capable of providing real-time data to users.
- Virtual reality is employed over the Internet to take users to places they physically cannot reach or view things they typically cannot see in reality.
- True multimedia is accomplished over the Internet via browser plugins for presentation software and audio/video compression schemes.

Try It Out!

1. Get tuned in. Download an Internet audio program or plugin for your World Wide Web browser. Once you are configured, a good place to visit to catch up with science news is National Public Radio's "Science Friday" show (**URL - http://www.realaudio.com/contentp/npr/scifri.html**).

2. Check out the rain forest of Central America by connecting to the "MayaQuest" home page (**URL - http://www.mecc.com/mayaquest.html**). Before doing so, make sure you're using a World Wide Web browser that supports VRML and Macromedia Shockwave to achieve the full experience of this site.

3. "Visit" the mountains west of Denver with KCNC Televsion's "Mountain Cam" (**URL - http://www.kcncnews4.com/cgi-bin/citycam.exe?6**). How well you can see the mountains is affected by the air's visibility. Visibility refers to the horizontal extinction of light. Sulfate aerosols and particulates are air pollutants that reduce visibility. Air pressure systems also impact visibilty. Visibility tends to be poor under the influence of high pressure, which inhibits vertical dispersion. How is the visibility west of Denver? What are (were) the weather conditions at the time of observation? Do you think the weather at the time of your observation had any effect on the visibility?

CHAPTER 10

Internet Resources for Earth Science

The list below represents only a small number of the resources available on the Internet. Sites are undoubtedly missing, as it is impossible to catalog all resources. A more extensive, up-to-date list of resources can be found on the ***Earth Online*** World Wide Web home page. Web sites are listed in alphabetical order. If you don't find what you're looking for in this list, go to one of the general earth science lists to check their resources. Turning to any of the better Internet search engines will likely provide you with the information you're looking for too.

Astronomy

Comet C/1996 B2 Hyakutake http://NewProducts.jpl.nasa.gov/comet/hyakutake
Comet Hale-Bopp http://www.eso.org/comet-hale-bopp/comet-hale-bopp.html
Comet Observation Home Page http://encke.jpl.nasa.gov/
Comet Shoemaker-Levy http://newproducts.jpl.nasa.gov/sl9/sl9.html
European Space Agency http://www.esrin.esa.it/htdocs/esa/esa.html
European Space Agency - ESA/ESRIN http://shark1.esrin.esa.it/
European Space Information http://mesis.esrin.esa.it/html/esis.html
Face of Venus Home Page http://stoner.eps.mcgill.ca/bud/first.html
Galileo Project Home Page http://es.rice.edu/ES/humsoc/Galileo/index.html
Giotto Information http://nssdc.gsfc.nasa.gov/planetary/giotto.html
Goddard Space Flight Center Library http://www-library.gsfc.nasa.gov/
Guide to NASA Online Resources http://naic.nasa.gov/naic/guide/
Lunar and Planetary Institute http://cass.jsc.nasa.gov/lpi.html
Milankovitch Cycles—Insolation and Orbital Parameters ftp://ngdc1.ngdc.noaa.gov/paleo/insolation/
NASA Home Page http://hypatia.gsfc.nasa.gov/NASA_homepage.html
NASA *Hot Topics* http://www.nasa.gov/nasa/nasa_hottopics.html
NASA Intelligent Mechanisms Group http://img.arc.nasa.gov/
NASA Internet Connection http://www.jsc.nasa.gov/nasa/NASAInternet.html
NASA Langley Research Center http://mosaic.larc.nasa.gov/nasaonline/gov.html
NASA Press Release Photographs gopher://images.jsc.nasa.gov/70
NASA Press Release Photographs http://images.jsc.nasa.gov/
NASA Press Release Photographs ftp://ftp-images.jsc.nasa.gov
NASA Questions & Answers http://www.nasa.gov/hqpao/questions_answers.html
NASA Solar Images http://umbra.gsfc.nasa.gov/images/latest.html
NASA SpaceLink telnet://spacelink.msfc.nasa.gov
NASA Technical Reports Server http://techreports.larc.nasa.gov/cgi-bin/NTRS
The Nine Planets: A Multimedia Tour of the Solar System http://seds.lpl.arizona.edu/nineplanets/nineplanets/nineplanets.html
Planetary Image Finders http://ic-www.arc.nasa.gov/fia/projects/bayes-group/Atlas/
Project Galileo: Bringing Jupiter to Earth http://www.jpl.nasa.gov/galileo/

Shuttle Payload Gopher gopher://sspp.gsfc.nasa.gov/1/
SkyView http://skyview.gsfc.nasa.gov/skyview.html
Solar/Magnetic Images http://www.sel.bldrdoc.gov/
Space Science and Engineering Center (SSEC) http://www.ssec.wisc.edu/
Space Telescope Science Institute/Hubble Space Telescope Public Information http://marvel.stsci.edu/public.html
Views of the Solar System http://www.c3.lanl.gov/~cjhamil/SolarSystem/homepage.html
WebStars: Astrophysics in CyberSpace http://www.Stars.com/WebStars/
Welcome to the Planets http://stardust.jpl.nasa.gov/planets/

Atmospheric Science (*see also* Climatology, Climate Change, Meteorology)

Center for Atmospheric and Space Science at Utah State University http://www.cass.usu.edu/
Centre for Atmospheric Science—Chemistry Department, Cambridge University http://www.atm.ch.cam.ac.uk/
Institute for Atmospheric Science, ETH Zurich, Switzerland http://dumnw.ethz.ch/LAPETH/lapeth.html
Lawrence Livermore National Laboratory (LLNL) Atmospheric Research http://www-ep.es.llnl.gov/www-ep/atm.html
Rosenstiel School of Marine and Atmospheric Science Home Page http://www.rsmas.miami.edu/
UCAR Gopher gopher://gopher.ucar.edu:70/1

Biogeography

Biosciences Gopher gopher://Info.bio.cmu.edu/1
Ecosystem Complexes by Carbon in Live Vegetation (NDP-017) http://www-eosdis.ornl.gov/
Henderson-Seller's Global Vegetation and Soils Data ftp://ncardata.ucar.edu/datasets/ds767.0
Landscape Ecology and Biogeography Page http://life.anu.edu.au/landscape_ecology/landscape.html
Olson's CDIAC World Ecosystems by Carbon Vegetation Data ftp://ncardata.ucar.edu/datasets/ds769.0
Satellite Tracking of Endangered Species http://sdcd.gsfc.nasa.gov/ISTO/satellite_tracking/
Video of the "Greening Up" of the Northern Hemisphere Through the 1986 Year http://xtreme.gsfc.nasa.gov/movies/FAST_NAMER86.mpg

Career Information

Bio Online Career Management http://cns.bio.com/hr/search/search_1.html
Department of the Interior Automated Vacancy Announcement Distribution System http://info.er.usgs.gov/doi/avads/index.html
Environmental Careers World Online http://www.infi.net/~ecw/
Geotimes Classifieds Employment American Geological Institute http://jei.umd.edu/agi/geotimes/ads.html
GIS Job Clearinghouse, U. of Minnesota Remote Sensing Lab http://walleye.forestry.umn.edu:70/0/www/rsgisinfo/jobs.html
GIS Jobs Clearinghouse gopher://gopher.gis.umn.edu:70/11/rsgis/gisjobs
Riley Guide—Employment Opportunities and Job Resources on the Internet http://www.jobtrak.com/jobguide/
Worldwide Register of Positions Vacant in Geology/Earth Sciences http://www.anu.edu.au/psychology/Academia/geol.htm

Cartography and Mapping

Cartography http://geog.gmu.edu/gess/jwc/cartogrefs.html
CIA World Fact Book Reference Maps http://www.ic.gov/94fact/fb94toc/fb94toc.html#refmap
Color Landform Atlas of the United States http://fermi.jhuapl.edu/states/states.html
Datasets ftp://spectur.xerox.com/pub/map
Making Maps Easy to Read http://acorn.educ.nottingham.ac.uk/ShellCent/maps/
National Mapping Information http://www-nmd.usgs.gov/
USGS National Mapping Information http://www-nmd.usgs.gov/
Xerox PARC Map Viewer http://pubweb.parc.xerox.com/map

Climate Change (*see also* Climatology)

Agricultural Genome World Wide Web Server http://probe.nal.usda.gov/
Animal and Plant Health Inspection Service (APHIS) gopher://gopher.aphis.usda.gov/
Biodiversity and Ecosystems Network http://straylight.tamu.edu/bene/bene.html
Global Change Master Directory http://gcmd.gsfc.nasa.gov
Global Warming Update http://www.ncdc.noaa.gov/gblwrmupd/global.html
National Biological Impact Assessment gopher://gophisb.biochem.vt.edu/
National Biological Service Division of Research: Global Change Research Program http://www.nbs.gov/nbii/gcrp/
NOAA/NASA Pathfinder Program http://pegasus.nesdis.noaa.gov/pathfinder.html
Program for Climate Model Diagnosis and Intercomparison (PCMDI) http://www-pcmdi.llnl.gov/
USGS Global Change Research Program http://geochange.er.usgs.gov/

Climatology

Atlantic Tropical Weather Center http://www.neosoft.com/citylink/blake/tropical.html
Atmospheric Research (NCAR) http://http.ucar.edu/metapage.html
Carbon Dioxide Information Analysis Center (Oak Ridge National Lab) (FTP) file://cdiac.esd.ornl.gov/pub/
Carbon Dioxide Information Analysis Center http://cdiac.esd.ornl.gov/cdiac/home.html
Climate Diagnostics Center http://www.cdc.noaa.gov/
Drought Palmer Index by State or Division (U.S.) http://www.ncdc.noaa.gov/onlineprod/drought/xmgr.html
Earth Space Research Group http://www.crseo.ucsb.edu/esrg.html
East Anglia Home Page Oceanography, Meteorology, Climatology http://www.mth.uea.ac.uk/climateinfo.html
EcoNet's Climate Resources Directory http://www.igc.apc.org/igc/www.clim.html
El-Nino Conditions, Forecasts gopher://cmits02.dow.on.doe.ca/11/climate/nino
El Nino Scenario http://www.crseo.ucsb.edu/geos/el_nino.html
Global Instrumental Climate Data (Atlas) ftp://cdiac.esd.ornl.gov/pub/images/ce
Global Historical Climatology Network ftp://cdiac.esd.ornl.gov/pub/ndp041/
Global and Hemispheric Air Temperature ftp://cdiac.esd.ornl.gov/pub/ndp022r2/
Global and Hemispheric Air Temperature, 1854-1991(Jones et al.) ftp://feature.geography.wisc.edu/pub/phys/global_temp.gif
Global Change—Assisted Search for Knowledge (GC-ASK) http://ask.gcdis.usgcrp.gov:8080/
High Plains Climate Center http://hpccsun.unl.edu/
Hurricane Page from Purdue, Historical Storm tracks http://thunder.atms.purdue.edu/hurricane.html
Lamb's Dust Veil Index, 1500-1983 ftp://cdiac.esd.ornl.gov/pub/ndp013/
Mauna Loa Atmospheric CO2, 1958-1992 ftp://feature.geography.wisc.edu/pub/phys/maunaloa_co2.gif

Matthew's GSFC Global Wetlands and Methane Emission Data, 1-DEGR ftp://ncardata.ucar.edu/datasets/ds765.5
Mauna Loa Atmospheric CO2, 1958-1992 ftp://cdiac.esd.ornl.gov/pub/ndp001r4/
Mean Sea Surface Temperatures http://geochange.er.usgs.gov/pub/magsst/magsst.html
Minnesota Climatology Working Group (Gopher) gopher://nx1.soils.umn.edu:70/1
National Center for Computer Hardware, Advanced Mathematics, and Model Physics (CHAMMP) http://www.esd.ornl.gov/programs/chammp/chammp.html
National Center for Atmospheric Research Home Page http://http.ucar.edu/metapage.html
National Climatic Data Center http://www.ncdc.noaa.gov
National Data Buoy Center http://seaboard.ndbc.noaa.gov/
NOAA Air Resources Laboratory ftp://arlrisc.ssmc.noaa.gov/pub/Home1.html
NOAA/PMEL/TAO El Nino Theme Page http://www.pmel.noaa.gov/toga-tao/el-nino/home.html
NOAA/PMEL/TAO—What Is an El Nino (ENSO)? http://www.pmel.noaa.gov/toga-tao/el-nino-story.html
Ozone http://icair.iac.org.NZ/ozone/ozone.html
Ozone Action Page http://www.essential.org/orgs/Ozone_Action/Ozone_Action.html
Ozone Variations, 1958-1986 ftp://cdiac.esd.ornl.gov/pub/ndp023/
PaleoClimate Data ftp://ngdc1.ngdc.noaa.gov/paleo/climate1500/
SSEC Real-Time Data http://www.ssec.wisc.edu/data/index.html#special
Upper Atmosphere Research Satellite (UARS) Home Page http://daac.gsfc.nasa.gov/CAMPAIGN_DOCS/UARS_project.html
US Global Change Research Program http://www.usgcrp.gov/usgcrp/MULTMAIN.html
USGS Global Change Research Program http://geochange.er.usgs.gov/
U.S. Historical Climatology Network ftp://cdiac.esd.ornl.gov/pub/ndp019r1/
Wilcox Solar Observatory—Stanford University (Telnet) file://solar.stanford.edu/

Earth Science: Education (*see also* Earth Science: General Topics)

EarthEd: Earth Science Education Resources http://www-hpcc.astro.washington.edu/scied/earth.html
Earth Science Educators Gopher Hole gopher://jei.umd.edu/
Earth Science Exercises http://athena.wednet.edu/curric/land/
Eyes on Earth Education Newsletter http://sdcd.gsfc.nasa.gov/ESD/eeenews.html
Geographer's Craft Project http://wwwhost.cc.utexas.edu/ftp/pub/grg/gcraft/contents.html
Image Processing for Teaching http://ipt.lpl.arizona.edu/
Meteorology Exercises http://athena.wednet.edu/curric/weather/
NASA SIR-C Education Program http://ericir.syr.edu/NASA/nasa.html
Ocean Exercises http://athena.wednet.edu/curric/oceans/index.html
Planetary Sciences Exercises http://athena.wednet.edu/curric/space/
Science and the Environment—A Learning Tool http://www.voyagepub.com/publish
Seismology Resources for Teachers http://www.geo.purdue.edu/seismology_resources.html
Space Physics Textbook http://www.oulu.fi/~spaceweb/textbook/
UK Earth Science Courseware Consortium http://info.mcc.ac.uk/Geology/CAL/index.html
U.S. Federal Education Resources http://www.ed.gov/EdRes/EdFed.html#others
Virtual Department (UT-Austin): Course List http://www.utexas.edu/depts/grg/virtdept/courses/courselist.html

Earth Science: General Topics

Clearinghouse for Subject-Oriented Internet Resource Guides http://www.lib.umich.edu/chhome.html
Earth and Environmental Sciences Connections from the USGS http://www.usgs.gov/network/science/earth/index.html
Earth Pages http://epserver.gsfc.nasa.gov/earth/earth.html

Earth Sciences Division (NASA/ARC) http://geo.arc.nasa.gov/esd
Earth Sciences Site of the Week http://agcwww.bio.ns.ca/misc/geores/sotw/sotw.html
Earth System Science Resource Center http://zelda.thomson.com/rcenters/earthnet/earth_sci.html
GeoClio: Webserver for the History of Geology and the Geosciences http://geoclio.st.usm.edu/
Geo Exchange: List of Applied and Commercial Geoscience Sites http://giant.mindlink.net/geo_exchange/geology.html
Geographical and Geological Sites http://www.abdn.ac.uk/~u01rpr/geo.html
Geosciences FAQ http://www.cs.ruu.nl/wais/html/na-dir/geology-faq/.html
Geosciences Information Group from the UK Geol. Society http://www.bris.ac.uk/Depts/Geol/gig/gig.html
GeoScience: K-12 Resources http://www.cuug.ab.ca:8001/~johnstos/geosci.html
Geosciences Link at Einet http://galaxy.einet.net/galaxy/Science/Geosciences.html
Internet Resources for Geographers and Geologists (UW-SP) http://www.uwsp.acaddept/geog/res.htm
Mike's Earth Science Web Pointers http://www.covis.nwu.edu/storage/Mike.html
NASA/GSFC Earth Sciences Directorate http://sdcd.gsfc.nasa.gov/ESD/
NASA Info by Subject http://hypatia.gsfc.nasa.gov/nasa_subjects/nasa_subjectpage.html
NOAA Geosciences Lab http://www.grdl.noaa.gov/
Online Resources for Earth Scientists (ORES) http://www.calweb.com/~tcsmith/ores/
Planet Earth Home Page Virtual Library http://www.nosc.mil/planet_earth/everything.html
Special Internet Connections http://www.uwm.edu/Mirror/inet.services.html
TradeWave Galaxy http://galaxy.einet.net/galaxy.htm
USGS Earth and Environmental Science Index http://www.usgs.gov/network/science/earth/earth.html
Virtual Earth http://wombat.es.mq.edu.au/0c:/v_earth.html
WWW Virtual Library http://www.w3.org/hypertext/DataSources/bySubject/Overview.html
Yahoo!—Science:Earth Sciences http://www.yahoo.com/Science/Earth_Sciences/

Earthquakes and Seismicity

Alaska Public Seismic Network http://www.polarnet.com/Users/APSN
Crustal Deformation Measurements in California http://quake.wr.usgs.gov/QUAKES/crustaldef/
Current Earthquake Activity http://quake.wr.usgs.gov/QUAKES/CURRENT/current.html
Earthquake Information from Menlo Park http://quake.wr.usgs.gov/
Earthquake Social Data, NGDC, Boulder, CO http://www.ngdc.noaa.gov/seg/hazard/resource/eqsoc.html
Frequently Asked Questions about Earthquakes http://quake.wr.usgs.gov/more/eqfaq.html
Kobe City http://www.shiga-pc.ac.jp:8080/~ohno/quake/kobe-city/disaster.html
Kobe Earthquake information http://www.niksula.cs.hut.fi/~haa/kobe.html
San Andreas Fault and the Bay Area http://sepwww.stanford.edu/oldsep/joe/fault_images/BayAreaSanAndreasFault.html
Memphis Public Seismic Network http://gandalf.ceri.memphis.edu/~rond/psn
National Earthquake Information Center http://wwwneic.cr.usgs.gov/
National Strong Motion Program http://agram.wr.usgs.gov/
Northern California Data Center, Berkeley, CA http://quake.geo.berkeley.edu/
ORES: Earthquakes Seismology Resources http://calweb.calweb.com/~mtnsweet/ores/geology/eq/
Public Seismic Network Home Page http://psn.quake.net/
San Francisco Earthquake of 1906 http://www.slip.net/~dfowler/1906/museum.html
Southern California Data Center, Pasadena, CA http://scec.gps.caltech.edu/
Surfing the Internet for Earthquake Data http://www.geophys.washington.edu/seismosurfing.html
UCR—Earthquake Information http://smaug.ucr.edu/Quakes/quake_page.html

USGS Internet Resources on Earthquakes http://www.usgs.gov/network/science/earth/earthquake.html
World-Wide Earthquake Locator http://geovax.ed.ac.uk/quakes/quakes.html

Ecology and Environment

Biodiversity Servers http://kaos.erin.gov.au/other_servers/category/Biodiversity.html
Bioregion Information Bank: University of Illinois http://W3.ag.uiuc.edu/AIM/Discovery/Issues/bioregion.html
Central Plains Exp. Range Long Term Ecological Research Site http://agropyron.cfnr.colostate.edu:3793/homepage.html
Ecosytem Home Page http://www.gold.net/ecosystem/
Environment Index of the WWW Virtual Library http://ecosys.drdr.virginia.edu/Environment.html
Long-Term Ecological Research (LTER) http://lternet.edu/
Man and the Biosphere http://ice.ucdavis.edu/MAB/
ToxFAQs™ http://atsdr1.atsdr.cdc.gov:8080/toxfaq.html
Tree of Life http://phylogeny.arizona.edu/tree/phylogeny.html
University of East Anglia, Norwich, England, School of Environmental Sciences http://www.env.uea.ac.uk/

Energy

Asian Oil and Gas Internet Resources http://www.ntu.ac.sg/~asreid/asianog.htm
Department of Energy Climate Data wais://ridgisd.er.usgs.gov
International Geothermal Association http://www.demon.co.uk/geosci/world.html
Investigating Wind Energy http://sln.fi.edu/tfi/units/energy/windguide.html
Risø:AMV: European Wind Atlas http://risul1.risoe.dk:80/amv/ewa/
sci.geo.petroleum Internet Resources http://cg.ensmp.fr/pointeurs/petroleum.html
Surface Exploration Techniques for Oil and Gas Exploration http://www.csn.net/~jamesf/ssiweb/ssiweb.html
Utilities Report Action Alert http://www.great-lakes.net:2200/0/partners/NWF/toxics/ut-alert.html

Erosion

Agricultural Research Service Wind Erosion Research Unit http://www.weru.ksu.edu
National Soil Erosion Research Laboratory http://soils.ecn.purdue.edu:20002/

Geochemistry

USGS Branch of Geochemistry http://helios.cr.usgs.gov/
Yale—Geochemical cycles http://stormy.geology.yale.edu/kgl/Brochure/Geochemistry/5_1.html

Geodata

Aerological Reference Data Set (CARDS) http://www.ncdc.noaa.gov/cards/cards_homepage.html
Air Temperatures—Suface, Troposphere, Stratosphere, 1958-1992 ftp://cdiac.esd.ornl.gov/pub/ndp008r3/
Atmospheric Radiation Measurement (ARM) Program http://info.arm.gov/
Carbon Emissions, Fossil (Global, Regional and National) 1950-1990 ftp://cdiac.esd.ornl.gov/pub/ndp006/

Central European Environmental Data Request Facility (CEDAR) http://pan.cedar.univie.ac.at/
Climate Monitoring and Diagnostics Laboratory (NOAA/OAR) http://www.cmdl.noaa.gov
CLIMVIS—Global Summary of the Day http://www.ncdc.noaa.gov/onlineprod/drought/xmgr.html
Cooperative Interactive Atmospheric Catalog System (CODIAC) http://www.ofps.ucar.edu/codiac-www.html
Datasurge: A Geotechnical Software Company http://www.usa1.com/datasurg
Digital Elevation Models (30-second) http://info.er.usgs.gov:80/data/noaa/global_relief_cd_rom/topo/topo30/
Earth Observation Satellites International Directory Network http://gcmd.gsfc.nasa.gov/ceos_idn.html
ETOPO5 World Topographic Dataset (N Hemisphere) ftp://walrus.wr.usgs.gov/pub/data/etopo5.northern.bat.Z
ETOPO5 World Topographic Dataset (S Hemisphere) ftp://walrus.wr.usgs.gov/pub/data/etopo5.southern.bat.Z
Fault Mapping Data—USGS file://alum.wr.usgs.gov/pub/map/
Federal Geographic Data Committee http://fgdc.er.usgs.gov/gdc/html/fgdc.htm
Federal Geographic Data Products http://info.er.usgs.gov/fgdc-catalog/title.html
FGDC—Manual of Geographic Data Products http://www.usgs.gov/fgdc-catalog/title.html
Fossil Fuel Emissions (Global), 1860-1989 ftp://cdiac.esd.ornl.gov/pub/ndp006/
GeoData Products Index http://www.usgs.gov/doc/edchome/ndcdb/ndcdb.html
Geophysical Data from the Solid Earth http://www.ngdc.noaa.gov/seg/segd.html
Geophysical On-Line Data (GOLD) http://ngdc.noaa.gov.4096/index.html
Global Change Data and Information System http://www.gcdis.usgcrp.gov/
Global Change Data at NGDC http://www.ngdc.noaa.gov/seg/globsys/global_c.html
Global Change Master Directory: Data Set Information Query http://gcmd.gsfc.nasa.gov/mainquery.html
Global and Hemispheric Air Temperature, 1854-1991 (Jones et al.) ftp://cdiac.esd.ornl.gov/pub/ndp022r2/
Global Historical Climatology Network—GHCN http://www.ncdc.noaa.gov/ghcn/ghcn.html
Global 1-Degree DEM ftp://feature.geography.wisc.edu:21/pub/phys/scripps/
Global 5-Minute DEM http://info.er.usgs.gov:80/data/noaa/global_relief_cd_rom/topo/etopo5/
Great Lakes Regional Environ. Information Sys. Metadata http://epaserver.ciesin.org/glreis/metadata/metasearch.html
Hydro-Climatic Data Network Streamflow Data Set, 1874-1988 http://wwwrvares.er.usgs.gov/hcdn_cdrom/1st_page.html
Lamont-Doherty Earth Observatory http://rainbow.ldgo.columbia.edu/
Langley Research Center (LaRC) EOSDIS Distributed Active Archive Center (DAAC) http://eosdis.larc.nasa.gov/
NASA Earth Observing System Data and Information System (EOSDIS) http://gcmd.gsfc.nasa.gov/gcmdeos.html
National Biological Information Infrastructure http://www.nbs.gov/nbii/
National Geophysical Data Center Digital Terrain Data http://www.ngdc.noaa.gov/seg/globsys/topo.html
National Geospatial Data Clearinghouse http://fgdc.er.usgs.gov/clearover2.html
National Geospatial Data Clearinghouse http://nsdi.usgs.gov/nsdi/
National Geospatial Data Clearinghouse USGS Node http://edcwww.cr.usgs.gov/nsdi/genselct.htm
National On-Line Data and Information Service (NODIS) telnet://nssdca.gsfc.nasa.gov
NBS EMTC Aerial Photo Server http://www.emtc.nbs.gov/http_data/aerial_photos/ap.html
NGDC Topographic Data http://www.ngdc.noaa.gov/seg/globsys/topo.html
Nimbus-7 TOMS Data ftp://jwocky.gsfc.nasa.gov/pub/nimbus7
NOAA Monthly Data http://ferret.wrc.noaa.gov/ferret/main-menu.html
OASIS http://www.ncdc.noaa.gov/oasis/oasis.html

OSCAR http://www.ncdc.noaa.gov.sdsd.oscar.html
Sea-Viewing Wide-Field Sensor (SeaWIFS) http://seawifs.gsfc.nasa.gov/SEAWIFS.html
Shaded (5-Minute) Relief Images http://ageninfo.tamu.edu/apl-us
Socioeconomic Data and Applications Center: Model Visualization http://sedac.ciesin.org/sedac-2.3/mvas.home/mvas-home.html
Soil and Surface Slope Data GISS (Staub and Rosenweigs) ftp://ncardata.ucar.edu/datasets/ds770.0
Trends 93: CDIAC http://cdiac.esd.ornl.gov/cdiac/trends_html/trends/co2/contents.htm
Tropical Database (Brazil) http://www.ftpt.br/
US Climate Division Drought Data http://www.ncdc.noaa.gov/onlineprod/drought/main.html
USGS Data Available Online http://internet.er.usgs.gov/index.html
US Dept. of Agriculture: Current Research Information System (CRIS) http://www.sura.net/main/members/usda.shtml
US GeoData FTP Access http://edcwww.cr.usgs.gov/doc/edchome/ndcdb/ndcdb.html
USGS Geographic Names Database gopher://gopher.peabody.yale.edu:71/1
US Summary of the Day http://www.ncdc.noaa.gov/onlineprod/tfsod/climvis/main.html
Vegetation and Soils (Global) Data (Henderson-Seller's) ftp://ncardata.ucar.edu/datasets/ds767.0
World Data Center—A for Marine Geology and Geophysics http://www.ngdc.noaa.gov/mgg/mggd.html
World Data Center—A for Paleoclimatology http://www.ngdc.noaa.gov/paleo/paleo.html
World Data Center—A for Solid Earth Geophysics http://www.ngdc.noaa.gov/wdcmain.html
Worldwide Organic Soil Carbon and Nitrogen Data (NDP-018) http://www-eosdis.ornl.gov/DATASET_DOCS

Geographic Information Systems

Beginners Guide to Geographic Information Systems (Tutorial) http://info.er.usgs.gov/research/gis/title.html
DMSP Home Page http://www.ngdc.noaa.gov/./dmsp/dmsp.html
Frequently Asked Questions About GIS http://www.census.gov/geo/gis/faq-index.html
GIS Analysis with ArcInfo (University of Buffalo) http://www.geog.buffalo.edu//arcinfo/aiwwwtut/ARChome.html
GIS Dictionary http://www.geo.ed.ac.uk/root/agidict/html/welcome.html
GIS-Related Internet Sites ftp://gis.queensu.ca/pub/gis/docs/gissites.html
National Atlas Information Service http://www-nais.ccm.emr.ca/
National Topographic Map Service, Geomatics Canada http://www.geocan.nrcan.gc.ca/topo/public_html/info.html
Tiger Mapping Service http://tiger.census.gov
WDB-II World Data Bank ftp://sepftp.stanford.edu/pub/World_Map

Geography

Desert Research Institute http://www.dri.edu/ASC
Geographer's Craft Project http://wwwhost.cc.utexas.edu/ftp/pub/grg/gcraft/contents.html
Geographic Name Server telnet:// martini.eecs.umich.edu 3000
Geography Resources on the Internet http://ncgia.geog.buffalo.edu/GIAL/netgeog.html
GeoWeb http://wings.buffalo.edu/geoweb/
New South Polar Times Project http://139.132.40.31/NSPT/NSPThomePage.html
WWW Virtual Library: Geography http://hpb1.hwc.ca:10002/WWW_VL_Geography.html

Geology

Geology and Geophysics Number Crunchers Forum http://www.glg.ed.ac.uk/crunch

Image Finder http://www.cm.cf.ac.uk/Misc/wustl.html
Smithsonian Gem & Mineral Collection http://galaxy.einet.net/images/gems/gems-icons.html
Mathematical Geology ftp:// www.iamg.org/pub/MG
Mathematical Geology and Computers in Geosciences http://www.geosc.uh.edu/anon.html
Numerical Analysis for Geological Sciences, Jim Carr ftp://www.iamg.org/pub/Carr
USGS Network Resources Page http://www.usgs.gov/network/index.html
The Very-Low-Grade Metamorphism WWW Server http://www.uni-erlangen.de/docs/FAU/fakultaet/natIII/geo_min/vlgm/

Glaciology

Benchmark Glaciers http://orcapaktcm.wr.usgs.gov/BenchmarkGlaciers/bmg.html
Glaciotectonic Bibliography http://www.emporia.edu/s/www/earthsci/biblio/biblio.htm
Satellite Images: Glaciers http://geochange.er.usgs.gov/pub/info/facts/atlas/index.html

Global Positioning

National Geodetic Survey Division (GPS Programs, Etc.) http://www.ngs.noaa.gov/

Government (*see also* Organizations and Surveys)

NOAA Home Page http://www.noaa.gov/
U.S. Geological Survey http://www.usgs.gov/

Grants

Grants Web http://infoserv.rttonet.psu.edu/gweb.htm
National Science Foundation World Wide Web Server http://www.nsf.gov/

Hydrology

EOSDIS Hydrologic Cycle Distributed Active Archive Center (DAAC) http://wwwdaac.msfc.nasa.gov/
Great Lakes Info http://h2o.seagrant.wisc.edu/greatlakes/greatlakes.html
The Great Mississippi River Flood of 1993 http://www.nohrsc.nws.gov/flood.html
Hydrologic Cycle DAAC at Marshall SpaceFlight Center http://wwwdaac.msfc.nasa.gov/
Hydrology Web http://terrassa.pnl.gov:2080/EESC/resourcelist/hydrology.html
Midwest Flood Images 1993 ftp://climate.gsfc.nasa.gov/pub/gumley/
National Operational Hydrologic Remote Sensing Center http://www.nohrsc.nws.gov/
National Snow and Ice Data Center http://nsidc.colorado.edu/NSIDC/data_announcements/ice_concentration_01-90.html
National Water Resources http://wwwdilurb.er.usgs.gov/pub/resources.html
1993 Midwest Flood Images ftp://climate.gsfc.nasa.gov/pub/gumley
Universities Water Information Network http://www.uwin.siu.edu/
US Army Corps of Engineers 1993 Flood Home Page http://www.wes.army.mil/EL/flood/fl93home.html
USGS Earth and Environmental Science: Water http://info.er.usgs.gov/network/science/earth/water.html
USGS Gauge Data ftp://srv1rvares.er.usgs.gov/hcdn92/
USGS Real-Time Hydrologic Data http://h2o.usgs.gov/public/realtime.html
USGS Water Resources of the United States http://h2o.usgs.gov/
USGS Water Resources Publications http://h2o.usgs.gov/public/wrd012.html

U.S. Water News http://www.mother.com/uswaternews
Water Management Research Laboratory http://asset.arsusda.gov/wmrl/wmrl.html
WRCS Hydrology and Hydraulics http://users.aol.com/h2oengr/index.htm

Internet

Awesome Lists http://www.clark.net/pub/journalism/awesome.html
DejaNews (Search Usenet Articles) http://www.dejanews.com/
Email Mailing Lists gopher://liberty.uc.wlu.edu:70/11/internet/searchlistserv
FTPmail Servers http://src.doc.ic.ac.uk/ftpmail-servers.html
Gopher gopher://gopher.tc.umn.edu
HaLsoft HTML Validation Service http://www.hal.com/~connolly/html-test/service/validation-form.html
Inter-Links http://www.nova.edu/Inter-Links/
Internet Resources http://bramble.er.usgs.gov/internetresources.html
Internet Resources Meta-Map http://www.ncsa.uiuc.edu/SDG/Software/Mosaic/Demo/metamap.html
NCSA Software Tools http://www.ncsa.uiuc.edu/SDG/Software/SDGSoftDir.html
Resources Classified by Type of Service http://www.w3.org/hypertext/DataSources/ByAccess.html
Usenet News gopher://liberty.uc.wlu.edu:70/11/internet/usenet/readers
WWW Primer http://www.vuw.ac.nz/who/Nathan.Torkington/ideas/www-primer.html
Yahoo! http://www.yahoo.com/

Meteorology

ACCU-WEATHER http://accuwx.com/berlin.de/english/index.html
Australian National University http://life.anu.edu.au/weather.html
Canadian Weather Forcasts (Gopher) gopher://gopher.nstn.ca:70/1
Cooperative Institute for Meteorological Satellite Studies (CIMSS) http://cloud.ssec.wisc.edu/
Global Grid Point Air Temperature ftp://cdiac.esd.ornl.gov/pub/ndp020r1/
Heat Index Chart http://thunder.atms.purdue.edu/heat.html
Meteor-3 TOMS Data ftp://jwocky.gsfc.nasa.gov/pub/meteor3
Michigan State University—Current Weather Maps/Movies http://rs560.cl.msu.edu/weather
Michigan State University—Current Weather Maps/Movies http://rs560.cl.msu.edu/weather
MSU Weather Maps, Satellite Images, Movies http://rs560.cl.msu.edu/weather/index.html
NASA Optical Transient (Lightning) Detector http://rimeice.msfc.nasa.gov:5678/otd.html
National Geophysical Data Center (NGDC)—Defense Meteorological Satellite Program Home Page(DMSP) http://web.ngdc.noaa.gov/dmsp/dmsp.html
NCEP Storm Prediction Center http://www.awc-kc.noaa.gov/spc/storm_prediction_center.html
NOAA Network Information Center http://www.nnic.noaa.gov/NIC/NNIC.html
NOAA Network Information Center WWW Page http://www.nnic.noaa.gov/
NSF Geoscience Unidata Intergrated Earth Information Server http://atm.geo.nsf.gov/
NSF Weather Station Information http://atm.geo.nsf.gov/atd/station.html
Purdue Weather Processor gopher://meteor.atms.purdue.edu/1
Purdue Weather Processor http://thunder.atms.purdue.edu
Realtime Satellite Data from SSEC http://www.ssec.wisc.edu/data/
Storm Chaser Home Page http://taiga.geog.niu.edu/chaser.html
Tropical Meteorology http://www.neosoft.com/citylink/blake/tropical.html
Tornado Debris Project Home Page http://geowww.gcn.uoknor.edu/WWW/Debris/Debris.html
University of Illinois—The Daily Planet http://www.atmos.uiuc.edu
University of Michigan Weather Underground http://groundhog.sprl.umich.edu/
University of Edinburgh (Meteorology) (Gopher) gopher://gopher.ed.ac.uk:70/1ftp%3acu.met.ed.ac.uk%40/

U.S. Cities Weather and Forecasts http://www.mit.edu:8001/weather/usa.html
U.S. Monthly Sunshine and Cloud, ca. 1900-1987 ftp://cdiac.esd.ornl.gov/pub/ndp021r1
Weather Center http://geowww.gcn.uoknor.edu/WWW/WxCenter/WxCenter.html
Weather World http://www.atmos.uiuc.edu/wxworld/html/detailed.html
Wind Chill Chart http://thunder.atms.purdue.edu/wchill.html
World Data Center A, Meteorology http://www.ncdc.noaa.gov/wdcamet.html
Worldwide Daily Surface Meteorological Data ftp://hurricane.ncdc.noaa.gov/pub/data/globalsod

Mineralogy

Crystallography Index of the WWW Virtual Library http://www.unige.ch/crystal/crystal_index.html
Mineralogical Sites at Clausthal Institute http://www.immr.tu-clausthal.de/
USGS Minerals Page http://minerals.er.usgs.gov

Museums

Electronic Prehistoric Shark Museum http://turnpike.net/emporium/C/celestial/epsm.htm
The Field Museum Online http://www.bvis.uic.edu/museum/Dna_To_Dinosaurs.html
National Museum of Natural History (Smithsonian) http://nmnhgoph.si.edu/
Natural History Museum London, England http://www.nhm.ac.uk/
Ocean Planet: Smithsonian Institute http://seawifs.gsfc.nasa.gov/ocean_planet.html
Ontario Science Center http://www.osc.on.ca/
Royal Tyrrell Museum http://freenet.calgary.ab.ca/science/tyrrell/
Smithsonian Institution http://www.si.edu
U.C. Berkeley Museum of Paleontology http://ucmp1.berkeley.edu:80/welcome.html

Oceanography

Altimetry Atlas of Indian and Atlantic Oceans by Delft University http://dutlru8.lr.tudelft.nl/
Global Ocean Heat Budget Data (Monthly) http://ferret.wrc.noaa.gov/ferret/main-menu.html
Hydro Atlas of the Southern Oceans from Alfred Wegener Institute http://www.awi-bremerhaven.de/
Interactive Hydrographic Map from the Levitus's 1982 Data Set http://www.ori.u-tokyo.ac.jp/fujio/Levitus-map.html
JPL Physical Oceanography Archive http://seazar.jpl.nasa.gov/
Levitus Annual Data Ocean T, Salinity, Oxygen http://ferret.wrc.noaa.gov/ferret/main-menu.html
Marine Geology, National Marine and Coastal Geology Program http://walrus.wr.usgs.gov
Physical Oceanography Distributed Active Archive Center http://podaac-www.jpl.nasa.gov/
RIDGE Multibeam Synthesis Project—Sea Floor Images http://imager.ldeo.columbia.edu/ridgembs/ne_pac/html/home.html
Sea Floor Imagery http://imager.ldeo.columbia.edu/ridgembs/ne_pac/html/home.html
Sea Surface Temperatures http://www.rsmas.miami.edu/images.html
USGS Marine Server http://marine.usgs.gov/
Woods Hole, USGS Atlantic Marine Geology http://bramble.er.usgs.gov/">
World Ocean Circulation Experiment WOCE http://www.coaps.fsu.edu/WOCE/

Organizations and Surveys

Aberdeen Department of Geology and Petroleum Geology http://hutton.geol.abdn.ac.uk/">
American Association of Petroleum Geologists http://www.geobyte.com/
American Association of Stratigraphic Palynologists http://www.geology.utoronto.ca/AASP

American Geological Institute http://agi.umd.edu/agi/agi.html
American Geophysical Union Home Page http://earth.agu.org
Association of Polish Geomorphologists http://hum.amu.edu.pl/~sgp/welcome.html
Atlantic Geoscience Center http://agcwww.bio.ns.ca/
Australian Geological Survey (Geological Survey of Canada) Organisation http://www.agso.gov.au/
British Geological Survey http://www.nkw.ac.uk/bgs/index.html
Geological Survey of Canada http://emr1.emr.ca/gsc/
Geological Survey of Finland http://www.gsf.fi/
Geological Survey of Japan http://www.aist.go.jp:7128/
Geologists Home Page http://www.geobyte.com
Geomagnetism Group http://ub.nmh.ac.uk
Paleontological Society http://www.uic.edu/orgs/paleo/homepage.html
Seismological Society of America http://www.seismosoc.org/ssa
Structural Engineers Association of California http://www.seaoc.org/seaoc/seaoc1.htm
UK Geoscience Information http://www.bris.ac.uk/Depts/Geol/gig/gig.html
University of Texas El Paso Department of Geological Sciences gopher://dillion.geo.utexas.edu
US Army Corps of Engineers http://www.usace.mil:80/usace.html
Volcanological Society of Japan Home Page http://loki.eri.u-tokyo.ac.jp/~kazan/VSJ1E.html

Paleontology

Dino Russ's Lair http://jacobson.isgs.uiuc.edu/
Dinosaurs Index http://www.yahoo.com/Science/Earth_Sciences/Paleontology/Dinosaurs/
Dinosaurs in Hawaii! http://www.hcc.hawaii.edu/dinos/dinos.1.html
Dinosaur and Vertibrate Paleontology Links from Journal of Geoscience Education http://www.geology.uiuc.edu/~schimmri/geology/vertebrate.html
Electronic Prehistoric Shark Museum http://turnpike.net/emporium/C/celestial/epsm.htm
The Field Museum Online http://www.bvis.uic.edu/museum/Dna_To_Dinosaurs.html
Invertebrate Paleontology and Evolution http://www.geology.uiuc.edu/~schimmri/geology/invertebrate.html
Radiolaria Home Page http://mindlink.net/fabrice_cordey/rad.htm>
Royal Tyrrell Museum http://freenet.calgary.ab.ca/science/tyrrell/
Russian Paleontological Institute http://ucmp1.berkeley.edu/exhibittext/pinentrance.html
U.C. Berkeley Museum of Paleontology http://ucmp1.berkeley.edu:80/welcome.html

Plate Tectonics

Crustal Dynamics Data Information System (CDDIS) http://cddis.gsfc.nasa.gov
Geodynamics Branch (NASA/GSFC) http://denali.gsfc.nasa.gov/
NCEER's Strong Motion Server telnet://duke.ldgo.columbia.edu:23

Publications

Astrophysics Data System Abstract Service http://adsabs.harvard.edu/ads_abstracts.html
Computers and Geosciences ftp:// www.iamg.org/pub/CG
Earth Science Publications, US GPO http://www.access.gpo.gov/su_docs/sale/sb-160.html
Earth Science Journals http://www.ldeo.columbia.edu/journal.html
Electronic Green Journal ftp.uidaho.edu/pub/docs/publications/EGJ
Electronic Green Journal http://gopher.uidaho.edu
Free Online Geophysics Books from the Samizdat Press http://cwp.mines.colorado.edu:3852/samizdat
GIS World http://www.gisworld.com/

Journal of Paleolimnology (Online Abstracts) http://www.umanitoba.ca/geosci/PALEOLIM/jopl.html
National Disaster Reference Database http://ltpwww.gsfc.nasa.gov/ndrd/ndrd2.html
Online Earth Science Journals (Official Site) http://www.ncpgg.adelaide.edu.au/journals.htm
Publications http://www.usgs.gov/data/geologic/index.html
Science and the Environment http://www.voyagepub.com/publish/voyage.htm
U.S. Geological Survey—Earth Science Publications http://internet.er.usgs.gov/fact-sheets/index.html
Volcano Systems Center Univ. Washington: Journal List http://www.vsc.washington.edu/resources/journals.html
VSC: Volcanology Publications http://www.vsc.washington.edu/resources/pubs.html

Reference (*see also* Earth Science: General)

CARL UnCover database telnet://database.carl.org
Clearing House for Subject-Oriented Resource Guides http://www.lib.umich.edu/chhome.html
Colorado Alliance of Research Libraries telnet://pac.carl.org
Digital Library (University of Michigan) http://www.lib.umich.edu/libhome/electres.html
Earthquake Hazards Bibliography, Utah http://utstdpwww.state.ut.us/~ugs/eqhazbib.htm
Geographic Name Server/Xerox Map Gateway http://wings.buffalo.edu/geogw
German Virtual Library Branch http://www.rz.uni-karlsruhe.de/Outerspace/VirtualLibrary/
Global Electronic Library gopher://marvel.loc.gov/11/global
INFO-MINE, Mining Information Service http://www.info-mine.com/
National Biological Service Libraries http://www.its.nbs.gov/nbs2/nbshp23.html
Server http://www.nalusda.gov/
Sunrise/Sunset/Twilight and Moonrise/Moonset/Phase http://tycho.usno.navy.mil/srss.html
U.S. Geological Survey Library http://internet.er.usgs.gov/education/library.html
USGS Library System http://internet.er.usgs.gov/education/library.html
WWW Virtual Library of Science http://coombs.anu.edu.au/SpecialProj/ASAP/WWWVL-HSTM.html

Remote Sensing (*see also* Cartography and Mapping, Geographic Information Systems)

Canada Centre for Remote Sensing http://www.ccrs.emr.ca:80/gcnet/
Distributed Active Archive Center (EDC DAAC) http://sun1.cr.usgs.gov/landdaac/landdaac.html
Earth Observing System (EOS) Home Page http://spso.gsfc.nasa.gov/spso_homepage.html
Earth Resources Observation Systems (EROS) Data Center EOSDIS Land Processes
EROS Data Center http://sun1.cr.usgs.gov/eros-home.html
EROS Data Center Catalog telnet://anonymous@glis.cr.usgs.gov
ESA Earth Observation http://tracy.esrin.esa.it/
ISS 2D Browser—Interactively View High-Resolution Satellite Imagery http://www-itg.lbl.gov/ISS/browser/iss2d.html
NASA Goddard Space Center: Biospheric Sciences Branch http://ltpwww.gsfc.nasa.gov/bsb/Home.html
NASA: SeaWifs Project http://seawifs.gsfc.nasa.gov/SEAWIFS.html
Public Use of Remote Sensing Data http://rsd.gsfc.nasa.gov/rsd/
Remote Sensing http://www.vtt.fi/aut/ava/rs/virtual/
Remote Sensing Meta Home Page http://geog1.geog.nott.ac.uk/hypertex/home.htm
Remote Sensing Organizations http://www.vtt.fi/aut/ava/rs/virtual/organizations.html
Shaded Relief Images: 5-Minute http://ageninfo.tamu.edu/apl-us/
World Wide Web Virtual Library: Remote Sensing http://www.vtt.fi/aut/ava/rs/virtual/

Search (Internet)

Archie Request Form: Search FTP http://hoohoo.ncsa.uiuc.edu/archie.html
Excite http://www.excite.com/
InfoSeek http://www2.infoseek.com/
Jughead gopher://liberty.uc.wlu.edu:3002/7
Lycos http://www.lycos.com/
Veronica gopher://veronica.scs.unr.edu/11/veronica
WAIS—Directory of Sources ftp://bash.cc.keio.ac.jp/pub/inet/wais-sources
WebCrawler http://webcrawler.com/
Whole Internet Catalog http://nearnet.gnn.com/gnn/wic/index.html
World Wide Web Worm http://wwww.cs.colorado.edu/wwww/

Seismicity (*see* Earthquakes and Seismicity; Plate Tectonics)

Software (*see also* Geodata)

Environmental Simulations Inc. http://www.us.net/evisim/links.html
Erlangen Public Domain Software Collection http://www.rrze.uni-erlangen.de/docs/FAU/fakultaet/natIII/geo_min/geologie/soft.html
Free Public-Domain Groundwater-Modeling Programs http://scribe.geol.lsu.edu/rbwinston.html
Geochemistry Software ftp://sparky2.esd.mun.ca
Groundwater Modeling Dept. Brigham Young Univ. http://www.et.byu.edu/~geos/staff/owens/groundwater.html#ModelsEnviroMod
Internet Browsers and Client Software http://life.anu.edu.au/links/syslib.html
Molecular Models http://ds.internic.net/indigo/molecular_models/index.html
Software Server http://199.227.7.95/ehisrvr.html
USGS Models Source Code ftp://kilburn.keene.edu/Kilburn/ftp/GWM-L/
Virtual Software Library: Master Site http://vsl.cnet.com/

Soil Science

National Soil Survey Center http://www.ncg.nrcs.usda.gov/soils/nssc.html
Soil Information System: Purdue University http://dynamo.ecn.purdue.edu/~biehl/SoilInfo/Index.html
Soil Science Page: Soil Science Dept. Massey Univ. http://www-aghort.massey.ac.nz/departs/soilsc/cybsoil/soildep1.htm

Virtual Field Trips

International Arctic Project 1995 http://scholastic.com:2005/public/IAP/IAP-Home.html
Virtual Field Trip: Ice Age Trail Project, Wisconsin http://www.uwsp.edu/acaddept/geog/vftrip/iat/
Virtual Field Trip: Oneonta to the Hudson River http://www.hartwick.edu/geology/work/VFT-so-far/VFT.html
Virtual Field Trip: Tomorrow River, Wisconsin http://www.uwsp.edu/acaddept/geog/vftrip/toriv/
Virtually Hawaii: Virtual Field Trips http://www.satlab.hawaii.edu/space/hawaii/virtual.field.trips.html
Virtual Tourist http://wings.buffalo.edu/world/

Volcanology (see also Plate Tectonics)

Alaska Volcano Observatory http://volcano.und.nodak.edu/vwdocs/current_volcs/shishaldin/shishaldin.html
Big Island Page http://www.satlab.hawaii.edu/space/hawaii/kilauea.virtual.field.trip.html
Electronic Volcano (Dartmouth University) http://www.dartmouth.edu/pages/rox/volcanoes/elecvolc.html
Global Volcanism Network, Bulletin of http://nmnhgoph.si.edu/gvn.html
IRIS EOS Volcanogy Team's Home Page http://www.geo.mtu.edu/eos/
Long Valley Volcano Page http://quake.wr.usgs.gov/VOLCANOES/LongValley/index.html
Stromboli Volcano Page http://udgtls.dgt.uniud.it/seismol/strombol.htm
U.K. Vulcanologists Group http://exodus.open.ac.uk/volcano/volc_index.html
USGS Hawaii Volcano Watch Reports http://www.soest.hawaii.edu/hvo/
Volcano Information Center http://magic.geol.ucsb.edu/~fisher
Volcanic Simulation Group (Pisa, Italy) http://www.dst.unipi.it/index.html
Volcanic Topography at the Mid-Atlantic Ridge http://humm.whoi.edu/debbie.html
Volcano World http://volcano.und.nodak.edu/vw.html
Volcanoes of the World http://volcano.und.nodak.edu/volc_of_world.html
What's Erupting Now! http://volcano.und.nodak.edu/vwdocs/current_volcs/current.html

Wetlands

Classification of Wetlands Manual, U.S. Fish and Wildlife Service http://www.nwi.fws.gov/classman.html
National Wetlands Inventory—Ecology Section http://www.nwi.fws.gov/Ecology.html
U.S. National Wetlands Survey http://www.nwi.fws.gov/

APPENDIX 1

Internet Glossary

application Software that performs a function for the user.

Archie A system for searching out publicly available files located on anonymous FTP servers (see Chapter 6, "Searching the Internet").

ARPAnet Computer network created by the Advance Research Projects Agency of the United States Army, out of which evolved the Internet. No longer in existence

bandwidth The capacity of a network to transfer over a network connection. Usually measured in bits per second.

baud The number of times per second a signal can change on a transmission line. For instance, a 28,800-baud modem changes the state of the signal 28,880 times per second.

bits per second (bps) The speed at which data, measured as bits, passes over a communication line.

browser A client program to navigate the World Wide Web (e.g., Netscape Navigator, NCSA Mosaic, Internet Explorer).

client A software application that requests the services of a server located in another location. For instance, to download data from an FTP server you must use an FTP client program that can issue the appropriate commands to an FTP server.

dial-up A means of communicating with a computer by dialing it up over a phone line.

DNS Domain Name System; the system used to translate computer domain names into numerical Internet Protocol (IP) numbers.

domain The suffix of an Internet address; .edu is the domain of the address **www.uwsp.edu**. The domain indicates the type of organization or country of origin (e.g., org, net, com, gov, uk, fi).

download To transfer data from a server to your desktop computer

emoticon A symbol used to indicate emotion in a message. For example, :-o indicates the emotion of surprise.

FAQ Frequently asked questions. A file compiled by a member of an email list or Usenet user group of frequently asked questions and answers about a particular topic.

flame Derogatory remark issued to someone via electronic mail or a Usenet group. "Flame Wars" occur when a hotly contested issue continues for a period of time.

Freenet A community-based bulletin board system or organization that provides free Internet access to a particular community. Limited access is available for outsiders as a guest via Gopher or Telnet.

FTP File Transfer Protocol. FTP is the service that enables Internet users to transfer files between computers. FTP software lets users rename and delete files on the client computer and, with permission, the FTP server.

Gateway A computer systems that enables the transfer of information between incompatible applications or computer networks. For example, a gateway enables the transfer of data between the Internet and Bitnet.

Gopher A menu-based browsing service on the Internet (see Chapter 2, "Browsing the Internet with Gopher and the World Wide Web").

hypermedia Media in the form of text, audio or video that are linked together.

HyperText Markup Language The language used to code documents for the World Wide Web.

hypertext Documents that contain links to other information either in the same document or in other files.

IP Internet Protocol. The protocol that enables data packets to travel through the Internet from your local computer to the destination computer.

listserv Software capable of sending multiple copies of electronic mail messages to different destinations at once. The software behind electronic mailing lists.

mailing list An electronic mail address for a list of recipients belonging to an electronic mail discussion group. Postings are sent to each subscriber's electronic mailbox rather than a "centralized" bulletin board like Usenet.

mail reflector A special address used to distribute electronic mail messages to a group of people. Often used to maintain an electronic mail discussion group.

modem The device that translates digital computer information into an analog tone for transmission over a telephone line. It also converts the analog telephone tones into digital pulses for a computer to understand.

Newsgroup Usenet interest group. Participants post news to the newsgroup, where it is archived.

NREN National Research and Education Network.

NSFNET Computer network created by the National Science Foundation.

packet Informal name for the unit of data that is transmitted across the Internet. Actually an Internet datagram.

port (1) An input/output channel on a computer; (2) a number that identifies a particular Internet application in an Internet packet.

posting A message sent to an electronic mail discussion list or a Usenet interest group.

PPP Point-to-Point Protocol; a protocol that enables a computer to use the TCP/IP protocols of the Internet over a conventional phone line and a modem. Permits the computer to have an IP number allocated to it.

protocol The definitions or rules by which computers will act when communicating with one another.

router A system that moves data between two computer networks that use the same protocols.

service provider (Internet) An organization that provides a connection to the Internet.

shell Software that activates an operation on a server in response to keyboard input.

signature A file that contains information about the originator of a message. A signature file usually contains the person's name, surface address and email address.

SLIP Serial Line Internet Protocol. SLIP is the protocol that enables a local computer to use Internet protocols by dialing in to an Internet service provider to gain access to the Internet. Being phased out in favor of PPP.

Smiley *See* emoticon.

TCP Transfer Control Protocol. The method by which Internet packets are transferred across the Internet.

Telnet The remote login service of the Internet.

terminal emulation A method to transform your keyboard to operate like another kind of keyboard so that the keystrokes you type are the same as the keystrokes on the keyboard type you desire.

UNIX A popular operating system for computers attached to the Internet.

upload To transfer data from your desktop computer to a computer server.

Usenet User network. A network of newsgroups or bulletin boards using the Internet to distribute network news. Other networks carry Usenet news feeds as well.

Veronica A Gopher space search service. Boolean searching is permitted.

WAIS Wide Area Information Server. A method for locating documents from indexed databases using full text queries and keywords.

white pages A list of Internet users accessible through the Internet.

World Wide Web Distributed hypermedia environment for accessing information over the Internet. Uses context-sensitive hyperlinks to connect Internet resources.

APPENDIX 2

Common HTML Tags

DOCUMENT	
<HTML> . . . </HTML>	HTML Document
HEAD	
<HEAD> . . . </HEAD>	Document Head
<BASE>	Base URL
<ISINDEX>	Searchable Document
<TITLE>	Document Title
Body	
<A HREF="filename"> . . . </A>	Hyperlink Reference Anchor
<BODY> . . . </BODY>	Document Body
 	Line Break
<ADDRESS></ADDRESS>	Address Information
<BLOCKQUOTE></ BLOCKQUOTE>	Block Quotation
<H1></H1>	First-Order Heading
<H2></H2>	Second-Order Heading
<H3></H3>	Third-Order Heading
<H4></H4>	Fourth-Order Heading
<H5></H5>	Fifth-Order Heading
<H6></H6>	Sixth-Order Heading
<HR>	Horizontal Rule
<DL> . . . </DL>	Description List
<LI> . . . </LI>	List Item
<OL> . . . </OL>	Ordered List
<DIR> . . . </DR>	Directory List
<MENU> . . . </MENU>	Menu List
<P> . . . </P>	Paragraph Break
<PRE> . . . </PRE>	Preformatted Text
<img src="filename">	Inline Image
TABLES (placed in body of HTML document)	
<TABLE> . . . </TABLE>	Define Table
<CAPTION> . . . </CAPTION>	Table Caption
<TR> . . . </TR>	Table Row
<TD> . . . </TD>	Table Element

Text Formatting

<B> . . . </B>	Bold Type
<I> . . . </I>	Italic Type
<TT> . . . </TT>	Fixed Width
<U> . . . </U>	Underline

REFERENCES

Beatty, J. K. (1994). Instant science on the Internet. *Sky and Telescope,* Vol. 88, 21.

Bresnahan , Tom. (1994). The Computer Oriented Geological Society: Background and purpose of COGS. http://www.csn.net/~tbrez/cogs/index.html.

Butler, J.C. (1995). An introduction to geoscience education resources on the Internet. *Computers & Geosciences,* Vol. 21, No. 6, 817–824.

Cobb, Flora Shrode, and Edward F. Lener. (1995). Internet resources for the earth sciences. *College & Research Libraries News,* Vol. 56, 319–321, 325.

Comer, D. E. (1995). *The Internet Book*. Prentice-Hall, New Jersey, 312.

Dern, D. P. (1994). *The Internet Guide for New Users*. McGraw-Hill, New York, 570.

Ellsworth, J. H. (1994). *Education and the Internet*. Sams Publishing, 591.

Foster, Steven. (1995). Frequently-asked questions (FAQs) about Veronica. gopher://gopher.scs.unr.edu:70/hh/veronica/About/vfaq%28html%29.

Frequently asked questions. (1994). [FAQ] (with answers comp.infosystems.wais). http://sunwww.informatik.uni-tuebingen.de:8080/Archive/WAISFAQ.html.

Gilster, Paul. (1994). *Finding It on the Internet*. John Wiley, New York, 302.

Gittings, B.M., and A.L. Towers. (1995). Earthquakes and GIS on the information superhighway. *GIS World,* 68–71.

Guide to Network Resources: NETFIND. http://www.cuhk.hk/guides/earn/netfind.html.

Guide to Network Resources: WHOIS. http://www.earn.net/gnrt/whois.html.

Hemingway Jr., D. F. (1996). Internet users select favorite web sites. *GIS World,* January, 42–47.

Kemp, Karen. (1996). About the NCGIA core curriculum. http://www.ncgia.ucsb.edu/education/curricula/giscc/giscc.html#intro.

Krol, Ed. (1992). *The Whole Internet User Guide and Catalog*. O'Reilly & Associates New York.

Krol, E. (1994). *The Whole Internet Catalog and User's Guide*. O'Reiley & Associates, New York.

Lemay, Laura. (1995). *Teach Yourself Web Publishing with HTML in a Week*. Sams Publishing, Indianapolis, 397.

LTER. (1995). Mission and Goals. http://lternet.edu/about/program/mission.htm.

LYCOS. (1995). http://www.lycos.com/reference/faq.html.

Norman, Kent L. (1995). Teaching in the switched on classroom: An introduction to electronic education and hypercourseware. http://www.lap.umd.edu/SOC/sochome.html.

Ostler, Paul. (1994). Revolution in realty. *Geographical,* May, 12–14.

Pinkerton, B. (1994). Finding what people want: Experiences with the WebCrawler. Paper delivered at the second International World Wide Web Conference. http://info.webcrawler.com/bp/WWW94.html.

Pool, T. S., S.M. Blanchard, S.A. Hale. (1995) From over the Internet: Users discuss a new direction for learning. *Techtrends,* January/February, 24–28.

Ramshaw, R. S. (1995). Geoscience listservs and newsgroups. *Computers & Geosciences,* Vol. 21, No. 6, 787–790.

Rheingold, H. (1995). The Virtual Community. Minerva, London, 325.

Robin, B. (1995). Supporting geoscience with graphical-user-interface Internet tools for the Macintosh. *Computers and Geosciences,* Vol. 21, No. 6, 737–751.

Scotchmoor, J. and J.H. Lipps. (1995). Where is the real Museum of Paleontology? *Geotimes,* December, 27–28.

Sproul, L.S. (1986). Using electronic mail for data collection in organizational research. *Academy of Management Journal,* 29, 159–169.

Tach, L. (1995). Using electronic mail to conduct survey research. *Educational Technology,* March/April, 27–31.

Thoen, B. (1994). Online resources for earth scientists. ftp://ftp.csn.org/COGS/ores.txt.

Thoen, B. (1996). GIS communities flourish. *GIS World,* January, 48–51.

Van Helden. (1995). The Galileo Project. http://es.rice.edu/ES/humsoc/Galileo/index.html.

Walker, Janice R. MLA-style citation of Electronic sources. http://www.cas.usf.edu/english/walker/mla.html.

Walsh, J.P., S. Kiesler, L.S. Sproull, & B. W. Hesse. (1992). Self-selected and randomly selected respondents in a computer network survey. *Public Opinion Quarterly,* Vol. 56, 241–244.

Watson, Ellen. (1995). Campus forum. *EduTech Exchange,* Spring/Summer, 14

Wehmeyer, L. B.(1996) Wide-angle searching on the World Wide Web. *Syllabus,* June, 34–37.

Woronow, A. and Dare, Scott. (1995). On the Internet with a PC. *Computers and Geosciences,* Vol. 21, No. 6, 753–757.

INDEX

Notes, New Addresses and Revised URLs

Notes, New Addresses and Revised URLs

Notes, New Addresses and Revised URLs

Notes, New Addresses and Revised URLs

Notes, New Addresses and Revised URLs

Notes, New Addresses and Revised URLs